FILM as LITERATURE, *LITERATURE as FILM*

Recent Titles in
Bibliographies and Indexes in World Literature

Psychocriticism: An Annotated Bibliography
Joseph P. Natoli and Frederik L. Rusch, compilers

Olaf Stapledon: A Bibliography
Harvey J. Satty and Curtis C. Smith, compliers

Spanish Literature, 1500-1700: A Bibliography of Golden Age
Studies in Spanish and English, 1925-1980
William W. Moseley, Glenroy Emmons, and Marilyn C. Emmons, compilers

Monthly Terrors: An Index to the Weird Fantasy Magazines
Published in the United States and Great Britain
Frank H. Parnell, compiler, with the assistance of Mike Ashley

The Independent Monologue in Latin American Theater:
A Primary Bibliography with Selective Secondary Sources
Duane Rhoades, compiler

J.R.R. Tolkien: Six Decades of Criticism
Judith A. Johnson

Bibliographic Guide to Gabriel García Márquez, 1979-1985
Margaret Eustella Fau and Nelly Sfeir de Gonzalez, compilers

Eastern Europe in Children's Literature: An Annotated Bibliography
of English-language Books
Frances F. Povsic

The Literary Universe of Jorge Luis Borges: An Index to References and
Allusions to Persons, Titles, and Places in His Writings
Daniel Balderston, compiler

FILM as LITERATURE, LITERATURE as FILM

An Introduction to and Bibliography of Film's Relationship to Literature

Harris Ross

Bibliographies and Indexes in World Literature, Number 10

Greenwood Press
New York • Westport, Connecticut • London

016.7914
R82f

Library of Congress Cataloging-in-Publication Data

Ross, Harris.
  Film as literature, literature as film.

  (Bibliographies and indexes in world literature,
ISSN 0742-6801 ; no. 10)
  Includes indexes.
  1. Moving-pictures and literature—Bibliography.
2. Moving-pictures and literature. I. Title. II. Series.
Z5784.M9R66 1987 [PN1995.3] 016.79143'01'5 87-132
ISBN 0-313-24595-9 (lib. bdg. : alk. paper)

Library of Congress Catalog Card Number: 87-132
ISBN: 0-313-24595-9
ISSN: 0742-6801

First published in 1987

Greenwood Press, Inc.
88 Post Road West, Westport, Connecticut 06881

Printed in the United States of America

The paper used in this book complies with the
Permanent Paper Standard issued by the National
Information Standards Organization (Z39.48-1984).

10 9 8 7 6 5 4 3 2

Contents

vi   Contents

Preface

Film as Literature, Literature as Film is intended
for those interested in the relationship of film to literature.
The bibliography, which lists almost 2500 articles and
books published from 1908 to 1985, demonstrates the durability
of interest in the comparison of film to drama, prose fiction,
and poetry. This comparison began early in the history
of the motion picture and was primarily directed toward
discovering the expressive capabilities of the "flickers"
and differentiating them from the established arts, particularly
drama. Now that film has established itself as an art
and is studied in high schools and colleges, its kinship
to the other arts remains an important scholarly concern.
One academic journal, Literature/Film Quarterly, is devoted
entirely to articles on film's relationship to literature,
and the recent interest in narratology, the study of narrative
structure, once again has focused attention on the shared
attributes of all narrative forms and the importance of
medium in determining just how and what narratives can
express.
     The introduction is not intended to discuss every
issue raised by every writer represented in the bibliography.
Such an enterprise would require several book-length treatments.
Rather, it is intended to explain and evaluate the issues
raised most frequently by major writers on the subject,
particularly issues concerning film's relationship to the
other narrative arts, drama and prose fiction. As such, it
should prove useful not only to newcomers to the field but
also to those familiar with the criticism on literature and
film. Publication information for material noted or quoted
in the introduction is provided by reference to their entry
numbers in the bibliography and page numbers in the source
work. For works that are quoted but not cited in the
bibliography, publication information is given directly in
the text of the introduction.
     The chapters of the bibliography concern broad subject
areas, and, while their contents may be self-evident from
their titles, some explanation might be helpful.

Chapter 1.   Articles and books that concern film's
                   relationship to prose fiction, drama, and
                   poetry. (Entry nos. 0001-0135)

Chapter 2.   Articles and books that analyze film using
              linguistic methods and that concern film
              as language or as having linguistic
              characteristics (Entry nos. 0136-0205)

Chapter 3.   Articles and books that concern film's
              relationship to the novel and the short story.
              (Entry nos. 0206-0282)

Chapter 4.   Articles and books that concern film's
              relationship to drama. (Entry nos. 0283-0460)

Chapter 5   Articles and books that concern film's
              relationship to poetry. (Entry nos. 0461-0484)

Chapter 6   Articles and books that concern cinematic
              adaptations and adaptation theory. Includes
              articles and books that concern a number
              of adaptations. Articles on single adaptations
              entered under the author's name in chapters
              8-11, 13-14. (Entry nos. 0485-0589)

Chapter 7   Articles and books that concern the motion
              picture careers of writers. Includes works
              that consider the careers of a number of
              writers. Studies of The careers of individual
              writers entered under the author's name in
              chapters 8-14. (Entry nos. 0590-0608)

Chapter 8   Articles and books on film and individual
              American writers. Includes the writer's
              statements about motion pictures, studies
              of the writer's career in motion pictures,
              analyses of film adaptations of the writer's
              works, and analyses of the "cinematic" qualities
              of the writer's work. (Entry nos. 0609-1181)

Chapter 9   Articles and books on film and individual
              writers of the United Kingdom. Includes
              the writer's statements about motion pictures,
              studies of the writer's career in motion
              pictures, analyses of film adaptations of
              the writer's works, and analyses of the
              "cinematic" qualities of the writer's work.
              (Entry nos. 1182-1599)

Chapter 10.   Articles and books on film and William
              Shakespeare. First section includes general
              studies of Shakespeare and the cinema, and
              articles and books that concern a number
              of film adaptations of Shakespeare's plays.
              Second section sub-divided by titles of
              the plays and includes works on adaptations
              of individual plays. (Entry nos. 1600-1859)

Chapter 11.   Articles and books on film adaptations of
              individual writers of classical Greek and
              Latin literature and the writers' influence
              upon filmmakers. (Entry nos. 1860-1872)

Chapter 12.   Articles and books on film and individual
               European writers. Includes the writer's
               statements about motion pictures, studies
               of the writer's career in motion pictures,
               analyses of film adaptations of the writer's
               works, and analyses of the "cinematic"
               qualities of the writer's work. (Entry nos.
               1873-2236)

Chapter 13.   Articles and books on film and individual
               writers of Latin America. Includes the writer's
               statements about motion pictures, studies
               of the writer's career in motion pictures,
               analyses of film adaptations of the writer's
               works, and analyses of the "cinematic" qualities
               of the writer's work. (Entry nos. 2237-2265)

Chapter 14.   Articles and books on film and individual
               writers of Asia and Africa. Includes the
               writer's statements about motion pictures,
               studies of the writer's career in motion
               pictures, analyses of film adaptations of
               the writer's works, and analyses of the
               "cinematic" qualities of the writer's work.
               (Entry nos. 2267-2276)

Chapter 15   Scripts of film adaptations of literary works
               and scripts by literary figures. (Entry
               nos. 2277-2449)

Chapter 16.   Articles and books on the use of adaptation
               study and comparisons of film and literature
               in the classroom. (Entry nos. 2450-2477)

Chapter 17.   Bibliographies of works on film's relationship
               to literature and filmographies of adaptations
               of literary works. (Entry nos. 2478-2495)

    While the bibliography is intended to be comprehensive,
some limitation was necessary. Film reviews and articles
from newspapers are not usually cited except in cases of
particular interest and merit. Foreign-language articles
and books are also not cited. Entries are annotated only
in three instances: when the title does not clearly indicate
subject matter, when several literary works are discussed
in depth, or when the title of a film adaptation differs
from the title of the source work. While the chapters
provide a reliable guide to the content of works cited,
users wishing to make a thorough search for works on a
particular subject are encouraged to use the author and
subject indexes. In the subject index, numbers preceded
by "p," or "pp." refer to page numbers within the introduction;
other numbers refer to entry numbers within the bibliography.

Acknowledgments

I wish to thank the staffs of the University of Delaware
and the Library of Congress for their assistance. I would
like to thank the University of Delaware for awarding me
a research grant that allowed me to complete most of the
work on the bibliography during the summer of 1985. Special
thanks are due to Dennis Jackson, Fleda Jackson, Mark Amsler,
and, above all, Kathleen Duke.

Introduction

"Film has nothing to do with literature; the character
and substance of the art forms are usually in conflict,"
Ingmar Bergman says (0008, p. xvii). This might seem an
odd statement from a director whose films are often called
"literary," whose scripts are regularly published, and
whose chief influence is playwright August Strindberg.
A teacher of film in a literature program or a compiler
of a bibliography of works on film and literature might
respond to Bergman that film has everything to do with
literature. He might say that drama and fiction were used
as models for early filmmakers struggling to make the flickers
tell stories. After all, didn't the father of the motion
picture, D.W. Griffith, defend his use of cross-cutting
on the grounds that Dickens had already done it? When
someone said novel writing was different from filmmaking,
Griffith responded that movies are "picture stories; not
so different."
      The scholar, sounding like the "Radcliffe tootsie"
who dared criticize Bergman to Woody Allen in Manhattan,
might add that film's appearance in the first decades of
the century shaped both drama and the novel; didn't the
drama shift from realism to theatricalism and didn't the
novel shift from realism to impressionism at least partly
in response to film? At the same time, poetry, drama,
and the novel appropriated various filmic techniques, such
as montage in Joyce's Ulysses, the "camera eye" in Dos
Passos' U.S.A. trilogy, and the "lap dissolves" in
Robbe-Grillet's novels. The scholar might note the number
of literary figures that have been involved in filmmaking
as writers or as directors: Agee, Fitzgerald, West, Faulkner
and Mailer in the United States; Shaw, Wells, Osborne,
and Pinter in Great Britain; Malraux, Cocteau, Sartre,
Robbe-Grillet in France. And what about the thousands
of cinematic adaptations of literary works? That connection
began early in the history of American film, in 1896, when
Edison excerpted The Widow Jones, and has been maintained
through film history. In the mid-sixties, Harry Geduld
estimated that around forty percent of Hollywood films
were literary adaptations (0043, p. 12) and in the late
seventies Morris Beja estimated that more than seventy-five
percent of the Academy Awards for "best picture" went to
literary adaptations (0006, p. 78). This scholar might
also contend that the differences between literature and

film are secondary to their common goal, meeting the imaginative
needs of their audiences and, because film, drama, and
prose fiction are all narratives, they meet those needs
by using the same elements, characters moving through space
and actions occurring across time. Nothing to do with
literature? Hardly.

Bergman, if he has not become thoroughly bored or
drifted into a Scandinavian funk, might respond that he
was drawing the distinction between literature and film
purely in terms of media and the way the audience apprehends
a work because of the means of expression. A filmmaker
adapting a literary work must convey what was verbal by
means of visual images. Because of the differences in
verbal and visual media, the reader of a novel assimilates
the fiction "by a conscious act of will in alliance with
the intellect," while a spectator puts aside will and intellect
to accept the film's illusion. Film is an art of emotion
and rhythm like music, Bergman says, not an art of words
and ideas like literature. Everything to do with literature?
Scarcely.

This mini-docudrama indicates at least some of the
connections often made between film and literature, and
the two common attitudes toward that relationship. Bergman's
position, or at least the position that he takes in his
essay "Bergman Discusses Film-Making," establishes boundaries
between the arts based upon their respective means of
expression, the word and the photographed image. The most
highly elaborated statements of this position are Siegfried
Kracauer's Theory of Film and Rudolph Arnheim's Film as
Art, both of which seek a radical separation of film from
literature, particularly film from drama. Their working
method, as indicated by a chapter title in Arnheim's book,
"A New Laokoon," is that drawn from Gotthold Lessing, who
in Laokoon argued for a radical separation of poetry from
painting and sculpture. Lessing's aim was to derive the
expressive capabilities of an art from the physical
characteristics of its medium and, consequently, to show
that the eighteenth-century taste for ut pictura poesis
had forced poetry to step over the natural boundary separating
it from the visual arts. His argument, essentially, was
that poetry is a temporal art, sculpture is a spatial art;
a temporal medium should depict actions through time while
a space art should depict bodies within space.

When Lessing's argument is directly applied to film
and literature, strange paradoxes are revealed. Prose
fiction is a temporal art; film is a spatial and temporal
art. They should have different expressive capabilities,
but film is usually considered to have more in common with
prose fiction than with theater, which, like film, is both
a spatial and temporal art. The reason for this apparent
contradiction is that theorists using Lessing's method
derive film's physical properties from the photographed
image. Arnheim notes that, because the image falls short
of reproducing reality and because its expressiveness is
tied to these limitations, elements such as dialogue and
color which bring film nearer to reality undercut its expressive
capabilities. By contrast, drama is the text which "does
not require staging--it merely permits it" (0288, p. 217).
Kracauer deduces the expressive capablilities of film from

its basis in photography, but he draws somewhat different
conclusions. Because a single photograph records only
a segment of reality, film gravitates toward certain kinds
of subject matter: the everyday, the unstaged (or that
which appears unstaged), the fortuitous, and the open-ended.
By contrast, through stylization, drama announces itself
as a performance, a metaphor for life--like life rather
than lifelike--and gravitates toward subject matter that
reaches definite closure.

For all their differences, Arnheim and Kracauer believe
that each art has unique expressive capabilities, which
artists must exploit to avoid being "unfaithful" to their
medium. Generally speaking, this position can be reduced
to the notion that good films, those that are "cinematic,"
convey their stories through images, and bad films, those
that are "uncinematic," borrow methods from the theater,
particularly a reliance on dialogue.

This purist view of film's relationship to literature
is riddled with a number of contradictions and peculiarities.
It rests upon deriving the unique capabilities of the art
from the physical properties of the medium, but, as Donald
Crawford says, "What is required is an enumeration of specific
expressive properties of the medium, or more usually, an
explanation of how these physical properties give rise
to expressive possibilities. And these seem elusive indeed"
(0026, p. 453). Even if this could be done, this approach
faces another hurdle. This position is predicated on the
notion that an art, particularly an art as complex as film,
can express itself not only in its own "natural" voice
but also in the voices of other arts. Film is, as Susan
Sontag says, a "pan-art" in that it "can use, incorporate,
engulf virtually any other art: the novel, poetry, theater,
painting, sculpture, dance, music, architecture" (1089,
p. 243). Still, it must be shown that using unique expressive
capabilities produces good films and using other expressive
capabilities, elements shared, let us say, with the theater,
produces bad films. This theory runs aground on films
that are generally thought to be successful but fail to
meet the criterion of exploiting the uniqueness of film.
For example, Kracauer praises Fred Astaire's films, which
surely used theatrical methods, because Astaire bases his
dance routines on everyday experience. But he banishes
from the cinematic promised land two cinematic mainstays,
fantasy and historical films, although most of these films
meet his standard of being derived from everyday experience
at least as well as Astaire's.

The second general approach to film's relationship
to literature is a modified version of the purist theory
that Crawford calls "the Weak Uniqueness Theory." This
theory is also concerned with differences among the arts,
differences accounted for by their materials of expression,
but it claims only that certain effects are easier to accomplish
in one art than in another. This approach has a number
of virtues, not the least of which is that it acknowledges
that artists may and often do step beyond the boundaries
of their arts and that a work may be thought successful
precisely because it achieves effects associated with other
arts.

These two general views of the relationship of film

and literature provide a handy way of classifying the writers discussed in this introduction, those who have drawn firm lines between film and literature and those who have kept their distinctions, to use Charles Eidsvik's phrase, "soft-edged." To organize the staggering number of observations made about the relationship of film to literature since the turn of the century, I shall discuss this relationship in terms of three major topics: narration, time, and space. Time and space are the most frequently cited formal qualities of film and are entailed in any narrative. Narration concerns a basic distinction drawn between prose fiction and drama, that of direct presentation versus mediation. While these three topics are important for analyses of filmic adaptations, adaptation theory per se will not be discussed in this introduction.

In the course of discussing narration, time, and space, I shall consider a number of questions often raised in writings on film's relation to literature: In what way is the camera the film's narrator? Can film be narrated in the first person? Can enunciation theory be successfully applied to film? What does it mean to speak of film as a "present tense" art and prose fiction as a "past tense" art? Can film describe? Are the temporal levels of film comparable to those of drama and prose fiction? Are film and the modern novel connected by the "metaphysical" qualities of film technique? Is there anything in prose fiction comparable to the shot? Is filmic space similar to dramatic space? Can film and drama be distinguished by means of differences in dramatic illusion?

This introduction will summarize some of the answers which have been given to these questions. These are by no means the only issues that have been posed concerning the relationship of the arts, but these are the ones which have been most frequently raised and fully discussed.

A. CAMERA EYE, NARRATOR'S VOICE

Prose fiction and drama are usually distinguished
by the way their fictional worlds are created. In prose
fiction, the fictional world is stipulated from without,
by a narrator separated from the counterfactual world either
ontologically, in the case of the third-person narrator,
or temporally, in the case of the first-person narrator.
The fictional world is not directly represented to the
reader; rather, it is signified by the narrator's words.
By contrast, the fictional world of the drama is stipulated
from within, by the action and dialogue of the characters.
Unlike prose fiction, drama works by ostension, by a direct
showing of the fictional world to the spectator. As Keir
Elam has written, "Dramatic worlds...are presented to the
spectator as 'hypothetically actual' constructs, since
they are `seen' in progress 'here and now' without narrational
mediation. Dramatic performance metaphorically translates
conceptual access to possible worlds into 'physical' access,
since the constructed world is apparently shown to the
audience, that is, ostended. . . ." (The Semiotics of Theatre
and Drama [London: Methuen, 1980], p. 111).
The difference between drama and prose fiction involves
the classic distinction between diegesis and mimesis, between
mediation by a narrator and direct presentation to the
spectator. Film would seem to be mimetic and, therefore,
closer to drama than to prose fiction because the spectator
directly apprehends the fictional world; it is presented,
ostended, to him. As in the theater, visual aspects of
the fiction are rendered visually and aural aspects are
rendered aurally.
Nevertheless, the majority of critics and theoreticians
have found that film shares a closer relationship to prose
fiction, particularly the novel, than to drama. Robert
Nathan, for example, flatly states that the film "is like
a novel, but a novel to be seen instead of told" (0255,
p. 130). Margaret Thorp finds that "it is not to the theater
but to the novel that we must turn when we wish to find
analogies useful to the development of the film" (0277,
p. 196). And Morris Beja notes "the widespread conviction
that film is essentially closer to the novel than to drama"
(0006, p. 54).
This conviction is based on a number of factors: the
broader scope of the plots of film and prose fiction, and
the ease with which the two manipulate time and space.

The connection has often been seen in terms of mediation,
in terms of the presence of a narrator. Many critics have
seen the film not in terms of presentation, ostension,
but in terms of enunciation, telling through images. As
early as 1894, H.G. Wells and Herbert Paul described the
new art of cinema as "telling stories by means of pictures"
(quoted in Ivor Montagu, Film World [Baltimore: Penguin
Books, 1968], p. 34). Early in the history of film, critics
began to equate the presentation of stories through images
with the telling of stories through words. In some sense,
it was felt, both involved enunciation and thus an enunciator.
More recent critics and theorists have expanded on Wells
and Paul's idea that film does not present a fictional
reality but, in some sense, tells it. For instance, Louis
Giannetti writes, "The cinematic equivalent to the 'voice'
of the literary narrator is the 'eye' of the camera" (0044,
p. 324). Similarly, Gerald Mast states, "Like a novel
it [film] uses focused narration (lens parallels
narrator)...." (0079, p. 18). James Monaco finds that
both film and prose fiction tell stories by means of a
narrator, the filmic narrator being the "objective image"
(0249, p. 30). Colin MacCabe equates the narrator's intrusions
in what he calls the "classic realist text" of the nineteenth-
century novel with camera work and editing (1922, p. 10).
Roy Huss and Norman Silverstein argue that the camera in
Tony Richardson's Tom Jones (1963) functions as a self-conscious
narrator (0231, p. 113). In the recent Double Exposure:
Fiction Into Film, Joy Gould Boyum argues that the camera,
by controlling the spectator's attention, "becomes the
equivalent of a narrator, a cinematic storyteller itself"
(0503, p. 38).
     In terms of its narration, film would seem to be a
rather curious hybrid, lying somewhere between the mimesis
of drama and the diegesis of prose fiction. On the one
hand, the filmic spectator directly apprehends the
counterfactual world. On the other hand, standing between
this world and the spectator is a narrating agent who chooses
one vantage point over another, who chooses to display
one action rather than another to the spectator. The argument
advanced for the filmic narrator runs this way: film "tells"
its story through images as prose fiction does through
words; because telling implies a teller, both film and
prose fiction have agents of mediation, narrators, who
control the flow of information about the fictional world
to the spectator. What sanctions the idea that film represents
a kind of telling closely akin to that of prose fiction?
In other words, what allows these critics to assume a similarity
between conveying information through images and information
through words?
     That film must have a narrator like that of prose
fiction and that film "tells" its stories as prose fiction
does is sanctioned by the modern, that is pre-structuralist,
view of the fictional narrator. This is hardly the place
to trace the history of the concept of point of view, but
it is important to note that the opinions advanced by Henry
James and refined by Percy Lubbock and Norman Friedman
are essentially mimetic. In their opinion, the narrator
must dramatize rather than tell his story so that the reader
can "see" the story through the narrator's eyes. In other

words, the foundation of their conception of the novel
as "showing" rather than "telling" rests on various spatial
and optical metaphors. In "Point of View in Fiction: The
Development of a Critical Concept," for example, Norman
Friedman writes that narrators can be distinguished on
the basis of their angle on the narrative (above, center,
front, shifting, periphery) and by the way they situate
the reader at some distance from the story. Even the term
he uses to designate the narrator's relationship to the
story, "point of view," is an optical metaphor.

It is easy to understand how the two kinds of "telling"
were equated and, consequently, how easily a narrator for
film was postulated. In the Jamesian view, prose fiction's
narration was seen in terms of showing, of vision, of space,
and so it seemed only natural to apply the traditional
pronominal categories of literary point of view to film.
Third-person film denoted films or parts of film in which
the vantage point of the camera could not be assigned to
a character. First person film denoted those films in
which a character's spatial position was assigned to the
camera. The delineation of both film and literary narrators
was made in terms of whose perception the spectator shared.

Most writers dealing with the relationship of film
to literature agree that film can narrate in the third
person but not in the first. Of the standard subdivisions
of third person, omniscient is the "natural" filmic point
of view. Richard L. Stromgren and Martin F. Norden argue
that the novel is told from a single point of view, third
or first, while film avoids the use of the latter. William
Jinks finds that film has occasionally experimented with
first-person narration, but, he notes, this technique is
usually used sparingly. Film generally relies on third-person
omniscient narration because that point of view allows
film to exploit its ability to rapidly shift perspective.
Similarly, Louis Giannetti argues that first-person narration
is unworkable in the film because "the camera would have
to record all the action through the eyes of the character,
which, in effect would also make the viewer the protagonist"
(0044, p. 324).

The traditional view of filmic point of view is that
first-person is actually a sub-category of third-person
because the very nature of film demands that the first-person
shots be "embedded" in third person narration. Gerald
R. Barrett sums up this position in his introduction to
the From Fiction to Film series. He argues that film can
adopt a third-person limited point of view by revealing
information to the spectator only as it is made available
to a character, but, he says, it naturally inclines to
a third-person omniscient point of view: "In such cases,
the camera shifts back and forth from the role of the detached
observer (objective) to the point of view of one of the
participants (subjective)" (0631, p. 29).

The failure of first-person narration in film has
been examined by Julio L. Moreno in "Subjective Camera
and the Problem of Film in the First Person." His analysis
of The Lady in the Lake (1946) remains the most detailed
explanation of the failure of first-person cinema and suggests
how the metaphorical basis of point of view has led to
a misunderstanding of the literary narrator's relationship

to the story. Moreno ascribes the failure of first-person
film to the inability of film to duplicate human perception
and the undermining of the spectator's identification with
the protagonist. Most significantly, Moreno writes that
first-person filmic narration and first-person literary
narration are not at all alike. When film attempts first-person
narration, it produces results that are precisely the opposite
of those obtained in literature. In first-person prose
fiction, the narrator and the protagonist, while nominally
identical, are temporally distinct. The retrospective
nature of first-person narration means that "the narrator
and the protagonist function in fact as two distinct persons,
perfectly discernible to the reader" (0250, p. 355). In
first-person film, however, the narrator and the protagonist
are the same, and the retrospective nature of first-person
literary narration is lost. Moreno suggests that first-person
literary narration is conceptual while first-person filmic
narration is perceptual.
      Moreno's thirty-year-old article foreshadows current
theories of narration which clearly distinguish the narrator's
relationship to the story from vantage point or perception.
In Story and Discourse, Seymour Chatman, drawing on Gérard
Genette's discussions of "voice" and "point of view,"
distinguishes the narrator's expression of the story from
a character's perception within the story:

> . . .what the narrator reports from his perspective
> is almost always outside the story (heterodiegetic)
> even if only retrospective, that is, temporally distant.
> Typically, he is looking back at his own earlier
> perception-as-a-character. But that looking-back
> is a conception, no longer a perception. The completely
> external narrator presents an even more purely conceptual
> view. . . . He did not 'perceive' in the same direct
> or diegetic sense that any character did. Literally
> speaking, he cannot have 'seen' anything in that other
> world (0215, p.155)

Perception, in other words, is the province of character,
not the narrator. Expression, enunciation, is the province
of the narrator, even when the narrator is also a character
within the story.
      Current narrative theory has gone a long way toward
clearing up the confusion about what precisely defines
point of view by rejecting the traditional mimetic
theories. Genette argues that point of view, what he terms
"focalization," concerns the source and the type of information
conveyed within the narrative, but it does not concern
the source of the narration itself, that is, the narrator.
For Genette, the narrator is not, of course, synonymous
with the author but is rather a fictional presence that
the reader recognizes by such traces in the text as personal
pronouns and verb tenses. Voice concerns the way a story
directly reaches the reader. Point of view concerns the
way the story information reaches the narrator, whether
by way of a single character or a host of characters.
      Current literary theory demands that we abandon the
old notion of equating camera and narrator on the grounds
of perception and invites us to detect the filmic narrator

in terms of "traces," cinematic equivalents for pronouns,
verb tenses, and other elements that indicate the presence
of a narrator.
     In Mindscreen, the first book-length study of filmic
point of view, and in a subsequent article, "Voices of
Filmic Narration," Bruce Kawin attempts to devise for film
the equivalent of language's pronominal code and to demonstrate
that film has no less facility in using narrative voice
than has literature. Essentially, Kawin attempts to rescue
first-person film from the critical junk heap and to establish
that first-person film is and has been an important genre
in the history of film.
     Kawin asserts that film, like fiction, tells its stories,
but he admits that film lacks equivalents for the traces
used to determine narrators in enunciation theory. "To
introduce the concept of telling into the passive system
of vision," he writes, "some encoding is necessary. There
must be ways to establish whether deliberate, personalized
narration is taking place, whether a given view is objective
or subjective, whether whatever subjectivity does appear
is authorial, and so on. And in the interest of sustained
narrative complexity, there ought to be a more useful and
comprehensive master code available than that of POV [point
of view shot] and voice-over for subjectivity, everything
else for objectivity" (0237, p. 39).
     Because it lacks systems of pronouns and verb tenses,
film must indicate narrators contextually. He argues that
an audience's understanding of the filmic narrator derives
from an assumption that the film's images are purposefully
ordered, and from "reading" the relationships among filmic
elements in terms of a narrator. A filmmaker indicates
first-person narration, what Kawin calls "mindscreen,"
not by shooting the film from the vantage point of a single
character or by directly indicating through voice-over
narration that a character is a narrator but by cuing the
spectator that the source of the image is a character's
mind. "One is alerted by camera position, montage, etc. to
narrative intent," Kawin argues, "and what emerges as the
logic of their changes to narrative bias" (0236, p. 14).
     When Kawin defines second- and third-person film,
however, he abandons the idea that the interplay of filmic
elements constitutes voice. Second-person films are classifed
on the basis of coerciveness, the degree to which the film
attempts to influence its audience. Third-person films
are classified on the basis of film styles which either
mask or reveal the perspective of the author, "the real
point of origin of the discourse" (0237, p. 44). They are
subdivided in terms of what is known in communications
theory as the "conglomerate communicator," that is, whether
the film has one author, several authors, or ideology as
author. Apparently, one determines whether a film has
one author or several authors simply by checking the credits,
but Kawin never explains how one differentiates the authors'
beliefs from ideology. The idea of a narrator is involved,
obviously, in only one of these classifications. The other
two concern the implied author, or the actual "speaker"
of the film; second person apparently concerns the film
as a perlocutionary act and third person concerns film
as an illocutionary act. Confusingly, under Kawin's system,

a given film could be classified as first-, second-, **and** third-person.

"Mindscreen," or subjective film, is the only classification that could reasonably be called a filmic "voice." Kawin sees subjective cinema in terms of character subjectivity and self-consciousness. The major difference between the two is that in the former the spectator shares the mental activity of a character while in the latter the spectator is aware of the film's artifice, the arbitrary nature of the narrative conventions upon which narrative's "reality" is founded. In many self-conscious works, the spectator traces this undermining of illusion to the author, but Kawin believes that in some films we assign this authority to the text itself. A film like Ingmar Bergman's Persona (1966), he claims, "appears to be aware of the fact it is a deliberate discourse--or a resonant center of consciousness within the narrative structure appears to be aware of being presented within a deliberate discourse--and this imitative awareness is not passed back to the real or implied author" (0237, p. 42). Precisely in what instances this self-consciousness is not ascribed to the author is never clarified. Given the allusions to Bergman's other films, his brief oral narration, and his appearance in Persona, most viewers, I think, would make the natural assumption that the narrator is Bergman, or "Bergman," the viewer's conception of the filmmaker. Interestingly, this idea of "text as consciousness" is most common among writers who reject the idea of a filmic narrator and so must anthropomorphize the text to account for unusual narrative effects.

Kawin's prime example of a character's mindscreen is, not surprisingly, Citizen Kane (1941). Because the temporal shifts in Welles' film are made by voice-over narration, the film invites an analysis of film as enunciation, and Kawin argues that these voice-overs and the flashbacks' "vision and emphasis" cue the spectator to ascribe the narrational authority to a character. The subject matter and its treatment within the episodes are congruent with what the spectator knows of the character/narrator. Thatcher, the banker, for example, recalls Kane's financial dealings and stresses Kane's financial shortcomings, his recklessness, and his rebelliousness.

Kawin's definition of first-person film avoids the mistake of equating narration with perception. Instead, he sees first-person narration in terms of textual organization. His analysis of Citizen Kane falls short of demonstrating just how a spectator should "read" the film in terms of first-person narration. Because he deals largely with the subject matter of each episode, he ignores the elements of "vision and emphasis" that he argues constitute first-person narration.

Because he deals largely with subject matter, he skirts some troubling questions that have to be answered in identifying Welles's film as first person. To consider the Thatcher episode as first-person narration, it would be necessary to reconcile Thatcher's egoism with the fact that space in the first part of this flashback is organized first around Mrs. Kane and then around Charlie. Further, Thatcher's obvious distaste during the congressional hearings at the mention of his being attacked by Charlie would have to

be reconciled with the elegiac tone of the shot of the
sled that ends the scene at the Kane boarding house, and
Thatcher's self-seriousness with the farcical tone of the
short scenes of his outrage at Kane's increasingly daring
headlines.

For a thorough reading of film as space and mise-en-scene
organized in terms of a narrator, it is necessary to turn
to Tony Pipola's "The Aptness of Terminology: Point of
View Consciousness and Letter From an Unknown Woman."
Unlike Kawin, Pipola makes no claims that there is a large
body of such films. Instead, he offers a close reading
of the Max Ophul's film to show how a director has linked
such filmic elements as camera angle, camera movement,
and editing to the consciousness of a single character.
He argues, however, that Ophul's film is not first person
in a literary sense. Rather, the film has a third-person
point of view "superimposed" over a first-person point
of view, a strategy akin to Henry James's use of the "central
consciousness."

Pipola and Kawin make the same assumptions about film:
that filmic narrators must be contextually signalled and
that "reading" a first-person film entails linking what
the spectator knows of the character/narrator to the film's
formal strategies. Although Kawin assumes that film is
capable of a first-person narration like literature's,
while Pipola does not. The reasons for their disagreement
indicate the difficulties in applying literary terms to
film.

The disagreement derives from the similarities and
differences in first-person narration and central consciousness
narration. Gèrard Genette's analysis of narration clarifies
these similarities. Central consciousness uses a single
character within the story for focalization, and this is
frequently true as well of first-person narration in which
the narrator and the character share the same identity.
In other words, the two kinds of narration are often connected
by their means of focalization. As Roland Barthes observes,
internally focalized narratives can be rewritten in the
first person with only a change in pronouns (see "Introduction
to the Structural Analysis of Narratives" in Image, Music,
Text. Trans. Stephen Heath. New York: Hill and Wang,
1977, pp. 79-124). The essential difference between the
first- and third-person narration, then, rests on whether
the narrator shares the same identity as the character,
that is whether the first-person pronoun refers to a character
within the story.

For Pipola, any first-person film must have the dual
structure of fiction's central consciousness because, basically,
film has no equivalent to the first-person pronoun. Even
when a film, like Letter From an Unknown Woman (1948),
signals through voice-over or other means that a character
is narrating, there is no way to sustain the impression
of first-person narration as prose fiction can by the repetition
of the pronoun "I." For Kawin, the connection between
the formal strategy of a film and a character is sufficient
to indicate first-person filmic narration; for Pipola,
it is not. Further, Pipola argues that the photographic
nature of film works against the sense of restriction
characteristic of much first-person prose fiction. Because

of its medium, a film will always convey more than can
be understood in terms of a single character's vantage
point. "The director's extensive visualization in filmic
terms of what one character sees or thinks always amounts
to what James calls a 'commentary [which] constantly attends
and amplifies,'" Pipola writes. "He, i.e., the director,
is always 'taking advantage of...things better than [the
character] herself [or himself]'" (0258, p. 168). Kawin
argues that narrators in first-person prose fiction often
present information that could not have been gathered first-hand
(his example: Ishmael in Moby Dick), and it is true, Genette
notes, that such shifts in focalization are not unknown
in prose fiction.

Edward Branigan in Point of View in the Cinema offers
an explanation of subjective filmic sequences that is similar
to Pipola's. Branigan is interested in how we "read" filmic
structures and therefore in what sanctions a viewer's assigning
the origin for a shot or a scene to a character. He notes
that the viewer will assign the authority for a sequence
to a character and will read shots in terms of character
psychology even though certain shots are from "neutral"
angles. He explains this subjective interpretation by
analogy with the "free indirect" style of prose fiction.
"In literature, a parallel case might be the telling of
a story as if by a character," he writes, "but told in
the third person, for example the third person 'reflectors'
of Henry James. This formulation suggests yet another
approach to the problem of explaining reflection and projection
sequences--through analogy with the discursive style known
as the 'free indirect.' The indirect is a way of reporting
the speech or thought of a character without direct quotation.
It is intimately connected to character without stating
exactly the character's speech or thought" (0211,
pp. 125-126). In free indirect style, because the speech
tag has been omitted, the reader may hesitate about assigning
a statement to the narrator or to a character; similarly,
Branigan says, a spectator may hestitate about assigning
shot sequences to a narrating agency or to a character.

In his "Tense, Mood, and Voice in Film (Notes After
Genette)," Brian Henderson applies Genette's categories
of mood and voice to film, particularly to John Ford's
How Green Was My Valley (1941) and Joseph Mankiewicz's
All About Eve (1950). Henderson identifies focalization
exclusively in terms of visual perspective. He may have
been led to equate focalization with visual perspective
because Genette often speaks of focalization in terms of
a character's seeing and because of a footnote in Genette's
Narrative Discourse in which he equates pure internal
focalization with the way the camera occupies the protagonist's
position in Robert Montgomery's Lady in the Lake.

But when he initially defines the term, Genette warns
against taking "focalization" in purely visual terms.
His three classes of focalization--variable, internal and
external--are based upon two criteria: the way information
comes to the narrator, whether through a single character
or many, and the kinds of information that come to the
narrator. Focalization concerns whether the narrator knows
more than, less than, or the same as his characters at
any given point in the text. Consequently, the first order

of business in discussing focalization in film should be
to establish whether film is mediated, that is, whether
film is narrated. Henderson does not offer an extended
discussion of the problem. He says that films "usually
present the direct imitation of speech and action but do
so in a mediated, or diegetic way" (0230, p. 13). He does
discuss first-person film, but he finds that it has little
to do with first-person narration in prose fiction, calling
it "a narrative convenience used and dropped by the film
to suit its purposes" (0230, p. 15). Because Henderson
has identified the image track with focalization, it is
not at all clear what he would consider the marks of the
narrator.

     In his analysis of a scene from John Ford's How Green
Was My Valley, Henderson argues that the scene is not internally
focalized, although internal focalization might be expected
in a "first-person" film. It is variably focalized, he
argues, because it is not shot from the perspective of
a single character but from the perspectives of a number
of characters. Variable focalization, he argues, is typical
of the "classical cinema." Henderson apparently equates
a series of point of view shots from the perspectives of
several characters with Genette's first category of
focalization, nonfocalized narrative, point of view shots
from the perspective of a single character with Genette's
second category, internal focalization, and an absence
of point of view shots with Genette's third, objective
focalization. Henderson's argument, when applied to various
"classical films," yields very odd results. If, for instance,
the flashback to Paris in Casabalanca (1942) is considered
in Henderson's terms, what is clearly indicated to be Rick's
memory is objectively focused because the sequence is not
consistently shot from a character's perspective or several
characters' perspectives. Genette argues that objective
focalization concerns the narrator's (and so the reader's)
inablility to read a character's thoughts or feelings directly,
which is certainly not the case in this flashback from
Casablanca. It would seem, then, that Henderson's orginal
identification of focalization with perspective is faulty.
I suspect that if Genette's definition of focalization
is applied to film, even the "classical film" would display
a greater variety of focalizations than Henderson admits.

     Most writers on film and literature simply presume
the presence of a narrator, generally because they identify
camera work and editing with mediation. If film is assumed
to be equivalent to prose fiction, if film is a process
of "telling" through images, then it should be possible
to apply various theories of utterance to uncover evidence
of a narrator's presence. Recent literary theory has been
concerned with locating these "traces" of the narrator
in the text, with isolating those elements that constitute
what Genette calls the "narrating instance." Most analyses
posit a distinction between discours, those parts of the
text strongly marked by the narrator's presence, and histoire,
those parts of the text free from the narrator's presence.
Emile Benveniste distinguishes the two by verb tense and
pronouns: discourse is marked by the absence of the aorist
and the presence of first- and second-person pronouns.
All utterances presuppose a narrator, a source, but only

some utterances display the narrator's marks.

As Jonathan Culler argues, Benveniste's linguistic
method has distinct limitations when applied to prose fiction;
a passage may lack the linguistic signs of histoire and
still imply the presence of a narrator (Structuralist Poetics
[Ithaca: Cornell University Press, 1975], p. 198). The
discours/histoire distinction is even more troublesome
when applied to film. Mark Nash in "Vampyr and the Fantastic"
and Steve Seidman in "The Innocents: Point of View as an
Aspect of the Cinefantastic System" apply Benveniste's
distinction to substantiate a connection between the two
films and Tzvetan Todorov's literary genre of the fantastic.
Because Seidman follows Nash's method, I will comment only
on Nash's article. Nash must, of course, ignore Benveniste's
primary means of distinguishing the two planes of utterance,
verb tenses. His application of Benveniste's distinction,
then, entirely depends upon the presence of "filmic shifters,"
the cinematic equivalent, he belives, of linguistic pronouns.
Using Roland Barthes's commutation test to distinguish
personal from a-personal narration, Nash divides various
kinds of shots into instances of discours and histoire
to show that Dreyer's Vampyr (1932) displays the same sort
of confusion of subject and narrator that distinguishes
works in the genre of the fantastic. First-person shots
attributable to both character and narrator are instances
of discourse; in essence, by making the shot of the source
ambiguous, the film itself performs the commutation test.
Descriptive shots with "personal marks" of the narrator,
primarily tracking shots, are also instances of discours.
Character point of view shots and descriptive shots without
those "personal marks" are instances of histoire.

David Bordwell argues that Nash fails to rigorously
apply Benveniste's method because he cannot find a cinematic
equivalent for the second-person pronoun (direct address
to the reader) save for two titles in the film that present
questions to the viewer (0015, p. 23). Nash implies that
certain close-ups have attributes of second-person, but
he is unable to substantiate what would make one close-up
second person and another third. He argues that some close-ups
are imperative; a shot of the pages of a book, he says,
is equivalent to "read this!" But this distinction is
so loose that it could be argued that every shot is
second-person because every shot is equivalent to "look
at this!" Nor can Nash substantiate what constitutes the
"personal marks" of the narrator, a critical factor in
distinguishing discours from histoire. His argument rests
on a norm of cinematic expression; those features that
violate that norm constitute the "personal marks" of discourse,
the cinematic equivalent of the narrator's "I." I agree
with Bordwell that attempts such as Nash's to apply enunciation
theory to film have led to "an intuitive, ad hoc spotting"
of discourse because film lacks equivalents for tense and
person (0015, p. 24).

From the beginning of film criticism, writers have
noted that film "tells" a story much as prose fiction does.
Prose fiction's mediation through language, it was felt,
was analogous to film's selection through camera work and
editing. The apparent similarity between film and prose
fiction was strengthened by the optical metaphor woven

into a number of categories of point of view. Though we
can understand why some have been tempted to analyze film
in terms of a narrator and the narrator's position relative
to the fictional world, such analyses have been fraught
with difficulties owing to the differences between prose
fiction and film. Such differences have blocked the direct
application of literary analyses, and those analyses that
have succeeded--Pipola's and Branigan's, for instance--have
done so by not forcing the analogy between prose fiction
and film.

The shortcomings of analyses of film in terms of a
narrator and point of view have led some writers to discard
the whole concept of narrator. George Wilson in his "Film,
Perception and Point of View" asserts that "we simply have
no clear, general idea of film narrative being rendered
by a kind of 'visual' narrator in the required sense.... But
neither of these notions [an implied author and subjective
shots] is sufficient to generate an aesthetically central
concept of narrative 'voice' which may be importantly distinct"
(0281, p. 1027). In <u>Narration in the Fiction Film</u>, David
Bordwell discards the notion of the filmic narrator for
a number of reasons. He notes the failure of such writers
as Mark Nash and Christian Metz to apply enunciation theory
to film. Spectators, are seldom aware of mediation by
a filmic narrator. Most importantly, he argues that the
concept of a narrator is not needed to "read" a film.
(In this, he parts company with Edward Branigan, whose
approach otherwise resembles Bordwell's in many ways.)
Though Bordwell admits that filmic narration can sometimes
suggest a narrator, he rejects that a narrator is an inherent
part of filmic narration because "to give every film a
narrator or an implied author is to indulge in an
anthropomorphic fiction" (0015, p. 62).

The application of the standard pronominal divisions
of point of view to film is fraught with difficulties simply
because of the different expressive means of film and
literature. While interpreting a literary work involves
identifying the first person pronoun with a narrator either
from inside or outside the fictional world and then interpreting
the fiction in terms of the narrator's identity, interpreting
film, at least according to Bruce Kawin and others, involves
the reverse. One can indentify the nature of the narrator
only after one has interpreted the entire film because
it lacks the clear narrational marks of literature that
allow for an easy identification of the narrator.

As this discussion has indicated, the major stumbling
block to applying the categories of literary point of view
to film is first person narration. If filmic first person
is reserved only for those films told from the optical
vantage point of a single character, then first person
narration is either a category containing a single film,
<u>Lady in the Lake</u>, or a series of deviations within a third-
person film. In the latter case, the point-of-view shots
which constitute the first-narration function something
like direct quotations in third-person prose fiction. If
filmic first person is extended to those films that cue
the spectator by means of dialogue, music, and such optical
devices as lap dissolves to interpret images in terms of
character retrospection, then, as Tony Pipola notes, one

must account for the excess of information that lies outside
the understanding or control of the narrator.

   If applying the concept of narrator to film presents
a number of problems, Wilson and Bordwell demonstrate
the difficulties of attempting to interpret filmic narrative
without recourse to the idea of a narrator. The idea of
a narrator, or a source, is so fundamental to an understanding
of narration that, even though both writers banish the
term "narrator" from their basic formulations of film,
the concept of a narrator is still very much a part of
their understanding of how film conveys its narrative.
Wilson, for instance, describes narrative in terms of
"reliability," a moral judgment applicable to people, or
in the case of fiction, narrators. In his view, the narrative
itself withholds information and misleads its spectators
for aesthetic affect. While Bordwell rejects the concept
of narrator as "an anthropomorphic fiction," it is clear
that he has subsumed the idea of a narrator under the term
"narration," which itself amounts to creating an anthropomorphic
fiction. Throughout his book, Bordwell describes the process
of conveying the fiction as "forgetting," "withholding,"
"delaying," in short, as doing the very things that are
usually accounted for by reference to a narrator.

B. TIME

A narrator must tell something, and he must tell it in a certain order. Attributes of this temporal narrative order can been seen in E.M. Forster's familiar example of a plot: "The king died, and then the queen died of grief." This is a plot because of temporal order, first that happened and then this happened, and because of an inferred causal sequence, first that happened which caused this to happen. While Forster's concern is the novel, temporal order is a basic characteristic of any narrative. By definition, drama, film, and prose fiction share temporal manipulation because all narrative involves "the representation of at least two real or fictive events or situations in a time sequence. . . ." (Gerald Prince, _Narratology: The Form and Functioning of Narrative_ [New York: Mouton, 1982, p. 4]). A consideration of Forster's example reveals that the order of the events as presented by the narrator and the order of the events as they happened in the fictional world are the same. But this need not be so. The narrator might have reported: "The queen died of grief after the king died." The order of the events as they happened in the fictional world has been reversed in the narrator's report. In this report, the actual order of the events is signalled by verb tense and by the preposition "after," which denotes time.

Two further observations are worth making about Forster's example. Each event occurs only once in the narrative although, the narrator might have reported one event twice: "The king died, and after he died, the queen died of grief." Also, the narrator's report of these events takes much less time to read than the events did to occur. These simple observations can give us a foothold in analyzing time in film, prose fiction, and drama. These seem to be the significant issues concerning time in the three arts: the means by which events are ordered; the various ways the events can be ordered; the duration of the events as they are presented versus their duration in the fictional world; the number of times the events occur in the narrative versus the number of times they occur in the fictional world. I shall begin by discussing time in film and prose fiction and then proceed with time in film and drama.

Perhaps the most widely held view is that film is in the present tense while prose fiction is in past tense; this distinction is based upon the observation that film

lacks any inherent means comparable to language's tense
system. While both film and drama are present tense arts,
many have argued that film's system of optical "punctuation"
and the ease with which its medium can be manipulated enables
film to use time in more ways and with greater ease than
can drama.

The traditional view of the present tense in film
is best exemplified by George Bluestone in his Novels Into
Film. Bluestone argues the novel has three tenses, the
film only one, and from this "follows almost everything
one can say about time in both media" (0498, p. 48). Because
of language's tense system, he says, the novel has three
chronological levels: the duration of the reading of the
text, the duration of the narrator's time, and the duration
of the narrated events. Film, however, has but two levels,
two "present" time frames—the duration of the "reading"
of the text and the duration of the depicted events—because
the filmic narrator is always the camera. Because film
is not a recounting of an event but a recording of an event
as it happens, Bluestone implies, the filmmaker cannot
derive effects by opposing the second and third levels;
such effects are typical of a novel like Tristram Shandy
in which Sterne juxtaposes the time it takes events to
transpire versus the longer time it takes to narrate them.

Other writers agree with Bluestone. Bela Balazs writes,
"They [pictures] show only the present. They cannot express
either a past or a future tense" (0004, p. 120). Evelyn
Riesman characterizes camera-work in terms of "telling
a story in the present tense" (0263, p. 358). Even flashbacks,
she says, are experienced by the audience as being in the
present. Prose fiction, on the other hand, is "an account
of something, a remembrance, told in the past tense" (0263,
p. 358). William Jinks characterizes filmic time as "present
tense" because film must rely on context to convey temporal
order while the "verbs alone will signal you that these
events occurred some time ago" (0232, p. 18). More recently,
Bruce Kawin has noted that the lack of a past tense is
one of film's "most decisive limitations" (0236, p. 77).
The filmmaker who uses a flashback "goes against the inherent
present tense of the image" and renders not the past but
the past as something present, he says.

This traditional view of time in film and literature
confuses the order of the events as reported by the narrator,
that is, the plot, and one of the means for creating that
order in prose fiction, verb tense. Verb tense is an attribute
of language, not images. As Alexander Sesonske in "Time
and Tense in Cinema" points out, to argue that film has
only a single tense is tantamount to arguing that it has
no tense at all because tense can only be defined by opposition
(past, not past). Perhaps when Bluestone and others refer
to film's present tense, they are actually referring to
its immediacy, the impression it gives of presenting its
story in the here and now. For instance, George Linden
in Reflections on the Screen writes that, though film is
"tenseless," it "directly displays the present." Even
a novel concerned with the present, he argues, "is still
written and experienced in the reflective mode and hence
never quite reaches the present. The film, on the other
hand, "collapses all its elements into a fluid present....The

essence of film is its immediacy, and this immediacy is grounded in its tenselessness" (0241, p. 32).

The weakness in Linden's argument can be seen when basic questions are posed about the novel's grounding in the past and film's ability to directly display the present. Whose past, whose remembrance, does a reader encounter in prose fiction? Certainly not the reader's nor the author's because the events in prose fiction are just that, fiction. The events are presented as though they occurred in the narrator's past. Whose present does the film directly depict? Drawing on Stephenson and Debrix, Linden says that the sense of the present derives from the image's immediacy. Because of this immediacy, it becomes difficult, if not impossible, for a film to establish past time, to say "then." As Stephenson and Debrix note, "when we watch a film, it is just something that is happening--now..." (0241, p. 33). In one respect this is true. The sense of the present derives from the spectator's presence before the film image, the spectator's experience of the film image; it is "here" and "now" because the spectator can only see and hear now, not retrospectively. But this distinction between prose fiction and film rests on a confusion between fictional time--the temporal relationship between fictional events and narrator--and actual time--the temporal relationship between the unfolding of the filmic narration and the spectator. More generally, it can be said that the former is purely artificial, the product of a reader's or viewer's projection of the characteristics of actual time onto the artwork to establish before and after relationships. The latter concerns not the work, but the spectator's engagement with the work, the spectator's sense of the duration of his experience with the film. As Sesonske notes, "The fact that I am watching an event in a film does not determine its location in action-time [story time] in relation to the other events I have seen or will see in the same film. But without this implication, immediacy no longer identifies the moment as the present, and therefore does not imply a present tense" (0195, p. 424).

In fact, if the experiential, or discourse, times of film and prose fiction are compared with their story times, the radical distinction between the temporality of film and of prose fiction disappears. As Joan Dagle notes in her "Narrative Discourse in Film and Fiction," the sense of presentness that derives from encountering a narrative is common to both readers of prose fiction and viewers of films. "To read is also to be subjected to the temporal, sequential unfolding of a series of units, each of which is present or absent at any given moment," she writes. "In other words, the act of either reading or viewing a narrative must necessarily take place in the present tense. Thus, any attempt to differentiate the tense of film narrative from that of fictional narrative cannot rest on an appeal to the process of encountering that narrative" (0151, 48). If their discourse times are similar in that both create a sense of presentness, then their story times are likewise similar. In both instances, the narratives provide the reader/spectator with cues to establish a present and cues to establish events as before or after that present. Unlike discourse time, which is

independent of the meaning of the work, these temporal
relationships derive from the work as a semantic system.

To summarize, the separation of film and prose fiction
on the basis of verb tense seems faulty on a number of
grounds. As Edward Branigan has written, film and prose
fiction are comparable with respect to time rather than
tense. Both film and literature, he writes, acquire temporal
reference through "a series of marks none of which is in
itself time but to which we apply temporal labels" (0211,
p. 218). To argue that film is tenseless and experienced
as present while the novel is experienced as past
confuses the spectator's experience of the work with temporal
indicators within the work. It may understood that what
is being read or viewed is past in terms of narrative or
plot order but still experienced as present, as though
the events were happening in here and now.

The mistakes that have marred discussions of time
in film and prose fiction have come from confusing the
reader's or viewer's present with that of the narrative's
present, the starting point of the narrative's event chain.
It is this narrative chain that need to be examined. It
is common in the study of narrative to distinguish plot
from story. The former concerns the order of the events
within the work itself, and the latter concerns the events
placed in another temporal order by the reader or the viewer.
Plots may correspond more or less closely to the story,
but the "reading," the basic understanding, of a narrative
entails converting the structure of the plot into the
chronological structure of the story. The basic assumption
in this operation is that fictional time must resemble
natural time, and, as Alexander Sesonske notes, this means
that in reading prose fiction or in viewing a film, it
must be possible to establish before and after relationships.
For example, to understand a flashback in film or in prose
fiction, the viewer must identify it as having occurred
before the present and must be able to place it in the
chronological order of the story.

A basic understanding of narrative involves establishing
before and after relationships. Verb tenses in verbal
discourse create a base-line, a "present," and so do
narratives. In rearranging the order of events in the
work into the chronological order of story, the reader
must discover the starting point, the base-line, which
establishes some events as before, some as after and some
as simultaneous. This "present" has been variously described.
Sesonske notes that "some point or duration becomes the
present time within the work; events may be described as
occurring in this present and other events related to them
as past or future, with tenses functioning to indicate
these relations" (0195, pp. 422-423). In Story and Discourse,
Seymour Chatman explains, "Narratives establish a sense
of a present moment, narrative NOW, so to speak. If the
narrative is overt, there are perforce two NOWs, that of
the discourse, the moment occupied by the narrator in the
present tense. . .and that of the story, the moment that
the action began to transpire, usually in the preterite.
If the narrator is totally absent or covert, only the story-NOW
emerges clearly" (0215, p. 63). Some writers have described
this sense of fictive present in terms of the emotional

reaction of the reader, but Meir Sternberg offers perhaps
a more precise definition when he says that the end of
the exposition in the story marks the beginning of the
fictive present in the plot (<u>Expositional Modes and Temporal
Ordering in Fiction</u> [Baltimore: The Johns Hopkins University
Press, 1978], p. 210).

   To clarify time in film and drama, I have distinguished
at least three "presents": that of the reader, that of
the narrator, and that of the story. But what are the
means which prose fiction and film use to create temporal
order? As I have said, one of the primary means writers
of prose fiction have at their disposal for ordering events
is verb tense, one aspect of language's deictic properties.
It is able, as Roger Fowler says, to "orient the propositions
and their parts in relation to time and place established
by the speech act" (<u>Understanding Language</u> [Boston: Routledge
and Kegan Paul, 1974, p. 112]). The speaker or the reader
establishes what Fowler calls a "temporal base-line," that
is, a present; tenses and other deictic elements locate
propositions in terms of this base-line. While language
enables a speaker to refer to a number of temporal points,
Fowler notes that formally the tense of English verbs has
but two values: past or not past. The reason that Fowler
discounts such values as the present, which can be expressed
by English, is that present tense alone is insufficient
to establish whether one is speaking about the present
or the past (as in instances of the "historical present").

   Verb tenses and other deictic elements in sentences
that refer to actual events or states establish real points
in time, but in fiction verb tenses and other deictic elements
establish fictional points in time within the narrative. By
far the most frequently used tense in narratives is the
past, the preterite, but then should it be assumed that
prose fiction is an art of past time and film an art of
the present? What value should be assigned to verb tenses
in fiction? Should it be assumed that past tense refers
to the past? That makes sense in a number of novels. For
instance, in first-person narration and the personalized
third-person narration characteristic of such eighteenth-
and nineteenth-century writers as Fielding and Thackeray,
the past tense indicates that the actions within the narrative
are past with respect to the base-line established by the
narrator. The past tense seems also to help establish the
reality of the fictional event, which "happened" before
the narrator related them to the reader.

   But some have attacked the whole idea that past tense
in fiction indicates past time by noting some narratives's
troublesome shifts from past to present tense, the so-called
historical present. For example, on the first page of
Joyce Cary's <u>Mister Johnson</u> we read, "Bamu said nothing.
She saw that Johnson was a stranger." But a paragraph
later we read, "Bamu pays no attention. She throws the
pole, places the top between her breasts against her crossed
palms and walks down the narrow craft." Especially in
works with effaced narrators, the reader's sense of the
past time of the events may be slight. And, if it is assumed
that the past tense primarily signals that a narrative's
events "occurred some time ago," as William Jinks says,
it must be considered that a number of literary theorists,

including Käte Hamburger and Roman Ingarden, have seen
the primary purpose of the past tense as indicating not
past time but the fictionality of the narrative.
    Tense is an important means by which prose fiction
establishes temporal order, but it is not the only one.
Adverbs, adjectives, context also play their parts.
Significantly for this discussion, past tense often designates,
not past time within the narrative, but the story-NOW,
that moment that establishes a temporal base-line for the
developing action. Sesonske writes, "When one tense, usually
the past, predominates in a fictional work, its continuous
usage does not explicitly indicate relations of before
and after, but rather sustains our sense of the regular
flow of time in the world of the work" (0195, p. 423).
    Both film and drama, of course, lack any formal means
for indicating temporal order. Film has a kind of "grammar,"
a system of "punctuation" consisting of the cut and various
optical devices such as the fade and the lap dissolve,
but, though they have sometimes been likened to prepositions
and adverbs that denote time, these "cinematic punctuation
marks" lack the stable meanings associated with language's
deictic elements. None of these devices alone denote the
order of events within the story. Rather, these devices
depend for their meaning on the general context of the
plot events. As David Bordwell remarks, "The temporal
relations in the fabula [story] are derived by inference;
the viewer fits schemata to the cues proferred by the narration"
(0015, p. 77). Because film lacks any inherent means of
indicating temporal order and so must rely on context to
indicate such order, devices that indicate shifts in time
are generally highly redundant.
    Are these optical devices the only means that film
has for indicating temporal order? Dialogue might seem
a prime means, but critics have generally not considered
language as important, preferring to see film in terms
of its pure visual "essence." George Bluestone, for instance,
notes that sound can indicate past, present, and future
relationships, but he asserts that "sound is a secondary
advantage which does not seriously threaten the primacy
of the spatial image" (0498, p. 57).   Joan Dagle has advanced
a number of arguments against seeing film purely in terms
of image, but the best case against the visual essence
argument is be made by conventional film practice itself.
Preston Sturges' The Miracle of Morgan's Creek (1944),
for example, begins with a phone call from the local newspaper
editor to the governor about a "miracle" that has occurred
in the small town, and most of the film concerns the editor's
explanation of the events leading up to this miracle, the
birth of sextuplets. What interests us is how Sturges
manages the shift from present to past. As the editor
recalls that he himself began the whole chain of events
one day when he was looking out the window, there is a
lap dissolve from the editor (time present) to what he
saw that day, the local police officer (time past). The
temporal shift is implied by an optical effect and directly
indicated by the tenses in the editor's dialogue ("I was
looking out the window....") and by its meaning.
Similarly, in Robert Hamer's Kind Hearts and Coronets (1949),
dialogue provides the means to distinguish present from

past. In the opening scene, Louis Dascoigne awaits execution
and prepares to spend his last night reading over his memoirs.
As he is seen reading, his voice-over is heard explaining
that he should "begin at the beginning." He says, "I was
a healthy baby," and the film cuts from the duke in his
cell to a young baby held by his nurse. Again, the temporal
order is specifically indicated by the tense of the dialogue.
The early part of the movie, in fact, proceeds through
frequent cuts back to the duke in his cell to establish
the duke's NOW and the duke's voice-over narration whose
meaning and tense uses identify scenes as flashbacks.
Lacking any equivalent of tense, film has often used tense
in dialogue as a way of specifically indicating temporal
order. As Brian Henderson notes, "Analepses [flashbacks]
in the cinema have nearly always involved the use of language,
sometimes explicit dialogue setting up a return to the
past, more often the direct intervention of language in
the form of titles or voice-over. . . .Classical cinema
reacts to a tense shift as though to a cataclysm; the viewer
must be warned at every level of cinematic expression,
in sounds, in images, and in written language, lest he/she
be disoriented" (0230, p. 6).
        If one considers film purely in terms of image, it
might seem that it simply has no way of indicating time
shifts with the facility and subtlety that language affords
prose fiction. But once film is seen in terms of both
image and sound, then the gap between their ability to
indicate temporal order narrows considerably. Language
offers the means of clarifying the present through reference
to the past and, occasionally, it shows the result of an
event as the event develops. In regard to this latter
point, Joan Dagle notes that film has the ability to order
time by using sound not just to enhance or complete the
image but to convey information different from that of
the image. This "superimposition" of time frames through
the use of film's double register can be seen in any number
of films in which dialogue evokes the past while showing
the effect of the past on the present. In Ingmar Bergman's
Persona, the double register is used to create the simultaneous
unfolding of events in two time frames; the viewer reconstructs
through Alma's dialogue her seduction at the beach by a
young boy, and the viewer deduces through the images of
her face the effect this memory has upon her. The use
of language to recount, to loop back and to establish the
effects of past events on the present, represents perhaps
the most significant and obvious means that film and drama
have to structure events. While many think of both film
and drama as arts of the present moment and assume that
everything in film must be visualized, narratives must
have some means for presenting expository material, and
given that the performance time of both is, generally speaking,
much shorter than the time of the events covered by the
artwork, recounting is a necessary tool for story-telling.
        Film can also use sound effects to signify a past
event and the image to embody an event in story-NOW. In
Alfred Hitchcock's _Strangers on a Train_ (1951), Bruno is
seen showing a dowager how easy it is to murder someone,
while the strains of "After the Ball" are heard, an aural
"flashback" to the murder of Guy's wife.

Events may be enacted rather than recounted or implied, and such instances provide interesting examples of how film can use its double register to structure time. For instance, in Bergman's <u>Autumn Sonata</u> (1978), Eva tells her mother of her childhood loneliness. As she says, "You'd shut yourself in and work," a lap dissolve draws the connection between the image of Eva's face in the story-NOW and the shot of a young girl outside a door; the verb tense locates the image of the child in the past, and the dialogue identifies the girl as Eva. The image then continues in the past, and the dialogue continues in the story-NOW. Later, we see Eva with her father, and the deixis in the voice-over establishes the recurring nature of what we see only once: "Sometimes he would say, 'Let's go to the movies this evening or get ice cream'....Occasionally Uncle Otto would be sitting on the sofa...."

In Phillip Kaufmann's western <u>The Great Northfield, Minnesota Raid</u> (1972) we find a similar superimposition of time. The James gang discovers that the Missouri legislature has not granted them amnesty. A drummer's account of the vote is heard in the story-NOW which establishes the images of the vote as past action and identifies the figures within the image as the members of the legislature and their actions as the amnesty vote.

In <u>Autumn Sonata</u>, Bergman uses the voice-over to establish the time frame, to summarize dialogue, to identify the nature of the depicted actions, and to establish Eva's attitude toward the past, particularly toward her mother. The images of past action are used chiefly to validate those attitudes; the indifference she ascribes to her mother in the voice-over is enacted in the image of past actions, and, because the images are not obviously stylized, they are assumed to represent what actually happened rather than Eva's memories of them. Kaufmann uses the voice-over for much the same reasons but with this difference: the images contradict what is said in the voice-over. As the drummer speaks of his admiration for the courage of the speaker of the house for rejecting the amnesty vote, the speaker is seen accepting a bribe from the railroad detectives. In other words, both directors use enacted images to convey the truth--"seeing is believing" is the relevant cliché--but Kaufmann uses the temporal juxtapositions as a means of establishing the shortcomings of the opinions expressed in the story-NOW; the enjambment of past and present underlines the difference between the irretrievable past truth and its present distortions.

If the outdated notion that the silent image is the essence of film is rejected, as Dagle argues, then it is evident that film has a number of ways to use its double register to indicate temporal order, not all of them dependent on context. Past events can be recounted through character dialogue or through commentary by a narrator or enacted and situated within the past by voice-over or implied by sound and situated within the past by prior context and by contrast with images in story-NOW. Events can be situated within the past purely by context, by the enjambment of images in story NOW with images in the past, as in Fellini's <u>8 1/2</u> (1963). This mixing of past and present in film is analogous to much modern fiction in which shifts from present

to past are made without any obvious temporal cues (change
in verb tense, prepositions, adverbs); in William Faulkner's
fiction, for instance, the shifts are indicated purely
by context, just as in the Fellini film. Finally, events
can be situated within the past by the conventional rhetorical
strategy of dialogue, music, and optical effects to signify
a temporal shift.

Therefore, both prose fiction and film have a number
of means to indicate temporal order. Before the possible
kinds of orderings used in both are considered, one final
difference posed between time in film and fiction needs
to be discussed: context. In terms of this argument, in
the novel, verb tense is a constant indicator of past time,
while in the film, once a time shift has been signalled
by dialogue, music and optical effects, the image in the
past is visually indistinguishable from those in the present.
In other words, in prose fiction, the altered signifier
that results from a change in verb form, is a constant
reminder of pastness, but film lacks any inherent means
to alter the signifiers, the images, to indicate the temporal
nature of an event. William Jinks in The Celluloid Literature
argues that a reader opening a novel to any passage will
know that the events belong to the past because of the
verb tense, but a spectator beginning to watch a film in
progess will have no way of knowing whether the images
belong to the present or to the past. "Certainly, given
enough time you would figure it out," he writes, "but the
point is that without the additional context, you'd have
no way of knowing" (0232, p. 18).

Film can use its double register to consistently anchor
a series of images in the past by means of voice-over.
As Joan Dagle notes, film can alter the image to indicate
time. For example, in Herbert Ross's The Seven Percent
Solution (1976), the edges of the images are blurred during
the final flashback when the cause of Sherlock Holmes's
cocaine addiction is revealed, constantly reminding the
viewer that the images signify past time. Though this
modification of the signifier may indicate past time, it
does lack any the settled, conventionalized meaning of
the modified linguisitic signifier in prose fiction. As
a result, the meaning of the blurred edges in the Ross
film is context-dependent. The viewer makes the connection
between such visual elements and time, not because of
conventional, stable relationships between these elements
and time, but because the context of a particular film
has led the viewer to assign the element such a meaning.
In the Herbert Ross film, we assign to the blurred image
the meaning of past time, of remembrance, primarily because
of the dialogue that explicitly identifies the image of
the murder as past, as Holmes' memory. In prose fiction,
we understand an episode is in the past because we understand
the meaning of the change in signifier, but in Dagle's
example, we understand the meaning of the altered signifier
only because we have been cued by other means that the
episode is in the past.

At any rate, such modifications of the image to indicate
time are rather rare. The standard means which film uses
to indicate time shifts, as Dagle notes, is to bracket
scenes in the past with images and sound that indicate

a shift from present to past and then a shift from past
back to present. But within these brackets, a flashback
looks no different than images in present time. While
she admits that a differece between film and prose fiction
is that the signifier which indicates a shift in time disappears
once the shift is made, Dagle argues that "it is possible
to conceive of a written narrative" that also employs this
bracketing technique (0151, p. 49).

It is not difficult to find examples from prose fiction
that illustrate this notion. Such works are just as dependent
upon context to indicate time as is film. Consider these
two passages from William Styron's Sophie's Choice:

>   She returned to the table, straining with the
>   effort as she lowered the lead German contraption
>   to the floor, replacing it with the Polish model. . .She
>   began to type, translating as she went from the shorthand
>   message Höss had dictated to her the previous afternoon.
>   It concerned a minor but vexing problem, one having
>   to do with community relations.
>
>   She lay down for what she thought would be a nap,
>   but in her exhaustion slept for a long time, although
>   restlessly. Waking up in the dark, she saw by the
>   alarm clock's green eyes that it was past ten o'clock
>   and she was seized by grave, immediate alarm ([New
>   York: Bantam Books, 1980], p. 276, 387-388).

Those familiar with the novel or with the film adaptation
will recognize that the second passage concerns Sophie's
relationships with Nathan and Stingo in story-NOW and the
first passage concerns her past experiences in the concentration
camp. A reader unfamiliar with the novel might be able
to deduce the temporal order after a while from the context,
but, contrary to Jinks, a reader would not be able to deduce
the temporal order purely by verb tense because in these
two passages Styron uses the preterite to indicate both
story-NOW and past. How, then, in the novel is the pastness
of the first passage indicated? The past tense locates
the two events--the typing, the nap--generally within the
narrator's, Stingo's, past, but it does not indicate the
temporal relationship between the two events. The pastness
of the first event is indicated by a bracketing technique
that loosely corresponds to the conventional rhetorical
strategy of film. The section from which the first passage
is drawn begins in story-NOW, and takes the form of indirect
discourse: "she described it to me. . .she blurted out
to me." Once the temporal relationship is established,
the section becomes free indirect discourse in which the
speech tags (she said, she recalled, she remembered) are
omitted. The section ends in direct quotations, which
returns the time frame to story-NOW: "'It stopped then,
the music,' Sophie said to me."

This strategy is typical of a number of novels employing
free indirect discourse: a bracketing in which story-NOW,
indicated by speech tags, mixes with past events, conveyed
by the dependent clauses, just as film mixes images from
story-NOW and images of past events by means of lap dissolves,
music, and dialogue. Certainly, the analogy between these

verbal and cinematic means cannot be pushed too far, but
the way such novels and films create temporal relations
are quite similar, though their means are different. In
both cases, incidents in the past are indistinguishable
from incidents in the present; in film, the images of past
and present are the same, and in the novel the temporal
signifier, the verb, remains the same in both past and
present events. Further, the temporal order is established
by bracketing the past material, by mixing past with present.
     The ease with which David Bordwell, Brian Henderson,
and Seymour Chatman apply to film Gérard Genette's categories
of temporal order in prose fiction indicates that the possible
orderings of large structures, such as scenes in film and
prose fiction, are quite similar as well.
     In general, Genette argues that the order runs from
the zero degree of chronology (a correspondence between
temporal order in plot and story) to deviations from chronology,
anachronies (disjunctions between the temporal order of
plot and story). Such anachronies include analepses (an
event happens later in the plot than in the story, such
as a flashback), and prolepses (the plot leaps ahead to
present an event that occurs much later in the story, a
flashforward). Despite the oddity of Genette's nomenclature,
his classifications, which I have simplified for this
discussion, should be familiar to students of film and
literature.
     Drawing on Genette's categories, David Bordwell posits
four classifications of the relationship between plot and
story. His first classification consists of simultaneous
events in the story presented simultaneously in the plot.
An example of this is the scene in Alfred Hitchcock's Marnie
(1964) in which on the right side of the screen we see
Marnie attempting to sneak out of the office after she
has robbed the safe and on the left side of the screen
a cleaning woman mopping the floor. Bordwell's second
classification consists of successive events in the story
presented as simultaneous events in the plot. An example
of this unusual relationship between plot and story is
the scene in which the friends in Lawrence Kasdan's The
Big Chill (1983) watch a videotape made by William Hurt's
character; a past event, in other words, is presented
simultaneously with a present event. It is quite obvious
that neither of these relationships has an analogue in
prose fiction for the simple reason that both depend on
the simultaneous presentation of events in the discourse.
While examples of successive events presented simultaneously
could be found in drama, the linguistic base of prose fiction
necessitates that events be unfolded in a linear fashion.
Thus, not surprisingly, this relationship between plot
and story constitutes a significant difference between
film and prose fiction which derives from the different
expressive capabilities of a digital medium and an analogic
medium.
     Literature shares with film Bordwell's third and fourth
classifications which entail the successive presentations
of events in the plot. His third classification consists
of simultaneous events in the story presented as successive
events in the plot. In film, of course, this is achieved
by crosscutting, the preferred technique for conveying

the chase. This relationship is just as common in prose
fiction, certainly in prose fiction since the nineteenth
century. Perhaps the prime example of this relationship
of plot and story is the fair scene in Flaubert's Madame
Bovary, which Eisenstein called "one of the finest examples
of cross-montage of dialogues," noting that the "method
is used with increasing popularity by Flaubert's artistic
heirs" (0324, pp. 12-13).

Bordwell's final classification contains the presentation
of successive events in the story presented as successive
events in the plot. This classification includes both
Genette's anachronies and straight chronology.

While writers have seen a close connection between
prose fiction's and film's ability to shuffle time, drama's
presumed inability to manipulate temporal order has been
seen as signficantly different from film. For example,
Jan Mukarovsky situates film between drama and prose fiction
because in the drama "the possibility of simultaneous plots
or even the displacement of segments of temporal series
(the performance of what happened earlier after what happened
later) is very limited, whereas the exploitation of simultaneity
and temporal shifts are normal in the narrative" (0085,
p. 192). Hugo Munsterberg says that the theater, unlike
film, "presents its plot in the time order of reality"
and that "the drama would give up its mission if it told
us in the third act something which happened before the
second act" (0087, pp. 77-78). Allardyce Nicoll characterizes
temporal manipulation in the drama as "freakish" and cautions
that the playwright must structure his plot on a "direct
and rectilinear path" (0409, pp. 96-97).

The ease with which film manipulates time, Robert
Gessner argues, has freed it from the theatrical tradition.
While film can easily shuffle between past and present
and can expand or contract time, in drama, he says, "the
time spent on stage between the rising and falling of the
curtain--or blackouts (a cinematic acquisition)--approximates
the watches of the audience" (0335, p. 13). More recently,
Edward Murray makes a similiar point when he says that
"continuity of space and time" are characteristic of the
drama whereas "discontinuity of space and time" are
characterisitc of the film" (0088, p. 10).

None of these writers argue that there need be a strict
correspondence between dramatic plot and story. Obviously,
the time covered by story seldom corresponds to the two
or three hours of performance. Drama has traditionally
begun its plot shortly before the crisis and used expositional
dialogue to recount events that led up to it; thus the
order of events in the plot does not correspond to the
order of events in the story. To cite one famous example,
the event that initiates the story in Oedipus the King,
the prophecy that leads to the abandonment of the baby,
appears late in the plot and is recounted by the shepherd.
However, such temporal reordering does not violate the
"mission" of theatre because, as Munsterberg writes, such
expositional passages are "an enclosure of the past in
the present, which corresponds exactly to the order of
events" (0087, p. 78).

The objection is not to reordering in terms of expositional
passages, but to reordering in terms of enactment. These

writers see the only proper temporal relationship between
events in the plot as chronological. But why should this
be so? Mukarovsky's argument is typical. He notes that
in any narrative there are at least two temporal levels,
plot time--the temporal order and duration of the enacted
events and spectator time--the duration of the spectator's
engagement with the art work. These two temporal levels
are separate in prose fiction; the order and duration of
fictional events are in no way affected by the speed by
which a text is read; the time of the fictional events
is the same whether the text is read in one hour or five
hours. But the two levels are intimately connected in
drama in that the drama unfolds in an actual time and space
shared by the spectator. "The time of the perceiving subject
and that of the plot thus elapses side by side in the drama;
therefore, the plot of a drama takes place in the viewer's
present, even if the theme of the drama is temporally located
in the past (a historical drama)" (0085, p. 192).

This seems intuitively accurate. Dramatic signs--the
actor's body, gesture, words, actions--are ostended in
actual space and time; the actor's present is naturally
the spectator's present. Thus, because the time of events
upon the stage takes place in actual time and space--in
the spectator's here and now--dramatic time must share
the same characteristics as real time. So Munsterberg
rejects the idea of a flashback in drama because it violates
one of the characteristics of real time: directionality.
Like actual time, dramatic time must move forward. The
past, of course, cannot be experienced in the here and
now, but only recalled through memory, through dialogue.
Only the present is directly accessible, and only through
the present can the future be reached.

However, these critics also acknowledge that plot
time, unlike actual time, is discontinuous. For instance,
a spectator assumes that, when the curtain rises on the
third act, a certain segment of time may have been omitted.
If plot time differs from actual time in this respect,
can it not differ in terms of directionality? Does the
drama have the means to indicate the temporal reordering
of events within the plot? There are a sufficient number
of plays that violate chronological order to support the
notion that spectator time and plot time are not necessarily
parallel. Consider for a moment Jean Anouilh's Becket
or The Honor of God. The play begins as Henry II kneels
before Beckett's tomb, waiting to be flogged in penance,
but, before the first scene ends, the action moves back
several years to dramatize the king's friendship with Beckett
and his eventual betrayal of him. At the end of act four,
the play comes full circle with a return to the "present,"
the conclusion of the initial action. In the play, the
shift from past to present is effected much as it is in
film. The verb tense in the dialogue signals the movement
from present to past : "Ah, those were happy times. . . . At
the peep of dawn. . .you'd come to may room, as I was emerging
from the bath house. . ."([New York: Coward-McCann, 1960],
p. 13). A change in the lighting, much like the optical
effects in film, reinforces the change in time frame, and
the change is confirmed by having the initial action in
the past be an enactment of the event recounted in the

dialogue. (Henry has emerged from his bath when Becket
enters.)

The well-known deformation of chronological order
in Arthur Miller's Death of a Salesman is more complex
than one usually finds in film. In the first act, for
instance, the play moves from story-NOW to past (Willy
talks to his sons about his dream of owning his own business)
and then the play shifts to another past event (Willy talks
to the woman in his hotel room in Boston), which is presumably
nearer in time to story-NOW. In other words, this is a
flashback within a flashback, or what Genette might call,
I suppose, a prolepsis within an analepsis.

With some effort, examples from drama can be found
to fit Bordwell's outline of temporal ordering. Examples
of simultaneous events in the story presented as simultaneous
events in the plot are, of course, numerous; a good example
of this is the sword fight and the drinking of the poisoned
wine in the last act of Hamlet. Simultaneous events in
the story presented as successive actions in the plot are
rarer. Bernard F. Dick in "At the Crossroads of Time:
Types of Simultaneity in Literature and Film" notes that
Acts I and II of Jean Cocteau's The Infernal Machine are
simultaneous (0027, pp. 425-426). Examples of successive
events in the story presented as simultaneous events in
the plot are again rare, but one example is Ed Bullins's
A Son Come Home, in which events from the mother's life
are enacted as she and her son discuss them. Examples
of successive events in the story presented as successive
events in the plot are more numerous because this class
includes, obviously, those plays whose plots are chronological.

Several points need to be made about temporal ordering
in drama. First of all, several critics noted above, such
as Nicoll and Munsterberg, couched their objections to
such deviant temporal structures in terms of what drama
not only can do but what it should do. Their objections
are based on the "purity" of each art form, the idea that
aesthetic worth derives from utilizing those techniques
"natural" to each art. Thus, they object because they
see such temporal organizations as impurities the drama
has borrowed from film. Second, the relative scarcity
of examples of temporal reordering suggests that drama
has more difficulty with temporal reordering than does
prose fiction and film. Third, a good many critics have
argued that drama's inability to reorder time is a primary
difference between film and drama. Considering the number
of examples of plays that reorder time, small though they
may be in comparison to examples from film and fiction,
this distinction seems too strong. More temperate and
accurate is Donald W. Crawford's contention that "compared
to the necessity in theater to change sets or utilize some
mechanism, which rarely goes unnoticed, whereby space and
time can be modified with ease and speed, the greater facility
of the film becomes apparent" (0026, p. 460).

Frequency and duration are Genette's other characteristics
of time, and the latter raises some interesting issues
with respect to the relationship of film to literature.
Duration is familiar in literary study as the distinction
between summary and scene. In the former a great expanse
of story time is compressed into a relatively brief span

of reading time. In the latter, the duration of the scene closely matches that of the duration of the reading. Duration has to do with the relationship of story time to reading time, or as it is more commonly called, discourse time. This immediately suggests some differences between film and drama, on the one hand, and prose fiction, on the other.

Genette notes that the concept of duration in prose fiction is based on two admittedly vague ideas. On the one hand, the only temporality the narrative text actually has is the rate by which it is read, which quite obviously varies considerably from reader to reader. On the other hand, duration is based upon some idea of the span of an action, an event, or a scene within the plot that is almost never indicated with precision by the narrative. Genette concludes that speed must be established by the relationship of the duration of the plot events measured in days, years, etc. to the length of the text measure in lines or pages. Duration is therefore expressed as a ratio.

In prose fiction, the temporal progression of the plot is "borrowed" from the act of reading, but in both drama and film temporal progression can be precisely measured. One major difference between the duration of prose fiction and that of film and drama is that the latter is independent of the spectator. Quite obviously, one spectator cannot view a film or a play at a slower rate than another spectator.

To these two temporal dimensions--discourse time and story time--David Bordwell adds a third, the entire time of the story. He notes that the time covered by the story may be several years; the time dramatized, or the plot time, may be several months; and the running time of the film or the play may be several hours. In some cases, discourse and plot time (what he calls screen time and syuzhet time) may be equal, but story time is usually longer than both.

What then are the possible relationships between events within the plot and discourse time? Genette lists five: summary, in which discourse time is shorter than story time; ellipsis, in which discourse time is zero; scene, in which discourse time equals story time; stretch, in which discourse time is shorter than story time; and pause, in which story time is zero. Ellipsis, for instance, is identical in all three arts; a gap occurs in the discourse (sometimes signalled by the curtain falling in the theatre, a fade or a cut in film, the end of a chapter in prose fiction), but story time is presumed to continue. A particularly dramatic use of ellipsis occurs in Stanley Kubrick's 2001: A Space Odyssey (1968), which cuts from a shot of a bone hurled by a caveman to a shot of a space ship; discourse time is zero, while story time is several million years.

Language provides prose fiction with a number of means to indicate summary with relative ease. The temporal span of summary can be specifically marked by lexical features or more generally indicated by grammatical features. Seymour Chatman notes that "film has trouble with summary" and so "directors often resort to gadgetry" (0215, p. 69). Among the gadgets he mentions are the "montage-sequence," voice-over narrators, and the split conversation, in which a continuous dialogue is heard over shots of the characters

in various locales. More generally, events in film and
drama can be summarized through dialogue. While the effect
of such dialogue may be the same as summary in prose fiction,
its temporal structure is not. Summary dialogue in film
and drama involves discourse time equaling story time;
summary by the narrator in prose fiction involves discourse
time being less than story time.

Film has a number of ways of compressing time, so
that story time outruns discourse time. Ellipsis is perhaps
the most obvious. Film can also use language, sound effects,
or visual context to imply a disjunction between discourse
time and story time. In Steven Spielberg's <u>Close Encounters</u>
<u>of the Third Kind</u> (1977) a change in lighting implies that
an indeterminate stretch of story time has been squeezed
into a few seconds of discourse time. The central character
falls asleep sometime during the night; as soon as he closes
his eyes, sunlight fills the room, implying that several
minutes or hours of story time has passed in only several
seconds of discourse time. David Bordwell notes that the
restaurant scene in Jacques Tati's <u>Playtime</u> (1967) lasts
several hours in story time but only 45 minutes in screen
time. Because every shot is a continuity cut, because
no action has obviously been deleted, story time is compressed
(0015, p.82).

A correspondence between story time and discourse
is usually assumed to be inevitable in drama. Renato Poggioli,
for instance, states that a clock on stage would "calculate
precisely the actual length of a dialogue or scene" (0417,
p. 63). While it is true that discourse time is usually
equivalent to story time, something of the same effect
as compression can be achieved in the theatre by marking
the duration of action by means of dialogue or such theatrical
devices as lighting and sound effects. Marlowe uses lexical
items to indicate time at the end of <u>Doctor Faustus</u>, and
the effect is much like the compressed time found in film;
Faust's final soliloquy of 53 lines occupies one hour of
story time, dialogue and sound effects marking the interval
between 11 o'clock and midnight.

Film has a number of ways of stretching time. For
instance, a single, discreet action can be stretched by
having shots overlap segments of the action, just as action
can be abridged by removing segments through editing.
Alternately, time can be expanded by inserting material
within sections of the action. In Hitchcock's <u>Strangers</u>
<u>on a Train</u>, discourse time is expanded by cuts from Bruno's
attempts to retrieve the cigarette lighter to the tennis
game. We see Bruno's outstretched fingers as he strains
to retrieve the lighter from the storm drain, and, after
we see the tennis match for a number of seconds, we again
see Bruno's hand in the same position. Interestingly,
in this sequence, Hitchcock uses crosscutting to expand
one line of action while compressing the other. During
the shots of the tennis match, Bruno's story time stops,
but during the shots of Bruno's recovering the lighter,
the time involving the tennis match presumably continues.
Insertion can also be found in the theatre. For instance,
in Eugene O'Neill's <u>Strange Interlude</u>, story time stops
during the soliloquies, the inserted material, while discourse
time continues. In <u>Becket</u>, as previously discussed, a

few minutes of story time is stretched to several hours
of discourse time by the insertion of the retrospective
material that traces the course of Henry and Beckett's
friendship.

Compression and expansion of time in prose fiction
are interesting issues because, while the reader may have
a sense of two different time frames, no time is actually
involved. How can the reader's sense of compression and
expansion in prose fiction be accounted for? Gerald Prince
says that such relationships entail not so much the relationship
of the length of the discourse and narrated time but rather
what the narrative might or might not have included. "We
know or feel things worth mentioning must have happened
during an exciting fight," he writes, "and we know or feel
that drinking a cup of coffee can and should be presented
in much less detail" (p. 57). Thus, compression concerns
actions implied but unspecified by the narrative, while
expansion concerns the reader's sense of how actions are
usually signified in a narrative. For instance, a reader
recognizes that some actions are usually named (walking,
running, etc.) instead of analyzed or described in detail.

Pause in prose fiction involves the old distinction
between showing and telling. In the former, story time
continues, in the latter, story time halts, but discourse
time continues as the narrator cites attributes of objects
or characters or comments upon actions within the fictional
world. Sterne has a great deal of fun with suspending
story time in _Tristram Shandy_, the characters frozen in
this or that position, while the narrator digresses on
some topic or other that has occurred to him during the
process of narration. In Chapter XXI of the first volume,
Uncle Toby takes his pipe from his mouth, taps it on his
thumb and begins a sentence. The narrator then interrupts
to tell his readers something of Uncle Toby's character
and continues this digression until he realizes that poor
Uncle Toby has been trying to finish his sentence for some
two or three pages: "But I forget my uncle Toby, whom all
this while we have left knocking the ashes out of his tobacco
pipe."

The pause in prose fiction occurs when the fictional
world fades from view and the narrator assumes center stage.
In drama, pauses can occur only in plays that have characters
who are not part of story time or characters that step
outside of story time. Such pauses are unusual, but there
are examples in plays with narrators, such as Wilder's
Our Town or in plays with characters who also function
as narrators, such as Miller's _View From a Bridge_. Even
in these plays the pauses generally come at the beginning
of acts, before story time begins, or are very brief
interruptions in the ongoing action.

A number of critics have assumed that a narrative
pause can occur in film. The Russian Formalist Juri Tynjanov
argues that the close-up abstracts an object from its spatial
relationship to other objects and from the temporal sequence
(0278, p. 88). Mukarovksy argues that close-ups do not
necessarily abstract details from a temporal progression
but that description in the cinema is possible because
of the independence of discourse time (what he calls "pictorial
time") from plot time: "Plot time can stop because even

at the moment of its suspension 'pictorial' time flows
parallel to the viewer's time..." (0085, p. 198).
     More recently, Christian Metz includes description
as one of his eight syntagmatic types. Unfortunately,
the example he gives is hypothetical. "It [the descriptive
syntagma] is the only case of consecutiveness on the screen
that does not correspond to any diegetic consecutiveness.
(Remember that the screen is the location of the signifier,
and the diegesis is the location of the significate),"
he explains. "Example: the description of a landscape
(a tree, followed by a shot of a stream running next to
the tree, followed by a view of a hill in the distance,
etc." (0180, pp. 127-128). In other words, the relationship
between signifiers, the shots, is consecutiveness, but
the relationship between signifieds is space, not time.
Description occurs even in shots of action, he argues,
when the spectator cannot link the images together in a
temporal sequence.
     The opening of <u>2001</u> would seem to satisfy Metz's criteria.
Those opening shots of the desert can be linked spatially,
not temporally. Some critics have noted that establishing
shots have a descriptive function; James Monaco, in fact,
cites the opening shot of <u>Rear Window</u> (1954) as an example
of Metz's descriptive syntagma (0249, p.189). But quite
clearly in that shot (not a series of shots, but a single,
complicated pan) the viewer is aware that plot time has
begun.   The viewer can see a number of progressive actions
(the composer attempting to write his song, Miss Torso
exercising, etc.), and can establish the temporal relationship
between this shot and the one that follows. The next shot
not only succeeds the establishing shot but is actually
later than the first shot in plot time.
     It may be that film can describe only in special instances,
and perhaps there is something about the film medium that
makes description, if not impossible, at least difficult.
In "What Novels Can Do That Films Can't," Seymour Chatman
convincingly argues that films cannot describe, at least
in the precise way that prose fiction can. A novelist
can assert the properties of objects ("the sky is blue"),
but the film image renders in pictorial form. While Chatman
admits that some establishing shots at the beginning of
films seem to function as description, he writes, "they
seem to enjoy that status only because they occur at the
very beginning of the films, that is to say, before any
characters have been introduced....It is not that story-time
has been arrested. It is just that it has not yet begun"
(0216, 129). Once story time begins, he argues, it cannot
be arrested, as it can be in prose fiction, because of
the iconic nature of film. Even if we cannot link shots
in precise temporal order, we still assume that story time
progresses like a taxi meter running during a traffic jam.
Brian Henderson makes much the same point. All film shots,
he says, are in a sense descriptive, but no film shot is
entirely descriptive. "Even if no action occurs in this
shot or in this setting," he writes, "the time devoted
to them builds expectations for action to come; they too
are ticks on the dramatic clock" (0230, p. 10).

C. SPACE

    Some theorists have seen film as a space/time art
and prose fiction as a time art. We can see the logic
of this differentiation if we reconsider E.M. Forster's
example of plot: "The king died and then the queen died
of grief." Prose fiction narrative is comprised of actions,
agents, and temporal and causal relationships. The only
necessary spatial component is that of the text itself,
the level of representation. In film, spatial context
is crucial; after all, the camera must always be put somewhere.
The implication is that space is a more significant formative
element for the film than for the novel. As Edward Branigan
says, "Thus in a verbal narrative the temporal determinations
of the narrating act are more salient than the spatial
determinations. By contrast, this dissymetry is exactly
reversed in pictorial narration" (0211, p. 45).
    Two kinds of spatial relationships are certainly optional
in prose fiction--that between narrator and his surroundings,
and the narrator and the work he is narrating. In some
narratives, such as Tristram Shandy, the space occupied
by the narrator is evoked and the space of composition
is distinguished from the space of the narrated events.
In many other narratives, such as Hemingway's "Hills Like
White Elephants," the space of composition and its relation
to the space of the narrated events remain unspecified.
However, the evocation of story space is optional only
in a theoretical sense. If we add to Forster's plot those
two fictional mainstays, dialogue and setting, we will
have inevitably begun to specify spatial relationships.
Most verbal narratives do specify this space with varying
degrees of exactitude. Film must, as Branigan says, "disclose
its spatial determinations for the reason that the picture
must necessarily be taken from some angle and location"
(0211, p. 45).
    Because of the centrality of spatial properties in
cinematic narration, the emergence of film has been used
as a benchmark in the evolution of the novel. Keith Cohen
in Film and Fiction, and Alan Spiegel in Fiction and the
Camera Eye describe a tradition that begins with the nineteenth
century novel, particularly with Flaubert, and extends
through the modern novels of Virginia Woolf, James Joyce,
and William Faulkner. These books by Cohen and Spiegel
and by others such as Claude-Edmonde Magny's Age of the
American Novel, seek to define and account for this tradition

by establishing links between the realistic and modern
novels and film. This often-quoted section from Flaubert's
Madame Bovary indicates the "cinematic" quality of the
realistic novel:

> One day he arrived about three o'clock. Everyone
> was in the fields. He went into the kitchen and at
> first didn't see Emma. The shutters were closed;
> the sun, streaming between the slats, patterned the
> floor with long thin stripes that broke off at the
> corners of the furniture and quivered on the ceiling.
> On the table, flies were buzzing as they struggled
> to keep from drowning in the cider at the bottom.
> The light coming down the chimney turned the soot
> on the fireback to velvet and gave a bluish cast to
> the cold ashes. Between the window and the hearth
> Emma sat sewing; her shoulders were bare, beaded with
> little drops of sweat (Quoted in 0272, pp.28-29).

What are the "cinematic" characteristics of Flaubert's
prose? The passage gives a hint of his impassibilité,
the objectivity that many have associated with the camera
eye. More significantly for these studies are the qualities
of the observed objects and their spatial relationships
that are conveyed without apparent authorial intrusion.
In Balzac's novels, there is an interest in situating objects
in space and in describing the qualities of these objects.
His narrator dresses the stage before the entrance of the
characters; the narrator usually takes the reader on a
guided tour of the characters' house, describing objects
room by room, explaining what those objects connote about
the owners, before the action commences. Balzac's novels
are typical of the novel before Flaubert in the stop-start
nature of story time. They halt for authorial comment
and description and start when the action commences. But
in this passage from Flaubert, we feel the smooth flow
of story time, because most of the work of setting the
scene has been delegated to a character who perceives the
objects and whose gaze helps us to infer spatial relationships.
The first two sentences are clearly the narrator's. The
rest of the passage seems to be Charles' perceptions.
Understood in that way, the passage is an example of what
Seymour Chatman has called "indirect free perception" because
the subject and perceptual verb, "he saw," have been been
deleted from each sentence. The objects "emerge" as Charles'
gaze rests on one, then on another, and they are rendered
as they appear to him at that moment, through precise sensuous
detail: the play of light upon the table, the beads of
sweat on Emma's bare shoulders. Spiegel writes that in
this passage Flaubert creates both a seer and an object
seen, "an object that is rendered as seen at a specific
point in space ('next to' something, 'above' something,
and the like) and at a specific moment in time..." (0272,
p. 30).
    Spiegel finds a number of even more specifically
"cinematic" passages in Conrad and Joyce, in which the
visual field is more obviously circumscribed than in the
passage by Flaubert, more precisely "framed" in the manner
of the cinema. For example, in A Portrait of the Artist,

Joyce writes, "Stephen. . . gazed at the fraying edge of
his shiny black coat sleeve. . . . Across the threadbare
cuffedge, he saw the sea hailed as a great mother by the
wellfed voice beside him" (Quoted in 0272, p. 63). Whether
Joyce's later novels and other stream of consciousness
novels are "cinematic" is open to question; Spiegel, Cohen,
Magny and a number of others believe so.
    What is evident is that contemporary literature offers
examples of the cinematic novel par excellence. Found
in Robbe-Grillet's The Voyeur is a passage strikingly similar
to the one from Madame Bovary, one less voluptuously rendered,
but more conscious of the justified point of view, more
painstaking in defining the spatial context:

        He did not have time to recognize the landscape,
        for his attention was immediately drawn in the opposite
        direction by the noise of some utensil falling, a
        kitchen implement, probably. In the corner farthest
        from the window he could make out two silhouettes,
        one the fisherman's and the other, which he had not
        noticed up to now, that of a girl or young woman--
        slender, graceful and wearing a close-fitting dress
        that was either black or very dark. Her head did
        not reach to the man's shoulder. She leaned over,
        bending her knees, to pick up the fallen object.
        Motionless above her, his hands on his hips, the sailor
        bent his head a little, as if to gaze at her (Trans.
        Richard Howard, [New York: Grove Press, 1958, p. 114]).

    Robbe-Grillet carefully locates the objects in space.
In the passage from Madame Bovary, it is possible to place
the objects in relation to each other but much more difficult
to place Charles within the scene. Is he by the door,
or has he moved into the room? But there is no trouble
placing Mathias; he is by the window, at the farthest point
from the other two characters. It may not be clear why
Charles failed to see Emma at all at the beginning of the
passage when he sees her clearly enough at the end to notice
the droplets of sweat. But in the Robbe-Grillet passage,
it is not difficult to link the various equivocations
(girl? young woman? kitchen implement?) to the observer's
position in the room, his inability to see clearly because
the other two characters are in shadow, away from the light
coming through the window, and his inability to understand
the fisherman's ambiguous movement. Nothing in the passage
is specified independently of the character's perception,
no information is conveyed independently of the character's
understanding.
    These passages typify the novel's progression toward
a cinematic ideal of grounding the narrative in perception,
of making the reader "see," as both Joseph Conrad and
D.W. Griffith claimed was the purpose of their narratives.
In fact, because these scenes are rendered through visual
imagery, it could be argued that little if anything would
be lost if they were adapted for the screen.
    The claims for a connection between film and literature
are modest and have a comfortable, familiar ring. Both
arts, in their own way, can represent experience. Both
arts can render space with precision and fluidity. Film

must and prose fiction can "show" rather than "tell."
As Herbert Read said, the aim of film and literature is
to "project on to that inner screen of the brain a moving
picture of objects and events, events and objects moving
towards a balance and reconciliation of a more than usual
state of emotion with more than usual order" (0483, p. 231).

Magny, Cohen, and Spiegel seek more precise correspondences
between film and prose fiction than a general recognition
that both are mimetic arts. If the Robbe-Grillet passage
is considered in terms of a filmic adaptation, a great
deal would be added in the transfer from the "imaginary"
space of prose fiction to the "literal" space of film.
In the Robbe-Grillet passage, the locations of the observer
and the observed can more or less be pinpointed, but where
exactly is the reader? The film spectator is always situated
within the film's story space by the camera, but is the
reader similarly situated within the novel's story space?
I suspect that Cohen, Magny, and Spiegel would say that
the reader assumes the observer's position, or, the reader
sees through the character's eyes. If this is so, then
"cinematic" is being defined exclusively in terms of those
instances in film where the spectator shares the position
of a character, that is, in terms of subjective or point
of view shots. But under this definition, the only "cinematic"
film is Robert Montgomery's Lady in the Lake (1946) or
perhaps some yet-to-be-made motion picture composed entirely
of subjective shots that represent the perception of not
one but a number of characters. While point of view shots
are not uncommon in the cinema, they are rarely used to
the degree implied by these writers. In a given film,
these shots, if present at all, are understood to be deviations
from those that are detached from any character's perception.

Since Harry Levin's seminal work on James Joyce, it
has been customary to speak of Joyce's novels, to say nothing
of the modern novel in general, in terms of montage. Montage
provides a convenient starting point for discussing and
evaluating what writers have seen as correspondences between
fictional and cinematic space. "Montage" is a notoriously
slippery term even in film studies. Generally speaking,
it has two distinct, though allied meanings. The first
involves the stylistic system of film, the way one shot
is joined to another. Montage, or editing, in this sense
is concerned with the formal relations of shots; it includes
such "rules" of continuity editing as matching eyelines
and corresponding positions of objects within the frame,
as well as Eisenstein's principles of conflict among the
graphic elements of shots. The second meaning is the basis
of tables of montage devised by Rudolph Arnheim, V.I. Pudovkin,
Christian Metz, and others. Such tables classify segments
of film not in terms of shot relations per se but rather
in terms of the way the film orders scenes or events.

Montage tables are based upon narrative order; their
categories are clear and noncontroversial ways of establishing
correspondences between film and prose fiction. For instance,
Alan Spiegel quotes a passage from A Portrait of the Artist
as a Young Man to demonstrate the cinematic movement of
modern fiction, what he calls "movement with a gap between
its phases"; the passage concerns two brief, enjambed scenes,
one of Stephen's meeting a prostitute on the roadway, a

second of Stephen in her room. By consulting Christian
Metz's syntagmatic categories, one could discover that
Joyce is using "the ordinary sequence," short scenes often
in different locations that represent portions of an action.
These categories could be applied to any number of nineteenth-
and twentieth-century novels to confirm what other writers
have found: that prose fiction and film often order their
narratives in much the same way. This, of course, was
Eisenstein's point when he cited instances of crosscutting
in Flaubert and Dickens. This is John Fell's point in
Film and the Narrative Tradition when he compares Frank
Norris's juxtaposition of scenes in The Octopus to Porter's
use of parallel editing in The Kleptomaniac (1905).
     If film and prose fiction are considered in terms
of our second meaning of montage, the linking of one shot
with another, severe problems of comparison crop up. Some
writers have been tempted to equate signifier with signifier,
word with image. In the late twenties, André Levinson argued
that the novel had the equivalent of shots, but he confusingly
identified the shot with paragraphs and chapters (0070,
p. 693). Both Eisenstein and Pudovkin equated shot and
word, and in the late sixties, Robert Richardson wrote,
"The vocabulary of film is the simple photographed image;
the grammar and syntax of film are the editing, cutting,
or montage processes by which the shots are arranged" (0103,
p. 65). Christian Metz has scotched such easy comparison
of signifiers by pointing out that film lacks a vocabulary;
each image is unique, and images are ordered by aesthetic
choices, not grammatical rules.
     Still the temptation remains to find fictional analogues
for the shot, located at higher levels of organization
than the word. Seymour Chatman attempts to devise two
categories for fictional and filmic space that correspond
to discourse and story time. He says that discourse-space
"is the framed area to which the implied audience's attention
is directed by the discourse, that portion of the total
story-space that is remarked or closed in upon, according
to the requirements of the medium--through a narrative
or through a camera eye--literally, as in film, or figuratively,
as in verbal narrative" (0215, p. 102). The nature of
the categories changes when he applies them to film and
fiction.
     He seems to say that discourse space in film is the
two-dimensional space of the film image and the graphic
elements of the image from which the spectator infers
three-dimensional space. Therefore story space is the
three-dimensional space we infer from discourse space.
It is "the segment of the world actually shown on the screen"
and the segment of the world not actually shown but implied
by sound or dialogue. Because Chatman has defined discourse
space in terms of the shot, he runs aground trying to find
an analogous category for prose fiction. He claims that
verbal discourse space is that segment of space actually
evoked by the text; it is the portion of space, as he says,
"remarked" or closed-in on by the narrative which would
seem to be analogous to film's story space. Verbal story
space is "what the reader is prompted to create in his
imagination. . . on the basis of the character's perceptions
and/or the narrator's reports" (0215, p. 104). It would

seem to be part of film's story space also because Chatman
has included in film's story space not only space actually
depicted but space implied by sound effects or dialogue.
Both verbal discourse and story space are apparently what
he is calling story space in film; film's discourse space
would not seem to be analogous to anything in prose fiction.
Even more confusingly, when he discusses prose fiction,
he drops the category of discourse space entirely and labels
space "framed" by the narrative as story space.   Cohen,
Spiegel, and Magny present similar problems.   Cohen tries
to find verbal analogues for such cinematic traits as camera
angle and distance from camera to object.   His aim is to
isolate "isomorphic structures" of film and the modern
novel, and one of these is a novelistic analogue for camera
work: "Though changes in distance, angle, and set-up cannot
take place in the novel with the facility and automatism
of the cinema because of the fundamental differences in
the production and articulation of their signs, experiments
with such changes do nonetheless become more and more frequent
in the postcinema novel. . . . Distance and angle are built
into the image, whereas in any discursive, literary art,
such as the novel, they are subtle and constantly varying
factors that are determined at another level, so to speak,
of production" (0217, p. 170).   Unfortunately, the topic
of "ismorphic structures" at other levels is never broached
again throughout his sensitive analyses of passages from
Woolf's <u>To the Lighthouse</u> and Joyce's <u>Ulysses</u>, and film
is mentioned only as a source for terminology to indicate
certain types of narrative organization in the novels
(crosscutting in Woolf, for instance).
     Spiegel follows essentially the same strategy but
makes a disastrous mistake by forcing his analogies.   The
various properties of the single photographed image--the
indeterminacy of detail, the reduction of three to two
dimensions, and vantage point--he likens to the depiction
of character, setting, or action, that is, description.
He links montage to the form of modern narrative, "the
movement from one point in time to another, from one
concretized perspective to another" (0272, p. 164).   Because
the connections between novelistic and filmic vantage points
are drawn on the basis of a single photographed image,
and because he has defined both film and novelistic forms
as shifts from one perspective to another, he is forced
to see film as simply a succession of photographs: "Montage,
then, is finally the essential difference between the single
photograph and the finished motion picture comprised of
many photographs, between the solitary angle of vision
and the composite perspective, between what can loosely
be called still photography and what can strictly be called
the cinema" (0272, p. 164).   Montage, as describes it,
is not the joining of single images, but the joining of
shots, and the essential difference between the single
image and the finished film is not montage, composite
perspective, but apparent movement.   By trying for too
tight a fit between film and the modern novel, he ends
up comparing the novel, not to film, but to the <u>photo roman</u>.
     Cohen speaks of locating angle and distance at "other
levels" in the psychological fiction of Joyce and Woolf.
Spiegel and Magny equate montage with the composite perspective

of the modern novel; Magny refers to the modern novel's
shift in point of view as "cutting." Both equate changing
points of view in film with changing points of view in
fiction, a confusion which has already been discussed and
which arises from various spatial metaphors used to describe
conceptual activity such as "taking a closer look" and
"seeing things from another angle." The metaphorical base
of the terminology allows Cohen and Spiegel simply to assert
the equivalence of changes in camera angle and changes
in voice or focalization and perhaps allows them to avoid
countering the commonsense argument that changes in camera
angle and changes in focalization often do very different
narrative work, that, in fact, the two serve different
ends. The changes in focalization in the modern novel
are meant to create a clash of subjectivities, to create
conflicting "pools of consciousness." Changes in camera
angle need not, and often do not, imply changes in
focalization. Rather they serve to create fictional space,
or to single out an object important for the narration;
in "subjective" shots they enable the spectator to infer
character psychology. These do not necessarily involve
the shifts in focalization and the competing subjectivities
that Cohen finds typical of the modern novel. The modern
novel has a good deal in common with certain films, Kurosawa's
Rashomon (1951) being an obvious example. But to explicate
this film and comparable novels, a good deal more than
changing camera positions would have to be examined.
     Film and literature can be examined on the basis of
formal correspondences, "isomorphic structures," the method
of Robert Richardson's Literature and Film, William Jinks's
The Celluloid Literature and, indeed, this introduction.
Spiegel, Cohen, and Magny attempt to draw a tighter connection
between film and the novel by explaining the formal similarities
of film and the novel, particularly the modern novel, in
terms of various "metaphysical" qualities of film technique.
Instead of pursuing the impossible goal of accounting for
analogous techniques in terms of direct influence, they
attempt to account for them by presenting film as the embodiment
of the modern Zeitgeist. Spiegel asserts that film technique
"embodies values and attitudes which are vital outside
of film; that film technique as such relates to a way of
thinking and feeling--about time, space, being and relation--
relates, in short, to a body of ideas abut the world that
has become part of the mental life of an entire epoch in
our culture" (0272, p. xii). Cohen writes that "the cinema
represents not simply another element in the turn-of-the-
century Zeitgeist but a privileged precedent, aesthetically,
and epistemologically, to the experiments carried out by
the classic modern novel" (0217, p. x). Similarly, Magny
speaks of the film as being "better adapted" to the modern
era than the novel, particularly the French novel (0246,
p. 98).
     All three books are, in a sense, extensions of Arnold
Hauser's view that the twentieth century is "the film
age" because film embodies, among other things, distinctly
modern views of time, space, relativity, and subjectivity.
Of relativity, Spiegel writes that, though the camera can
"objectively" record the "surface of physical reality,"
it can do so only by means of a series of views from certain

spatial positions. "This means that the images produced
by the motion picture camera will only allow us to experience
the object through a series of perspectives; that the ontology
of the image itself will never allow for an apprehension
of the object as a whole. In this sense no other art is
less equipped to present a godlike and omniscient view
of human experience than the cinema, and no other art form,
therefore, presents a more accurate embodiment of a modernist
and relativist metaphysics than cinematographic form" (0272,
p. 32). Editing and specific types of editing such as
crosscutting are endowed with specific meaning congruent
with the aims of the modern novel.

Even the nature of the film image has specific metaphysical
characteristics. Like other writers, Spiegel notes that
the film image reduces human beings to the same status
as things. The dehumanizing effects of the film image,
he argues, parallel the existential, anti-pyschological
aspects of the modern novel in which "the character fuses
with the brutal material components of his environment
and becomes virtually indistinguishable from the objects
associated with him" (0272, p. 136). Similarly, Cohen
argues that film reverses the mode of existence of subject
and object by making people seem more like things and things
seem more like human beings.

However, as James Goodwin in "Literature and Film:
A Review of Criticism" points out, this alignment of technique
and meaning assumes that the technique is "univocal" in
meaning (0047, p. 235), and these metaphysical meanings
make a close relationship between film and the modern novel
more apparent than real. It seems dubious that narrative
techniques have meaning outside their use in particular
works of art and their place in particular narrative
traditions. Editing and crosscutting, for instance, are
used by the conventional film to convey, not relativity,
but omniscience. The conventional Hollywood film makes
much the same assumption about reality as the eighteenth-
and nineteenth-century novel: reality is knowable, and
individual mistakes about the nature of reality are explicable
in terms of partial knowledge. But full knowledge is possible
if one can gather enough of the pieces. While his method
is questionable, Colin McCabe in "Realism in the Cinema:
Notes on Some Brechtian Theses" is correct in assuming
that the "classical realist text" and the classical Hollywood
film proceed by an additive process: the partial understandings
of each character added together by means of the narrator
and juxtaposed with the narrator's judgement in the novel
or added together by means of editing in the film equal
full understanding for the spectator.

With regard to subjectivity, these writers confuse
the reduction of person to object with the reduction of
self to object. Film generally shares with the nineteenth
century novel the presumption that external reality, characters'
actions and words, even setting, are indexes to character
psychology. While the characters are seen from without,
their internal nature is clearly implied by what they do
or say; they are, to use Käte Hamburger's phrase, self-
revealing. By contrast, the modern novel presumes a split
between external and internal reality. This is most evident
in the contemporary anti-novel in which external reality

does not clearly index character because such novels follow
the Sartrean notion that there is no psychological essence
to index.
   That the meaning of such techniques as crosscutting
and objective presentation of character are dependent upon
the ways particular artists working within certain traditions
have used them should not imply that film or the modern
novel are inevitably different. In fact, such films as
those by Alain Resnais demonstrate that these techniques
can be used for many of the same ends as those of the modern
novel. The point is that shared techniques do not necessarily
imply shared themes or world views as Magny and Spiegel
argue.
   Film is a space/time art; prose fiction is essentially
a temporal one. Therefore, it might be assumed that film
is closer to drama than to prose fiction. After all, whether
drama is considered in terms of playscript or performance,
space is a crucial formative element. Most writers, however,
have made radical distinctions between film and drama based
upon their use of space. In fact, for all the characteristics
the two arts seem to share--actors, costumes, makeup, scenery--
most writers have argued that film and drama are means
of expression that result in totally different experiences
for the spectator. Few writers would agree with Charles
Eidsvik who has argued that "every attempt to find some
'essential' nature in either medium always founders" (0323,
p. 165). However,this assumption of some essential difference
between film and the drama is the premise of many film
histories which describe the development of the film from
medium to art form in terms of its emancipation from the
theater. In this view, the fledgling art of the movies
was tempted by the theatrical tradition to stray from the
path that would lead to the development of its natural,
inherent means of expression. Consequently, two possibilities
emerged in the early years of film--the "false" theatrical
method and the "true" cinematic method. The history of
film is shaped by the conflict between these two.
   Thus, in Lewis Jacobs' <u>The Rise of the American Film</u>,
the standard history of American movies, the French pioneer
Georges Méliès is said to have led film along the "theatrical
way" while the American pioneer Edwin S. Porter pioneered
the "cinematic way" (New York: Teachers College Press,
1968, p. 35). Jacobs notes that even the trailblazer of
the path to genuine cinematic expression often was tempted
to emulate the methods of the stage in his movies. Films
such as those produced in France by the Société Film d'Art
in the first decade of the century and in the United States
by Adolph Zukor's Famous Players in Famous Plays Company
during the next decade have been seen by film historians
as examples of the disaster that results when film embraces
the temptation of the theatrical manner and abandons its
"true" methods. For instance, in 1916, Hugo Munsterberg
called for the liberation of film from theater because
"as long as the photoplays are fed by the literature of
the stage, the new art can never come to its own and can
never reach its real goal" (0087, p. 84). Succeeding writers
have depicted the theatrical influence in much the same
manner: a constant temptation to abandon film's essential
nature in favor of a foreign and destructive aesthetic.

This conflict between methods can be detected in the demands
of modern writers that film be "visual" because the true
cinematic method is to convey stories through images rather
than by the stage's method of conveying stories through
words.

Because of the widely held view that the methods of
theater are hostile to film's essential nature, the pejorative
terms "theatrical" and "literary" have been applied to
films to indicate those works that have attempted to go
beyond the inherent limitations of the medium. André Bazin,
while admitting that drama was "a false friend" to film,
argued that adaptations of drama and prose fiction have,
at the very least, given to film a greater sense of complex
characters and themes, an awareness of a more unified structure,
and a clarification of the true differences between the
art forms (0494, p. 66-67). In his recent A History of
Narrative Film, David Cook argues along similar lines that
the film d'art movement was quickly superseded by more
sophisticated, more "cinematic" works, but the movement
did give to film a degree of respectability and a greater
awareness of the differences between drama enacted on a
stage and drama projected on a screen (New York: W.W. Norton,
1981, p. 53).

Generally speaking, theater and film have been seen
as mutually exclusive means of expression. For one art
to embrace the methods of the other leads it to abandon
its essential means of expression and to transgress the
boundaries separating the arts. But determining the essential
means of expression, those methods that make an art unique,
and the subject matter best suited to these methods has
proved to be problematic. As Gregory Waller has pointed
out, there has been little agreement on what actually
constitutes the essence of the two art forms or on their
proper subject matter (0452, p. 100). Some have cited
film's command over time and space as its essential
characteristic, others its realism, its independence from
dialogue, its independence from the actor. Some have argued
that modern life is film's proper subject matter, while
others have cited everyday life, fantasy, horror, the dream,
and observable reality.

Perhaps the most frequently made distinction between
film and drama has centered upon film's ability to reconstruct
space and time through editing, or montage. In one of
the first critical studies of the new art of film published
in the United States, Rollin Summers, while admitting
similarities between film and drama, cites the manipulation
of space, the ease with which locales can be shifted, as
the critical difference between the two (0439, p. 11).
Similary, René Clair notes that film's facility in manipulating
time and space makes it closer to the novel than drama,
where the action is held "prisoner" by the set (0311, p. 175).
V.I. Pudovkin argues that film became an art only when
film avoided recording scenes that were "already arranged
and definitely planned" in the manner of the theater and
allowed the camera to become an active observer (0422,
p. 54). "The theatrical producer works with real actuality,
which he may remould, yet forces him to remain bound by
the laws of real space and real time," he writes. "The
film director on the other hand, has as his material the

finished piece of celluloid. . . .He does not adapt reality, but uses it for the creation of a new reality, and the most characteristic and important aspect of this process is that, in it, laws of space and time invariable and inescapable in work with actuality become tractable and obedient. The film assembles the elements of reality to build from them a new reality proper only to itself. . . ." (0422, pp. 61-62).

Arnold Hauser believes that theater is similar to film in that both are arts of space and time. Yet film demolishes the boundaries between space and time so that space takes on a quasi-temporal character and time a quasi-spatial character; in other words, filmic space is constructed by means of the progression of individual shots and filmic time is constructed by means of individual images that, by necessity, fragment space. Filmic space, then, is "fluid, unlimited, unfinished," while theatrical space is static and homogenous (0056, p. 940). Hauser's distinction between film and theater is similar to Erwin Panofsky's formulation of film's unique capabilities as the "dynamization of space and the spatialization of time." Whereas the filmic spectator's relationship to the screen action changes from shot to shot, he writes, the theatrical spectator's position to the stage action is always fixed (0410, p. 18). Louis Giannetti locates the difference between film and drama in their uses of space and time; unlike film, the theater can manipulate dramatic space and time only between scenes (0336, p. 250).

André Bazin's theory of screen realism is based upon the link between our experience of space in everyday life and our perception of space in film. It is not surprising then that his analysis of space in film and theater is particularly thorough and evocative. The elements of drama--costumes, makeup, decor, footlights--are all means to distinguish it from nature. Because the theatrical performance exists in real time and space, without such conventions, such ways to distinguish the reality of the characters on stage from the reality of the spectators, the performance would be "under penalty of being absorbed by her [nature] and ceasing to be" (0495, p. 104). The stage itself, though, is the primary means of erecting a barrier between these two realities because it is "an area materially enclosed, limited, circumscribed, the only discoveries of which are in our collusive imagination" (0495, p. 104).

Modern dramatic theory can help us to structure and evaluate Bazin's remarks on the methods the theater uses to define space. Kier Elam notes three such methods: (1) fixed feature space defined by the architecture of the theater that cannot be altered; (2) semi-fixed feature space defined by such items as furniture and lighting that can be altered from performance to performance; (3) informal space defined by the distance between actors or between actors and the audience that changes from moment to moment during the course of a performance (The Semiotics of Theatre of Drama [London: Methuen, 1980, pp. 62-63]). Bazin emphasizes the first of these, for he sees the stage itself and the distance between the audience and the performance as the theater's chief means of distinguishing performance from reality. He notes that whatever is enacted on the stage

is transformed into a spectacle, like something seen in
a shop window. Like many writers on theater and film,
Bazin seems to focus his discussion on the proscenium theater.
But modern theatrical practice, such as theater-in-the-round,
attempts to bridge the gap between spectator as observer
and the actor by emphasizing semi-fixed feature space and,
particularly, informal space. Rather than a stage that
demarks fictional space, modern theater creates acting
areas by means of the actors' bodies; the actors' bodies
occupy and define the actual space that signifies the fictional
space. As Elam notes, "The centre of the theatrical transaction
has become, during this century and particularly in recent
decades, less an absolute stage-auditorium divide than
a flexible and, occasionally, unpredictable manipulation
of body-to-body space" (p. 63).

Focus on the proscenium arch stage, a number of writers
have distinguished theater from film based upon the great
distance that separates the theatrical audience from actors
and have noted that to bridge this gap theatrical actors
have had to use exaggerated acting styles. By contrast,
the intimacy afforded by the camera allows film actors
to use a more subtle, more "realistic" acting style. This
distinction is valid in regard to large proscenium arch
auditoriums but not for theater in general; no single acting
style can truly be said to distinguish drama from film.

While many of his comments concern conventional staging
procedures, Bazin seeks the defining characteristic of
theatrical space, regardless of specific theatrical practices.
Essentially, he argues that however dramatic space is defined,
the idea of a locus for dramatic action is central to any
style of theatrical performance, whether, as he says, the
performance occurs in a fairground, a cathedral square,
or the palace of the Popes. In any theatrical performance,
the actual space of the locus dramaticus must be defined
in some way, and because it must stand for the space within
the fictional work, the space evoked by the performance
must be circumscribed by the space available for that
performance. This locus of dramatic action exists, he
argues, "by virtue of its reverse side and of anything
beyond, as the painting exists by virtue of its frame"
(0495, p. 105). Therefore, theatrical performance incorporates
the limits of dramatic space, the separation of dramatic
space from "anything beyond." Whether through the design
of the auditorium, stylized decor, lighting, or the movement
of the actors, Bazin argues, theatrical performance directs
the spectator's attention to that segment of space inhabited
by the actors, that segment of space that stands for space
within the drama.

Theater limits space and directs the spectator's attention
to action occurring within it. Bazin describes theatrical
space as "centripetal" in which the lines of force converge
on the actor; theater is like a crystal chandelier, "which
refracts the light which plays around its center and holds
us prisoners of its aureole..." (0495, p. 107). Film "is
the little flashlight of the usher, moving like an uncertain
comet across the night of our waking dream, the diffuse
shape or frontiers that surround the screen" (0495, p. 107).
According to Bazin, the light of the theater is directed
inward, while the light of the cinema is directed outward.

In film the space occupied by the spectator is not
an extension of the space occupied by the actors; these
two spaces are distinct and unbridgeable. So film has
no need to define a locus dramaticus; indeed, Bazin argues
that such a concept of unified, limited dramatic space
contradicts the basic nature of film. If theater directs
the spectator's attention within dramatic space, film directs
the spectator's attention outside cinematic space. When
a character moves offstage, Bazin says, he becomes an actor
waiting in the wings; he has moved outside fictional space.
But when a character moves offscreen, "he continues to
exist in his own capacity at some other place in the decor
which is hidden from us" (0495, p. 105). This is so because
the edges of the screen do not form the limits of fictional
space but rather are a mask that allows only a part of
the action to be seen. Because each shot implies a limitless
space beyond the boundaries of the screen, Bazin describes
cinematic space as
"centrifugal."

       Bazin is typical of a number of writers who have
distinguished film from drama on the basis of extended
space. Stanley Kauffmann argues this distinction grows
from a desperate attempt to separate the art forms and
to grant to film "an unimaginative exclusivity that is
invalid except to the dull-minded" (0365, p. 356). In
his view, both film and drama involve two spaces: actual
space beyond which are technicians, equipment, and dressing
rooms, and imaginative space that stretches beyond the
stage or the screen. When an actor leaves the stage, he
may go to his dressing room or he may wait in the wings
for his next cue, just as when an actor moves out of frame
he may stand with the technicians to wait for the shot
to end. In both instances, fictional space is limited
by the acting area and the camera. However, just as spectators
assume that film characters continue to exist outside the
frame, so too spectators who are imaginatively engaged
assume that theatrical characters continue to exist when
they leave the stage--in Hamlet Cornelius and Voltimand
are on their way to Norway with a dispatch from the king
and in A Doll's House Christine is searching for Krogstad.
In both cases, what spectators know to be true and what
they choose to believe to enjoy the fiction is the same;
they choose to believe that space extends beyond the space
evoked before them.

       It can be argued that at a certain level of generality
the two types of space in film and drama are similar, but
that should not overshadow their real differences. After
rejecting a number of arguments about the differences between
film and drama, Susan Sontag finds "an irreducible distinction"
between theater's use of continuous space and film's reinvention
of space. She writes, "In drawing a line of demarcation
between theater and films, the issue of the continuity
of space seems to me more fundamental than the difference
that might be pointed out between theater as an organization
of movement in three-dimensional space (like dance) versus
cinema as an organization of plane space (like painting)" (1090,
p. 108). Her distinctions are much more pronounced when
film is compared to the proscenium stage. Here the actual
space of the stage and the space within the fictional world

correspond rather closely; the stage represents, at any
given moment, a single locale demarked by the architecture
of the theater, the decor, the lighting, and the movement
of the actor. Further, the performance begins with a display
of stage space as the curtain goes up and before the action
begins. In other words, the establishment of space, the
locus dramaticus, precedes and prepares the way for the
dramatic action.
     In film, cinematic space is defined from without by
the position of the camera and is constructed by the spectator
from cues provided by the film's images. The fact that
cinematic space is constructed by the spectator is by no
means a new idea in film theory; it is an integral part
of Eisenstein's definition of montage. In recent years,
the activity of the spectator in constructing cinematic
space has been analyzed in detail in such works as David
Bordwell's Narration in the Fiction Film, Nick Browne's
The Rhetoric of Filmic Narration, Edward Branigan's Point
of View in the Cinema, and Jean-Pierre Oudart's article
on "suture" in Screen. While these writers disagree on
a number of fundamental issues, all seek to account for
the way the spectator derives a sense of total space from
the partial views of each shot by understanding the logic
of the narrative and by applying conventions specific to
film. Generally speaking, then, cinematic space is not
displayed to the spectator but is presented discontinuously
and linearly. We should also note that in films by such
directors as Welles and Wyler, in which the emphasis is
placed upon movement before the camera rather than the
movement from shot to shot through editing, the use of
space is similar to that in drama; in such films as The
Magnificent Ambersons (1942), or at least in parts of such
films, space is demarked and displayed in a theatrical
manner rather than reinvented from shot to shot.
     Dramatic space need not be the unifed space familiar
from the proscenium arch theater. The total space available
for performance can be divided into various playing areas
to stand for different locales within the fiction, allowing
theater to approximate techniques commonly associated with
film, such as crosscutting. If film is compared only to
the proscenium arch theater, then film's use of space seems
quite different from theater's. But if other performance
practices are considered, then film's use of space seems
to differ from theater's in degree rather than kind. Theater
simply cannot manipulate space as dexterously as film.
Whatever the performance practice, theater is dependent
on actual space, and so there are practical limits to what
the theater can depict. Theater must rely on lighting
and stage position to direct the spectator's attention,
all of which are less precise than the camera. As Sontag
says, "The theatre's capacities for manipulating space
and time are, simply, much cruder and more labored than
film's" (1090, p. 109).
     The relative ease with which film can manipulate time
and space may not suggest a radical distinction between
the two, but some writers have attempted to establish firm
boundaries between film and theater by exaggerating the
significance of editing. This exaggeration has had unfortunate
consequences for film theory. Early theorists were anxious

to establish an artistic pedigree for film and to do so
they had to demonstrate that film had unique expressive
capabilities. They had to counter at least two objections
if film were to be accepted as a legitimate art. They
had to show that film was the product of human creation,
not mechancial reproduction and that film differed significantly
from the other arts, particularly theater. Especially
common in film's early years was the notion that film was
simply drama's mute, idiot cousin, or, in Roman Ingarden's
words, "corrupted theater" (0061, p. 326).

An emphasis on editing seemed to answer both objections.
Many film advocates argued that the art of film began not
with the recorded image but with that image being arranged
in sequence with other images, in the process of editing.
Film was not to be identified with the mechanically reproduced
photographic image, which was simply the film artist's
raw material. Film was, rather, the organization of shots
to create an artistic pattern. In a number of defenses
of cinema, writers equate the shot with the word, both
inexpressive until they are linked sequentially to convey
the artist's ideas or emotions. In this view, editing
was the tool within the artist's shaping hand.

Editing, the cinematic technique par excellence, seemed
unquestionably to differentiate film from drama. Film
was identified with the edited image, drama with all that
threatened the primacy of the image--spatial uniformity
and dialogue. This characterization of film and theater
has become commonplace in a number of standard works on
film. In this view, those elements that film shares with
drama, such as the arrangment of elements before the camera
and dialogue, are either ignored or condemned as "uncinematic."
V.F. Perkins argues that the overemphasis on editing has
obstructed a full understanding of the ways in which film
communicates. "If we isolate cutting from the complex
which includes the movement of the actors, the shape of
the setting, the movement of the camera, and variations
of light and shape--which change within the separate shots
as well as between them--we shall understand none of the
elements (and certainly not the editing) because each of
them derives its value from its relationship with the other"
(0096, p. 23).

In their attempt to find a radical, decisive difference
between film and theater, these early theorists created
a dogma that in effect would make narrative filmmaking
an impossiblilty. Rudolph Arnheim, for instance, demanded
that all effects possible on the stage must be rejected
by film. Raymond Spottiswoode took the more generous view
that stage techniques were permissible in film only if
no cinematic technique would produce the same effect. The
logical implication of Arnheim's position is that the only
legitimate film is the abstract film, a conclusion Arnheim
himself refuses to draw. The implication of Spottiswoode's
argument is that there are, in a sense, a dual set of narrative
means, one cinematic, the other theatrical. As Perkins
notes, once film is seen as both the edited image and the
arrangement of elements to be filmed, the radical distinction
between film and drama vanishes: "When he works with actors
the film director assumes many of the functions of his
theatrical counterpart. He organizes the space in front

of the camera much as the stage director controls the space beyond the proscenium. Gesture, grouping, pace, intonation and movement become vitally significant" (0096, p. 25).

The search for the boundaries of film and drama has also had unfortunate consequences for film history. I have noted that in the view of a number of standard histories, the story of film has been the story of a struggle for emancipation from the theater. Film, even through the beginning of the sound era, had to struggle to resist the temptation of the way of the drama, a way that led to aesthetic failure. Many of these histories have accepted what Eisenstein termed a belief in the virgin birth of the film. The early cinema owed a debt to painting and sculpture, perhaps, and certainly to reality from which it drew its subject matter, but not to drama or prose fiction. The temptation to adopt the methods of these art forms could, they felt, only stifle film's struggle to create its own methods of expression. Benjamin Hampton speaks of early filmmakers as forging their own artistic tradition; the only beneficial connection between film and theater is that the relaxing of moral strictures against the legitimate stage benefitted film. Lewis Jacobs speaks of the early film drawing its subject matter from American life; when filmmakers turned to literature, they were "forced" to do so by the demand for story material and threats of censorship. At the same time, he argues, though film may have shared subject matter with literature, its means of expression was unique, and so film became an art only when it freed itself from the theater.

The contention that film began rather than continued an artistic tradition has been challenged by A. Nicholas Vardac's From Stage to Screen and by John L. Fell's Film and the Narrative Art. Vardac analyzes the impact upon film of what he terms the romantic-realistic movement in the nineteenth century theater; Fell analyzes part of that movement, the melodrama, and other narrative forms such as pulp fiction, engraving, and painting. Both advance the same argument: film and nineteenth-century theater shared not only the same aims but essentially the same means. In fact, they argue that the very techniques that are usually considered distinctly cinematic were in actuality analogous to the techniques of the nineteenth-century popular theater. In the last three decades of the century, men like David Belasco, Henry Irving, and Steele McKay stretched the capabilities of the stage to the limit to satisfy the audience's demand for pictorial realism, speed, and suspense. Advancements in stagecraft made possible the use of huge three-dimensional sets without the sacrifice of rapid scene changes, nor was the stage bound to the uniform, static space typical of later realistic plays. The climax of numerous melodramas was the culmination of several lines of action, a prefigurement of cinema's "parallel montage." Staging techniques allowed for prefigurations of the shifting vantage points of the camera. For instance, Belasco's Girl of the Golden West opened with a painted panorama moving vertically across the proscenium opening. The audience saw a mountain range and then, as the panorama was rolled, a valley, a trail, a cabin and a saloon; after a fade out and fade in, the audience saw a set for the saloon's interior.

Both Fell and Vardac identify this opening with a pan and
a tracking shot. This movement from exterior to interior
foreshadows the editing structure of the rescue sequence
in Edwin S. Porter's <u>Life of an American Fireman</u> (1903),
often cited as one of the first films to take a step away
from the theatrical mode.
     Two more examples should suffice to indicate the nature
of Vardac's and Fell's argument. They note that the popular
theater linked scenes by means of the fade out and fade
in, a device they believed was borrowed by the film; further,
during transformation scenes, one scene would fade out
and another would fade in, a technique suggestive of film's
lap dissolve.
     According to Vardac, film arrived just as the nineteenth-
century theater had pushed the idea of pictorial realism
as far as stagecraft would allow. Because film could achieve
the same effects more cheaply and more convincingly for
a broader audience, film supplanted the popular theater.
 When David Belasco had an entire room dismantled and
reconstructed upon his stage, he was striving for a scrupulous
realism that filmmakers would achieve by simply turning
on their cameras. Indeed, Vardac describes the popular
theater as a preparation for the cinema, an imperfect
realization of methods that have come to be thought of
as "cinematic." Vardac writes that Edwin S. Porter, usually
credited with beginning the emancipation of film from theater,
"merely translated the idiom of the motion-picture camera
into the aims and methods" of melodorama (0449, p. 67).
D.W. Griffith, often credited with completing this process
of emancipation, fully realized the ideals toward which
the theater had been striving for a century.
     If both Fell and Vardac establish a link between film
and drama through aims and means, however, neither makes
claims for theatrical influence on filmmakers. As is well
known, Griffith and Porter, men of both the theater and
the cinema, strongly rejected any suggestion that their
methods were connected to the theater. Instead of direct
influence, Fell accounts for the similarity in terms of
a "narrative tradition," techniques in the public domain
that were avaliable to all artists but belonging to no
particular art. Vardac accounts for the similarity by
reference to social forces that shaped both arts; he argues
that "the need for cinema and for greater pictorial realism
in the theater came in response to a single stimulus,"
science, which created for both arts "a similar aesthetic"
(0449, p. xxi).
     In Fell's and Vardac's view, film could more easily
and more convincingly achieve the photographic realism
imperfectly realized by the popular theater, but a number
of writers have used film's more nearly complete illusion
of reality to set boundaries between film and theater.
Vachel Lindsay pointed out early in the history of film
theory: "The stage interior is large. The motion-picture
interior is small. The stage out-of-doors scene is at
best artificial and little and is generally at rest, or
its movement is tainted with artificiality. The waves
dash, but not dashingly, the water flows but not flowingly.
The motion picture out-of-doors is as big as the universe"
(0963 pp. 164-165). More recently, Robert Steele wrote:

> We step into the theater mentally prepared to see
> actors and sets through the proscenium arch. We are
> fully aware of and even inured to the artificiality
> of the whole form. We must see through the artifice
> to experience the reality of the drama. . . .In film
> we meet nothing but the illusion of reality, but the
> illusion seems to have more to do with a projector
> and a screen rather than what is put on the screen.
> We accept what we see up there, even if it is fantasy,
> for reality. Real persons in real places doing natural
> things constitute most of our better films. We do
> not think of actors as actors or sets as sets (0437,
> pp. 17-18).

The half-century that separates these two writers indicates
the durability of this distinction between drama and film.
"Theatrical" is stylized, approximate, counterfeit; "cinematic"
is natural, precise, genuine. The theatrical experience
depends upon convention, the suspension of disbelief and
the acceptance of make-believe. It is a product of the
imagination. The filmic experience, though, is a product
of perception. Instead of accepting a dramatic illusion,
the movie spectator recognizes an exact reproduction of
actuality, and the intensity of the illusion depends on
the material of expression, not on the content. A movie
fantasy seems more real than an Ibsen play.
     This point is made by Allardyce Nicoll in his Film
and Theatre, when he writes, "Dramatic illusion is never
(or so rarely as to be negligible) the illusion of reality;
it is always imaginative illusion, the illusion of a period
of make-believe" (0409, p. 166). In theater, he notes,
the spectator is aware of the "falsity" of the spectacle,
and so demands "a theatrical truth"; but, in film, the
audience assumes the illusion to be reality and the characters
to be actual human beings. While all three writers argue
that film offers the more complete illusion, they account
for that in quite different ways. Lindsay bases his argument
on film's ability to use actual locales rather than stage
sets and its ability to simulate motion. Steele too bases
his argument on the photographic nature of film, its ability
to create reality through concrete detail. But he also
stresses the obviousness of the means to illusion. Both
film and theater may use sets, but in film, shots of sets
can be intermingled with shots of actual locales so that
"the keenest observer will not have the film spoiled by
his perceiving the way it was brought together" (0437,
p. 22). In other words, photography and editing are the
sleight-of-hand by which film hides its method; theater,
taking place in the here and now of the spectator, has
less opportunity and less need to hide its methods because
the spectator expects artifice in the theater, Steele believes.
Nicoll rests his argument on what the audience knows about
drama and film, or rather what he thought the audience
of 1936 knew about drama and film. Quite simply he thinks
the suspension of disbelief is more complete in film because
the audience knows more about dramatic methods than about
cinematic methods. The audience knows that drama, like
painting and sculpture is a human creation, but the methods
of film are so unfamiliar and mysterious, that audiences

fall back on the old prejudice that "the camera never lies."
     Perhaps film audiences of thirty years ago knew as
little about film as Nicoll believes, but today, when ten-
year-olds can discuss stop-motion photography and their
older brothers and sisters take film courses, Nicoll's
argument seems questionable. Lindsay and Steele, on the
other hand, raise points that still have currency in discussions
of literature's relation to film.
     Film's photographic basis, its facility in creating
the illusion of motion, and its unobtrusive recreation
of space are major factors in the distinctions between
film and drama drawn by the contemporary film theorist
Christian Metz. He attempts to account for film's greater
sense of reality, its greater believability. Arguments
on behalf of film's greater sense of reality generally
rest on the verisimilitude of the film image; because it
is photographically based, film makes a stage of the world.
The film audience's relationship to the fictional world
is different from that of the dramatic audience. The film
audience is temporally and spatially separated from the
projected images that convey the fiction; the theatrical
audience is temporally and spatially connected to the actors
and objects that signify the fiction. Both arts fall short
of providing a complete identification of the vehicle of
representation with the represented, but theater comes
closest, in one respect. Because theater represents objects
by objects, bodies by bodies, there is in the theater the
possibility of total identification of vehicle and whatever
the vehicle represents. A gun can be represented by a
gun, a crown by a crown in the theater, but, because film
must always represent by images, there is always a gap
between the two-dimensional vehicle and the represented
three-dimensional world.
     Defining the two distinct spaces of the film--that
of the audience and that of the image--is precisely how
Metz approaches the problem of believability. He distinguishes
film's illusion from drama's on the basis of film's being
a photographically based art, but he does not do so in
the conventional manner of noting that photography gives
film greater versatility in representing locale or that
the mobility of the camera enables film to present aspects
of reality that are too large or too small to represent
on the stage. Instead, he argues that it is the very unreality
of film's vehicle that allows its fiction to be believed,
to assume the status of reality.
     Like Arnheim, Metz defines film by contrast with
photography and drama, and he argues that film occupies
a midpoint between an art whose vehicle has too few connections
with reality to create a believable illusion and an art
whose vehicle has too many connections. To pinpoint the
nature of the photograph, Metz draws upon Roland Barthes's
contention that photography has created a new space-category,
spatial immediacy and temporal anteriority. The message
of the photograph is simply literal reality, captured through
mechanical means rather than rendered through human means.
The photograph is not simply a copy of reality that differs
from, say, a drawing with respect to the fidelity of the
reproduction, nor is it an illusion that the scene photographed
is actually present. Because the image is automatically,

mechanically registered on film, the photograph presents
evidence that something has been there. Rather than a
copy or an illusion, it is, in André Bazin's description,
a fingerprint of reality. The photograph becomes paradoxically
both "here-now" because it is a reproduction of the scene
and "there-then" because it is the result of an object's
having been at one time before the camera's lens.
    Like Barthes, Metz argues that the distinction between
film and photography is not merely one of degree but of
radical difference. A single film image is, of course,
a photograph, but a film is a series of projected images
that create the illusion of motion, and motion, according
to Metz, always implies present action. Like the objects
in a photograph, the objects in a film are "apparently
only effigies" but "their motion is not the effigy of motion--
it seems real" (0180, p.8). Because motion implies something
is actually there, the unreality of the photograph's here
and there gives way to the apparent reality of here and
now.
    In Metz's view, film meets the two conditions necessary
for the vehicle of representation to be identified by the
spectator with the represented, the fictional world. The
narrative film can present only images of actors, objects,
setting, and, therefore, its vehicle is "already imaginary
in its own way" and "tends to be swallowed up" by the fictional
world. In other words, the photographic nature of film
narrows the gap between film's means of representation
and the represented fiction. But to confer reality on
the represented fiction, the vehicle must have some connection
to reality, and that connection is movement. Apparently,
by Metz's standards, a film of a theatrical performance
would be more believable than the performance itself.
    David Lodge reaches the same conclusion as Metz but
by different means. Using Roman Jakobson's categories
of metaphoric and metonymic arts, Lodge argues that film
is a metonymic art because it stresses syntagmatic
relationships--that is, spatial, temporal, and causal
relationships--and is perceived as an "illusion of life"
while drama stresses metaphorical relationships--similarity
and dissimilarity and is perceived in terms of a performance.
He states "our pleasure in the play depends on our continuous
and conscious awareness that we are spectators not of reality
but of a conventionalized model of reality, constructed
before us by actors who speak words not their own but provided
by an invisible dramatist" (0380, p. 83).
    Metz, Lodge, and the rest do not really argue their
case that film is more believable; they assume it is and
then attempt to account for its believability in terms
of the ontology of the image, or relationships within the
narrative, or its ability to use actual locations. What
supports their premise is a widely, deeply held belief
that film is more believable, more engrossing, more emotionally
affecting than drama or prose fiction. The Production
Code of 1934 that imposed self-censorship on the Hollywood
film industry was premised on the notion that greater care
had to be taken with the content of motion pictures than
with drama because "the grandeur of mass settings, large
action, spectacular features, etc. affect and arouses more
intensely the emotional side of the audience." A number

of studies in the social sciences, particularly during
the 1930s, investigated film's apparent ability to present
a heigtened sense of reality, often described in terms
of film's hypnotic effect, and its ability to influence
audiences' values. While the findings of these studies
have been largely discounted, they do indicate the longevity
and the tenacity of the assumption that the film audience
in some sense believes what it sees and hears.
     It might be beneficial to consider the minority report.
In answer to Nicoll's <u>Film and Theatre</u>, Eric Bentley writes,
"In short, and Mr. Nicoll to the contrary notwithstanding,
there is no radical difference between stage and screen
illusion. At best the difference is one of degree. The
usual Hollywood product does seek a convincing illusion
of actuality, but so does the usual Broadway product.
This is a matter not of stage or screen but of the style
chosen by the director or author or producer" (0302, p. 54).
He raises two interesting points. First, if film audiences
do identify the vehicle with the diegesis, as Metz says,
or if film audiences are not aware of film as performance,
as a conventionalized model of reality, as Lodge suggests,
then we might expect a number of deviant reactions by film
audiences. Both film and dramatic audiences become emotionally
involved, but, if film audiences lose sight of the film
as performance, then they might be expected to react as
they would to real life events: by calling the police,
by rushing to help the emperiled heroine. But this does
not seem to be the case. Second, Bentley's insistence
on style rather than medium raises an interesting point
about the implication of Metz's and Lodge's arguments.
By basing them almost entirely on the nature of the film
image, its "naturally metonymic" character, they come
dangerously close to assuming that illusionist film is
not the result of the predilections of the film audience
but rather the result of the inherent nature of film itself.
In other words, Metz does not offer a realist agenda, but
he does imply that maintaining dramatic illusion is more
inherently cinematic, in fact, almost inevitable. He explains
believability in terms of a kind of automatic transference
of image content to fiction instead of in terms of the
calculations of certain filmmakers and the reactions of
certain spectators to certain conventional ways of patterning
narrative. Since believabilty is a characteristic of how
something is perceived, of how something is identified,
rather than simply a matter of what is perceived, it might
be more fruitful to compare the mindsets of film spectators
and dramatic spectators rather than film and drama. In
this regard, it is interesting to note that in <u>The Dynamics
of Literary Response</u> Norman Holland presumes that responses
to film, drama, and prose fiction are similar enough to
warrant a single psychoanalytic model of the audience's
engagement with art works.

                    * * * * * *

     Before the rise of narratology in the 1960s, most
articles and books on film and literature focused, often
haphazardly, on the differences in their methods. These
discussions sometimes distorted the ways film and literature

communicate to underline the autonomy of each art; for
instance, the role of dialogue in film was minimized or
ignored altogether to draw a firm boundary between film
and drama. Narratology shifted the focus of the discussion
to the elements common to all narrative and provided a
framework for a more systematic comparison of film to
literature. Genette's classes of temporal articulations
in prose fiction, for example, offer a convenient and
comprehensive framework for the comparison of plot structure
in film, drama, and prose fiction.

Even though such narratologists as Seymour Chatman
have broken ground in the systematic analysis of narrative
and in turn a systematic comparison of film and literature,
much is left to be done in this area, even considering
the work represented by the nearly 2500 articles and books
listed in the bibliography. It is commonplace that film
must "tell" its story through images rather than through
dialogue. Ideally, dialogue completes what has been
substantially conveyed by images or it risks using methods
better suited to theater. The kind of dialogue used in
film differs from that of theater and prose fiction; filmic
dialogue, as such writers as Edward Murray have argued,
is less "literary" and more "realistic" than that of drama
or prose fiction. However, such arguments are often based
upon the unsuitability for film of highly metaphoric dialogue
and ignore that obviously "literary" dialogue does not
typify a great deal of modern literature and that some
film genres, such as <u>film noir</u>, typically employ highly
stylized, "unrealistic," dialogue. Rather than arguing
the proper mix of images and words or the proper type of
dialogue for film, a systematic analysis of how dialogue
actually functions in film and literature is needed.

A clearer understanding of the role of the narrator
in film and in prose fiction is needed as well. Because
film lacks any equivalent of pronouns and because we lack
any dependable means for determining the traces of narration
in film, some writers such as David Bordwell have rejected
both the application of enunciation theory to film and
the idea of the narrator as fundamental to filmic narrative.
At the same time, Bordwell admits that some idea of source--
whether narrator, author, director or "grand image maker"--is
necessary in interpreting a good many "art" films. Bordwell's
work suggests that an analysis of film in terms of the
spectator's use of a narrator as a reading strategy would
be more fruitful than the application of the pronominal
categories of literary point of view to film. The idea
that the literary text should be interpreted in the light
of an origin, a narrator, has been fundamental to literary
criticism since Henry James. With that in mind, an analysis
of film would attempt to determine whether a spectator
customarily uses the notion of an origin for the image
and sound tracks in understanding film. Further, such
a study might determine whether this reading strategy is
specific to particular film genres rather than to film
in general.

This introduction began with Ingmar Bergman's assertion
that film has nothing to do with literature. However,
it has been demonstrated that film and literature share
the same vocation, that of narrative, which has been the

foundation of numerous articles and books on the relationship
of these arts from the early years of this century to the
present. These works are based on the notion that spectators
of film and drama and readers of novels share the same
task, to create a coherent story from the information provided
by the art work. It seems to me that the similar tasks
of story creation posed by both film and literature account
for the "unified field of imaginative response beyond the
page and the image" postulated by Bruce Morrissette in
his "Aesthetic Response to Novel and Film" (0251, p. 27).
While spectators are posed analogous tasks by film and
literature, they encounter some different methods and different
kinds of information because of the various materials of
expression. For example, the dramatic spectator may or
may not encounter problems unifying fragmentary space,
but the filmic spectator must moment by moment construct
a unified space for the fiction from the cues offered by
the fragmentary views of each shot. What, on the one hand,
is specific to a particular work of art is, on the other,
customary for the expressive system of film. These expressive
similarities and differences have and will continue to
interest writers on these partners in narrative, film and
literature.

1

Literature and Film:
General Studies

0001. Adams, Robert H. "Pictures and the Survival of
       Literature." <u>Western Humanities Review</u>, 25 (1971),
       79-85.

0002. Adler, Mortimer J. "Form and Matter" and "Criticism
       and Taste." In his <u>Art and Prudence: A Study
       in Practical Philosophy</u>. New York: Longmans,
       Green and Co., 1937, pp. 457-512 and pp. 545-585.

0003. Arnheim, Rudolph. "Epic and Dramatic Film." <u>Film
       Culture</u>, 3, No. 1 (1957), 9-10. Reprinted in
       <u>Film: A Montage of Theories</u>. Ed. Richard MacCann.
       New York: E.P. Dutton, 1966, pp. 124-128. Reprinted
       in <u>Film and/as Literature</u>. Ed. John Harrington.
       Englewood Cliffs: Prentice-Hall, 1977,
       pp. 323-326.
       Arnheim applies Goethe's theory of the epic to film.

0004. Balázs, Béla. "The Script." In his <u>Theory of the
       Film: Character and Growth of a New Art</u>. Trans.
       Edith Bone. New York: Dover Publications, 1970,
       pp. 246-257.

0005. Barnes, Walter. <u>The Photoplay As Literary Art</u>.
       Newark, N.J.: Educational and Recreational Guide,
       1936.

0006. Beja, Morris. <u>Film and Literature</u>. New York: Longman,
       1979.
       On comparison of film with literature and on adaptations.
       Contains brief essays on <u>Rashomon</u>, <u>A Clockwork Orange</u>,
       <u>Blow-Up</u>, <u>Great Expectations</u>, <u>The Third Man</u>, <u>The Innocents</u>
       (adaptation of Henry James's <u>Turn of the Screw</u>),
       <u>The Trial</u>, <u>Death in Venice</u>, <u>Lolita</u>, <u>Jules and Jim</u>,
       <u>Hamlet</u>, <u>Henry V</u>, <u>The Grapes of Wrath</u>, <u>The Treasure
       of the Sierra Madre</u>, <u>The Pawnbroker</u>, and <u>Cat on a
       Hot Tin Roof</u>.

0007. Berger, Carole. "Viewing as Action: Film and Reader
       Response." <u>Literature/Film Quarterly</u>, 6 (1978),
       144-151.

0008.   Bergman, Ingmar. "Bergman Discusses Film-Making."
         In Four Screenplays by Ingmar Bergman. Trans.
         Lars Malmstrom and David Kushner. New York: Simon
         and Schuster, 1960, pp. xiii-xxii. Shortened
         version reprinted as "Film Has Nothing to Do With
         Literature." In Film: A Montage of Theories.
         Ed. Richard MacCann. New York: E.P. Dutton, 1966,
         pp. 142-146.

0009.   Blaine, Allan. "The New American Cinema and the
         Beat Generation, 1956-1960." DAI, 45 (1985),
         1894A (Northwestern University).
         Influence of the Beat writers on avant-garde
         film with a discussion of Jack Kerouac's participation
         in the filming of Pull My Daisy.

0010.   Blakeston, Oswell. "Our Literary Screen." Close
         Up, 6, No. 4 (1930), 308-310.

0011.   Block, Ralph. "A Literature of the Screen?" Bookman,
         60 (Dec. 1924), 472-473.

0012.   _____. "Not Theatre, Not Literature, Not
         Painting." Dial, 82 (Jan. 1927), 20-24. Reprinted
         in Film: A Montage of Theories. Ed. Richard
         MacCann. New York: E.P. Dutton, 1966, pp. 154-159.

0013.   _____. "Those Terrible Movies: A Medium
         Surpassing the Theatre and the Novel."
         Theatre, 43 (Feb. 1926), 35, 52.

0014.   Borde, Raymond and Etienne Chaumeton. "The Sources
         of Film Noir." Film Reader 3 (1978), 58-66.

0015.   Bordwell, David. Narration in the Fiction Film.
         Madison: The University of Wisconsin Press,
         1985.

0016.   Boud, Jean. "Film Among the Arts." Sequence,
         No. 1 (Dec. 1946), pp. 2-4.

0017.   Browne, Nick. The Rhetoric of Filmic Narration.
         Ann Arbor: UMI Research Press, 1982.

         On point of view.

0018.   Brownell, Baker. "Drama, the Novel, the Movie."
         In his Art Is Action: A Discussion of Nine Arts
         in a Modern World. New York: Harper, 1939,
         pp. 159-170; rpt. Freeport, N.Y.: Books for
         Libraries Press, 1969.

0019.   Carpenter, Lynette. "`The Stuff That Dreams Are
         Made of': American Culture and Its Literature
         and Film, 1940-1953." DAI, 40 (1980), 4033-4034A
         (Indiana Univeristy).
         Evolution of fantasy in film and literature.

0020.   Carter, Huntley. "Cinema Activities of Five English
        Leading Men of Letters: Bernard Shaw, John
        Galsworthy, H.G. Wells, Arnold Bennett, and
        Sir James Barrie" and "The Cinema as an Art
        Form: Answers to Questions Addressed to Bernard
        Shaw and John Galsworthy." In his The New Spirit
        in the Cinema. London: Harold Shaylor, 1930,
        pp. 374-376 and pp. 376-379; rpt. New
        York: Arno Press, 1970.

0021.   Caughie, John, ed.   Theories of Authorship: A Reader.
        London: Routledge and Kegan Paul, 1981.
        A number of essays on the position of authors
        within literary and filmic texts.

0022.   Charney, Hanna. "Eric Rohmer's Le Genou de Claire:
        Rousseau Revisited?" Symposium, 27 (1973),
        101-110.
        Influence of such literary figures as Laclos,
        Rousseau, and Montaigne upon Rohmer.

0023.   Comito, Terry. "Notes on Panofsky, Cassier, and
        the `Medium of the Movies.'" Philosophy and
        Literature, 4 (Fall 1980), 229-241.

0024.   Conger, Syndy M. and Janice R. Welsch, eds. Narrative
        Strategies: Original Essays in Film and Prose
        Fiction. Macomb: Western Illinois University,
        1980.
        See 0151, 0247, 0485, 1099, 1414, 2244..

0025.   Connor, Edward. "Of Time and Movies." Films in
        Review, 12 (1961), 131-142, 181.

0026.   Crawford, Donald. "The Uniqueness of the Medium."
        The Personalist, 51 (1970), 447-469.

0027.   Dick, Bernard F. "At The Crossroads of Time: Types
        of Simultaneity in Literature and Film." Georgia
        Review, 33 (1979), 423-432.

0028.   _____. "Narrative and Infra-Narrative In
        Film." Literature/Film Quarterly, 3 (1975),
        132-144.

0029.   Durgnat, Raymond. "This Damned Eternal Triangle."
        Films and Filming, 15 (Feb. 1969), 56-60.

0030.   _____. "The Mongrel Muse." In his Films
        and Feeling. Cambridge: M.I.T. Press, 1967,
        pp. 19-30. Reprinted in Film and Literature:
        Contrasts in Media. Ed. Fred H. Marcus. Scranton:
        Chandler Publishing Co., 1971, 71-82. Portion
        reprinted in Film and/as Literature. Ed. John
        Harrington. Englewood Cliffs: Prentice-Hall,
        1977, pp. 350-354.

0031.   Dworkin, Martin S. "The Writing on the Screen."
        Antigonish Review, No. 24 (Winter 1976), pp. 75-88.

0032.   Eidsvik, Charles.   "Cinema and Literature."   In
        his Cineliteracy: Film Among the Arts.   New
        York: Random House, 1978, pp. 145-158.

0033.   _____.   "Demonstrating Film Influence."
        Literature/Film Quarterly, 1 (1973), 113-121.
        Film's influence on John Dos Passos, Iris Murdoch,
        and the Imagists.

0034.   _____.   "Soft Edges: The Art of Literature,
        the Medium of Film."   Literature/Film Quarterly,
        2 (1974), 16-21.   Reprinted in Film and/as
        Literature.   Ed. John Harrington.   Englewood
        Cliffs: Prentice-Hall, 1977, pp. 306-313.

0035.   Eikhenbaum, Boris.   "Literature and Cinema (1926)."
        In Russian Formalism.   Ed. Stephen Bann and
        John E. Bowlt.   New York: Harper and Row, 1973,
        pp. 122-127.

0036.   Feldman, Joseph and Harry Feldman.   "The Film and
        Literature."   In their Dynamics of the Film.
        New York: Arno Press, 1972, pp. 11-22.

0037.   Fell, John L.   "Verbal Arts."   In his Film and
        the Narrative Tradition.   Norman: University
        of Oklahoma Press, 1974, pp. 3-86.
        Influence of nineteenth-century popular drama and
        fiction on the movies.

0038.   _____.   "Vladimir Propp in Hollywood."   Film
        Quarterly, 30, (Spring 1977), 19-28.
        Propp's "grammar" of folk tales applied to film.

0039.   Frongia, Eugenio.   "The Literary Roots of Cinematic
        Neo-Realism."   Forum Italicum, 17 (1983), 176-195.
        Influence of literary training on film directors.

0040.   Frye, Northrop.   Anatomy of Criticism: Four Essays.
        Princeton: Princeton University Press, 1973,
        pp. 13, 107, 164, 179, 288-289.

0041.   Gallagher, Brian.   "Film Imagery, Literary Imagery:
        Some Distinctions."   College Literature, 5 (1978),
        157-173.

0042.   Gassner, John.   "The Screenplay as Literature."
        In Twenty Best Film Plays.   New York: Crown
        Publishers, 1943, pp. VII-XXX.

0043.   Geduld, Harry M., ed.   Authors on Film.   Bloomington:
        Indiana University Press, 1972.
        Responses of 41 playwrights and fiction writers
        to film, from the silent era to the present.

0044.   Giannetti, Louis.   "Literature."   In his Understanding
        Movies.   Englewood Cliffs: Prentice-Hall, 1982,
        pp. 289-332.

0045. Giles, Dennis Leslie. "The Retrieve: A Theory
       of Narrative Structure with Application to Film."
       <u>DAI</u>, 37 (1977), 6810A (Northwestern University).
       Vladimir Propp's "grammar" of narrative applied
       to film.

0046. Golden, Leon, ed. <u>Transformations in Literature
       and Film</u>. Tallahassee: University Presses of
       Florida, 1982.
       See 0543, 0864, 2240.

0047. Goodwin, James. "Literature and Film: A Review
       of Criticism." <u>Quarterly Review of Film Studies</u>,
       4 (1979), 227-246.
       Essay-review of Richardson, Magny, and Spiegel.

0048. Graham, John. "`Damn Your A Priori Principles--
       Look!' W.R. Robinson Discusses Movies as a
       Narrative Art." <u>The Film Journal</u>, 1 (Summer
       1971), 49-52.

0049. Grossvogel, David I. "The Play of Light and Shadow:
       A Directorial Error." <u>Yale French Studies</u>,
       No. 17 (1956), pp. 75-85.
       Film's relation to the other arts; the growth of
       the French film.

0050. Hamburger, Käte. "Cinematic Fiction." In her
       <u>The Logic of Literature</u>. Trans. Marilyn J. Rose.
       Bloomington: Indiana University Press, 1973,
       pp. 218-231.
       In this study of the defining characteristics of
       fiction, Hamburger finds film closer to prose
       fiction than drama.

0051. Hamilton, Harlan. "Using Literary Criticism to
       Understand Film." <u>Exercise Exchange</u>, 14
       (1966-67), 16-17.

0052. Hammond, Paul, ed. <u>The Shadow and Its Shadow:
       Surrealist Writing on Cinema</u>. London: British
       Film Institute, 1978.
       Contains brief essays on film by Louis Aragon,
       Andre Breton, Antonin Artaud, and Robert Desnos.

0053. Hannon, William Morgan. <u>The Photodrama: Its Place
       Among the Fine Arts</u>. New Orleans: The Ruskin
       Press, 1915. Reprinted in <u>Screen Monographs
       II</u>. New York: Arno Press, 1970.

0054. Hargrave, Harry. "Film as Literature." <u>Southern
       Humanities Review</u>, 9 (1975), 233-239.
       Imagery, symbolism, point of view, and the manipulation
       of time in film and literature.

0055. Harrington, John, ed. <u>Film and/as Literature</u>.
       Englewood Cliffs: Prentice-Hall, 1977.
       See 0003, 0030, 0034, 0068, 0495, 0514, 1166.

0056.   Hauser, Arnold. "The Film Age." In his The Social
         History of Art. Volume 2. New York: Alfred
         A. Knopf, 1951, pp. 927-959.

0057.   Hitchcock, Alfred M. "Relation of the Picture
         Play to Literature." English Journal, 4 (May
         1915), 292-298.

0058.   Holland, Norman N. The Dynamics of Literary Response.
         New York: Oxford University Press, 1968,
         pp. 162-190. Excerpted in Film and/as
         Literature. Ed. John Harrington. Englewood
         Cliffs: Prentice-Hall, 1977, pp. 336-349.
         On psychological response to literature and film.

0059.   Horton, Andrew. "Film and Literature." In Encyclopedia
         of World Literature in the 20th Century. Volume
         2. Ed. Leonard S. Klein. New York: Frederick
         Ungar, 1982, pp. 93-99.

0060.   Huss, Roy and Norman Silverstein. "Film Study:
         Shot Orientation for the Literary Minded."
         College English, 27 (1966), 566-568.

0061.   Ingarden, Roman. "The Cinematographic Drama [the
         Film]." In his The Literary Work of Art: An
         Investigation on the Borderline of Ontology,
         Logic, and Theory of Literature. Trans. George
         G. Grabowicz. Evanston: Northwestern University
         Press, 1973, pp. 323-327.
         Unless visual events are used to tell its stories,
         film will be a parasite of drama and fiction.

0062.   Jahiels, Edwin. "Literature and Film." Books
         Abroad, 45 (1971), 259-261.
         Essay-review of Richardson's Film and Literature
         and Wollen's Signs and Meaning in the Cinema.

0063.   Jakobson, Roman. "Is the Cinema in Decline?"
         In Russian Formalist Film Theory. Ed. Herbert
         Eagle. Ann Arbor: University of Michigan Slavic
         Publications, 1981, pp. 161-166.

0064.   Kawin, Bruce. Telling It Again: Repetition in
         Literature and Film. New York: Cornell University
         Press, 1977.
         Robbe-Grillet, Genet, Stein, and Beckett are among
         the artists discussed.

0065.   Kerr, Walter. "Film, Stage, Novel." In Thirty
         Plays Hath November: Pain and Pleasure in the
         Contemporary Theater. New York: Simon and Schuster,
         1968, pp. 93-120.

0066.   Khatchadourian, Haig. "Family Resemblances and
         the Classification of Works of Art." The
         Journal of Aesthetics and Art Criticism, 28
         (1969), 19-90.

0067.   _____. "Film as Art." The Journal of Aesthetics
         and Art Criticism, 33 (1975), 271-284.

0068.   Klein, Michael. "The Literary Sophistication of
         Francois Truffaut." Film Comment, 3 (Summer
         1965), 24-29. Reprinted in The Emergence of
         Film Art. Ed. Lewis Jacobs. New York: Hopkinson
         and Blake, 1969, pp. 303-312. Reprinted in
         Film and/as Literature. Ed. John Harrington.
         Englewood Cliffs: Prentice-Hall, 1977, pp. 327-335.
      The French director's techniques compared to those
   of Brecht, Ionesco, and Joyce.

0069.   Krows, Arthur Edwin. "Literature and the Motion
         Picture." The Annals of the American Academy
         of Political and Social Science, 128 (Nov. 1926),
         70-73.

0070.   Levinson, André. "The Nature of Cinema." Theatre
         Arts Monthly, 13 (1929), 684-693.

0071.   Lewis, Brian. "Film as Art." In his Jean Mitry
         and the Aesthetics of the Cinema. Ann Arbor:
         UMI Research Press, 1984, pp. 50-60.

0072.   Lillard, Richard G. "Movies Aren't Literary."
         The English Journal, 29 (1940), 735-743.

0073.   Lindgren, Ernest T. The Art of the Film. New
         York: The Macmillan Co., 1963.

0074.   McConnell, Frank. The Spoken Seen: Film and the
         Romantic Imagination. Baltimore: Johns Hopkins
         University Press, 1975.

0075.   _____. Storytelling and Mythmaking: Images
         From Film and Literature. New York: Oxford
         University Press, 1979.

0076.   MacDonald, George B. "An Application of New Critical
         Methodology to the Study of the Narrative Film."
         DAI, 32 (1972), 6435A (Lehigh University).

0077.   McLuhan, Marshall. "Movies: The Reel World."
         In his Understanding Media: The Extensions of
         Man. New York: McGraw-Hill, 1964, pp. 284-296.
         Reprinted in Film and/as Literature. Ed. John
         Harrington. Englewood Cliffs: Prentice-Hall,
         1977, pp. 295-305.

0078.   Marcus, Fred H., ed. Film and Literature: Contrasts
         in Media. Scranton: Chandler Publishing Co.,
         1971.
      See 0030, 0103, 0231, 0241, 0409, 0422, 0654,
   0885, 0915, 1135, 1526, 1840

0079.   Mast, Gerald. Film/Cinema/Movie: A Theory of
         Experience. New York: Harper and Row, 1977.

0080.   Michalczyk, John J.   "Alain Resnais: Literary Origins
         from Hiroshima to Providence." Literature/Film
         Quarterly, 7 (1979), 16-25.

0081.   _____. The French Literary Filmmakers. Cranbury,
             N.J.: Associated University Presses, 1980.
         Contains essays on Jean Cocteau, Sacha Guitry,
         Marcel Pagnol, Jean Giono, Andre Malraux, Alain
         Robbe-Grillet, and Marguerite Duras.

0082.   Moeller, Hans-Bernhard. "Literature in the Vicinity
             of Film: On German and Nouveau Roman Authors."
         Symposium, 28 (1974), 315-335.
         Film's influence on such writers as Bertolt Brecht,
         Wolfgang Bauer, Peter Weiss, and Peter Handke.

0083.   Morris, C.B.   This Loving Darkness: The Cinema
             and Spanish Writers, 1920-1936. New York: Oxford
             University Press, 1980.
         Influence of film on such literary figures as Rafael
         Alberti, Federico García Lorca, Luis Cernuda, Benjamín
         Jarnès, and Francisco Ayala.

0084.   Morsberger, Robert E. and Katharine M. Morsberger.
             "Screenplay as Literature: Bibliography and
             Criticism." Literature/Film Quarterly, 3 (1975),
             45-59.

0085.   Mukarovsky, Jan.   "A Note on the Aesthetics of
             Film" and "Time in Film." In his Structure,
             Sign, and Function. Ed. John Burbank and Peter
             Steiner. New Haven: Yale University Press,
             1978, pp. 178-190 and pp. 191-199.

0086.   Munro, Thomas.   The Arts and Their Interrelations.
             New York: The Liberal Arts Press, 1949, pp. 501-504.

0087.   Munsterberg, Hugo. "The Aesthetics of the Photoplay."
             In his The Film: A Psychological Study. New
             York: Dover Publications, 1970, pp. 57-100.
             Section of chapter, "The Means of the
             Photoplay," reprinted in Film Theory: Introductory
             Readings. Ed. Gerald Mast and Marshall Cohen.
             New York: Oxford University Press, 1974, pp. 239-248.

0088.   Murray, Edward.   The Cinematic Imagination. New
             York: Frederick Ungar, 1972.
         Cinematic techniques in and filmic adaptations
         of works by Samuel Beckett, Bertolt Brecht,
         John Dos Passos, Theodore Dreiser, William Faulkner,
         F. Scott Fitzgerald, Graham Greene, Ernest Hemingway,
         Eugene Ionesco, James Joyce, Thomas Mann, Arthur
         Miller, Eugene O'Neill, Alain Robbe-Grillet, John
         Steinbeck, and Nathanael West.

0089. Nichols, Bill.   "The Cinema: Movement, Narrative,
       and Paradox." In his <u>Ideology and Image: Social
       Representation in the Cinema and Other Media</u>.
       Bloomington: Indiana University Press, 1981,
       pp. 69-103.

0090. Nichols, Dudley.   "The Writer and the Film."   In
       <u>Twenty Best Film Plays</u>. Ed. John Gassner and
       Dudley Nichols. New York: Crown Publishers,
       1943, pp. XXXI-XL.

0091. Oakes, Philip. <u>The Film Addicts Archive</u>. London:
       Elm Tree Books, 1977.
       An anthology of literature with film as its subject
       matter; includes works by Kipling, Fitzgerald,
       Vidal, Lowell, and Shapiro.

0092. Ortman, Marguerite G., ed. <u>Fiction and the Screen</u>.
       Boston: Marshall Jones, 1935.
       Contains four essays on film and literature: film
       and Greek drama by Lewis Worthington Smith; film
       and fiction by Marguerite Ortman; Cukor's adaptation
       of <u>David Copperfield</u> by Lewis Worthington Smith;
       and detail in film production by Mrs. Lewis Worthington
       Smith.

0093. Palesis, Ioannis Antonios. "At the Crossroads
       of Cinema and Literature: A Study of the Scenario
       as a Genre." <u>DAI</u>, 40 (1979), 3342A (The University
       of Pennsylvania).

0094. Patterson, Frances Taylor. "The Author and Hollywood."
       <u>The North American Review</u>, 244 (1937), 77-89.

0095. Perez, Gilberto. "The Narrative Sequence." <u>Hudson
       Review</u>, 30 (1977), 80-92.

0096. Perkins, V.F. <u>Film as Film: Understanding and
       Judging Movies</u>. Baltimore" Penguin Books, 1974.

0097. Perlmutter, Ruth. "Add Film to Rhetoric."
       <u>Literature/Film Quarterly</u>, 3 (1975), 316-326.

0098. Phillips, Henry Albert. "Differentiation." In
       his <u>The Photodrama</u>. Larchmont, N.Y.: The
       Stanhope-Dodge Publishing Co., 1914, pp. 32-38;
       rpt. New York: Arno Press, 1970.

0099. Piotrovskij, A. "Towards a Theory of Cine-Genres."
       In <u>Russian Formalist Film Theory</u>. Ed. Herbert
       Eagle. Ann Arbor: University of Michigan Slavic
       Publications, 1981, pp. 131-146.

0100. Poague, Leland. "Literature vs. Cinema: The Politics
       of Aesthetic Definition." <u>Journal of Aesthetic
       Education</u>, 10 (1976), 75-91.

0101.   _____. "The Problem of Film Genre: A Mentalist
         Approach." Literature/Film Quarterly, 6 (1978),
         152-161.

0102. Reynolds, Leslie M. "Film as a Poetic Art and
         Contemporary Fable." South Atlantic Bulletin,
         38, No. 2 (1973), 8-14.
       In its scope, film is related to the epic; in its
       use of language, it is related to poetry.

0103. Richardson, Robert Dale. Literature and Film.
         Bloomington: Indiana University Press, 1972.
         Portion reprinted in Film and Literature: Contrasts
         in Media. Ed. Fred H. Marcus. Scranton: Chandler
         Publishing Co., 1971, pp. 115-126.
       Finds literary techniques analogous to film techniques.
       Believes film is a part of literature.

0104.   _____. "Visual Literacy: Literature and
         Film." Denver Quarterly, 1 (1966), 24-36.
       Became a portion of Literature and Film.

0105. Ross, Harris E. Some Aspects of the Relationship
         of Film to Literature." DAI, 41 (1981), 3093A
         (The University of Arkansas).

0106. Ruhe, Edward. "Film: The `Literary' Approach."
         Literature/Film Quarterly, 1 (1973), 76-83.

0107. Sandro, Paul. "The Management of Destiny in Narrative
         Form." Ciné-Tracts, 4 (Spring 1982), 50-56.
       Frank Kermode's literary criticism applied to film.

0108. Schenck, Mary-Low Taylor. "Action Writing: A Study
         of Selected Works of Twentieth-Century Drama,
         Fiction, and Film Whose Theme is the Examination
         of Their Own Processes." DAI, 38 (1977), 257A
         (Brown University).
       Among the writers and filmmakers considered are
       Alain Robbe-Grillet, John Barth, Tom Stoppard,
       Jean Genet, Thomas Pynchon, Federico Fellini, and
       Ingmar Bergman.

0109. Scholes, Robert. "Narration and Narrativity in
         Film." Quarterly Review of Film Studies, 1 (1976),
         283-296.

0110. Scholes, Robert and Robert Kellogg. The Nature
         of Narrative. New York: Oxford University Press,
         1966, pp. 280-281.
       Contends that film is a narrative rather than a
       dramatic form.

0111. Scruton, Roger. "Fantasy, Imagination, and the
         Screen." In his The Aesthetic Understanding:
         Essays in the Philosophy of Art and Culture.
         New York: Methuen, 1983, pp. 127-136.

0112.   Seidman, Barbara Ann.   "The Filmgoing Imagination:
        Filmmaking and Filmgoing as the Subjects of
        Modern American Literature." DAI, 42 (1982),
        4827-4828A (The University of Illinois at
        Urbana-Champaign).
        Concerns fiction inspired by film. Among the authors
        discussed are H.D., F. Scott Fitzgerald, Theodore
        Dreiser, Eugene O'Neill, Walker Percy, David Madden,
        Thomas Pynchon, and Vladimir Nabokov. The works
        discussed include Percy's The Moviegoer, Nabokov's
        Lolita, and Pynchon's Gravity's Rainbow.

0113.   Sesonske, Alexander.   "Aesthetics of Film, Or a
        Funny Thing Happened on the Way to the Movies."
        Journal of Aesthetics and Art Criticism, 33
        (1974), 51-57.
        Author notes that film usually seen in terms of
        other arts; he seeks criteria to distinguish film
        from other arts.

0114.   Sevastakis, Michael George.   "Death's Love Songs:
        The American Horror Film (1931-1936) and Its
        Embodiment of Romantic Gothic Conventions."
        DAI, 40 (1979), 2308-2309A (New York University).
        Includes discussions of such films as Frankenstein,
        Dracula, Dr. Jekyll and Mr. Hyde, Mad Love, and
        The Mummy.

0115.   Shattuck, Roger.   "Fact in Film and Literature."
        Partisan Review, 44 (1977), 539-550.

0116.   Shklovsky, Viktor.   "Poetry and Prose in
        Cinematography." In Russian Formalism. Ed. Stephen
        Bann and John E. Bowlt. New York: Harper and
        Row, 1973, pp. 128-130.

0117.   Silverstein, Norman.   "Film and Language, Film
        and Literature." Journal of Modern Literature,
        2 (1971), 154-160.

0118.   Simmons, Steven Clyde.   "'Modernism' in Film: Essays
        on Jean-Luc Godard." DAI, 43 (1982), 956A (Stanford
        University).
        The relationship of Godard's films to the modern
        novel and the dramatic theory of Bertolt Brecht.

0119.   Siska, William C.   "Metacinema: A Modern Necessity."
        Literature/Film Quarterly, 7 (1979), 285-289.
        Reflexivity in literature and film.

0120.   Small, Edward S.   "Literary and Film Genres: Toward
        a Taxonomy of Film." Literature/Film Quarterly,
        7 (1979), 290-299.

0121.   Sobchack, Vivian.   "Tradition and the Cinematic
        Allusion." Literature/Film Quarterly, 2 (1974),
        59-65.

0122. Stam, Robert. _Reflexivity in Film and Literature:_
       From Don Quixote to Jean-Luc Godard. Ann Arbor:
       UMI Research Press, 1985.
       The artists covered include Hitchcock, Keaton,
       Balzac, Truffaut, Jarry, and Brecht; adaptations
       covered include _Tom Jones_, _Lolita_, _The French_
       Lieutenant's Woman, and _Macunaima_.

0123. Stolnitz, Jerome. "Kracauer: Thing, Word, and
       Inferiority in the Movies." _The British Journal_
       of Aesthetics, 14 (1974), 351-367.

0124. Stonier, George Walter. "Movie." In his _Gog Magog_
       and Other Critical Essays. London: Dent, 1933,
       pp. 177-189; rpt. Freeport, N.Y.: Books for
       Libraries Press, 1966.
       Influence of film on other arts.

0125. Suhor, Charles. "The Film/Literature Comparison."
       Media and Methods, 12, No. 4 (1975), 56-59.

0126. Thompson, George H. "The Four Story Forms: Drama,
       Film, Comic Strip, Narrative." _College English_,
       37 (1975), 265-280.

0127. Timberg, Bernard M. "`E=MC^2'and the Birth of Film."
       Texas Studies in Language and Literature, 22
       (1980), 263-285.
       Includes discussion of film and Gertrude Stein,
       H.G. Wells, and Vachel Lindsay.

0128. Toliver, Harold. "Mixed Modes: Lyric and Cinematic
       Narrative." In his _Animate Illusions: Explorations_
       of Narrative Structure. Lincoln: University
       of Nebraska Press, 1974, pp. 189-217.

0129. Torossian, Aram. _A Guide to Aesthetics_. Stanford:
       Stanford University Press, 1937, pp. 183-190.

0130. Wegner, Hart L. "Literary Influences on the Earliest
       Expressionist Film: _Der Student von Prag_."
       West Virginia University Philological Papers,
       26 (Aug. 1980), 1-6.

0131. _____. "The Literate Cinema." _Western Humanities_
       Review, 24 (1970), 279-282.

0132. Weitz, Morris. _Philosophy of the Arts_. Cambridge:
       Harvard University Press, 1950, pp. 126-129.
       Film is ancillary to story plot, character.

0133. White, Eric Walter. _Parnassus to Let: An Essay_
       About Rhythm in the Film. London: Hogarth Press,
       1928. Reprinted in _Screen Monographs I_. New
       York: Arno Press, 1970.

0134. Williams, Linda. "The Image." In her _Figures_
       of Desire: A Theory and Analysis of Surrealist
       Film. Urbana: University of Illinios Press,
       1981, pp. 3-52.
       André Breton's, Antonin Artaud's and Guillaume
       Apollinaire's views of film.

0135. Winston, Douglas Garrett. _The Screenplay as_
       Literature. Cranbury, N.J.: Associated University
       Presses, 1973.
       Film's debt to the novel, stream of consciousness
       in film and fiction, and Bresson's adaptation of
       Diary of a Country Priest.

2

Language and Film:
Linguistic Approaches to Film

0136.   Abramson, Ronald. "Structure and Meaning in the
        Cinema." In <u>Movies and Methods</u>. Ed. Bill Nichols.
        Berkeley: University of California Press, 1976,
        pp. 558-568.

0137.   Andrew, Dudley. "The Primacy of Figure in Cinematic
        Signification." In <u>Cinema and Language</u>. Ed.
        Stephen Heath and Patricia Mellenchamp. Frederick,
        MD.: University Publications of America, 1983,
        pp. 133-140.

0138.   _____. "Signification." In his <u>Concepts
        in Film Theory</u>. New York: Oxford University
        Press, 1984, pp. 57-74.
        Recent trends in semiotics.

0139.   _____. "The Structuralist Study of Narrative:
        Its History, Use, and Limits." <u>Bulletin of
        the Midwest MLA</u>, 8 (1975), 45-61. Reprinted
        in <u>The Horizons of Literature</u>. Ed. Paul Hernadi.
        Lincoln: University of Nebraska Press, 1982,
        pp. 99-124. Reprinted as "Narrative Structure."
        In his <u>Concepts in Film Theory</u>. New York: Oxford
        University Press, 1984, pp. 75-95.
        Discussion of recent developments in narratology
        with some attention to film.

0140.   Barthes, Roland. "The Third Meaning: Research
        Notes on Some Eisenstein Stills." In his <u>Image,
        Music, Text</u>. Trans. Stephen Heath. New York:
        Hill and Wang, 1977, pp. 52-68.

0141.   Bettetini, Gianfranco. <u>The Language and Technique
        of the Film</u>. Trans. David Osmond-Smith. The
        Hague: Mouton, 1973.

0142.   Brakhage, Stan. "Metaphors on Vision." <u>Film Culture</u>,
        30 (Fall 1963), 64 unnumbered pages.

0143.   Brewster, Ben. "Structuralism in Film Criticism."
        <u>Screen</u>, 12 (1971), 49-58.

0144.   Burke, Frank.   "The Natural Enmity of Words and
        Moving Images: Language, La Notte, and the Death
        of the Light." Literature/Film Quarterly, 7
        (1979), 36-46.

0145.   Cadbury, William and Leland Poague. Film Criticism:
        A Counter Theory. Ames: The Iowa State University
        Press, 1982.
        Book's first section includes an extensive critique
        of approaches to film that are derived from linguistics.

0146.   Carroll, John M. Toward a Structural Psychology
        of Cinema. Berlin: Mouton Publishers, 1980.
        Transformational linguistics and psycholinguistics
        applied to film.

0147.   Carroll, Noel. "Language and Cinema: Preliminary
        Notes for a Theory of Verbal Images." Millenium
        Film Journal, 7-9 (1980-81), 186-217.

0148.   Clifton, N. Roy. The Figure in Film. East Brunswich:
        Associated University Presses, 1983.
        Rhetorical figures in film.

0149.   Cook, David A. "Some Structural Approaches to
        Cinema: A Survey of Models." Cinema Journal,
        14 (Spring 1975), 41-54. Reprinted in Cinema
        Examined: Selections from Cinema Journal.
        Ed. Richard Dyer MacCann and Jack C. Ellis.
        New York: E.P. Dutton, 1982, pp. 269-282.

0150.   Cozyris, George Agis. Christian Metz and the Reality
        of Film. New York: Arno Press, 1980.

0151.   Dagle, Joan. "Narrative Discourse in Film and
        Fiction: The Question of the Present Tense."
        In Narrative Strategies: Original Essays in
        Film and Prose Fiction. Ed. Syndy Conger and
        Janice R. Welsch. Macombe: Western Illinois
        University, 1980, pp. 47-59.

0152.   Dart, Peter. "Figurative Expression in the Film."
        Speech Monographs, 35 (1968), 170-174.

0153.   Denkin, Harvey. "Linguistic Models in Early Soviet
        Cinema." Cinema Journal, 17 (Fall 1977), 1-13.

0154.   Dreyfus, Dina. "Cinema and Language." Diogenes,
        35 (Fall 1961), 23-33.

0155.   Durgnat, Raymond. "The Death of Cinesemiology
        (With Not Even a Whimper)." Cinéaste, 10, No. 2
        (1980), 10-13.

0156.   _____. "The Language of Film and Problems
        in Cinesemiotics." The British Journal of
        Aesthetics, 22 (1982), 64-269.

0157.   Eckert, Charles W.   "The English Cine-Structuralists."
         Film Comment, 9 (May-June 1973), 46-51.

0158.   Eco, Umberto.   "Articulations of the Cinematic
         Code." In _Movies and Methods_. Ed. Bill Nichols.
         Berkeley: University of California Press, 1976,
         pp. 590-607.

0159.   Eisenstein, Sergei.   "Film Language." In his _Film
         Sense: Essays in Film Theory_. Ed. Jay Leyda.
         New York: Harcourt, Brace, and World, 1949,
         pp. 108-121.

0160.   _____.   "Word and Image." In his _The Film
         Sense_. Ed. Jay Leyda. New York: Harcourt,
         Brace, and World, 1970, pp. 3-68.
         Montage explained in terms of language and memory.

0161.   Giannetti, Louis D.   "Cinematic Metaphors." _The
         Journal of Aesthetic Education_, 6 (Oct. 1972),
         49-61.   Reprinted in his _Godard and Others:
         Essays on Film Form_. Rutherford, N.J.: Fairleigh
         Dickinson University Press, 1975, pp. 89-131.

0162.   Gross, Larry.   "Introduction: Sol Worth and the
         Study of Visual Communication." In _Studying
         Visual Communication_ by Sol Worth. Ed. Larry
         Gross. Philadelphia: University of Pennsylvania
         Press, 1981, pp. 1-35.

0163.   Grundy, Dr. J.B.C.   "Language and Film: A Prophecy."
         Sight and Sound, 2 (Summer 1933), 45-46.

0164.   _____.   "Language and Film II: A Solution,."
         Sight and Sound, 2 (Autumn 1933), 85-86.
         Both articles are on dialogue.

0165.   Guzzetti, Alfred.   "Christian Metz and the Semiology
         of the Cinema." _Journal of Modern Literature_,
         3 (1973), 292-308.

0166.   Hale, Clarence Benjamin, Jr.   "The Application
         of Linguistic Principles to the Analysis of
         Film Surface-Structure." _DAI_, 41 (1980), 1253A
         (North Texas State University).

0167.   Hanhardt, John G. and Charles H. Harpole.   "Linguistics,
         Structualism, and Semiology: Approaches to the
         Cinema, With a Bibliography." _Film Comment_,
         9 (May-June 1973), 52-59.

0168.   Heath, Stephen.   "Language, Sight, and Sound."
         In _Cinema and Language_. Ed. Stephen Heath and
         Patricia Mellencamp. Frederick, MD.: University
         Publications of America, 1983, pp. 1-17.

0169.   Henderson, Brian.   "Critique of Cine-Structuralism,
         I and II." _Film Quarterly_, 26 (Fall 1973),
         25-34, and 27 (Winter 1973-74), 37-46.

0170. _____. "Metz: _Essais I_ and Film Theory."
      Film Quarterly, 28 (Spring 1975), 18-23.

0171. _____. "Segmentation." _Film Quarterly_,
      31 (Fall 1977), 57-65. This essay, 0169
      and 0170 are reprinted with an addtional essay,
      "Film Semotics as Semiotics," in _A Critique
      of Film Theory_. New York: E.P. Dutton, 1980,
      pp. 109-233.
      Critiques of Metz's semiotic analysis of film.

0172. Hervey, Sandor. "Semiotics of the Cinema: Christian
      Metz." In his _Semotic Perspectives_. Boston:
      George Allen and Unwin, 1982, pp. 234-243.

0173. Hudlin, Edward W. "Film Language." _The Journal
      of Aesthetic Education_, 13 (April 1979), 47-56.

0174. Johnson, William C., Jr. "Literature, Film, and
      the Evolution of Consciousness." _Journal of
      Aesthetics and Art Criticism_, 38 (1979), 29-38.

0175. Kinden, Gorham Anders. _Toward a Semiotic Theory
      of Visual Communication in the Cinema_. New
      York: Arno Press, 1980.

0176. Koch, Christian Herbert. "Understanding Film as
      a Process of Change: A Metalanguage for the
      Study of Film Developed and Applied to Ingmar
      Bergman's _Persona_ and Alan J. Pakula's _The
      Sterile Cuckoo_." _DAI_, 31 (1971), 4936-4937A
      (The University of Iowa).

0177. Lewis, Brian. "Film and Language" and "Poetics
      or Linguistics? Mitry and Metz." In his _Jean
      Mitry and the Aesthetics of the Cinema_. Ann
      Arbor: UMI Research Press, 1984, pp. 60-70 and
      pp. 70-84.

0178. Lotman, Jurij. _Semiotics of Cinema_. Trans. Mark
      E. Suino. Ann Arbor: University of Michigan
      Press, 1976.

0179. Metz, Christian. "Current Problems of Film Theory:
      Mitry's _L'Esthetique et Psychologie du Cinema_."
      Trans. Diana Matias. _Screen_, 14 (Spring-Summer
      1973), 40-87. Portion Reprinted in _Movies and
      Methods_. Ed. Bill Nichols. Berkeley: University
      of California Press, 1976, pp.568-578.

0180. _____. _Film Language: A Semiotics of the
      Cinema_. Trans. Michael Taylor. New York: Oxford
      University Press, 1974.

0181. _____. _The Imaginary Signifier: Psychoanalysis
      and the Cinema_. Trans. Celia Britton, Annwyl
      Williams, Ben Brewster, and Alfred Guzetti.
      Bloomington: Indiana University Press, 1977.

0182.   _____. Language and Cinema. Trans. Donna
        Jean Umiker-Sebeok. The Hague: Mouton Publishers,
        1974.

0183.   _____. "On the Notion of Cinematographic
        Language." In Movies and Methods. Ed. Bill
        Nichols. Berkeley: University of California
        Press, 1976, pp. 582-589.
        In this early essay, Metz draws distinctions between
        film and language.

0184.   Monaco, James. "The Language of Film: Sign and
        Syntax." In his How to Read a Film: The Art,
        Technology, Language, History, and Theory of
        Film and Media. New York: Oxford University
        Press, 1977, pp. 121-192.

0185.   Nash, Mark. "Vampyr and the Fantastic." Screen,
        17 (Autumn 1976), 29-67.
        Applies Todorov's definition of the genre, and
        Benveniste's definition of "discours" and "histoire"
        to Dreyer's film.

0186.   Nichols, Bill. "Style, Grammar, and the Movies."
        Film Quarterly, 28 (Spring 1975), 33-49. Reprinted
        in Movies and Methods. Ed. Bill Nichols. Berkeley:
        University of California Press, 1976, pp. 607-628.
        A critique of film semiology and a call for an
        approach not based upon a language model.

0187.   Pryluck, Calvin. "The Film Metaphor: The Use of
        Language-Based Models in Film Study."
        Literature/Film Quarterly, 3 (1975), 117-123.
        Argues that language-based models not appropriate
        in film study; argues that film's metaphors differ
        from those in language.

0188.   Rohdie, Sam. "Narrative Structures." Film Reader
        2. Evanston: Northwestern University, 1977,
        pp.11-14.

0189.   Russell, Lee. "Cinema--Code and Image." New Left
        Review, No. 49 (1968), pp. 65-81.

0190.   Salvaggio, Jerry Lee. A Theory of Film Language.
        New York: Arno Press, 1980.

0191.   Sandro, Paul. "Signification in the Cinema."
        Diacritics, 4 (Fall 1974), 42-50.
        On Christian Metz's semiotic approach to film.

0192.   Seidman, Steve. "The Innocents: Point of View
        as an Aspect of the Cinefantastic System."
        Film Reader 4. Evanston: Northwestern University,
        1979, pp. 201-213.
        Uses Mark Nash's approach for an analysis of Jack
        Clayton's film.

0193.   Selig, Michael Emil. "On Language/On Film:
         Deconstructing the Cinema." DAI, 44 (1984),
         2910-2911A (Northwestern University).

0194.   Seril, William. "The Language of the Screen."
         Sight and Sound, 17 (Spring 1948), 18-19.
         How film conveys the emotions of characters.

0195.   Sesonske, Alexander. "Time and Tense in the Cinema."
         Journal of Aesthetics and Art Criticism, 38
         (1980), 419-426.

0196.   Silverman, Kaja. The Subject of Semiotics. New
         York: Oxford University Press, 1983.

0197.   Silverstein, Norman. "Film and Language, Film
         and Literature." Journal of Modern Literature,
         2 (1971), 154-160.
         Essay/review of books by Christian Metz and Robert
         Richardson.

0198.   _____. "Film Semiology." Salmagundi,
         13 (Summer 1970), 73-80.

0199.   Van Wert, William F. and Walter Mignolo. "Julia
         Kristeva/Cinematographic Semiotic Practice."
         Sub-Stance, No. 9 (1974), pp. 97-114.

0200.   Willemen, Paul. "Cinematic Discourse: The Problem
         of Inner Speech." In Cinema and Language.
         Ed. Stephen Heath and Patricia Mellencamp.
         Frederick, MD.: University Publications of America,
         1983, pp. 141-167.

0201.   Wollen, Peter. "Cinema and Semiology: Some Points
         of Contact." In Movies and Methods. Ed. Bill
         Nichols. Berkeley: University of California
         Press, 1976, pp. 481-492.

0202.   _____. Signs and Meaning in the Cinema.
         Bloomington: Indiana University Press, 1972.

0203.   Worth, Sol. "The Development of a Semiotic of
         the Cinema." Semiotica, 1 (1969), 282-321.
         Reprinted in his Studying Visual Communication.
         Ed. Larry Goss. Philadelphia: University of
         Pennsylvania Press, 1981, pp. 36-73.
         Applying Chomsky's ideas, Worth argues that film
         is not a language.

0204.   _____. "Pictures Can't Say Ain't." Versus
         12 (1975), 85-108. Reprinted in his Studying
         Visual Communication. Ed. Larry Gross.
         Philadelphia: University of Pennsylvania Press,
         1981, pp. 162-184. Revised version in Film/Culture:
         Explorations of Cinema in Its Social Context.
         Ed. Sari Thomas. Metuchen: Scarecrow Press,
         1982, pp. 97-109.

0205.   Zholkovsky, Alexander.   "Eisenstein's Generative
          Poetics."   In his <u>Themes and Texts: Toward a
          Poetics of Expressiveness</u>.   Ithaca: Cornell
          University Press, 1984, pp. 35-52.

3

Prose Fiction and Film:
General Studies

0206. Armes, Roy. "Film and the Modern Novel." In his
Film and Reality: A Historical Survey. Baltimore:
Penguin Books, 1975, 208-214.

0207. Barr, Charles. "Cinemascope: Before and After."
Film Quarterly, 16 (Summer 1963), 4-24. Excerpt
reprinted in Film: A Montage of Theories. Ed.
Richard Dyer MacCann. New York: E.P. Dutton,
1966, 318-328. Reprinted in Film Theory and
Criticism. Ed. Gerald Mast and Marshall Cohen.
New York: Oxford University Press, 1979,
pp. 140-168.
Description in novel and film.

0208. Bazin, André. "An Aesthetic of Reality: Neorealism."
In his What Is Cinema? Volume Two. Trans. Hugh
Gray. Berkeley: University of California Press,
1971, pp. 16-40.
Bazin draws numerous parallels between neorealism
and the novels of Faulkner, Hemingway, and Malraux.

0209. Belson, James Ira. "Maps of Consciousness: Creating
an Inner Life for Character in Film and Novel."
DAI, 34 (1974), 4242A (University of Southern
California).

0210. Bond, Kirk. "Film as Literature." The Bookman,
84 (1933), 188-189.

0211. Branigan, Edward. Point of View in the Cinema:
A Theory of Narration and Subjectivity in Classical
Film. Berlin: Mouton Publishers, 1984.

0212. Burke, John. "The Book of the Film." Film, No. 33
(Autumn 1962), 48.
On the novelization of films.

0213. Campbell, Robert Ewing. "The Cameo Illusion."
DAI, 42 (1981), 209A (Oklahoma State University).
Film technique in the novel.

0214.   Chatman, Seymour. "What Is Description in the
        Cinema?" <u>Cinema Journal</u>, 23 (Summer 1984),
        4-11.

0215.   _____. <u>Story and Discourse: Narrative Structure
        in Fiction and Film</u>. Ithaca: Cornell University
        Press, 1978.
        Drawing on such theorists as Barthes and Gennette,
        Cohen analyzes the similar ways that film and fiction
        employ plot, character, and authorial distance.

0216.   _____. "What Novels Can Do That Films Can't
        (And Vice Versa)." <u>Critical Inquiry</u>, 7 (1980),
        121-140.
        Uses a portion of <u>A Day in the Country</u>, Jean Renoir's
        adaptation of Maupassant, to demonstrate the limits
        of film and fiction.

0217.   Cohen, Keith. <u>Film and Fiction: The Dynamics of
        Exchange</u>. New Haven: Yale University Press,
        1979.
        Impact of film on such novelists as Proust and
        Joyce.

0218.   _____. "Novel and Cinema: Dynamics of Literary
        Exchange." <u>Film Reader 2</u>. Evanston: Northwestern
        University Press, 1977, pp. 42-51.

0219.   Cook, Bruce. "Science, Fiction, and Film: A Study
        of the Interaction of Science, Science Fiction
        Literature, and the Growth of Cinema." <u>DAI</u>,
        37 (1977), 6810A (University of Southern California).
        Includes a study of the literary roots of the genre,
        with attention given to Shelley's <u>Frankenstein</u>.

0220.   Dittmar, Linda. "Fashioning and Re-Fashioning:
        Framing Narratives in the Novel and Film."
        <u>Mosaic</u>, 16, Nos. 1-2 (1983), 189-203.

0221.   Dreyer, Carl Theodor. "New Ideas About Film: Benjamin
        Christensen and His Ideas." In <u>Dryer in Double
        Reflection</u>. Ed. Donald Skoller. New York:
        E.P. Dutton and Co., 1973, pp. 30-35.

0222.   Durgnat, Raymond. "Images of the Mind--Part Two:
        Shapes and Stories." <u>Films and Filming</u>, 15
        (Feb. 1969), 56-60.

0223.   Eberwein, Robert T. "The Filmic Dream and Point
        of View." <u>Literature/Film Quarterly</u>, 8 (1980),
        197-203.
        First person narration and dream sequences in film.

0224.   Edel, Leon. "Novel and Camera." In <u>The Theory
        of the Novel: New Essays</u>. Ed. John Halperin.
        New York: Oxford University Press, 1974, pp. 177-188.

0225.   Eisenstein, Sergei. "Lessons from Literature."
        In his Film Essays and a Lecture. Ed. Jay Leyda.
        New York: Praeger Publishers, 1970, pp. 77-83.
        Film's connection to such authors as Zola and Balzac.

0226.   Fell, John. "Film and Prose." In his Film: An
        Introduction. New York: Praeger Publishers,
        1975, pp. 32-40.

0227.   Fiedler, Leslie. "The Death and Rebirth of the
        Novel." In The Theory of the Novel: New Essays.
        Ed. John Halperin. New York: Oxford University
        Press, 1974, pp. 189-209.
        Sees novel sharing "popular archetypes" with film.

0228.   Guzzetti, Alfred. "The Role of Theory in Films
        and Novels." New Literary History, 3 (1972),
        547-558.

0229.   Hanhardt, John G. "Boris Uspensky's A Poetics
        of Composition."   In Film Reader 4. Evanston:
        Northwestern University, 1979, pp. 189-192.

0230.   Henderson, Brian. "Tense, Mood, and Voice in Film
        (Notes After Genette)." Film Quarterly, 36
        (Summer 1983), 4-17.
        Applies Gerard Genette's Narrative Discourse to
        film.

0231.   Huss, Roy and Norman Silverstein. "Tone and Point
        of View." In their The Film Experience: Elements
        of Motion Picture Art. New York: Dell Publishing,
        1968, pp. 105-126. Reprinted in Film and Literature:
        Contrasts in Media. Ed. Fred H. Marcus. Scranton:
        Chandler Publishing Co., 1971, pp. 53-70.
        This introductory text uses literature as a point
        of reference. In this section, point of view in
        literature and film is described through an analysis
        of Tony Richardson's Tom Jones.

0232.   Jinks, William. The Celluloid Literature: Film
        in the Humanities. Beverly Hills: Glencoe Press,
        1974.
        A general introduction explains film in terms of
        the novel.

0233.   Jobst, John William II. "Cinematic Technique in
        the World War I American Novel." DAI, 39 (1979),
        4937-4938A (The University of Missouri at Columbia).
        Includes discussions of John Dos Passos, Laurence
        Stallings, Humphrey Cobb, William March, Thomas
        Boyd, and Ernest Hemingway.

0234.   Karageorge, Yuri Vidov. "Fictional and Cinematic
        Treatment of Time in Five French Authors,
        1955-1976." DAI, 40 (1979), 2046A (Indiana
        University).
        Discussions of Michel Butor, Marguerite Duras,
        Alain Resnais, Alain Robbe-Grillet, and Chris Marker.

0235.   Kawin, Bruce. "Authorial and Systemic Self-
         Consciousness in Literature and Film."
         Literature/Film Quarterly, 10 (1982), 3-12.

0236.   _____. Mindscreen: Bergman, Godard, and First
         Person Film. Princeton: Princeton University
         Press, 1978.
         Argues that film, like prose fiction, can be narrated
         in the first person.

0237.   _____. "An Outline of Film Voices." Film
         Quarterly, 38 (Winter 1984-85), 38-46.
         Answers Henderson's article. Argues that film
         is as capable as novel of narrating in first person.

0238.   Kracauer, Siegfried. "Interlude: Film and Novel."
         In his Theory of Film: The Redemption of Physical
         Reality. New York: Oxford University Press,
         1960, pp. 232-244.
         Finds similarity in how film and novel narrate
         and handle time, but believes the two share different
         "worlds," physical and mental.

0239.   Levinson, Julie R. "Self-Creating Narrative in
         Film and Fiction." DAI, 45 (1984), 977A (Boston
         University).

0240.   Linden, George W. "Films and a Novel Future."
         The Journal of Aesthetics and Art Criticism,
         8 (Jan. 1974), 55-64. Excerpt reprtined in
         Film and Literature: Contrasts in Media. Ed. Fred
         H. Marcus. Scranton: Chandler Publishing Co.,
         1971, pp. 157-163.

0241.   _____. "The Storied World." In his Reflections
         on the Screen. Belmont, Ca.: Wadsworth Publishing
         Co., 1970, pp. 32-59. Reprinted in Film and/as
         Literature. Ed. John Harrington. Englewood
         Cliffs: Prentice-Hall, 1977, pp. 156-170.

0242.   Losano, Wayne A. "The Horror Film and the Gothic
         Narrative Tradition." DAI, 34 (1974), 5221A
         (Rensselaer Polytechnic Institute).

0243.   Luhr, William and Peter Lehman. "The Function
         of Narrative in Film." In their Authorship
         and Narrative in the Cinema: Issues in Contemporary
         Aesthetics. New York: G.P. Putnam's Sons, 1977,
         pp. 173-195.

0244.   McGlynn, Paul D. "Point of View and the Craft
         of Cinema: Notes on Some Devices." The Journal
         of Aesthetics and Art Criticism, 32 (1973),
         187-195.

0245.   _____. "Rhetoric in Fiction and Film: Notes
         Toward a Cultural Symbiosis." English Record,
         21 (1970), 15-22.

0246.   Magny, Claude-Edmonde. _The Age of the American_
         Novel: The Film Aesthetic of Fiction Between
         the Wars. Trans. Eleanor Hochman. New York:
         Frederick Ungar Publishing, 1972.
         This seminal work, first published in 1948, concerns
         the impact of film on the novel. The book contains
         essays on film's influence on the novels of John
         Dos Passos, Ernest Hemingway, John Steinbeck, and
         William Faulkner.

0247.   Mayne, Judith. "Mediation, the Novelistic, and
         Film Narrative." In _Narrative Strategies: Original_
         Essays in Film and Prose Fiction. Ed. Syndy
         Conger and Jancie R. Welsch. Macomb: Western
         Illinois University, 1980, pp. 79-92.
         Film and fiction serve to mediate between the
         individual's public and private lives.

0248.   Mendilow, A.A. "Fiction and the Other Arts."
         In his _Time and the Novel_. New York: Humanities
         Press, 1965, pp. 53-59.

0249.   Monaco, James. "Film and the Novel." In his _How_
         to Read a Film: The Art, Technology, Language,
         History, and Theory of Film and Media. New
         York: Oxford University Press, 1977, pp. 29-33.

0250.   Moreno, Julio L. "Subjective Cinema: The Problem
         of Film in the First Person." _The Quarterly_
         of Film, Radio, and Television, 7 (Summer 1953),
         341-358.
         Film lacks genuine first-person narration.

0251.   Morrissette, Bruce. "Aesthetic Response to Novel
         and Film: Parallels and Differences." _Symposium_,
         27 (1973), 137-151. Shorter version printed
         in _Expression, Communication and Experience_
         in Literature and Language. Ed. Ronald G.
         Popperwell. Leeds: W.S. Manley and Son, 1973,
         pp. 215-218. Reprinted in his _Novel and Film:_
         Essays in Two Genres. Chicago: University of
         Chicago Press, 1985, 12-27.

0252.   _____. "The Cinema Novel." In his _Novel_
         and Film: Essays in Two Genres. Chicago: University
         of Chicago Press, 1985, 28-39.

0253.   _____. "Post-Modern Generative Fiction:
         Novel and Film." _Critical Inquiry_, 2 (1975),
         253-260. Reprinted in his _Novel and Film: Essays_
         in Two Genres. Chicago: University of Chicago
         Press, 1985, 28-39.

0254.   Morse, Margaret. "Paradoxes of Realism: The Rise
         of Film in the Train of the Novel." _Ciné-Tracts_,
         4 (Spring 1981), 27-37.
         Ian Watt's method in _The Rise of the Novel_ applied
         to film.

0255.   Nathan, Robert. "A Novelist Looks at Hollywood."
        Hollywood Quarterly, 1 (1946), 146-147. Reprinted
        in Film: A Montage of Theories. Ed. Richard
        Dyer MacCann. New York: E.P. Dutton, 1966,
        pp. 129-131.
Author says a film is a novel in images.

0256.   Noxon, Gerald. "The Anatomy of the Close-Up: Some
        Literary Origins in the Works of Flaubert, Huysmans,
        and Proust." Journal of the Society of
        Cinematographers, 1 (1961), 1-24.

0257.   _____. "Some Observations on the Anatomy
        of the Long Shot: An Extract from Some Literary
        Origins of Cinema Narrative." Journal of the
        Society of Cinematographers, 5 (1965), 70-80.

0258.   Pipolo, Tony. "The Aptness of Terminology: Point
        of View, Consciousness, and Letter from an Unknown
        Woman." In Film Reader 5. Evanston: Northwestern
        University, 1979, pp. 166-179.
Argues that film can be narrated in the first person.

0259.   Prill, Penelope Kay. "Point of View in Literature
        and Film." DAI, 40 (1980), 4208A (Ohio State
        University).
Based on Boris Upensky's theory of point of view
in literature.

0260.   Purdy, Strother B. "Can the Novel and the Film
        Disappear?" Literature/Film Quarterly, 2 (19174),
        237-255.

0261.   Rebolledo, Carlos. "Buñuel and the Picaresque
        Novel." In The World of Luis Buñuel: Essays
        in Criticism. Ed. Joan Mellen. New York: Oxford
        University Press, 1978, pp. 139-148.
Influence of Spanish literature, particularly Quevedo,
on the director.

0262.   Riesman, David. "The Oral Tradition, the Written
        Word, and the Screen Image." Film Culture,
        2 (1956), 1-5. Reprinted in Film and the Liberal
        Arts. Ed. T.J. Ross. New York: Holt, Rinehart
        and Winston, 1970, pp. 251-259.

0263.   Riesman, Evelyn T. "Film and Fiction." Antioch
        Review, 17 (1957), 353-363.

0264.   Roud, Richard. "Novel, Novel; Fable, Fable?"
        Sight and Sound, 31 (Spring 1962), 84-88.

0265.   See, Carolyn. "The Hollywood Novel: The American
        Dream Cheat." In Tough Guy Writers of the Thirties.
        Ed. David Madden. Carbondale: Southern Illinois
        University Press, 1968, pp. 199-217.
Discusses Nathanael West (Day of the Locust),
Raymond Chandler (Little Sister), Richard Sale
(Lazarus #7), and John O'Hara (Hope of Heaven).

0266.   _____. "The Hollywood Novel: An Historical
           and Critical Survey." DAI, 24 (1964), 5418A
           (University of California, Los Angeles).

0267.   Seldes, Gilbert. "The Cinema Novel." In his The
           Seven Lively Arts. New York: Harper and Row,
           1924, pp. 383-390.
         Film's influence on the French novel.

0268.   Shine, Carol Ellen Bolduan. "Montage: A Critical
           Technique in Selected Modern Novels and Narrative
           Films." DAI, 39 (1978), 2A (The University
           of Massachusetts).
         Among the works discussed are Citizen Kane, Hiroshima
         Mon Amour, Last Year at Marienbad, Rashomon, and
         three Faulkner novels: The Sound and the Fury,
         As I Lay Dying, and Absalom, Absalom!

0269.   Smith, Julian. "Orson Welles and the Great Dummy--Or,
           the Rise and Fall of Benjamin Franklin's Modern
           American." Literature/Film Quarterly, 2 (1974),
           196-206.
         Popular literature as a source for Citizen Kane.

0270.   Snyder, John R. "The Spy Story and Modern Tragedy."
           Literature/Film Quarterly, 5 (1977), 216-234.
         Discussion centers on Conrad's The Secret Agent.

0271.   Spencer, Sharon. "The Perspectives of the Camera."
           In her Space, Time and Structure in the Modern
           Novel. New York: New York University Press,
           1971, pp. 101-129.
         Film techniques in John Dos Passos, Alain Robbe-Grillet,
         and Gertrude Stein.

0272.   Spiegel, Alan. Fiction and the Camera Eye: Visual
           Consciousness in Film and the Modern Novel.
           Charlottesville: University of Virginia Press,
           1976.
         Discussion of "cinematic" novel includes Flaubert,
         Zola, Lawrence, Woolf, James, Conrad and Joyce.

0273.   _____. "Flaubert to Joyce: Evolution of
           Cinematographic Form." Novel, 6 (1973), 229-243.
         Material is included in Fiction and the Camera Eye.

0274.   _____. "The Mud on Napoleon's Boots: The
           Adventitious Detail in Film and Fiction." Virginia
           Quarterly Review, 52 (1976), 249-264.
         Centers on Joyce and Sartre. Material is included
         in Fiction and the Camera Eye.

0275.   Stromgren, Richard L. and Martin F. Norden. "Film
           and Literature." In their Movies: A Language
           in Light. Englewood Cliffs: Prentice-Hall,
           1984, pp. 167-182.
         Covers differences in prose fiction and film; considers
         adaptation and includes a list of works adapted
         to the screen.

0276.   Sweet, Frederick Joseph.   "Narrative in the Films
         of Alain Resnais and Contemporary Fiction."
         <u>DAI</u>, 34 (1973), 1870A (The University of Michigan).

0277.   Thorp, Margaret.   "The Motion Picture and the Novel."
         <u>American Quarterly</u>, 3 (Fall 1951), 195-203.

0278.   Tynjanov, Ju.   "On the Foundations of Cinema."
         In <u>Russian Formalist Film Theory</u>.   Ed. Herbert
         Eagle.   Ann Arbor: University of Michigan Slavic
         Publications, 1981, pp. 81-100.

0279.   Van Norstrand, Albert.   "Hollywood Pay-Off."   In
         his <u>The Denatured Novel</u>.   Indianapolis: Bobbs-
         Merrill, 1960, pp. 105-132.
         Hollywood's negative influence on the novel.

0280.   Van Wert, William.   <u>The Theory and Practice of
         the Cine-Roman</u>.   New York: Arno Press, 1978.
         Examination of the French literary filmmakers such
         as Resnais, Robbe-Grillet, and Varda.

0281.   Wilson, George.   "Film, Perception, and Point of
         View."   <u>Modern Language Notes</u>, 91 (1976), 1026-1043.
         First-person narration in film.

0282.   Wolfe, Charles.   "Fictional Realism: Watt and Bazin
         on the Pleasures of Novels and Films."
         <u>Literature/Film Quarterly</u>, 9 (1981), 40-50.

4

Drama and Film:
General Studies

0283. Allen, Jeanne Thomas. "Copyright, and Early Theater, Vaudeville, and Film Competition." In Film Before Griffith. Ed. John L. Fell. Berkeley: University of California Press, 1983, pp. 176-187.

0284. Alpert, Hollis. "Film and Theatre." In his The Dreams and the Dreamers. New York: The MacMillan Co., 1962, 233-251. Portion reprinted in Film: A Montage of Theories. Ed. Richard Dyer MacCann. New York: E.P. Dutton and Co., 1966, pp. 108-123.

0285. Altshuler, Thelma and Richard Paul Janaro. Responses to Drama: An Introduction to Plays and Movies. Boston: Houghton Mifflin, 1967.

0286. Anthony, Luther B. "The Talkies: Back to the Real Stage From the Reel Stage." The Dramatist, 19 (July 1928), 1372-1376.

0287. Arliss, George. "The Stage and the Screen." Journal of the Royal Society of Arts, 85 (30 July 1937), 862-865.

0288. Arnheim, Rudolph. "A New Laocoon: Artistic Composites and the Talking Film." In his Film as Art. Berkeley: University of California Press, 1957, pp. 199-230.

0289. Bakshy, Alexander. "The Cinematograph as Art." Drama, 22 (May 1916), 267-284.

0290. _____. "The Movie Scene: Notes on Sound and Silence." Theatre Arts Monthly, 13 (1929), 97-107.

0291. _____. "The New Art of the Moving Picture." Theatre Arts Monthly, 11 (1927), 277-282.

0292. _____. "The Road to Art in the Motion Picture." Theatre Arts Monthly, 11 (1927), 455-462.

0293.   Balfour, Betty. "The Art of the Cinema." The
         English Review, 37 (1923), 388-391.

0294.   Barry, Iris. "A Comparison of Arts." The Spectator
         (London), 132 (3 May 1924), 707.

0295.   _____. "Dolls and Dreams." In her Let's
         Go to the Movies. New York: Payson and Clark,
         1926, pp. 23-33; rpt. New York: Arno Press,
         1972.

0296.   Battle, Barbara Helen. "George Cukor and the American
         Theatrical Film." DAI, 33 (1972), 439A (Columbia
         University).

0297.   Beck, Warren. "Dumb Show into Drama." The English
         Journal (Regular Edition), 21 (1932), 220-228.

0298.   Beguiristain, Mario Eugenio. "Theatrical Realism:
         An American Film Style of the Fifties." DAI,
         38 (1978), 6991-6992A (The University of Southern
         California).
         A study of theatrical influence on the work of
         such filmmakers as Elia Kazan and Sidney Lumet.
         Among the works discussed: The Rose Tatoo, Bachelor
         Party, Edge of the City, A Face in the Crowd, and
         The Pawnbroker.

0299.   Belasco, David. "The Movies--My Profession's Flickering
         Bogy: A Famous Theatrical Manager Gives His
         Opinions on the Film Drama, and Tells What He
         Would Do If He Were to Direct a Motion-Picture
         Play." Munsey's Magazine, 63 (1918), 593-604.

0300.   Bell, Clive. "Cinema Aesthetics." Theatre Guild
         Magazine, 7 (Oct. 1929), 39, 62-63.

0301.   Bentley, Eric. "Monsieur Verdoux as Theater."
         The Kenyon Review, 10 (1948), 705-716.

0302.   _____. "Realism and the Cinema." In Focus
         on Film and Theatre. Ed. James Hurt. Englewood
         Cliffs: Prentice-Hall, 1974, pp. 51-58.
         In this excerpt from The Playwright as Thinker,
         Bentley contrasts cinematic and theatrical realism.

0303.   Blossom, Roberts. "On Filmstage." Tulane Drama
         Review, 11 (1966), 68-72.
         An actor and dramatist discusses the influence
         of film upon his work.

0304.   Boroff, Phil Dean. "Joshua Logan's Directorial
         Approach to the Theatre and Motion Pictures:
         A Historical Analysis." DAI, 37 (1976), 3270A
         (Southern Illinois University).

0305.   Brazier, Marion Howard. Stage and Screen. Boston:
         M.H. Brazier, 1920.

0306.   Budgen, Suzanne. "The Sources of `La Regle de
           Jeu.'" Take One, 1 (July-Aug. 1968), 10-12.
           Influence of French comedy on Renoir's film.

0307.   Callenbach, Ernest. "The Natural Exchange: From
           an Interview with Vito Pandolfi." Tulane Drama
           Review, 11 (1966), 137-140.
           Influence of film on drama.

0308.   Carter, Huntley. "Cinema and Theatre: The Diabolical
           Difference." English Review, 55 (1932), 313-320.

0309.   Casty, Allen. "The New Style in Film and Drama."
           Midwest Quarterly, 11 (Winter 1970), 209-227.
           On Truffaut, Godard, Bergman, Brecht, and Pinter.

0310.   Chenoweth, Stuart Curran. "A Study of the Adaptation
           of Acting Technique from Stage to Film, Radio,
           and Television." DA 18 (1958), 1143-1144
           (Northwestern University).

0311.   Clair, René. "Theatre and Cinema." In his Cinema
           Yesterday and Today. Trans. Stanley Appelbaum.
           New York: Dover Publications, 1972, pp. 159-169.

0312.   Collingnon, Jean. "Theatre and Talking Pictures
           in France." Yale French Studies, No. 5 (1950),
           pp. 34-40.

0313.   Craig, Gordon. "The Cinema and Its Drama." English
           Review, 34 (Feb. 1922), 119-122.

0314.   Darlington, William Aubrey. "Stage and Film
           Technique." In his Through the Fourth Wall.
           London: Chapman and Hall, 1922, pp. 110-114;
           rpt. Freeport, N.Y.: Books for Libraries Press,
           1968.

0315.   Dean, Basil. "The Future of Screen and Stage."
           In Footnotes to the Film. Ed. Charles Davy.
           London: Lovat and Dickson, 1937, pp. 172-184;
           rpt. New York: Arno Press, 1970.

0316.   De Casseres, Benjamin. "Are the Pictures and Stage
           Antagonistic?" Theatre, 47 (Jan. 1928), 23,
           68.

0317.   Denby, David. "Stranger in a Strange Land: A Moviegoer
           at the Theater." The Atlantic, 255 (Jan. 1985),
           37-50.

0318.   Dickinson, Thorold. "The Maturing Cinema." Cinema
           Journal, 4 (1964), 9-19.

0319.   Dreyer, Carl Theodor. "The Real Talking Film."
           In Dreyer in Double Reflection. Ed. Donald
           Skoller. New York: E.P. Dutton and Co., 1973,
           pp. 52-56.

0320. Durgnat, Raymond. "Images of the Mind--Part One:
       Throwaway Movies." Films and Filming, 14 (July
       1968), 4-10.

0321. _____. "Sensation, Shape and Shade." In
       his Films and Feelings. Cambridge: The M.I.T. Press,
       1967, pp. 43-60.

0322. Eaton, Walter Prichard. "The Latest Menace to
       the Movies." The North American Review, 212
       (1920), 80-87.

0323. Eidsvik, Charles. "Film, the Visual Arts, and
       Theater." In his Cineliteracy: Film Among the
       Arts. New York: Random House, 1978, pp. 159-166.

0324. Eisenstein, Sergei. "Through Theatre to Cinema."
       In Film Form. Ed. Jay Leyda. New York: Harcourt,
       Brace, and World, 1949, pp. 3-17. Reprinted
       in Focus on Film and Theatre. Ed. James Hurt.
       Englewood Cliffs: Prentice-Hall, 1974, pp. 116-129.
       Chronicles the Russian director's growing
       dissatisfaction with the theatre. Eisenstein uses
       a section of Madame Bovary to illustrate the principles
       of montage.

0325. Ejxenbaum, B. "Problems of Cinema Stylistics."
       In Russian Formalist Film Theory. Ed. Herbert
       Eagle. Ann Arbor: University of Michigan Slavic
       Publications, 1981, pp. 55-80.

0326. Embler, Jeffry Brown. "A Historical Study of the
       Use of Film to Provide Additional Content to
       Theatrical Productions on the Legitimate Stage."
       DAI, 32 (1971), 3473A (The University of Pittsburg).

0327. Faure, Elie. The Art of Cineplastics. Trans. Walter
       Pach. Boston: THe Four Seas Co., 1923. Reprinted
       in Screen Monographs I. New York: Arno Press,
       1970.

0328. Feldman, Joseph and Harry Feldman. "The Film and
       Drama" and "The Film and the Stage." In their
       Dynamics of the Film. New York: Arno Press,
       1972, pp. 22-30 and pp. 30-38.

0329. Fell, John L. "Dissolves by Gaslight." Film Quarterly,
       23 (Spring 1970), 22-34.
       Film's techniques analogous to those of
       nineteenth-century theatre. This article was
       subsequently incorporated into Film and the Narrative
       Tradition (see 0037).

0330. _____. "Film and Theater." In his Film:
       An Introduction. New York: Praeger Publishers,
       1975, pp. 28-32.

0331.   Frye, Northrop. "Specific Forms of Drama." In his
        Anatomy of Criticism: Four Essays. Princeton:
        Princeton University Press, 1957, pp. 282-293.
        Contains a brief comparison of film to masque.

0332.   Garrett, George. "Don't Make Waves." In Man and
        the Movies. Ed. W.R. Robinson. Baltimore:
        Penguin Books, 1967, pp. 227-260.

0333.   Gassner, John. "Film Perspectives." In his The
        Theatre in Our Time. New York: Crown Publishers,
        1954, pp. 565-588.

0334.   Gauteur, Claude. "A Frenzy of Images: An Interview
        with Roger Planchon." Tulane Drama Review, 11
        (1966), 133-136.
        Stage director's use of film techniques.

0335.   Gessner, Robert. "The Faces of Time: A New Aesthetics
        for Cinema." Theatre Arts, 46 (July 1962),
        13-17.
        Uses idea of montage to distinguish film from drama.

0336.   Giannetti, Louis. "Player" and "Spectacle." In
        his Understanding Movies. Englewood Cliffs:
        Prentice-Hall, 1982, pp. 201-248 and pp. 249-288.

0337.   Gilman, Richard. "About Nothing--With Precision."
        In his Common and Uncommon Masks. New York:
        Random House, 1971, pp. 30-37. Reprinted in Focus
        on Film and Theatre. Ed. James Hurt. Englewood
        Cliffs: Prentice-Hall, 1974, pp. 59-66.
        Contends that some modern directors like Antonioni
        have moved beyond theatrical influence.

0338.   Goodman, Paul. "The Shape of the Screen and the
        Darkness of the Theatre." In his Art and Social
        Nature. New York: Vinco Publishing Co., 1946,
        pp. 72-85.
        The differences in the way spectators perceive
        film and drama.

0339.   Grafe, Frieda. "Theatre, Cinema, Audience: Liebelei
        and Lola Montes." In Ophuls. Ed. Paul Willemen.
        London: British Film Institute, 1978, pp. 51-54.
        Max Ophuls's views on film and theatre.

0340.   Grau, Robert. "The `Talking' Picture and the Drama."
        Scientific American, 105 (Aug. 1911), 155-156.

0341.   _____. The Theatre of Science. New York:
        Broadway Publishing, 1914; rpt. New York: Benjamin
        Blom, 1969.

0342.   Gray, Paul. "Cinema Verite: An Interview with
        Barbet Schroeder." Tulane Drama Review, 11
        (1966), 130-132.
        Cinema verite seen as a means for overcoming theatrical
        influence.

0343.   _____. "Class Theatre, Class Film: An Interview
         with Lindsay Anderson." Tulane Drama Review,
         11 (1966), 122-129.

0344.   _____. "Growing Apart: From an Interview
         with Roger Blin." Tulane Drama Review, 11 (1966),
         115-116.

0345.   _____. "A Living World: An Interview with
         Peter Weiss." Tulane Drama Review, 11 (1966),
         106-114.

0346.   Griffith, D.W. "Moving Pictures Can Get Nothing
         From the Stage," "New Prophecies: Film and Theatre,
         Screenwriting, Education," and "The New Stage
         Supplants the Old." In Focus on D.W. Griffith.
         Ed. Harry Geduld. Englewood Cliffs: Prentice-Hall,
         1971, pp. 32, 34-35, and 48-49.

0347.   Hamilton, Clayton. "The Art of the Moving-Picture
         Play." The Bookman, 32 (1911), 512-516.

0348.   Harris, Celia. "The Movies and the Elizabethan
         Theatre." Outlook, 130 (4 Jan. 1922), 29-31.

0349.   Hatfield, Hurd. "Stage Acting Versus Film Acting."
         Films in Review, 1 (1950), 11-16, 47.

0350.   Helburn, Theresa. "Theatre Versus Pictures."
         American Association of University Women Journal,
         29 (Jan. 1936), 84-88.

0351.   Hinsdale, Harriet. "Writing for Stage and Screen."
         Films in Review, 2 (Jan. 1951), 25-28.

0352.   Holland, Norman. "Aristotle for Filmmakers."
         Films in Review, 9 (1958), 324-328.
         Relationship of film to the Greek theatre.

0353.   Howard, Trevor. "The Stage, the Screen, and the
         Actor." In International Film Annual, No. 1.
         Ed. Campbell Dixon. New York: Doubleday, 1957,
         pp. 90-92.

0354.   Hughes, Pennethorne. "The Historical Inception
         of Stage and Film." Close Up, 10 (Dec. 1933),
         341-346.

0355.   Hurt, James. "Film/Theatre/Film/Theatre/Film."
         In Focus on Film and Theatre. Ed. James Hurt.
         Englewood Cliffs: Prentice-Hall, 1974, pp. 1-15.

0356.   _____, ed. Focus on Film and Theatre. Englewood
         Cliffs: Prentice-Hall, 1974.
         See 0302, 0324, 0337, 0355, 0365, 0409, 0427, 0451,
         0963, 1489, 1528, 2027.

0357. Israel, Mary Catherine. "Film Takes Over the Theatre:
       An Historical Study of American Resident Stock
       Companies from 1920 to 1932." DAI, 40 (1980),
       4806A (City University of New York).

0358. Jaffe, Ira Sheldon. "Aristotle and the Movies:
       A Critical Study of Unity in the Film." DAI,
       36 (1977), 5604-5605A (The University of Southern
       California).

0359. Jones, Henry Arthur. "The Dramatist and the
       Photoplay." In Authors on Film. Ed. Harry
       M. Geduld. Bloomington: Indiana University
       Press, 1972, pp. 161-162. Reprinted in Film
       and/as Literature. Ed. John Harrington. Englewood
       Cliffs: Prentice-Hall, 1977, pp. 53-54.

0360. _____. "Drama Versus Film." In Fact, Fancy,
       and Opinion. Ed. Robert M. Gay. Boston: Atlantic
       Monthly Press, 1923, pp. 109-113.

0361. Jones, Robert Edmund. "A New Kind of Drama."
       In his The Dramatic Imagination. New York:
       Theatre Arts Books, 1941, pp. 131-148.

0362. Kallen, Horace M. "The Dramatic Picture Versus
       the Pictoral Drama: A Study of the Influences
       of the Cinematograph on the Stage." Harvard
       Monthly, 50 (March 1910), 22-31.

0363. Kantor, Bernard R., Irwin R. Blacker, and Anne
       Kramer. "Interview with Elia Kazan." In Focus
       on Film and Theatre. Ed. James Hurt. Englewood
       Cliffs: Prentice-Hall, 1974, pp. 130-148.

0364. Kauffmann, Stanley. "End of an Inferiority Complex."
       Theatre Arts, 46 (Sept. 1962), 67-70.
       Kauffmann feels that around 1958 films gained in
       power and the theatre lost power.

0365. _____. "Notes on Theater-and-Film." In Focus
       on Film and Theatre. Ed. James Hurt. Englewood
       Cliffs: Prentice-Hall, 1974, pp. 67-77. Reprinted
       in his Living Images. New York: Harper and
       Row, 1975, pp. 353-362.

0366. Kazanskij, B. "The Nature of Cinema." In Russian
       Formalist Film Theory. Ed. Herbert Eagle.
       Ann Arbor: University of Michigan Slavic
       Publications, 1981, pp. 101-129.

0367. Khatchadourian, Haig. "Movement and Action in
       Film." The British Journal of Aesthetics, 20
       (1980), 349-355.

0368. Kirby, Michael. "The Uses of Film in the New Theatre."
       Tulane Drama Review, 11 (Fall 1966), 49-61.

0369.   Kovács, Katherine Singer. "Georges Méliès and the
         Féerie." Cinema Journal, 16 (Fall 1976),
         1-13. Reprinted in Film Before Griffith. Ed. John
         L. Fell. Berkeley: University of California
         Press, 1983, pp. 244-257.
The filmmaker and nineteenth-century French theatre.

0370.   Kracauer, Siegfried. "Stage Acting Versus Screen
         Acting." Films in Review, 1 (1950), 7-11.

0371.   _____. "The Theatrical Story." In his Theory
         of Film: The Redemption of Physical Reality.
         New York: Oxford University Press, 1960,
         pp. 215-231.

0372.   Krempel, Daniel S. "A Place and No Place: Comparing
         Stage and Screen as Dramatic Media." Intellect,
         104 (1976), 396-399.

0373.   Kupier, John B. "The Stage Antecedents of the Film
         Theory of S.M. Eisenstein." Educational Theatre
         Journal, 13 (1961), 259-263.

0374.   Langer, Susanne. "A Note on the Film." In her
         Feelings and Form. New York: Charles Scribner's
         Sons, 1953, pp. 411-415.

0375.   Laufe, A.L. "Not So New in the Theatre." South
         Atlantic Quarterly, 46 (1947), 384-389.

0376.   Laurie, Edith. "Film--the Rival of the Theater."
         Film Comment, 1 (Fall 1963), 51-53.
Discussion by Peter Brook, Kenneth Tynan, and Alain
Robbe-Grillet.

0377.   Leech, Clifford. "Dialogue for Stage and Screen."
         The Penguin Film Review, 6 (1958), 97-103; rpt.
         Totowa, N.J.: Rowan and Littlefield, 1978.

0378.   Lehman, Peter. "Script/Performance/Text: Theory
         and Auteur Theory." Film Reader 3, Evanston,
         Ill.: Northwestern University, 1978, 197-206.

0379.   Linden, George. "The Staged World." In his Reflections
         on the Screen. Belmont, Ca.: Wadsworth Publishing
         Co., 1970, pp. 2-29.

0380.   Lodge, David. "Drama and Film." In his The Modes
         of Modern Writing: Metaphor, Metonymy, and the
         Typology of Modern Literature. Ithaca, N.Y.:
         Cornell University Press, 1977, pp. 81-87.

0381.   Loney, Glenn. "Bergman in the Theater." Modern
         Drama, 9 (1966), 170-177.

0382.   Macdonald, Dwight. "Our Elizabethan Movies." In
         his On Movies. New York: Berkeley Publishing,
         1969, pp. 89-93.
Compares film to Elizabethan drama.

0383.   MacDonald, Gerald. "From Stage to Screen." Films
        in Review, 6 (Jan. 1955), 13-18.
        Stage stars in films.

0384.   Macgowan, Kenneth. "Crossroads of Screen and Stage."
        Seven Arts, 1 April 1917, pp. 649-654.

0385.   _____. "The Movies--the Curtain Becomes the
        Stage." In his The Theatre of Tomorrow. London:
        T. Fisher Unwin, 1923, pp. 178-185.

0386.   McLaughin, Robert. Broadway and Hollywood: A History
        of Economic Interaction. New York: Arno Press,
        1974.

0387.   McVay, Douglas. "The Art of the Actor." Films
        and Filming, 12 (July 1966), 10.

0388.   _____. "The Art of the Actor." Films and
        Filming, 13 (Nov. 1966), 2.
        Both articles are on film versus stage acting.

0389.   Mamoulian, Rouben. "Recommended: A Divorce."
        Theatre Arts, 32 (June 1948), 22-23.

0390.   _____. "Stage and Screen." Screen Writer,
        2 (March 1947), 1-15.

0391.   Marker, Lise-Lone. Ingmar Bergman: Four Decades
        in the Theatrer. New York: Cambridge University
        Press, 1981.

0392.   _____. "The Magic Triangle: Ingmar Bergman's
        Implied Philosophy of Theatrical Communication."
        Modern Drama, 26 (1983), 251-261.
        Influence of Bergman's theatrical experience upon
        his films.

0393.   Marker, Frederick J. and Lise-Lone Marker. "Of
        Winners and Losers: A Conversation with Ingmar
        Bergman" Theatre, 13 (Summer-Fall 1982), 42-52.
        Reprinted in Ingmar Bergman: A Project for the
        Theatre. Ed. Frederick J. Marker and Lise-Lone
        Marker. New York: Frederick Ungar, 1983, pp. 1-18.

0394.   _____. "Love Without Lovers: A Commentary
        on the Bergman Project." In their Ingmar Bergman:
        A Project for the Theatre. New York: Frederick
        Ungar, 1983, pp. 19-45.
        On Bergman's staging of Ibsen's A Doll's House,
        Strindberg's Miss Julie, and his own Scenes from
        a Marriage.

0395.   Mason, James. "Back to the Stage." Films in Review,
        5 (1954), 327-332.

0396.   _____. "Stage Versus Screen." Films and
        Filming, 1 (Nov. 1954), 5.

0397.   _____. "Stage Versus Screen." Films and
              Filming, 1 (Dec. 1954), 7.
         Mason's articles are on film versus stage acting.

0398.   Matthews, Brander. "Are the Movies a Menace to
              the Drama?" The North American Review, 205
              (1917), 447-454.

0399.   Matthews, J.H. "Spectacle and Poetry: Surrealism
              in Theatre and Cinema." Journal of General
              Education, 27 (1975), 55-68.

0400.   Meyerhold, Vsevolod. "Two Lectures." Trans. Margorie
              L. Hoover. Tulane Drama Review, 11 (1966),
              186-195.

0401.   Miles, Bernard. "The Acting Art." Films in Review,
              5 (1954), 267-282.
         Film versus stage acting.

0402.   Monaco, James. "Film and Theater." In his How
              to Read a Film: The Art, Technology, Language,
              History, and Theory of Film and Media. New
              York: Oxford University Press, 1977, pp. 33-37.

0403.   Montale, Eugenio. "Report on the Cinema." In
              his The Second Life of Art. Trans. Jonathan
              Galassi. New York: The Ecco Press, 1982,
              pp. 217-220.

0404.   Nathan, George Jean. "The Cinema." In his The
              Theatre of the Moment: A Journalistic Commentary.
              New York: Alfred A. Knopf, 1936, pp. 97-118.

0405.   _____. "The Movies in Love." In his The
              Entertainment of a Nation, or Three-Sheets to
              the Wind. New York: Alfred A. Knopf, 1942,
              pp. 206-212.

0406.   _____. "Movies Versus the Stage." American
              Mercury, 58 (1944), 682-686.

0407.   _____. "Notes on the Movies." The American
              Mercury, 12 (1927), 117-122. Reprinted in his
              Art of the Night. New York: Alfred A. Knopf,
              1928, pp. 106-139.

0408.   _____. "On the Movies." In The World of
              George Jean Nathan. Ed. Charles Angoff. New
              York: Alfred A. Knopf, 1952, pp. 452-463.

0409.   Nicoll, Allardyce. Film and Theatre. New York:
              Thomas Y. Crowell, 1936. Selection, "Film Reality:
              The Cinema and the Theatre" reprinted in Film
              and Literature: Contrasts in Media. Ed. Fred
              H. Marcus. Scranton: Chandler Publishing Co.,
              1971, pp. 190-204. Reprinted in Focus on Film
              and Theatre. Ed. James Hurt. Englewood Cliffs:
              Prentice-Hall, 1974, pp. 29-50.

0410. Panofsky, Erwin. "Style and Medium in the Motion
           Picture." Critique 1 (1947), 5-18, 27-28.
           Reprinted in Film: An Anthology. Ed. Daniel
           Talbot. Berkeley: University of California
           Press, 1970, pp. 15-32. Reprinted in Film and/as
           Literature. Ed. John Harrington. Englewood
           Cliffs: Prentice-Hall, 1977, pp. 283-294.

0411. Paul, Norman. "Artistic Alliance." Sight and
           Sound, 8 (Autumn 1939), 116.

0412. Pemberton, Brock. "A Theatrical Producer's Reaction
           to the Movies." In The Movies on Trial: The
           Views and Opinions of Outstanding Personalities
           Anent Screen Entertainment Past and Present.
           Ed. William J. Perlman. New York: Macmillan,
           1936, 153-165.

0413. Petrie, Graham. "Theater Film Life." Film Comment,
           10 (May-June 1974), 38-43.

0414. Pfaff, Roland Leonard. "Bullough's `Physical Distance,'
           the Aesthetic Attitude, and Appreciation of
           Theater and Film." DAI, 35 (1974), 3064A.
           (The University of Michigan).
       On Artaud's and Brecht's theories.

0415. Pichel, Irving. "Character, Personality, and Image:
           A Note on Screen Acting." Howard Quarterly,
           2 (Oct. 1946), 25-29.

0416. Poggi, Gregory Joseph. "From Dramatic to Cinematic
           Standards: American Silent Film Theory and Criticism
           to 1929." DAI, 38 (1977), 1745A (Indiana
           University).

0417. Poggioli, Renato. "Aesthetics of the Stage and
           Screen." Journal of Aesthetics and Art Criticism,
           1 (1941), 63-69.

0418. Potamkin, Harry Alan. "The Film in the Theater."
           In The Compound Cinema: The Film Writings of
           Harry Alan Potamkin. Ed. Lewis Jacobs. New
           York: Teachers College Press, 1977, pp. 579-582.
       Use of film within the drama.

0419. Pratt, George. "Early Stage and Screen: A Two-Way
           Street." Cinema Journal, 14 (Winter 1974-1975),
           16-19.

0420. Przbylska, Krystyna Korvin. "An Interview with
           Andrezej Wajda." Literature/Film Quarterly,
           5 (1977), 2-16.

0421. Pudovkin, V.I. "The Actor's Work: Film Versus
           Stage." Trans. Vera Sonutchinsky. Close Up,
           10 (Sept. 1933), 227-234.

0422. _____. Film Technique and Film Acting.
Trans. Ivor Montagu. New York: Bonanza Books,
1949, pp. 227-234. Excerpt reprinted in Film
and Literature: Contrasts in Media. Ed. Fred
H. Marcus. Scranton: Chandler Publishing Co.,
1971, pp. 13-22.

0423. _____. "Stanislavski's System in the Cinema."
Trans. T. Shebunina. Sight and Sound, 22
(Jan.-March 1952), 115-118. Reprinted in
Pudovkin's Films and Film Theory by Peter Dart.
New York: Arno Press, 1974, pp. 186-206.

0424. Richie, Donald and Joseph L. Anderson. "Traditional
Theater and the Film in Japan." Film Quarterly,
12 (Fall 1958), 2-9.

0425. Roberts, Cecil Alden. "Stage v. Screen." Scenario,
1 (July 1934), 3-5.

0426. Roof, Judith Ann. "Oedipus in the Cave: Metaphors
of Seeing in Modern Drama and Film." DAI, 45
(1985), 2518-2519A (The Ohio State University).
The works discussed are Samuel Beckett's Play,
Jean-Luc Godard's La Chinoise, Eugène Ionesco's
The Killer, Michelangelo Antonioni's Blow-Up, Harold
Pinter's Betrayal, and Michelle Citron's Daughter
Rite.

0427. Ross, Lillian and Helen Ross. "The Player: Actors
Talk About Film Acting." In Focus on Film and
Theatre. Ed. James Hurt. Englewood Cliffs:
Prentice-Hall, 1974, pp. 99-115.

0428. Samuels, Charles Thomas. "Jean Renoir and the
Theatrical Film." In his Mastering the Film and
Other Essays. Ed. Lawrence Graver. Knoxville:
The University of Tennessee Press, 1977, pp. 42-68.

0429. Sarris, Andrew. "Film: The Illusion of Naturalism."
The Drama Review, 13 (Winter 1968), 108-112.

0430. Schare, Dore. "Literature and the Screen." The
English Journal, 43 (1954), 135-141.

0431. Seaton, George. "A Comparison of Playwright and
Screen Writer." The Quarterly of Film, Radio,
and Television, 10 (1956), 217-226.

0432. Segal, Mark. "Eye and Ear in the Theatre." Close
Up, 8 (March 1931), 38-43.

0433. Shelly, Frank. Stage and Screen. London: Pendulum
Publishers, 1946.
Among the topics covered in this monograph are
the differences in audiences, acting styles, and
expressive capabilities.

0434.   Snyder, John.   "Film and Classical Genre: Rules
        for Interpreting Rules of the Game."   Literature/Film
        Quarterly, 10 (1982), 162-169.
        Influence of French drama upon Renoir's film.

0435.   Spottiswoode, Raymond.   "The Relation of Cinema
        to Stage."   In his The Grammar of the Film:
        An Analysis of Film Technique.   Berkeley: University
        of California Press, 1950, pp. 104-107.

0436.   Steele, Robert.   "Screen and Theatre Reality."
        Journal of Screen Producers Guild, Dec. 1968,
        pp. 3-7.

0437.   _____.   "The Two Faces of Drama."   Cinema
        Journal, 6 (1966-67), 16-32.

0438.   Stromgren, Richard L. and Martin F. Norden.   "Film
        and Theatre."   In their Movies: A Language in
        Light.   Englewood Cliffs: Prentice-Hall, 1984,
        pp. 183-199.

0439.   Summers, Rollin.   "The Moving Picture Drama and
        the Acted Drama: Some Points of Comparison as
        to Technique."   Moving Picture World, 3 (19
        Sept. 1908), 211-213.   Reprinted in American
        Film Criticism.   Ed. Stanley Kauffmann.   New
        York: Liveright, 1972, pp. 9-18.

0440.   Thomson, David.   "Theatre."   In his Movie Man.
        London: Secker and Warburg, 1967, pp. 59-62.

0441.   Tibbetts, John Carter.   "The Stage/Screen Exchange:
        Patterns of Imitation in Art: 1896-1930."   DAI,
        43 (1983), 2500A (The University of Kansas).

0442.   Tonecki, Zygmunt.   "At the Boundary of Film and
        Theatre."   Close Up, 9 (March 1932), 31-35.

0443.   _____.   "The Preliminary of Film Art."   Close
        Up, 8 (Sept. 1931), 193-200.

0444.   _____.   "The Preliminary of Film Art II."
        Close Up, 8 (Dec. 1931), 321-324.

0445.   _____.   "The Theatre and the Future of the
        Talking Film."   Close Up, 8 (March 1931), 27-32.

0446.   Tyler, Parker.   "The Play Is Not the Thing."   In
        his The Hollywood Hallucination.   New York:
        Simon and Schuster, 1970, pp. 3-21.

0447.   Ubans, Mara Isaks.   "Expressionist Drama and Film:
        Filmic Elements in Dramas and Film Scripts by
        Selected Expressionist Authors."   DAI, 37 (1977),
        5864-5865A (The University of Southern California).
        Includes discussions of Carl Meyer, Max Brod, Walter
        Hasenclever, and Ernst Toller.

0448.   Van Wert, William. "Eisenstein and Kabuki." _Criticism_,
        20 (1978), 403-420.

0449.   Vardac, A. Nicholas. _Stage to Screen: Thearical
        Method From Garrick to Griffith_. Cambridge:
        Harvard University Press, 1949.

0450.   Vesselo, A. "Stage and Screen." _English Review_,
        62 (Feb. 1936), 194-196.

0451.   Von Sternberg, Josef. "Acting in Film and Theatre."
        Film Culture 1, Nos. 5-6 (1955), 1-4, 27-29.
        Reprinted in _Film Makers on Film Making_. Ed. Harry
        M. Geduld. Bloomington: Indiana University
        Press, 1967, pp. 238-256. Reprinted in _Focus
        on Film and Theatre_. Ed. James Hurt. Englewood
        Cliffs: Prentice-Hall, 1974, pp. 80-98.

0452.   Waller, Gregory A. _The Stage/Screen Debate: A
        Study in Popular Aesthetics_. New York: Garland
        Publishing, 1983.
        Studies the views on the relationship of film to
        drama of such critics as Kracauer, Nicoll, and
        Seldes.

0453.   Watts, Richard, Jr. "Stage Play and Screen Play:
        Two Art Forms Have Been Confused Anew by the
        Talkies." _Theatre Guild Magazine_, 6, No. 6
        (1929), 31-33, 64.

0454.   Williams, David. "Cinema Technique and the Theatre."
        Nineteenth-Century, 110 (Nov. 1931), 602-612.

0455.   Williams, Linda Paglierani. "Perceptual Ambiguity
        in Selected Modern Plays and Films." _DAI_, 38
        (1977), 2099A (Boston University).
        Includes discussions of Pirandello, García-Lorca,
        Pinter, Truffaut, and Albee.

0456.   Williams, Raymond and Michael Orrom. _Preface to
        the Film_. London: Film Drama, 1954.

0457.   Withers, Googie. "Acting for Stage and Screen."
        The Penguin Film Review, 4 (1947), 36-40;
        rpt. Totowa, N.J.: Rowan and Littlefield, 1978.

0458.   Wolfe, Humbert. "I Look at the Theatre." _Theatre
        Arts Monthly_, 15 (1931), 49-52.

0459.   Wright, Edward A. "Cinema and the Stage" and
        "Television, Cinema, and the Stage." In his
        _A Primer for Playgoers: An Introduction to the
        Understanding and Appreciation of Cinema-Stage-
        Television_. Englewood Cliffs: Prentice-Hall,
        1958, pp. 202-219 and pp. 220-241.

0460.   Youngblood, Gene. "Intermedia Theatre." In his
        Expanded Cinema. New York: E.P. Dutton, 1970,
        pp. 365-386.

5
Poetry and Film:
General Studies

0461. Abel, Richard. "The Contribution of the French
        Literary Avant-Garde to Film Theory and Criticism
        (1907-1924)." Cinema Journal, 14 (Spring 1975),
        18-40.

0462. Belz, Carl I. "The Film Poetry of Man Ray." Criticism,
        7 (1965), 117-130.

0463. Berman, Russell. "The Recipient as Spectator:
        West German Film and Poetry of the Seventies."
        German Quarterly, 55 (Nov. 1982), 499-510.

0464. Broughton, James. "What Magic in the Lanterns? Notes
        on Poetry and Film." Film Culture, No. 61
        (1975-1976), 35-40.

0465. Coates, Paul. "Cinema, Symbolism, and the
        Gesamtkunstwerk." Comparative Criticism, 4
        (1982), 213-229.

0466. Debrix, Jean. "Cinema and Poetry." Yale French
        Studies, No. 17 (1956), pp. 86-104.

0467. _____. "The Movies and Poetry." Trans. Dorothy
        Milburn. Films in Review, 2 (Oct. 1951), 17-22.

0468. Deren, Maya, Arthur Miller, Dylan Thomas, and Parker
        Tyler. "Poetry and Film." Film Culture Reader.
        Ed. P. Adams Sitney. New York: Praeger Publishers,
        1970, pp. 171-186. Reprinted in Film and/as
        Literature. Ed. John Harrington. Englewood
        Cliffs: Prentice-Hall, 1977, pp. 178-189.

0469. Durgnat, Raymond. "Mute Poetry in the Commercial
        Cinema." In his Films and Feeling. Cambridge:
        The M.I.T. Press, 1967, pp. 223-228.
        Not a comparison of film to poetry but a discussion
        of film in the light of its emotional qualities.

0470. Field, Edward. "The Movies as American Mythology."
       Concerning Poetry, 2, No. 1 (1969), 27-31.
       A poet's use of myth derived from the movies.

0471. Gaston, Karen Carmean. "Luis Buñuel's Use of
       Metaphysical Conceits." New Orleans Review,
       9 (Fall 1982), 40-44.
       Buñuel's use of conceits compared to T.S. Eliot's.

0472. Glaser, Carol. "Using Film Language to Understand
       Poetry." Media and Methods, 11, No. 7 (1975),
       38-40.

0473. Goldstein, Laurence. "The American Poet at the
       Movies: A Life and Times." Centennial Review,
       24 (1980), 432-452.
       Allen Ginsberg, Winfield Townley Scott, and Vachel
       Lindsay.

0474. Gwynn, R.S. "Cinematic Allusion and Twentieth
       Century Poetry." Lamar Journal of the Humanities,
       5, No. 1 (1979), 36-45.

0475. Kelman, Ken. "Film as Poetry." Film Culture,
       29 (Summer 1963), 22-27.

0476. Kovács, Steven. "The Poets Go to the Movies."
       In his From Enchantment to Rage: The Story of
       Surrealist Cinema. Cranbury, N.J.: Associated
       University Presses, 1980, pp. 15-47.
       On Robert Desnos, Louis Aragon, Guillaume Apollinaire,
       Jacques Vaché, Germaine Dullac, and André Breton.

0477. Leonard, Arthur Byron. "Poetry and Film: Aspects
       of the Avant-Garde in France (1918-1932). DAI,
       36 (1976), 6085A (Stanford University).
       Includes discussions of Man Ray, André Breton,
       Louis Aragon, Marcel Duchamp, and Antonin Artaud.

0478. Lewis, Brian. "In Defense of Symbol: Film Aesthetics
       and Symbolist Poetics." In his Jean Mitry and
       the Aesthetics of the Cinema. Ann Arbor: UMI
       Research Press, 1984, pp. 97-116.

0479. McMillen, Barbara Fialkowski. "A Study of the
       Formal and Thematic Uses of Film in the Poetry
       of Parker Tyler, Frank O'Hara, and Adrienne
       Rich." DAI, 37 (1976), 1549-1550A (Ohio
       University).

0480. Manvell, Roger. "The Poetry of the Film." In
       New Road 4: Directions in European Arts and
       Letters. Ed. Fred Marnau. London: Grey Walls
       Press, 1946, pp. 152-164. Reprinted in The
       Penguin Film Review, 6 (1948), 111-124; rpt. Totowa,
       N.J.: Rowan and Littlefield, 1978.

0481. Mekas, Jonas. "Hans Richter on the Nature of Film
       Poetry." Film Culture, 3 (1957), 5-8.

0482. Mistral, Gabriela.   "The Poet's Attitude Toward
       the Movies." Trans. Marion A. Zeitlin.   In
       The Movies on Trial: The Views and Opinions
       of Outstanding Personalities Anent Screen
       Entertainment Past and Present.   Ed. William
       J. Perlman.   New York: Macmillan, 1936,
       pp. 141-152.

0483. Read, Herbert.   "The Poet and the Film."   In his
       A Coat of Many Colors.   London: Routledge, 1945,
       pp. 225-231.

0484. Taylor, Henry.   "A Panel of Experts on `Blind Alley'
       Discuss the Influence of Cinema on Modern Poets."
       Film Journal, 1 (Fall-Winter 1972), 36-49.

6

Adaptation:
General Studies and Anthologies

0485. Andrew, Dudley. "The Well-Worn Muse: Adaptation
        in Film History and Theory." In <u>Narrative
        Strategies: Original Essays in Film and Prose
        Fiction</u>. Ed. Syndy M. Conger and Janice R. Welsch.
        Macomb: Western Illinois University Press,
        1980, pp. 9-17. Reprinted in his <u>Concepts
        in Film Theory</u>. New York: Oxford University
        Press, 1984, pp. 96-106.

0486. Archer, Jane Elizabeth. "Short Fiction/Short
        Film: A Comparative Analysis of the Formal
        Structures of American Short Stories and the
        Films Made From Them." <u>DAI</u>, 39 (1979), 6760A
        (The University of Texas at Austin).
        Includes discussions of Ambrose Bierce's "An Occurrence
        at Owl Creek Bridge", Robert Chambers's "Pickets,"
        Herman Melville's "Bartleby the Scrivener," and
        Flannery O'Connor's "The Comforts of Home," "Good
        Country People," "A Circle in the Fire," and "The
        Displaced Person."

0487. Asheim, Lester. "From Book to Film: Simplification."
        <u>Hollywood Quarterly</u>, 5 (1951), 289-304.

0488. _____. "From Book to Film: Mass Appeals."
        <u>Hollywood Quarterly</u>, 5 (1951), 334-349.

0489. _____. "From Book to Film: The Note of
        Affirmation." <u>The Quarterly of Film, Radio,
        and Television</u>, 6 (1952), 54-68.

0490. _____. "From Book to Film: Summary." <u>The
        Quarterly of Film, Radio, and Television</u>, 6
        (1952), 258-273.
        Using twenty-four adaptations of novels, Asheim
        distinguishes between the limitations imposed
        on filmmakers by the medium and those imposed
        on them by the conventions of film as a mass art.

0491.   Baláɀs, Béla. "Art Form and Material." In his
        Theory of Film: Character and Growth of a New
        Art. Trans. Edith Bone. New York: Dover
        Publications, 1970, pp. 258-265. Reprinted
        in Film and/as Literature. Ed. John Harrington.
        Englewood Cliffs: Prentice-Hall, 1977, pp. 6-12.

0492.   Barron, Arthur. "The Intensification of Reality."
        Film Comment, 6 (Spring 1970), 20-23.
        Discussion of adaptations centers on Moby Dick,
        Babbitt, and The Grapes of Wrath.

0493.   Bauer, Leda V. "The Movies Tackle Literature."
        American Mercury, 14 (July 1928), 288-294.

0494.   Bazin, André. "In Defense of Mixed Cinema."
        In his What Is Cinema? Volume One. Trans. Hugh
        Gray. Berkeley: University of California
        Press,1967, pp. 53-75.
        Mutual influence of film and literature and film
        adaptations.

0495.   _____. "Theatre and Cinema--Part One and
        Part Two." In his What Is Cinema? Volume One.
        Trans. Hugh Gray. Berkeley: University of
        California Press, 1967, pp. 76-124. Reprinted
        in Film and/as Literature. Ed. John Harrington.
        Englewood Cliffs: Prentice-Hall, 1977, pp. 93-105.
        The French director's controversial view that
        an adaptor's first allegiance must be to the source
        work rather than to the demands of the film medium.

0496.   Block, Maxine. "Films Adapted From Published
        Works." Wilson Library Bulletin, 10 (Feb. 1936),
        394-395.

0497.   _____. "Looking Backward and Looking Forward
        at Films." Wilson Library Bulletin, 12 (Nov. 1937),
        202.

0498.   Bluestone, George. Novels into Film: The Metamorphosis
        of Fiction into Cinema. Berkeley: University
        of California Press, 1971.
        In this seminal work, first published in 1957,
        Bluestone attempts to determine the limits of
        film through an examination of six Hollywood
        adapations: John Ford's The Informer (novel, Liam
        O'Flaherty), William Wyler's Wuthering Heights,
        (novel, Emily Bronte), Robert Z. Leonard's
        Pride and Prejudice (novel, Jane Austen), John
        Ford's The Grapes of Wrath (novel, John Steinbeck),
        William Wellman's The Ox-Bow Incident (novel Walter
        Van Tilburg Clark), and Vincente Minnelli's Madame
        Bovary (novel, Gustave Flaubert).

0499.   _____. "Time in Fiction and Film." Journal
        of Aesthetics and Art Criticism, 19 (1961),
        311-315.

0500. _____. "Word to Image: The Problem of the
        Filmed Novel." The Quarterly of Film, Radio,
        and Television, 11 (1956), 171-180.
        Both 0489 and 0490 are part of Novels into Film.

0501. Bodeen, Dewitt. "The Adapting Art." Films in
        Review, 14 (1963), 349-356.

0502. Bond, Kirk. "Film as Literature." Bookman, 84
        (July 1933), 188-189.
        General discussion of adaptations with emphasis
        on von Stroheim's Greed.

0503. Boyum, Joy Gould. Double Exposure: Fiction Into
        Film. New York: Universe Books, 1985.
        Essays on film adaptations: The Innocents (adaptation
        of Henry James's Turn of the Screw), The Great
        Gatsby (Jack Clayton's adaptation of F.Scott
        Fitzgerald's novel), The French Lieutenant's Woman
        (novel by John Fowles), Apocalypse Now (based
        on Joseph Conrad's Heart of Darkness), Women in
        Love (novel by D.H. Lawrence), Ragtime (novel
        by E.L. Doctorow), Tess (adaptation of Thomas
        Hardy's Tess of the d'Urbervilles), Daisy Miller
        (novella by Henry James), A Clockwork Orange (novel
        by Anthony Burgess), Lord of the Flies (novel
        by William Golding), Wise Blood (novella by Flannery
        O'Connor), Death in Venice (novella by Thomas
        Mann), Slaughterhouse-Five (novel by Kurt Vonnegut),
        Under the Volcano (novel by Malcolm Lowry), The
        Day of the Locust (novella by Nathanael West),
        Swann in Love (adaptation of Marcel Proust's
        Remeberance of Things Past), and The Magnificent
        Ambersons (novel by Booth Tarkington).

0504. Brandt, Carole Ann. "A Critical Consideration
        of the Transference of Playscripts into Films,
        with Particular Reference to the American Film
        Theatre's 1975 Series." DAI, 37 (1977), 5439A
        (Southern Illinois University).
        The plays discussed are Bertolt Brecht's Galileo,
        Mort Schuman's Jacques Brel Is Alive and Living
        in Paris, Jean Genet's The Maids, Robert Shaw's
        The Man in the Glass Booth, and David Storey's
        In Celebration.

0505. Brooks, Richard. "A Novel Isn't a Movie." Films
        in Review, 3 (1952), 55-59.
        The film director discusses the adaptation of
        his novel The Brick Foxhole.

0506. Butcher, M. "Look Upon This Picture: Books and
        Film." Wiseman Review, 238 (Spring 1964),
        55-64.

0507.   Byg, Barton Benjamin. "History, Narrative and
            Film Form: Jean-Marie Straub and Daniele Huillet."
            DAI, 43 (1983), 3901A (Washington University).
            Adaptations discussed include Not Reconciled (from
            Billiards at Half Past Nine by Heinrich Böll and
            History Lessons (from The Business Affairs of
            Mr. Julius C. by Bertolt Brecht).

0508.   Callenbach, Ernest. "The Filmed Novel: All the
            King's Men." In his Our Modern Art the Movies.
            Chicago: Center for the Study of Liberal Education
            for Adults, 1955, pp. 58-66.
            Concerns adaptations of novels with study questions
            on Robert Penn Warren's novel.

0509.   Crouch, William Pryor. "Satanism and Possession
            in Selected Contemporary Novels and Their Cinematic
            Adaptations." DAI, 37 (1976), 3966A (Northwestern
            University).
            Concerns Ira Levin's Rosemary's Baby, Fred Mustard
            Stewart's The Mephisto Waltz, Ramona Stewart's
            The Possession of Joel Delaney, Thomas Tryon's
            The Other, and William Peter Blatty's The Exorcist.

0510.   Dick, Bernard. "Authors, Auteurs, and Adaptations:
            Literature as Film/Film as Literature." Yearbook
            of American Comparative and General Literature,
            No. 27 (1978), pp. 72-76.

0511.   Dowdy, Andrew. "Adapted for the Screen." In
            his Movies Are Better Than Ever: Wide-Screen
            Memories of the Fifties. New York: William
            Morrow, 1973, pp. 204-220.
            Survey with brief evaluations of adaptations in
            American movies during the 1950s.

0512.   Dwan, Allan. "Filming Great Fiction: Can Literature
            Be Preserved in Motion Pictures?" The Forum,
            62 (1919), 298-305.

0513   Eidsvik, Charles. "Film and Theater." In his
            Cineliteracy: Film Among the Arts. New York:
            Random House, 1978, pp. 231-263.
            Adaptations: Peter Hall's A Midsummer Night's
            Dream (play, William Shakespeare), Clive Donner's
            The Caretaker (play, Harold Pinter), Peter Brook's
            King Lear (play, William Shakespeare) and Peter
            Brook's Marat/Sade (play, Peter Weiss).

0514.   _____. "Toward a `Politique des
            Adaptations'." Literature/Film Quarterly,
            3 (1975), 255-263. Reprinted in Film and/as
            Literature. Ed. John Harrington. Englewood
            Cliffs: Prentice-Hall, 1977, 27-37.

0515.   Fadiman, William. "Books into Movies." Publishers
            Weekly, 126 (22 Sept. 1934), 1085-1087.

0516.   _____. "But Compared with the Original."
         Films and Filming, 11 (Feb. 1965), 21-23.

0517.   _____. "The Great Hollywood Book-Hunt."
         In Hello Hollywood! A Book About the Movies
         by the People Who Make Them.   Ed. Allen Rivkin
         and Laura Kerr. New York: Doubleday, 1962,
         pp. 15-23.

0518.   _____. "The New Style Myth Makers." Films
         and Filming, 17 (Aug. 1961), 30.

0519.   Feyen, Sharon. "The Stage Play Adapted." In
         Screen Experience: An Approach to Film. Ed. Sharon
         Feyen. Dayton, Ohio: Geo. A. Pflaum, 1969,
         pp. 33-39.

0520.   Field, Alice Evans. "Adapting the Novel to the
         Screen" and "From Stage to Screen." In her
         Hollywood, U.S.A.: From Script to Screen.
         New York: Vantage Press, 1952, pp. 46-51 and
         pp. 52-59.

0521.   Ford, Frank Xavier. "The American Film Theatre:
         An Examination of the Process of Adaptation
         from Stage to Screen in Theory and Practice."
         DAI, 42 (1982), 4959A (The University of Southern
         California).

0522.   Fulton, A.R. "From Short Story to Film." In
         his Motion Pictures: The Development of an
         Art From Silent Films to the Age of Television.
         Norman: University of Oklahoma Press, 1960,
         pp. 249-263.
         Discussions of Coward's Brief Encounter, Benet's
         "Devil and Daniel Webster," and Maugham's "The
         Facts of Life."

0523.   _____. "It's Exactly Like the Play." Theatre
         Arts, 37 (March 1953), 78-83.
         On adaptations of drama and fiction, centering
         on a discussion of Greed.

0524.   Gaffney, Maureen. "Evaluating Attitude: Analyzing
         Point of View in Film Adaptations of Literature."
         Children's Literature, 9 (1981), 116-125.

0525.   Godfrey, Lionel. "It Wasn't Like That in the
         Book." Films and Filming, 13 (April 1967),
         12-16.

0526.   _____. "It Wasn't Like That in the Play."
         Films and Filming, 13 (Aug. 1967), 4-8.

0527.   Gow, Gordon.   "Novel into Film."   Films and Filming,
           12 (May 1966), 19-22.
        On Alan Sillitoe, Patricia Highsmith, and Rumer
        Godden.

0528.   Griffith, James John.   "Adaptations as Imitations:
           An Evaluative Study of Recent Adaptations of
           Novels."   DAI, 45 (1984), 1557A (The Ohio State
           University).
        Concerns the adaptations of James Dickey's Deliverance,
        Arthur C. Clarke's 2001: A Space Odyssey, and
        Judith Rossner's Looking for Mr. Goodbar.

0529.   Hanlon, Lindley Page.   "Narrative Structure in
           the Later Films of Robert Bresson."   DAI, 38
           (1978), 5761A (New York University).
        Discusses these adaptations: Mouchette (from the
        novel Nouvelle Histoire de Mouchette by Georges
        Bernanos), and Une femme douce (from the Dostoyevsky).

0530.   Hoch, Edward D.   "Mystery Movies: Behind the Scenes."
           In The Murder Mystique: Crime Writers on Their
           Art.   Ed. Lucy Freeman.   New York: Frederick
           Ungar, 1982, pp. 104-117.
        Adaptations of mystery stories from Doyle to Fleming.

0531.   Holmes, Winifred.   "The New Renaissance."   Sight
           and Sound, 5 (Summer 1936), 7-9.

0532.   Horne, William Leonard.   "`A Starting Point':
           A Critical Approach to the Role of the Screenplay
           in the Adaptation of Novels for the Cinema."
           DAI, 43 (1983), 3444A (The University of Wisconsin
           at Madison).

0533.   Horton, Andrew and Joan Magretta, eds.   Modern
           European Filmmakers and the Art of Adaptation.
           New York: Frederick Ungar Publishing, 1981.
        See 1863, 1888, 1894, 1897, 1973, 1976, 2011,
        2012, 2016, 2025, 2035, 2048, 2050, 2056, 2084,
        2085, 2089, 2113, 2127, 2189, 2203, 2205, 2252.

0534.   Huselberg, Richard A.   "Novels and Films: A Limited
           Inquiry."   Literature/Film Quarterly, 6 (1978),
           57-65.

0535.   Jay, Herman.   "Hollywood and American Literature:
           The American Novel on the Screen."   English
           Journal, 66 (Jan. 1977), 82-86.
        Concerns The Adventures of Huckleberry Finn and
        The Grapes of Wrath; contains brief list of
        adaptations.

0536.   Kennedy, Margaret.   The Mechanized Muse.   London:
           George Allen and Unwin, 1942.   Reprinted in
           Film: An Anthology.   Ed. Daniel Talbot.   Berkeley:
           University of California Press, 1966, pp. 80-109.
        Monograph on the plight of the scenarist, adaptations,
        and film's relationship to poetry and drama.

0537.   Kiernan, Maureen Brigid. "Novelists/Scenarists:
        Four Case Studies of Writers Adapting Their
        Own Fiction to Film." DAI, 45 (1985), 3350A
        (University of Illinois at Urbana-Champaign).
        Concerns Richard Wright's Native Son, Vladimir
        Nabokov's Lolita, James Dickey's Deliverance,
        and Joan Didion's Play It As It Lays.

0538.   Kinney, Judy Lee. "Text and Pretext: Stanley
        Kubrick's Adaptations." DAI, 43 (1982), 1A
        (University of California at Los Angeles).

0539.   Kittredge, William and Steven M. Krauzer, eds.
        Stories into Film. New York: Harper and Row,
        1979.
        Volume contains short stories that have been adapted
        to film: "Spurs" (Freaks), "Night Bus" (It Happened
        One Night), "Stage to Lordsburg" (Stagecoach),
        "Cyclists' Raid" (The Wild One), "Rear Window"
        (Rear Window), "The Hustler" (The Hustler), "The
        Man Who Shot Liberty Valance" (The Man Who Shot
        Liberty Valance), "Blow-Up" (Blow-Up), and "The
        Sentinel" (2001: A Space Odyssey).

0540.   Klein, Michael and Gillian Parker, eds. The English
        Novel and the Movies. New York: Frederick
        Ungar Publishing, 1981.
        See 1184, 1198, 1202, 1244, 1252, 1265, 1286,
        1289, 1292, 1338, 1339, 1386, 1408, 1410, 1422,
        1426, 1435, 1438, 1441, 1444, 1477, 1538, 1556,
        1559, 1567, 1574, 1591.

0541.   Kubrick, Stanley. "Words and Movies." Sight
        and Sound, 30 (Winter 1960-61), 14.
        The director discusses the kind of novel that
        lends itself to adaptation.

0542.   Kuhns, William and John Carr. "Fiction into Film."
        In Movies in America: Teaching in the Dark.
        Dayton, Ohio: Pflaum, 1973, pp. 49-78.
        Contains discussions of film adaptations of
        C.S. Forester's The African Queen, Richard Condon's
        The Manchurian Candidate, Shirley Jackson's The
        Haunting of Hill House, and Harper Lee's To Kill
        a Mockingbird.

0543.   Larsson, Donald. "Novel into Film: Some Preliminary
        Reconsiderations." In Transformations in Literature
        and Film. Ed. Leon Golden. Tallahassee: University
        Presses of Florida, 1982, pp. 69-83.
        Larsson raises issues that will lead, he believes,
        to a theory of adaptations.

0544.   Leyda, Jay. "Theatre on Film." Theatre Arts
        Monthly, 21 (March 1937), 194-207.
        History of adaptations.

0545. Luhr, William. "The Function of Narrative in
       Literature and Film." In <u>Ideas of Order</u> <u>in</u>
       <u>Literature and Film</u>. Ed. Peter Ruppert.
       Tallahassee: University Presses of Florida,
       1980, pp. 32-38.
       Luhr believes that adaptations have led to a
       misconception that film is more closely related
       to the novel than it actually is.

0546. _____. "Victorian Novels on Film." <u>DAI</u>,
       39 (1979), 7358A (New York University).
       Adaptations discussed: <u>Dr. Jekyll and Mr. Hyde</u>,
       <u>Wuthering Heights</u>, <u>David Copperfield</u>, <u>Becky Sharp</u>
       (adaptation of <u>Vanity Fair</u>), and <u>Nosferatu</u> (adaptation
       of <u>Dracula</u>).

0547. McCaffery, Donald W. "Adaptation Problems in
       the Two Unique Media: The Novel and the Film."
       <u>Dickinson Review</u>, 1 (Spring 1967), 11-17.

0548. McFarlane, Brian. <u>Words and Images: Australian</u>
       <u>Novels into Film</u>. Victoria, Australia: Heinemann,
       1983.
       Discusses <u>Wake in Fright</u> (from the novel by Kenneth
       Cook), <u>Picnic at Hanging Rock</u> (from the novel
       by Joan Lindsay), <u>The Getting of Wisdom</u> (from
       the novel by Henry Handel Richardson), <u>The Mango</u>
       <u>Tree</u> (from the novel by Ronald McKie), <u>The</u>
       <u>Chant of Jimmie Blacksmith</u> (from the novel by
       Thomas Keneally), <u>My Brilliant Career</u> (from the
       novel by Miles Franklin), <u>Monkey Grip</u> (from the
       novel by Helen Garner), <u>The Year of Living Dangerously</u>
       (from the novel by C.J. Koch), <u>The Night of the</u>
       <u>Prowler</u> (from the novel by Patrick White),
       <u>Lucinda Brayford</u> (from the novel by Martin Boyd),
       and <u>Outbreak</u> <u>of Love</u> (from the novel by Martin
       Boyd).

0549. Macgowan, Kenneth. "The Search for Story Material."
       In his <u>Behind</u> <u>the</u> <u>Screen:</u> <u>The</u> <u>History</u> <u>and</u> <u>Techniques</u>
       <u>of</u> <u>the</u> <u>Motion</u> <u>Picture</u>. New York: Delacorte
       Press, 1965, pp. 333-346.

0550. Madsen, Roy Paul. "Adaptation: Novels and Stage
       Plays into Cinema-Television." In his <u>The</u>
       <u>Impact of Film: How Ideas Are Communicated</u>
       <u>Through Cinema and Television</u>. New York: Macmillan
       Publishing, 1973, pp. 244-264.

0551. Manvell, Roger. <u>Theater and Film: A Comparative</u>
       <u>Study of the Two Forms of Dramatic Art And</u>
       <u>of the Problems of Adaptation of Stage Plays</u>
       <u>into</u> <u>Film</u>. Rutherford: Fairleigh Dickinson
       University Press, 1979.
       Contains essays on the adaptations of <u>Pygmalion</u>,
       <u>Electra</u>, <u>Three Sisters</u>, <u>Long Day's Journey into</u>
       <u>Night</u>, <u>A Streetcar Named Desire</u>, <u>Macbeth</u>, <u>A Midsummer</u>
       <u>Night's Dream</u>, <u>Hamlet</u>, <u>Henry V</u>, <u>Miss Julie</u>, <u>The</u>
       <u>Caretaker</u>, <u>Who's Afraid of Virginia Woolf</u>, <u>Marat-Sade</u>.

0552.   Mason, Ronald. "The Film of the Book." _Film_,
         No. 16 (March-April 1958), 18-20.

0553.   Melville, Clyde B., Jr. "Short Fiction on Film:
         The `Little Man' in Cinematic Adaptation."
         DAI, 41 (1981), 5098A (The University of Texas
         at Arlington).

0554.   Messenger, James R. "I Think I Liked the Book
         Better: Nineteen Novelists Look at the Film
         Version of Their Work." _Literature/Film Quarterly_,
         61 (1978), 125-134.

0555.   Miller, Gabriel. _Screening the Novel: Rediscovered
         American Fiction in Film_. New York: Frederick
         Ungar Publishing, 1980.
         Adaptations discussed: _Hester Street_ (from _Yekl_
         by Abraham Cahan), _Susan Lennox: Her Rise and
         Fall_ (from the novel by David Graham Phillips),
         The Postman Always Rings Twice (from the novel
         by James M. Cain), _They Shoot Horses, Don't They?_
         (from the novel by Horace McCoy), _The Treasure
         of the Sierra Madre_ (from the novel by B. Traven),
         Paths of Glory (from the novel by Humphrey Cobb),
         The Gangster (from _Low Company_ by Daniel Fuchs),
         and _The Pawnbroker_ (from the novel by Edward Lewis
         Wallant).

0556.   Mitry, Jean. "Remarks on the Problem of Cinematic
         Adaptation." Trans. Richard Dyer. _Midwest
         Modern Language Association Bulletin_, 12 (Spring
         1971), 1-9.

0557.   Morton, James. "From the Book of the Same Name."
         Contemporary Review, 219 (Aug. 1971), 100-104.
         On _Death in Venice_, _Little Big Man_, _Cotton Comes
         to Harlem_.

0558.   Nicoll, Alardyce. "Literature and Film." _English
         Journal_, 26 (1937), 1-9.
         Discusses material suitable for adaptation; article
         focuses on _A Midsummer Night's Dream_ and _Dodsworth_.

0559.   Niver, Kemp R. _Klaw and Erlandger Present Famous
         Plays_. Ed. Bebe Bergsten. Los Angeles: Locare
         Research Group, 1976.
         Adaptations of plays by the theatrical producers.

0560.   Palmer, James Wentworth. "Film and Fiction: Essays
         in Narrative Rhetoric." _DAI_, 37 (1976), 1-2A
         (Claremont Graduate School).
         Essays on _The Red Badge of Courage_, _Jane Eyre_,
         "The Turn of the Screw," "An Occurrence at Owl
         Creek Bridge," and their film adaptations.

0561.   Patterson, Frances Taylor. "Adaptation." In
         his _Cinema Craftsmanship: A Book for Playwrights_.
         New York: Harcourt, Brace, and Co., 1921, pp. 64-95.

0562. Peary, Gerald and Roger Shatzkin, eds. The Classic
       American Novel and the Movies. New York: Frederick
       Ungar Publishing, 1977.
       See 0634, 0647, 0665, 0711, 0712, 0716, 0723,
       0759, 0764, 0825, 0837, 0869, 0871, 0898, 0911,
       0925, 0929, 0930, 0936, 0959, 0961, 0962, 0965,
       0990, 0995, 1034, 1134, 1179.

0563. _____. The Modern American Novel and the
       Movies. New York: Frederick Ungar Publishing,
       1978.
       See 0636, 648, 0679, 0680, 0705, 0726, 0782, 0809,
       0850, 0857, 0883, 0908, 0910, 0912, 0943, 0970,
       0971, 0986, 1023, 1037, 1073, 1074, 1085, 1095,
       1100, 1136, 1138, 1140, 1147, 1150, 1152, 1180.

0564. Petrie, Graham. "The Films of Sidney Lumet: Adaptation
       as Art." Film Quarterly, 21 (Winter 1967-68),
       9-18.
       Adatations discussed include: Long Day's Journey
       into Night, A View from the Bridge, The Fugitive
       Kind, The Pawnbroker, and The Group.

0565. Phillips, Gene D. "The Play's the Thing: Drama
       on Film" and "From Page to Screen: Fiction
       on Film." In his George Cukor. Boston: Twayne
       Publishers, 1982, pp. 35-58 and pp. 129-145.
       Adaptations discussed are: Rockabye (play by Lucia
       Bronder), Our Betters (play by Somerset Maugham),
       Dinner at Eight (play by George S. Kaufman and
       Edna Ferber), Romeo and Juliet (play by William
       Shakespeare), Zaza (play by Pierre Berton and
       Charles Simon), Her Cardboard Lover (play by
       Jacques Deval), Gaslight (play by Patrick Hamilton),
       Winged Victory (play by Moss Hart), David Copperfield
       (novel by Charles Dickens), Gone With the Wind
       (novel by Margaret Mitchell), The Chapman Report
       (novel by Irving Wallace), Justine (novels by
       Lawrence Durrell), and Travels With My Aunt (novel
       by Graham Greene).

0566. Podheiser, Linda Ellen. "Filmed Theatre and Tragic
       Form in the Work of Carl Th. Dreyer." DAI,
       42 (1982), 4960A (New York University).
       Adaptations discussed are Day of Wrath (from
       the play Anne Pedersdotter by Hans Wiers-Jenssen),
       Ordet (from the play by Kaj Munk) and Gertrud
       (from the play by Hjalmar Söderberg).

0567. Powell, Dilys. "The Film of the Book." Essays
       by Divers Hands, 38 (1975), 93-111.
       On Olivier's Hamlet and Henry V, Welles's Othello,
       Russell's Women in Love, and Cukor's David Copperfield.

0568.   Reisz, Karel. "Substance into Shadow." The Cinema
         1952. Ed. Roger Manvell and R.K. Neilson Baxter.
         Harmondsworth, Middlesex: Penguin Books, 1952,
         pp. 188-205.
         On Dashiell Hammett's The Maltese Falcon, Ernest
         Hemingway's To Have and Have Not, and William
         Faulkner's Intruder in the Dust.

0569.   Robertson, E. Arnot. "Intruders in the Film World."
         Fortune, 145 (Feb. 1936), 194-198.
         Novelists on adaptations.

0570.   Ross, Theodore. "Gargoyles in Motion: On the
         Transmigration of Character From Page to Screen
         and Related Questions on Literature and Film."
         College English, 39 (1977), 371-382.
         Includes a discussion of Russell's Women in Love.

0571.   Roud, Richard. "Two Cents on the Rouble." Sight
         and Sound, 27 (Summer 1958), 245-247.
         General discussion of adaptations with comments
         on A Farewell to Arms, The Grapes of Wrath, The
         Ox-Bow Incident, The Magnificent Ambersons, and
         The Brothers Karamazov.

0572.   Saba, Behrouz. "The Knight Errant, Medieval and
         Modern: A Comparative Study of the Character
         in Medieval Literature and Contemporary Literature
         and Film." DAI, 40 (1980) 4782A (The University
         of Southern California).
         On novels by Hammett, Chandler and Cain and their
         film adaptations.

0573.   Schindel, Morton. "Children's Literature on Film:
         Through the Audiovisual Era to the Age of
         Telecommunications." Children's Literature,
         9 (1981), 93-106.
         On adaptations of film and filmstrips.

0574.   Schmidt, Nancy J. "African Literature on Film."
         Research in African Literatures, 13 (1982),
         518-531.

0575.   Seldes, Gilbert. "No More Swing?" Scribner's,
         100 (Nov. 1936), 71-72.
         Comments on adaptation in general and Odets' The
         General Died at Dawn in particular.

0576.   _____. "Vandals of Hollywood: Why a Good
         Movie Cannot Be Faithful to the Original Book."
         Saturday Review, 17 Oct. 1936, pp. 3-4.

0577.   Sobchack, Thomas and Vivian C. Sobchack. "The
         Source." In their An Introduction to Film.
         Boston: Little, Brown, and Co., 1980, pp. 313-328.
         Adaptations discussed: William Shakespeare's Henry
         V, Richard III, Hamlet, Joseph Heller's Catch-22,
         and Frank Norris's McTeague (Greed).

0578.   Stowell, H. Peter. "John Ford's Literary Sources:
        From Realism to Romance." Literature/Film
        Quarterly, 5 (1977), 164-173.

0579.   Street, Douglas, ed. Children's Novels and the
        Movies. New York: Frederick Ungar Publishing,
        1983.
        See 0635, 0639, 0645, 1163, 1182, 1325, 1427,
        1466, 1552, 1557, 1580, 2197.

0580.   _____. "An Overview of Filmic Adaptation
        of Children's Fiction." Children's Literature,
        7 (1982), 13-17.

0581.   Swain, Dwight V. "Adaptation and Its Problems."
        In his Film Scriptwriting: A Practical Manual.
        New York: Hastings House, 1976, pp. 187-192.

0582.   Taradash, Daniel. "Into Another World." Films
        and Filming, 5 (May 1959), 9, 33.
        On From Here to Eternity and Andersonville.

0583.   Tyler, Parker. "Magic-Lantern Metamorphosis II:
        "Revenge by Hollywood." In his Magic and Myth
        of the Movies. New York: Simon and Schuster,
        1970., pp. 117-131.
        A discussion of Hollywood's adaptation of Broadway
        plays, centered around Arsenic and Old Lace.

0584.   Wagner, Geoffery. The Novel and the Cinema.
        Rutherford: Fairleigh Dickinson University
        Press, 1975.
        Essays on Citizen Kane, Les Liaisons Dangereuses,
        Greed, The Blue Angel, The House of Usher (1960),
        Face to Face (1953), Wuthering Heights (1939),
        Jane Eyre, Madame Bovary (1949), Lord Jim, Hunger,
        Last Year at Marienbad, 1984 (1956), The Heiress,
        A Clockwork Orange, The Stranger (1967), Candide,
        The Trial, Cabaret, Death in Venice, Contempt,
        and Catch-22.

0585.   Wald, Jerry. "Jerry Wald on Filmed Authors."
        Film Culture, 3 (Dec. 1957), 16.

0586.   _____. "Screen Adaptation." Films in Review,
        5 (1964), 62-67.
        Producer of The Sound and the Fury discusses such
        problems as "opening up" plays, length of the
        source, and compressing action.

0587.   Walker, Alexander. "What About the Workers?" and
        "The Anglo-Italian Job." In his Hollywood
        U.K.: The British Film Industry in the Sixties.
        New York: Stein and Day, 1974, pp. 68-91 and
        pp. 107-132.
        On the adaptations of works by the "Angry Young
        Men," including discussions of Sillitoe's Saturday
        Night and Sunday Morning and The Loneliness of
        the Long Distance Runner.

0588.   Weinburg, Herman G.   "Novel into Film."
            Literature/Film Quarterly, 1 (1973), 98-102.
        Survey of adaptations.

0589.   Williams, W.E.   "Film and Literature."   _Sight
            and Sound_, 4 (Winter 1935-1936), 163-165.
        Film adaptations hampered by film's inability
        to create characters in depth and to use literary
        language; analyzes Reinhardt's _A Midsummer Night's
        Dream_.

7

Writers and the Film Industry

0590. Clurman, Harold. <u>The Fervent Years: The Story
   of the Group Theatre and the Thirties</u>. New
   York: Hill and Wang, 1957, pp. 158-160,
   pp. 167-171, pp. 188-192.

0591. Dardis, Tom. "The Myth That Won't Go Away: Selling
   Out in Hollywood." <u>Journal of Popular Film</u>,
   11 (1984), 167-171.

0592. _____. <u>Some Time in the Sun</u>. New York:
   Charles Scribner's Sons, 1976.
   Hollywood careers of Nathanael West, Aldous
   Huxley, James Agee, F. Scott Fitzgerald, and William
   Faulkner.

0593. Fiedler, Leslie. "What Shining Phantom: Writers
   and the Movies." In <u>Man and the Movies</u>.
   Ed. W.R. Robinson. Baltimore: Penguin Books,
   1967, pp. 304-323.
   On novels about Hollywood (West's <u>Day of the Locust</u>,
   Mailer's <u>Deer Park</u>, Fitzgerald's <u>The Last Tycoon</u>,
   and Viertel's <u>White Hunter, Black Heart</u>).

0594. Fine, Richard. <u>Hollywood and the Profession of
   Authorship 1928-1940</u>. Ann Arbor: UMI Research
   Press, 1984.
   William Faulkner, F. Scott Fitzgerald, Lillian
   Hellman, Nathanael West, John Dos Passos, Thornton
   Wilder, Maxwell Anderson, James M. Cain, W.R. Burnett,
   Ben Hecht, Budd Schulberg, and Dashiell Hammett.

0595. Graham, Sheila. <u>The Garden of Allah</u>. New York:
   Crown Publishers, 1970.
   John O'Hara, William Faulkner, Robert Benchley,
   Donald Ogden Stewart, and F. Scott Fitzgerald.

0596. Guiles, Fred Lawrence. <u>Hanging on in Paradise</u>.
   New York: McGraw Hill, 1975.
   Hollywood careers of F. Scott Fitzgerald, Robert
   Sherwood, Ben Hecht, and Dorothy Parker.

0597.   Hazel, Erik Richard. "The Hollywood Image: An
            Examination of the Literary Perspective."
            DAI, 35 (1974), 2991A (Case Western Reserve
            University).
        The image of Hollywood in works by writers who
        worked there; case study is Nathanael West's Day
        of the Locust.

0598.   Kazan, Elia. "Writers and Motion Pictures."
            Atlantic Monthly, 199 (April 1957), 67-70.

0599.   Kempton, Murray. "Day of the Locust: The Worker's
            Theater Goes to Hollywood." In his Part of
            Our Time: Some Ruins and Monuments of the Thirties.
            New York: Simon and Schuster, 1955, pp. 184-210.

0600.   Mayersberg, Paul. "The Great Rewrite." Sight
            and Sound, 36 (Spring 1967), 72-77.
        Hollywood experiences of Richard Brooks, Raymond
        Chandler, and Daniel Tardash.

0601.   Podeschi, John B. "The Writer in Hollywood."
            DAI, 32 (1972), 4629A (University of Illinois
            at Urbana-Champaign).
        The Hollywood careers of Clifford Odets, William
        Inge, Preston Sturges, Arthur Miller, Tennessee
        Williams, F. Scott Fitzgerald, Raymond Chandler,
        Budd Schulberg, Arch Oboler, Paddy Chayefsky,
        Dudley Nichols, and Robert Sherwood.

0602.   Schultheiss, John. "The `Eastern' Writer in
            Hollywood." Cinema Journal, 11 (Fall 1971),
            13-47. Reprinted in Cinema Examined: Selections
            from Cinema Journal. Ed. Richard Dyer MacCann
            and Jack C. Ellis. New York: E.P. Dutton,
            1982, pp. 41-75.
        Hollywood careers of Clifford Odets, Budd Schulberg,
        Donald Ogden Stewart, F. Scott Fitzgerald, and
        William Faulkner.

0603.   _____. "George Jean Nathan and the Dramatist
            in Hollywood." Literature/Film Quarterly,
            4 (1976), 13-27.

0604.   _____. "A Study of the `Eastern' Writer
            in Hollywood in the 1930's." DAI, 34 (1974),
            4473A (The University of Southern California).

0605.   Snyder, Stephen. "From Words to Images: Five
            Novelists in Hollywood." Canadian Review of
            American Studies, 8 (1977), 206-213.
        Essay-review of Dardis's Some Time in the Sun.

0606.   Spatz, Jonas. Hollywood in Fiction: Some Versions
            of the American Myth. The Hague: Mouton, 1969.
        Discussions of The Last Tycoon, The Deer Park,
        After Many a Summer, and What Makes Sammy Run?

0607.   Taylor, John Russell. <u>Strangers in Paradise:</u>
        <u>The Hollywood Emigres</u>. New York: Holt, Rinehart
        and Winston, 1983.
        Contains discussions of the experiences of Bertolt
        Brecht and Thomas Mann in Hollywood.

0608.   Wilson, Edmund. <u>The Boys in the Back Room: Notes</u>
        <u>on California Novelists</u>. San Francisco: The
        Colt Press, 1941.
        On James M. Cain, John O'Hara, William Saroyan,
        and Nathanael West.

8

Literary Figures
of
the United States

JAMES AGEE

0609. Barson, Alfred T. "Epiphany and Dream" and "The
Full Life Is Full of Crap." In his A Way of
Seeing: A Critical Study of James Agee. Amherst:
University of Massachusetts Press, 1972, pp. 107-127
and pp. 165-188.
On Agee's work for the screen.

0610. Bergreen, Laurence. James Agee: A Life. New York:
E.P. Dutton, 1984.
Contains new information on Agee's film career,
including contention that the published script of
Night of the Hunter is largely by Charles Laughton.

0611. Dardis, Tom. "James Agee: The Man Who Loved the
Movies." American Film, 1 (June 1976), 62-67.
A portion of Some Time in the Sun.

0612. Flanders, Mark Wilson. The Film Theory of James
Agee. New York: Arno Press, 1977.

0613. Fultz, James R. "A Classic Case of Collaboration:
The African Queen." Literature/Film Quarterly,
10 (1982), 13-24.

0614. _____. "Heartbreak at the Blue Hotel: James
Agee's Scenario of Stephen Crane's Story." Midwest
Quarterly, 21 (1980), 423-434.

0615. _____. "High Jinks at Yellow Sky: James Agee
and Stephen Crane." Literature/Film Quraterly,
11 (1983), 46-55.

0616. _____. "James Agee's Film Scripts: Adaptation
and Creation." DAI, 39 (1979), 3884A (The University
of Nebraska at Lincoln).

0617.   _____. "The Poetry and Danger of Childhood:
         James Agee's Film Adaptation of "Night of the
         Hunter." Western Humanities Review, 34 (1980),
         90-98.

0618.   Hammel, William Muller. "James Agee and Motion
         Pictures." DAI, 35 (1975), 5568A (The University
         of Texas at Austin).

0619.   Kramer, Victor A. "Agee and Plans for the Criticism
         of Popular Culture." Journal of Popular Culture,
         5, (1972), 755-766.

0620.   _____. "Agee's Projected Screenplay for Chaplin:
         Scientists and Tramps." Southern Humanities
         Review, 7 (1973), 357-364.

0621.   Macdonald, Dwight. "Agee and the Movies." Film
         Heritage, 3 (Fall 1967), 3-11.

0622.   Madden, Roberta. "`The Blue Hotel': An Examination
         of Story and Film Script." Film Heritage, 3
         (Fall 1967), 20-34.

0623.   Murray, Edward. "James Agee, `Amateur Critic'."
         In his Nine American Film Critics: A Study of
         Theory and Practice. New York: Frederick Ungar,
         1975, pp. 5-23.

0624.   Ohlin, Peter H. Agee. New York: Ivan Obolensky,
         1966.
         Discusses both scripts and film criticism.

0625.   Pechter, William S. "On Agee on Film." Sight and
         Sound, 33 (Summer 1964), 148-153.

0626.   Phelps, Donald. "James Agee as Film Critic." Film
         Comment, 1 (Summer 1955), 17-18.

0627.   Sieb, Kenneth. James Agee: Promise and Fulfillment.
         Pittsburg: University of Pittsburg Press, 1968.
         Discusses both scripts and film criticism.

0628.   Siegel, Joel. "On Agee on Film." Film Heritage,
         3 (Fall 1967), 12-19.

0629.   Silberberg, Elliot David. "The Celluloid Muse:
         A Critical Study of James Agee." DAI, 34 (1974),
         6662A (The University of Wisconsin).

0630.   Snyder, John J. James Agee: A Study of His Film
         Criticism. New York: Arno Press, 1977.

CONRAD AIKEN

0631.   Barrett, Gerald R. and Thomas L. Erskine. From
         Fiction to Film: Conrad Aiken's "Silent Snow,
         Secret Snow." Encino, Cal.: Dickenson Publishing,
         1972.
         Contains essays on the film by Martin A. Gardner,
         Jerry Herman, Lee R. Bobker, and Gerald R. Barrett.

EDWARD ALBEE

0632.   Leff, Leonard J. "Play into Film: Warner Brothers'
         Who's Afraid of Virginia Woolf?" Theatre Journal,
         33 (1981), 453-466.

0633.   Storrer, William Allin. "A Comparison of Edward
         Albee's Who's Afraid of Virginia Woolf as Drama
         and Film." DA 29 (1969), 3544-3545A (Ohio
         University).

LOUISA MAY ALCOTT

0634.   Ellis, Kate. "Life with Marmee: Three Versions."
         In The Classic American Novel and the Movies.
         Ed. Gerald Peary and Roger Shatzkin. New York:
         Frederick Ungar, 1977, pp. 62-72.
         On Little Women.

0635.   Gay, Carol. "Little Women at the Movies." In Children's
         Novels and the Movies. Ed. Douglas Street.
         New York: Frederick Ungar Publishing, 1983, pp. 28-38.

NELSON ALGREN

0636.   Rosen, Robert C. "The Man with the Golden Arm:
         Anatomy of a Junkie Movie." In The Modern American
         Novel and the Movies. Ed. Gerald Peary and Roger
         Shatzkin. New York: Frederick Ungar, 1978,
         pp. 189-198.

EDWARD ANDERSON

0637.   Kolker, Robert Phillip. "Night to Day." Sight
         and Sound, 43 (1974), 236-239.
         On two adaptations of Anderson's Thieves Like Us:
         Nicholas Ray's They Live by Night and Robert Altman's
         Thieves Like Us.

SHERWOOD ANDERSON

0638.   Sojka, Gregory S. "'I'm a Fool' on Film: Humor
         and Irony in Sherwood Anderson." The Winesburg
         Eagle, 5, No.1 (1979), 1-4.

WILLIAM H. ARMSTRONG

0639.   Deutsch, Leonard J. "Sounder: The Names and the
         Unnamed." In Children's Novels and the Movies.
         Ed. Douglas Street. New York: Frederick Ungar
         Publishing, 1983, pp. 214-226.

0640. Rutherford, Charles S. "A New Dog with an Old Trick:
       Archetypal Patterns in Sounder." Journal of
       Popular Film, 2 (Spring 1973), 155-163. Reprinted
       in Movies as Artifacts: Cultural Criticism of
       Popular Film. Ed. Michael T. Marsden, John
       G. Nachbar, and Sam L. Grogg, Jr. Chicago:
       Nelson-Hall, 1982, pp. 223-229.

JAMES BALDWIN

0641. Baldwin, James. The Devil Finds Work. New York:
       Dial Press, 1976.
       Essays on film, centering on the treatment of blacks
       in film.

0642. _____. "I Can't Blow This Gig." Cinema (US),
       No. 2 (Summer 1968), pp. 2-3.

JOHN BARTH

0643. Sragow, Michael. "End of the Road." Film Society
       Review, 5, No. 6 (1970), 36-39.

L. FRANK BAUM

0644. Baum, Frank. "The Oz Film Co." Films in Review,
       7 (1956), 329-333.
       On Baum's difficulties in selling his novels to
       the movies.

0645. Billman, Carol. "I've Seen the Movie: OZ Revisited."
       Literature/Film Quarterly, 9 (1981), 241-250.
       Reprinted in Children's Novels and the Movies.
       Ed. Douglas Street. New York: Frederick Ungar,
       1983, pp. 92-100.

0646. Harmetz, Aljean. ""The Script(s)." In her The
       Making of The Wizard of Oz. New York: Alfred
       A. Knopf, 1981, pp. 26-59.

0647. Juhnke, Janet. "The Wonderful Wizard of Oz: A Kansan's
       View." In The Classic American Novel and the
       Movies. Ed. Gerald Peary and Roger Shatzkin.
       New York: Frederick Ungar, 1977, pp. 165-175.

THOMAS BERGER

0648. Bezanson, Mark. "Berger and Penn's West: Visions
       and Revisions." In The Modern American Novel
       and the Movies. Ed. Gerald Peary and Roger Shatzkin.
       New York: Frederick Ungar, 1978, pp. 272-281.
       On Little Big Man.

0649. Braudy, Leo. "The Difficulties of Little Big Man."
       Film Quarterly, 25 (Fall 1971), 30-33.

0650. Turner, John W. "Little Big Man, the Novel and
       the Film: A Study of Narrative Structure."
       Literature/Film Quarterly, 5 (1977), 154-163.

JOHN BERRYMAN

0651.   Simons, John L.   "Henry on Bogie: Reality and Romance
        in `Dream Song No. 9' and High Sierra."
        Literature/Film Quarterly, 5 (1977), 269-272.

AMBROSE BIERCE

0652.   Barrett, Gerald R. and Thomas L. Erskine.   From
        Fiction to Film: Ambrose Bierce's "An Occurrence
        at Owl Creek Bridge."   Encino, Cal.: Dickenson
        Publishing Co., 1973.
        Essays on the films by Lewis Jacobs, James Welsh,
        Jack Shadoian, Julius Bellone, and Gerald R. Barrett.

0653.   Kwapy, William.   "Literary Adaptations."   In Screen
        Experience: An Approach to Film.   Ed. Sharon
        Feyen.   Dayton, Ohio: Geo. A. Pflaum, 1969, pp. 25-32.
        On "An Occurrence at Owl Creek Bridge."

0654.   Marcus, Fred H.   "Film and Fiction: `An Occurrence
        at Owl Creek Bridge.'"   In Film and Literature:
        Contrasts in Media.   Ed. Fred H.Marcus.   Scranton,
        Pa.: Chandler Publishing Co., 1971, pp. 260-271.
        Reprinted in California English Journal, 7 (1971),
        14-23.

0655.   Palmer, James W.   "From Owl Creek to La Riviere
        du Hibou: The Film Adaptation of Bierce's `Occurrence
        at Owl Creek Bridge.'"   Southern Humanities Review,
        11 (1977), 363-371.

0656.   Simonet, Thomas.   "Filming Inner Life: The Works
        of Robert Enrico."   Cinema Journal, 14 (Fall
        1974), 51-59.
        On In the Midst of Life.

WILLIAM PETER BLATTY

0657.   Blatty, William Peter.   "Introduction" and "Why
        Changes Were Made in the Screenplay."   In his
        William Peter Blatty on The Exorcist: From Novel
        to Film.   New York: Bantam Books, 1974, pp. 3-41
        and pp. 273-283.

0658.   Bowles, Stephen E.   "The Exorcist and Jaws."
        Literature/Film Quarterly, 4 (1976), 196-214.

0659.   McCormick, Ruth.   "`The Devil Made Me Do It!' A
        Critique of The Exorcist."   Cinéaste, 6, No. 3
        (1974), 18-22.

RAY BRADBURY

0660.   Carter, Douglas.   "A Cross Media Narrative Analysis
        of The Martian Chronicles: Novel, Radio, Theater,
        Film, and Television."   DAI, 44 (1984), 3531-3532A
        (Ohio University).

0661.   Ross, T.J. "Wild Lives." Literature/Film Quarterly,
        1 (1973), 218-225.
        Concerns Truffaut's adaptations of Fahrenheit 451
        by Ray Bradbury and The Bride Wore Black by William
        Irish (Cornell Woolrich).

0662.   Truffaut, Francois. "Journal of Fahrenheit 451."
        Cahiers du Cinéma in English, No. 5 (1967), pp. 11-22,
        No. 6 (1967), pp. 11-23, No. 7 (1967), 9-19.

                      W.R. BURNETT

0663.   Burnett, W.R.   "Afterward." In The Asphalt Jungle:
        A Screenplay by Ben Maddow and John Huston.
        Ed. Mathew J. Bruccoli. Carbondale: Southern
        Illinois University Press, 1980, pp. 145-147.

0664.   Gomery, Douglas.   "Introduction: Reworking the Classic
        Gangster Film." In High Sierra. Ed. Douglas
        Gomery. Madison: The University of Wisconsin
        Press, 1979, pp. 9-26.

0665.   Peary, Gerald. "Rico Rising: Little Caesar Takes
        Over the Screen." In The Classic American Novel
        and the Movies. Ed. Gerald Peary and Roger Shatzkin.
        New York: Frederick Ungar, 1977, pp. 286-296.

0666.   _____. "Introduction: Little Caesar Takes
        Over the Screen." In Little Caesar. Ed. Gerald
        Peary. Madison: The University of Wisconsin
        Press, 1981, pp. 9-28.

0667.   Poulos, Phil Johnston. "Benighted Eyes: W.R. Burnett
        and Film Noir." DAI, 44 (1983), 1451-1452A (The
        University of Tulsa).
        Discusses adaptations of Little Caesar, High Sierra,
        The Asphalt Jungle, and The Beast of the City.

                      ABRAHAM CAHAN

0668.   Michel, Sonya. "Yekl and Hester Street: Was Assimilation
        Really Good for the Jew?" Literature/Film Quarterly,
        5 (1977), 142-146.

                      JAMES M. CAIN

0669.   Allyn, John. "Double Indemnity: A Policy that Paid
        Off." Literature/Film Quarterly, 6 (1978), 116-124.

0670.   Brunette, Peter and Gerald Peary. "Tough Guys:
        James M. Cain Interviewed." Film Comment, 12
        (May-June 1976), 50-57.

0671.   Farrell, James T. "Cain's Movietone Realism."
        In his Literature and Morality. New York: Vanguard
        Press, 1947, pp. 79-89.
        On Mildred Pierce.

0672.   Graham, Allison.   "The Phantom Self: James M. Cain's
        Haunted America in the Early Neorealism of Visconti
        and Antonioni."   Film Criticism, 9 (Fall 1984),
        47-62.

0673.   Krutnik, Frank.   "Desire, Transgression, and James
        M. Cain: Fiction into Film Noir."   Screen, 23
        (May-June 1982), 31-44.

0674.   La Valley, Albert.   "Introduction: A Troublesome
        Property to Script."   In Mildred Pierce.   Ed. Albert
        La Valley.   Madison: University of Wisconsin
        Press, 1980, pp. 9-53.

0675.   Madden, David.   "James M. Cain and the Movies of
        the Thirties and Forties."   Film Heritage, 2
        (Summer 1967), 9-25.

0676.   Prigozy, Ruth.   "Double Indemnity: Billy Wilder's
        Crime and Punishment."   Literature/Film Quarterly,
        12 (1984), 160-170.

0677.   Spiegel, Alan.   "Seeing Triple: Cain, Chandler, and
        Wilder on Double Indemnity."   Mosaic, 16
        (Winter-Spring 1983), 83-101.

0678.   Tellotte, J.P.   "Visconti's Ossessione and the Open
        World of Neorealism."   New Orleans Review, 10
        (Summer-Fall 1983), 61-68.
        Visconti's film is based on The Postman Always Rings
        Twice.

ERSKINE CALDWELL

0679.   Gomery, Douglas.   "Three Roads Taken: The Novel,
        the Play, and the Film."   In The Modern American
        Novel and the Movies.   Ed. Gerald Peary and Roger
        Shatzkin.   New York: Frederick Ungar, 1978, pp. 9-18.
        On John Ford's Tobacco Road

TRUMAN CAPOTE

0680.   Clark, Leslie.   "Breakfast at Tiffany's: Brunch
        on Moon River."   In The Modern American Novel
        and the Movies.   Ed. Gerald Peary and Roger Shatzkin.
        New York: Frederick Ungar, 1978, pp. 236-246.

0681.   Murray, Edward.   "In Cold Blood: The Filmic Novel
        and the Problem of Adaptation."   Literature/Film
        Quarterly, 1 (1973), 132-137.

RAYMOND CHANDLER

0682.   Anderson, John Robert.   "`Hidden Fires': The Dimensions
        of Detection in American Literature and Film."
        DAI, 44 (1984), 2808A (Yale University).
        On Chandler's The Big Sleep and Hammett's The Maltese
        Falcon.

0683. Brackett, Leigh. "`The Big Sleep' to `The Long
          Goodbye' and More or Less How We Got There."
          Take One, 4, No. 1 (1974), 26-28.
       Scenarist discusses her two adaptations of Chandler's
       novels.

0684. Bruccoli, Matthew J. "Raymond Chandler and Hollywood."
          In The Blue Dahlia: A Screenplay by Raymond Chandler.
          Ed. Matthew J. Bruccoli. Carbondale: Southern
          Illinois University Press, 1976, pp. 129-137.

0685. Chandler, Raymond. "Chandler on the Film World
          and Television." In Raymond Chandler Speaking.
          Ed. Dorothy Gardiner and Kathrine Sorley Walker.
          Boston: Houghton Mifflin Co., 1962, pp. 115-144.

0686. _____. "Writers in Hollywood." Atlantic Monthly,
          176 (Nov. 1945), 50-54.

0687. French, Phillip. "Media Marlowes." In The World
          of Raymond Chandler. Ed. Miriam Gross. London:
          Weidenfeld and Nicolson, 1977, pp. 68-79.

0688. Gallagher, Brian. "Howard Hawks' The Big Sleep:
          A Paradigm for the Postwar American Family."
          North Dakota Quarterly, 51 (Summer 1983), 78-91.

0689. Gregory, Charles. "Knight Without Meaning?" Sight
          and Sound, 42 (1973), 155-159.
       On adaptations of Chandler's Phillip Marlowe novels.

0690. Houseman, John. "Lost Fortnight." In The World
          of Raymond Chandler. Ed. Miriam Gross. London:
          Weidenfeld and Nicolson, 1977, pp. 54-66.
       On Houseman's collaboration with Chandler on The
       Blue Dahlia.

0691. Houston, Penelope. "The Private Eye." Sight and
          Sound, 26 (Summer 1956), 22-23, 55.

0692. Jensen, Paul. "Film Noir: The Writer, the World
          You Live In; Raymond Chandler." Film Comment,
          10 (Nov.-Dec. 1974), 18-22.

0693. _____. "From Fiction to Fantasy with Howard
          Hawks." Film Comment, 10 (Nov.-Dec. 1974), 23.
       On The Big Sleep.

0694. Luhr, William. Raymond Chandler and Film. New
          York: Frederick Ungar Publishing Co., 1983.
       Chandler's scripts (Double Indemnity, Playback,
       The Blue Dahlia, and Strangers on a Train) and films
       adapted from his fiction: The Falcon Takes Over
       (from Farewell, My Lovely), Time to Kill (from The
       High Window), Murder, My Sweet (from Farewell, My
       Lovely), The Big Sleep (1946 and 1978), Lady in
       the Lake, The Brasher Doubloon(from The High Window),
       Marlowe (from The Little Sister), The Long Goodbye,
       and Farewell, My Lovely.

0695. _____. "Pre-, Prime-, and Post-Film Noir:
       Raymond Chandler's Farewell, My Lovely and Three
       Different Film Styles." Michigan Academician,
       15 (Fall 1982), 125-131.

0696. MacShane, Frank. "The Golden Graveyard." In The
       Life of Raymond Chandler. New York: E.P. Dutton,
       1976, pp. 104-128.
       Chandler's career in Hollywood.

0697. _____. "Raymond Chandler and Hollywood: An
       Uncomfortable Relationship." American Film,
       1 (April 1976), 62-69.

0698. _____. "Stranger in a Studio: Raymond Chandler
       and Hollywood." American Film, 1 (May 1976),
       54-60.
       Two articles are sections from MacShane's The Life
       of Raymond Chandler.

0699. Moffat, Ivan. "On the Fourth Floor of Paramount:
       Interview with Billy Wilder." In The World of
       Raymond Chandler. Ed. Miriam Gross. London:
       Weidenfeld and Nicolson, 1977, pp. 44-51.
       On Wilder's collaboration with Chandler on Double
       Indemnity.

0700. Monaco, James. "Notes on The Big Sleep/Thirty Years
       After." Sight and Sound, 44 (1975), 34-38.

0701. Oliver, Bill. "The Long Goodbye and Chinatown: Debunking
       the Private Eye Tradition." Literature/Film
       Quarterly, 3 (1975), 240-248.

0702. Pendo, Stephen. Raymond Chandler on Screen: His
       Novels into Film. Metuchen, N.J.: Scarecrow
       Press, 1976.
       Contains discussions of the films Murder, My Sweet
       (from Farewell, My Lovely), The Big Sleep (1946),
       Lady in the Lake, The Brasher Doubloon (from The
       High Window), Marlowe (from The Little Sister),
       and Farewell, My Lovely.

0703. _____. "Raymond Chandler's Phillip Marlowe:
       His Metamorphoses in Film." Films in Review,
       27 (1976), 129-136.
       A portion of Raymond Chandler on Screen.

0704. Ponder, Eleanor Anne. "The American Detective Form
       in Novels and Film, 1929-1947." DAI 40 (1980),
       4599A-600A (The University of North Carolina
       at Chapel Hill).
       On The Big Sleep and The Maltese Falcon.

0705. Shatzkin, Roger. "The Big Sleep: Who Cares Who
       Killed Owen Taylor?" In The Modern American
       Novel and the Movies. Ed. Gerald Peary and Roger
       Shatzkin. New York: Frederick Ungar, 1978, pp. 80-94.

0706. _____. "Double Indemnity: Raymond Chandler,
       Popular Fiction and Film." DAI, 45 (1985), 2105A
       (The State University of New Jersey at New Brunswick).

0707. Tuska, John. "A Conference with Raymond Chandler."
       In The Detective in Hollywood. New York: Doubleday,
       1978, pp. 301-337.
       On Chandler's literary career, his Hollywood experiences,
       and the adaptations of his novels.

0708. Van Wert, William. "Marlowe, The Long Goodbye,
       Phillip Marlowe: Hardboiled to Softboiled to
       Poached." Jump Cut, No. 3 (Sept.-Oct. 1974),
       pp. 10-13.

                    KATE CHOPIN

0709. Hoder-Salmon, Marilyn. "A `New-Born Creature,'
       The Authentic Woman in The Awakening: Novel to
       Screenplay as Critical Interpretation." DAI,
       45 (1985), 2567-2568A (The University of New
       Mexico).
       The screenplay was written by Hoder-Salmon.

              WALTER VAN TILBURG CLARK

0710. Crain, Mary Beth. "The Ox-Bow Incident Revisited."
       Literature/Film Quarterly, 4 (1976), 240-248.

                 SAMUEL L. CLEMENS
                   (MARK TWAIN)

0711. Brunette, Peter. "The Prince and the Pauper: Twain's
       Pauper, Warner's Prince." In The Classic American
       Novel and the Movies. Ed. Gerald Peary and Roger
       Shatzkin. New York: Frederick Ungar, 1977,
       pp. 105-113.

0712. Fuller, Dan. "Tom Sawyer: Saturday Matinee." In
       The Classic American Novel and the Movies. Ed. Gerald
       Peary and Roger Shatzkin. New York: Frederick
       Ungar, 1977, pp. 73-82.

0713. Reiber, Karen Jo. "Mark Twain and Buster Keaton:
       A Study in Comic Attitudes." DAI, 45 (1985),
       3351A (The University of Washington).

0714. Roman, Robert C. "Mark Twain on the Screen." Films
       in Review, 12 (1961), 20-33.
       Annotated filmography.

0715. Seelye, John D. Mark Twain in the Movies: A Meditation
       with Pictures. New York: Viking Press, 1977.
       Study of photographs and motion pictures of Clemens
       himself; not on adaptations of novels

JAMES FENIMORE COOPER

0716.   Horak, Jan-Christopher.   "The Last of the Mohicans:
         Maurice Tourneur's Tragic Romance."   In The Classic
         American Novel and the Movies.   Ed. Gerald Peary
         and Roger Shatzkin.   New York: Frederick Ungar,
         1977, pp. 10-19.

0717.   Merlock, James Raymond.   "From Flintlock to Forty-Five:
         James Fenimore Cooper and the Popular Western
         Tradition in Fiction and Film."   DAI, 42 (1982),
         3602A (Ohio University).

0718.   Scott, Kenneth W.   "Hawkeye in Hollywood."   Films
         in Review, 9 (1958), 575-579.
         Annotated filmography of adaptations of Cooper.

STEPHEN CRANE

0719.   French, Warren.   "Face to Face: Film Confronts
         Story."   In English Symposium Papers,IV.   Ed. Douglas
         Shepard.   Fredonia, N.Y.: State University College
         at Fredonia, 1974, pp. 43-74.
         On The Bride Comes to Yellow Sky and The Secret
         Sharer.

0720.   Reinhardt, Gottfried.   "Soundtrack Narration: Its
         Use Is Not Always a Resort of the Lazy or the
         Incompetent."   Films in Review, 4 (1953), 459-460.
         The producer of The Red Badge of Courage discusses
         the use of narration in the film.

0721.   Rollins, Janet Buck.   "Stephen Crane on Film: Adaptation
         as Interpretation."   DAI, 44 (1984), 1954-1955A
         (Oklahoma State University).
         On the adaptations of The Red Badge of Courage,
         "Three Miraculous Soldiers," "The Blue Hotel," and
         "The Bride Comes to Yellow Sky."

0722.   Ross, Lillian.   Picture.   New York: Rinehart, 1952.
         On the filming of John Huston's The Red Badge of
         Courage.

0723.   Silva, Fred.   "The Red Badge of Courage: Uncivil
         Battles and Civil Wars."   In The Classic American
         Novel and the Movies.   Ed. Gerald Peary and Roger
         Shatzkin.   New York: Frederick Ungar, 1977,
         pp. 114-123.

E.E. CUMMINGS

0724.   Seidman, Barbara.   "'Patronize Your Neighborhood
         Wake-Up-and-Dreamery': E.E. Cummings and the
         Cinematic Imagination."   Literature/Film Quarterly,
         13 (1985), 10-21.

JAMES DICKEY

0725.   Armour, Robert. "Deliverance: Four Variations of
        the American Adam." Literature/Film Quarterly,
        1 (1973), 280-285.

0726.   Beaton, James F. "Deliverance: Dickey Down the
        River." In The Modern American Novel and the
        Movies. Ed. Gerald Peary and Roger Shatzkin.
        New York: Frederick Ungar, 1978, pp. 293-306.

0727.   Coulthard, Ron. "From Manuscript to Movie Script:
        James Dickey's Deliverance." Notes on Contemporary
        Literature, 3, No. 3 (1973), 11-12.

0728.   Dempsey, Michael. "Deliverance: Boorman, Dickey
        in the Woods." Cinema (U.S.), 8, No. 1 (1973),
        10-17.

0729.   Dickey, James. "Afterward." In Deliverance.
        Ed. Matthew J. Bruccoli. Carbondale: Southern
        Illinois University Press, 1982, pp. 153-157.

0730.   Samuels, Charles Thomas. "How Not to Film a Novel."
        American Scholar, 42 (1972-73), 148-154. Reprinted
        in his Mastering the Film and Other Essays.
        Ed. Lawrence Graver. Knoxville: University of
        Tennessee Press, 1977, pp. 190-197.
        On Dickey's novel and Leonard Gardner's Fat City.

0731.   Wilson, Robert F. "Deliverance From Novel to Film:
        Where Is Our Hero?" Literature/Film Quarterly,
        2 (1974), 52-58.

JOAN DIDION

0732.   Bromwich, Peter. "Angst-Pushers and Austenites."
        Dissent, 20, No.2 (1973), 219-223.
        Concerns the adaptation of Play It As It Lays.

THOMAS DIXON

0733.   Cook, Raymond. "The Man Behind The Birth of a Nation."
        The North Carolina Historical Review, 29 (1962),
        519-540.
        Focuses on Dixon's relationship with D.W. Griffith.

0734.   Merritt, Russell. "Dixon, Griffith, and the Southern
        Legend: A Cultural Analysis of The Birth of a
        Nation." Cinema Journal, 12 (Fall 1972), 26-45.
        Reprinted in Cinema Examined: Selections from
        Cinema Journal. Ed. Richard Dyer MacCann and
        Jack C. Ellis. New York: E.P. Dutton, 1982,
        pp. 165-184.

0735.   Silverman, Joan L. "The Birth of a Nation: Prohibition
        Propaganda." Southern Quarterly, 18 (Spring-Summer
        1981), 23-30.

E. L. DOCTOROW

0736.   Dawson, Anthony B. "Ragtime and the Movies: The
         Aura of the Duplicable." Mosaic, 16 (Winter-Spring
         1983), 205-214.

0737.   Estrin, Barbara L. Recomposing Time: Humbolt's
         Gift and Ragtime." Denver Quarterly, 17 (Spring
         1982), 16-31.
         On the use of film in Saul Bellow's and E.L. Doctorow's
         novels.

0738.   Hague, Angela. "Ragtime and the Movies." North
         Dakota Quarterly, 50 (Summer 1982), 101-112.

0739.   Quart, Leonard and Barbara Quart. "Ragtime without
         a Melody." Literature/Film Quarterly, 10 (1982),
         71-74.

0740.   Rapf, Joanna. "Some Fantasy on Earth: Doctorow's
         Welcome to Hard Times." Literature/Film Quarterly,
         13 (1985), 50-55.

HILDA DOOLITTLE
(H.D.)

0741.   Doolittle, Hilda. "An Appreciation." Close Up,
         4 (March 1929), 56-68.

0742.   _____. "Boo: Sirocco and the Screen." Close
         Up, 2 (Jan. 1928), 38-50.

0743.   _____. "The Cinema and the Classics I: Beauty."
         Close Up, 1 (July 1927), 22-33.

0744.   _____. "The Cinema and the Classics II:
         Restraint." Close Up, 1 (Aug. 1927), 30-39.

0745.   _____. "The Cinema and the Classics III: The
         Mask and the Movietone." Close Up, 1 (Nov. 1927),
         18-31.

0746.   _____. "Conrad Veidt: The Student of Prague."
         Close Up, 1 (Sept. 1927), 34-44.

0747.   _____. "Expectation." Close Up, 2 (May 1928),
         38-49.

0748.   _____. "Joan of Arc." Close Up, 3 (Feb. 1928),
         15-22.

0749.   _____. "The King of Kings Again." Close Up,
         2 (Feb. 1928), 21-32.

0750.   _____. "Projector II." Close Up, 1 (Oct. 1927),
         35-44.
         A poem on the movies.

0751.   _____.   "Russian Films."   <u>Close Up</u>, 3 (Sept. 1928),
              18-29.

0752.   _____.   "Turksib."   <u>Close Up</u>, 5 (Dec. 1929),
              488-492.

0753.   Mandel, Charlotte.   "The Redirected Image: Cinematic
              Dynamics in the Style of H.D."   <u>Literature/Film
              Quarterly</u>, 11 (1983), 36-45.

JOHN DOS PASSOS

0754.   Larsson, Donald F.   "The Camera Eye: `Cinematic'
              Narrative in   <u>U.S.A.</u> and <u>Gravity's Rainbow</u>."
              In <u>Ideas of Order in Literature and Film</u>.   Ed. Peter
              Ruppert.   Tallahassee: University Presses of
              Florida, 1980, pp. 94-106.

0755.   Mottram, Eric.   "The Hostile Environment and the
              Survival Artist: A Note on the Twenties."   In
              <u>The American Novel in the Nineteen Twenties</u>.
              Ed. Malcolm Bradbury and David Palmer.   London:
              Edward Arnold Publishers, 1971, pp. 233-262.
         Discusses Dos Passos' debt to Griffith and Eisenstein.

THEODORE DREISER

0756.   Baird, James Lee.   "The Movies in Our Heads: An
              Analysis of Three Versions of Dreiser's <u>An American
              Tragedy</u>."   <u>DAI</u>, 28 (1967), 557A (The University
              of Washington).
         Discusses Eisenstein's proposed adaptation and Josef
         von Sternberg's and George Stevens's films.

0757.   Barbarow, George.   "Dreiser's Place on the Screen."
              <u>Hudson Review</u>, 5 (1952), 290-294.
         George Stevens's adaptation of <u>An American Tragedy</u>.

0758.   Bishoff, Robert Earl, Jr.   "Changing Perspectives:
              <u>An American Tragedy</u> from Literature to Film."
              <u>DAI</u>, 35 (1974), 440A (The University of
              Massachusetts).

0759.   Cohen, Keith.   "<u>An American Tragedy</u>: Eisenstein's
              Subversive Adaptation."   In <u>The Classic American
              Novel and the Movies</u>.   Ed. Gerald Peary and Roger
              Shatzkin.   New York: Frederick Ungar, 1977,
              pp. 239-256.

0760.   Dreiser, Theodore.   "Hollywood: Its Morals and
              Manners."   <u>Shadowland</u>, 5 (Nov. 1921), 37, 61-63;
              5 (Dec. 1921), 51, 61; 5 (Jan. 1922), 43, 67;
              5 (Feb. 1922), 53, 66.

0761.   _____.   "The Real Sins of Hollywood."   <u>Liberty</u>,
              9 (11 June 1932), 6-11.

0762. Eisenstein, Sergei. "An American Tragedy." In
       Notes of a Film Director. Trans. X. Danko.
       New York: Dover Publications, 1970, pp. 98-106.
       Concerns Eisenstein's proposed adaptation of Dreiser's
       novel.

0763. _____. "A Course in Treatment." In his Film
       Form: Essays in Film Theory. Ed. Jay Leyda.
       New York: Harcourt, Brace and World, 1949, pp. 84-107.
       On his adaptation of An American Tragedy.

0764. Geduld, Carolyn. "Wyler's Suburban Sister: Carrie
       1952." In The Classic American Novel and the
       Movies. Ed. Gerald Peary and Roger Shatzkin.
       New York: Frederick Ungar, 1977, pp. 152-164.

0765. Geist, Kenneth. "Carrie." Film Comment, 6 (Fall
       1970), 25-27.
       On William Wyler's adaptation of Sister Carrie.

0766. Hayne, Barrie. "Sociological Treatise, Detective
       Story, Love Affair: The Film Versions of An American
       Tragedy." Canadian Review of American Studies,
       8 (1977), 131-153.

0767. Kliman, Bernice. "An American Tragedy: Novel,
       Scenario, and Films." Literature/Film Quarterly,
       5 (1977) 258-268.

0768. Leonard, Neil. "Theodore Dreiser and the Film."
       Film Heritage, 2 (Fall 1966), 7-17.

0769. Montagu, Ivor. "Denouement: Sudden Death." In
       With Eisenstein in Hollywood: A Chapter of
       Autobiography. New York: International Publishers,
       1969, pp. 110-120.
       On Eisenstein's attempted adaptation of An American
       Tragedy.

0770. Morsberger, Robert E. "`In Elf Land Disporting':
       Sister Carrie in Hollywood." Bulletin of the
       Rocky Mountain Modern Language Association, 27
       (Dec. 1973), 219-230.

0771. Pichel, Irving. "Revivals, Reissues, and A Place
       in the Sun." The Quarterly of Film, Radio, and
       Television, 6 (1952), 388-393.
       On George Steven's adaptation of An American Tragedy.

0772. Potamkin, Harry A. "Novel into Film: A Case Study..."
       Close Up, 8 (Dec. 1931), 267-279. Reprinted
       in The Compound Cinema: The Film Writings of
       Harry Alan Potamkin. New York: Teachers College
       Press, 1977, pp. 186-196.
       On Eisenstein's attempt to adapt An American Tragedy.

HOWARD FAST

0773. Lillard, Richard G. "Through the Disciplines with
          Spartacus." American Studies, 16, No. 2 (1975),
          15-28.

WILLIAM FAULKNER

0774. Adams, Michael. "`How Come Everybody Down Here
          Has Three Names?': Martin Ritt's Southern Films."
          Southern Quarterly, 19 (Spring-Summer 1981),
          143-155.

0775. Anderson, Thomas Duncan. "Light in August: Novel;
          Chamber Theater; Motion Picture--The Role of
          Point of View in the Adaptation Process." DAI,
          34 (1974), 6161A (Southern Illinois University).
       The film script is by Anderson.

0776. Barbera, Jack. "Tomorrow and Tomorrow and Tomorrow."
          Southern Quarterly, 19 (Spring-Summer 1981),
          183-197. Reprinted in The South and Film. Ed. Warren
          French. Jackson: University Press of Mississippi,
          1981, pp. 183-197.

0777. Blotner, Joseph. Faulkner: A Biography. 2 vols.
          New York: Random House, 1974.

0778. _____. "Faulkner in Hollywood." In Man and
          the Movies. Ed. W.R. Robinson. Baltimore: Penguin
          Books, 1967, pp. 261-303.
       Both works contain information about Faulkner's
       Hollywood career.

0779. Degenfelder, E. Pauline Sutta. "Essays on Faulkner:
          Style, Use of History, Film Adaptations of His
          Fiction." DAI, 33 (1973), 5169A (Case Western
          Reserve University).
       Includes discussions of The Reivers, The Story of
       Temple Drake, The Long, Hot Summer, Sanctuary, and
       Today We Live.

0780. _____. "The Film Adaptation of Faulkner's
          Intruder in the Dust." Literature/Film Quarterly,
          1 (1973), 138-148.

0781. _____. "The Four Faces of Temple Drake: Faulkner's
          Sanctuary, Requiem for a Nun, and the Two Film
          Adaptations." American Quarterly, 28 (1976),
          544-560.

0782. _____."Rites of Passage: Novel into Film."In
          The Modern American Novel and the Movies. Ed. Gerald
          Peary and Roger Shatzkin. New York: Frederick
          Ungar, 1978, pp.178-186.
       On Intruder in the Dust.

0783. _____. "Sirk's The Tarnished Angels: Pylon
         Recreated." Literature/Film Quarterly, 5 (1977),
         242-251.

0784. Fadiman, Regina K. "Novel into Film," "The Novel,"
         "The Background of the Film," "The Scripts,"
         and "The Film." In Faulkner's Intruder in the
         Dust. Knoxville: University of Tennessee Press,
         1978, pp. 3-10, pp. 11-25, pp. 26-43, pp. 44-61,
         and pp. 62-81.

0785. Folks, Jeffrey. "William Faulkner and the Silent
         Film." Southern Quarterly, 19 (Spring-Summer
         1981), 171-182. Reprinted in The South and Film.
         Ed. Warren French. Jackson: University Press
         of Mississippi, 1981, pp. 171-182.

0786. Foote, Horton. "On First Dramatizing Faulkner."
         In Faulkner, Modernism, and Film: Faulkner and
         Yoknapatawpha, 1978. Ed. Evans Harrington and
         Anne J. Abadie. Jackson: University Press of
         Mississippi, 1979, pp. 49-65.
         Concerns a television production of "Old Man."

0787. _____. "Tomorrow: The Genesis of a
         Screenplay." In Faulkner, Modernism, and Film:
         Faulkner and Yoknaptawpha, 1978. Ed. Evans
         Harrington and Anne J. Abadie. Jackson: University
         Press of Mississippi, 1979, pp. 149-162.

0788. Garrett, George. "Afterward." In The Road to Glory:
         A Screenplay by Joel Sayre and William Faulkner.
         Ed. Matthew J. Bruccoli. Carbondale: Southern
         Illinois University Press, 1981, pp. 159-174.

0789. Hasseloff, Cynthia. "Formative Elements of Film:
         A Structural Comparison of Three Novels and Their
         Adaptations by Irving Ravetch and Harriet Frank."
         DAI, 33 (1972), 438A (The University of Missouri
         at Columbia).
         Discussions of adaptations of Faulkner (The Reivers
         and The Sound and the Fury) and McMurtry (Hud).

0790. Hayhoe, George F. "Faulkner in Hollywood: A Checklist
         of His Filmscripts at the University of Virginia."
         Mississippi Quarterly, 31 (Summer 1978), 402-419.

0791. _____. "Faulkner in Hollywood: A Checklist
         of His Filmscripts at the University of Virginia:
         A Correction and Some Additions." Mississippi
         Quarterly, 32 (Summer 1979), 467-472.

0792. Heller, Terry L. "Intruder in the Dust: The
         Representation of Racial Problems in Faulkner's
         Novel and the MGM Film Adaptation." Coe Review,
         No. 8 (1977), pp. 79-90.

0793. Hogue, Peter. "Hawks and Faulkner: Today We Live."
         Literature/Film Quarterly, 9 (1981), 51-58.

0794.   Hyams, Joe. "An Interview with `Pappy' Faulkner."
        Journal of the Screen Producers Guild, Sept. 1959,
        pp. 17-20.

0795.   Jones, Dorothy B. "William Faulkner: Novel into
        Film." _The Quarterly of Film, Radio, and Television_,
        8 (1953), 51-71.
        Clarence Brown's _Intruder in the Dust_.

0796.   Kauffmann, Stanley. "_The Sound and the Fury_: Signifying
        Nothing?" In _The Classic American Novel and
        the Movies_. Ed. Gerald Peary and Roger Shatzkin.
        New York: Frederick Ungar, 1977, pp. 305-308.

0797.   Kawin, Bruce. "Faulkner's Film Career: The Years
        with Hawks." In _Faulkner, Modernism, and Film:
        Faulkner and Yoknapatawpha, 1978_. Ed. Evans
        Harrington and Anne J. Abadie. Jackson: University
        Press of Mississippi, 1979, pp. 163-181.

0798.   _____. "A Faulkner Filmography." _Film Quarterly_,
        30 (Summer 1977), 12-21.

0799.   _____. _Faulkner on Film_. New York: Frederick
        Ungar, 1977.
        Film techniques in _The Sound and the Fury_, Faulkner's
        scripts, and adaptations of his fiction (_The Story
        of Temple Drake_, _Sanctuary_, _Intruder in the Dust_,
        The Tarnished Angels, _The Long, Hot Summer_, _The
        Reivers_, and _Tomorrow_).

0800.   _____. "The Montage Element in Faulkner's
        Fiction. In _Faulkner, Modernism, and Film: Faulkner
        and Yoknapatawpha, 1978_. Ed. Evans Harrington
        and Anne J. Abadie. Jackson: University Press
        of Mississippi, 1979, pp. 103-126.

0801.   Murray, Donald M. "Faulkner, the Silent Comedies,
        and the Animated Cartoon." _Southern Humanities
        Review_, 9 (1975), 241-257.

0802.   Neidhardt, Frances Elam. "Verbal-Visual Simultaneity
        in Faulkner's _The Sound and the Fury_: A Literary
        Montage Filmscript for Quentin." _DAI_, 39 (1978),
        1165A (East Texas State University).
        First part is a study of time in the novel; second
        is Neidhardt's scenario of Quentin's section.

0803.   Phillips, Gene. "Faulkner and Film: Two Versions
        of _Sanctuary_." _Literature/Film Quarterly_, 1
        (1973), 263-273.

0804.   Rollyson, Carl E., Jr. "Faulkner into Film: `Tomorrow'
        and `Tomorrow.'" _Mississippi Quarterly_, 32 (1979),
        437-452.

0805.   Savarese, Sister Paul C., C.S.J. "Cinematic Techniques
        in the Novels of William Faulkner." _DAI_, 33
        (1972), 1179A (St. Louis University).

0806. Sidney, George R. "Faulkner in Hollywood: A Study
      of His Career as a Scenarist." <u>DA</u>, 20 (1959),
      2810 (The University of New Mexico).

0807. _____. "William Faulkner and Hollywood."
      <u>Colorado Quarterly</u>, 9 (1961), 367-377.

0808. Skaggs, Merrill Maguire. "Story and Film of `Barn
      Burning': The Difference a Camera Makes." <u>Southern
      Quarterly</u>, 21 (Winter 1983), 5-15.

0809. Stern, Michael. "<u>Pylon</u>: From the Folklore of Speed
      to Danse Macabre." In <u>The Modern American Novel
      and the Movies</u>. Ed. Gerald Peary and Roger Shatzkin.
      New York: Frederick Ungar, 1978, pp. 40-52.

0810. Wald, Jerry. "Faulkner and Hollywood." <u>Films in
      Review</u>, 10 (1959), 129-133.
      Includes discussions of two adaptations produced
      by Wald, <u>The Long, Hot Summer</u> and <u>The Sound and
      the Fury</u>.

0811. Yellin, David and Marie Connors. "Faulkner and
      Foote and Chemistry" and "Conversations with
      the Creators." In <u>Tomorrow and Tomorrow and
      Tomorrow</u>. Ed. David G. Yellin and Marie Connors.
      Jackson: University Press of Mississippi, 1985,
      pp. 3-31 and pp. 163-184.
      Analysis of Foote's television and film adaptations
      of Faulkner's short story and interviews with the
      cast and crew of the film.

                    F. SCOTT FITZGERALD

0812. Adams, Michael. "Fitzgerald Filmography." <u>Fitzgerald-
      Hemingway Annual 1977</u>. Ed. Margaret M. Duggan
      and Richard Layman. Detroit: Gale Research,
      1977, pp. 101-109.

0813. _____. "<u>Gatsby</u>, <u>Tycoon</u>, <u>Islands</u> and Film
      Critics." <u>Fitzgerald/Hemingway Annual 1978</u>.
      Ed. Matthew J. Bruccoli and Richard Layman.
      Detroit: Gale Research, 1979, pp. 296-306.
      On screen adaptations of Fitzgerald's <u>The Great
      Gatsby</u> and <u>The Last Tycoon</u> and Hemingway's <u>Islands
      in the Stream</u>.

0814. Alpert, Hollis. "Fitzgerald, Hollywood, and <u>The
      Last Tycoon</u>." <u>American Film</u>, 1 (March 1976),
      8-14.
      On the making of Elia Kazan's adaptation.

0815. Arnold, Edwin T. "The Motion Picture as Metaphor
      in the Works of F. Scott Fitzgerald." <u>Fitzgerald-
      Hemingway Annual 1977</u>. Ed. Margaret M. Duggan
      and Richard Layman. Detroit: Gale Research,
      1977, pp. 43-60.

0816.   Atkins, Irene Kahn.   "Hollywood Revisited: A Sad
          Homecoming." Literature/Film Quarterly, 5 (1977),
          105-111.
        On The Last Tycoon.

0817.   _____. "In Search of the Greatest Gatsby."
          Literature/Film Quarterly, 2 (1974), 216-228.

0818.   Bahrenberg, Bruce. Filming The Great Gatsby. New
          York: Berkeley Books, 1974.

0819.   Bodeen, DeWitt. "F. Scott Fitzgerald and Films."
          Films in Review, 28 (1977), 285-294.

0820.   Callahan, John F. "The Unfinished Business of The
          Last Tycoon." Literature/Film Quarterly, 6 (1978),
          204-213.

0821.   Carringer, Robert L. "Citizen Kane, The Great Gatsby,
          and Some Coventions of American Narrative."
          Critical Inquiry, 2 (1975), 307-325.

0822.   Corliss, Mary and Charles Silver. "Hollywood Under
          Water--Elia Kazan on The Last Tycoon." Film
          Comment, 13, (Jan.-Feb. 1977), 40-44.

0823.   Cumbow, R.C. "East Egg, West Egg, Rotten Egg."
          Movietone News, No. 31 (April 1974), pp. 8-12.
        On Clayton's The Great Gatsby.

0824.   Dixon, Wheeler Winston. "The Cinematic Vision of
          F. Scott Fitzgerald." DAI, 43 (1982), 1150-1151A
          (Rutgers University).
        The relationship of Fitzgerald's fiction to his
        screenplays.

0825.   Farber, Manny. "East Egg on the Face: Gatsby 1949."
          In The Classic American Novel and the Movies.
          Ed. Gerald Peary and Roger Shatzkin. New York:
          Frederick Ungar, 1977, pp. 257-260.

0826.   Giannetti, Louis D. "The Gatsby Flap." Literature/Film
          Quarterly, 3 (1975), 13-22.

0827.   Houston, Penelope. "Visits to Babylon: F. Scott
          Fitzgerald and Hollywood." Sight and Sound,
          21 (April-June 1952), 153-156.
        Concerns Fitzgerald's Hollywood career and
        adaptations of his works.

0828.   Johnston, Kenneth G. "Fitzgerald's `Crazy Sunday':
          Cinderella in Hollywood." Literature/Film Quarterly,
          6 (1978), 214-221.

0829.   Jones, Edward T. "Green Thoughts in a Technicolor
          Shade: Revaluation of The Great Gatsby." Literature/
          Film Quarterly, 2 (1974), 229-236.

0830.   Latham, Aaron. <u>Crazy Sundays: F. Scott Fitzgerald</u>
         <u>in Hollywood</u>. New York: Viking Press, 1971.

0831.   LeVot, André. "Writer for Hire: Hollywood." In
         his <u>F. Scott Fitzgerald: A Biography</u>. Trans.
         William Byron. Garden City: Doubleday and Co.,
         1983, pp. 315-355.

0832.   Margolies, Alan. "F. Scott Fitzgerald's Work in
         the Film Studios." <u>Princeton University Library</u>
         <u>Chronicle</u>, 32 (Winter 1971), 81-110.

0833.   _____. "The Impact of Theatre and Film on
         F. Scott Fitzgerald." <u>DAI</u>, 30 (1970),3467A (New
         York University).

0834.   _____. "'Kissing, Shooting, and Sacrificing':
         F. Scott Fitzgerald and the Hollywood Market."
         In <u>The Short Stories of F. Scott Fitzgerald:</u>
         <u>New Approaches in Criticism</u>. Ed. Jackson R. Bryer.
         Madison: University of Wisconsin Press, 1982,
         pp. 65-73.
         On Fitzgerald's writing with an eye toward a sale
         to Hollywood.

0835.   _____. "Novel to Play to Film: Four Versions
         of <u>The Great Gatsby</u>." In <u>Critical Essays on</u>
         <u>F. Scott Fitzgerald's The Great Gatsby</u>. Ed. Scott
         Donaldson. Boston: G.K. Hall, 1984, pp. 187-200.

0836.   Martin, Robert A. "Hollywood in Fitzgerald: After
         Paradise." In <u>The Short Stories of F. Scott</u>
         <u>Fitzgerald: New Approaches in Criticism</u>. Ed. Jackson
         R. Bryer. Madison: University of Wisconsin Press,
         1982, pp. 127-148.
         Fitzgerald's treatment of Hollywood in his stories.

0837.   Maslin, Janet. "Ballentine's Scotch, Glemby Haircuts,
         White Suits, amd White Teflon: <u>Gatsby</u> 1974."
         In <u>The Classic American Novel and the Movies</u>.
         Ed. Gerald Peary and Roger Shatzkin. New York:
         Frederick Ungar, 1977, pp. 261-267.

0838.   Mass, Rosyln. "A Linking of Legends: <u>The Great</u>
         <u>Gatsby</u> and <u>Citizen Kane</u>." <u>Literature/Film Quarterly</u>,
         2 (1974), 207-215.

0839.   Mazzocco, Robert. "The Ghost of Gatsby." <u>The New</u>
         <u>York Review of Books</u>, 21 (2 May 1974), 35-37.

0840.   Michaels, I. Lloyd. "Auteurism, Creativity, and
         Entropy in <u>The Last Tycoon</u>." <u>Literature/Film</u>
         <u>Quarterly</u>, 10 (1982), 110-119.

0841.   Mizener, Arthur. <u>The Far Side of Paradise: A Biography</u>
         <u>of F. Scott Fitzgerald</u>. New York: Houghton Mifflin
         Co., 1951, pp. 270-286.
         On Fitzgerald's work in Hollywood.

0842.   Piper, Henry Dan. "Hollywood Script Writer" and
        "The Last Tycoon: The Hollywood Theme." In F.
        Scott Fitzgerald: A Criticial Portrait. New
York: Holt, Rinehart, and Winston, 1965, pp. 245-257
        and pp. 258-276.

0843.   Powell, Anthony. "Hollywood Canteen: A Memoir of
        F. Scott Fitzgerald in 1937." Fitzgerald/Hemingway
        Annual 1971. Ed. Matthew J. Bruccoli and
        C. E. Frazer Clark, Jr. Washington, D.C.: Microcard
        Editions, 1971, pp. 71-80.

0844.   Ring, Frances and R.L. Samsell. "Sisyphus in Hollywood:
        Refocusing F. Scott Fitzgerald." Fitzgerald/Hemingway
        Annual. Ed. Matthew J. Bruccoli and C.E. Frazer
        Clark. Washington, D.C.: Microcard Editions,
        1974, pp. 93-104.

0845.   Rosen, Marjorie. "I'm Proud of That Film." Film
        Comment, 10 (July-August 1974), 49-51.
        Interview with Jack Clayton, the director of The
        Great Gatsby.

0846.   Stewart, Lawrence P. "Fitzgerald's Film Scripts
        of `Babylon Revisited.'" Fitzgerald/Hemingway
        Annual, 1971. Ed. Matthew J. Bruccoli and C.E.
        Frazer Clark, Jr. Washington: Microcard Editions,
        1971, pp. 81-104.

0847.   Turnbull, Andrew. Scott Fitzgerald. New York:
        Charles Scribner's Sons, 1962, pp. 286-297.
        On Fitzgerald's work in Hollywood.

ERNEST J. GAINES

0848.   Callahan, John. "Image Making: Tradition and Two
        Versions of The Autobiography of Miss Jane Pittman."
        Chicago Review, 29, (Autumn 1977), 45-62.

0849.   Potter, Vilma Raskin. "The Autobiography of Miss
        Jane Pittman: How to Make a White Film From a
        Black Novel." Literature/Film Quarterly, 3 (1975),
        371-375.

ELLEN GLASGOW

0850.   Bathrick, Serafina Kent. "In This Our Life: Independent
        Woman, Doomed Sister." In The Modern American
        Novel and the Movies. Ed. Gerald Peary and Roger
        Shatzkin. New York: Frederick Ungar, 1978,
        pp. 143-55.

DAVID GOODIS

0851. Sherman, William Mark. "David Goodis: Dark Passage."
        Sight and Sound, 38 (Winter 1968-1969), 41.

0852. Török, Jean-Paul. "The Sensitive Spot." In Focus
       on Shoot the Piano Player. Ed. Leo Braudy.
       Englewood Cliffs: Prentice-Hall, 1972, pp. 67-75.
       On Truffaut's Shoot the Piano Player, an adaptation
       of Goodis's Down There.

0853. Truffaut, Francois. "Adapting Shoot the Piano Player."
       In Focus on Shoot the Piano Player. Ed. Leo
       Braudy. Englewood Cliffs: Prentice-Hall, 1972,
       pp. 123-126.

PAUL GREEN

0854. Daugherty, Frank. "Paul Green in Hollywood." Close
       Up, 9 (June 1932), 81-86.

0855. Green, Paul. "Theatre and the Screen." In his
       Hawthorne Tree: Some Papers and Letters on Life
       and the Theatre. Chaprl Hill: University   of
       North Carolina Press, 1943, pp. 37-50; rpt. Freeport,
       N.Y.: Books for Libraries Press, 1971.

DAVIS GRUBB

0856. Welch, Jack. "Art Is Long, Entertainment Short:
       Cinematic Composition in Two Films Made From
       Davis Grubb's Novels." West Virginia University
       Philological Papers, 26 (Aug. 1980), 43-52.
       On Night of the Hunter and Fools' Parade.

0857. Wood, Robin. "Night of the Hunter: Charles Laughton
       on Grubb Street." In The Modern American Novel
       and the Movies. Ed. Gerald Peary and Roger Shatzkin.
       New York: Frederick Ungar, 1978, pp. 204-214.

DASHIELL HAMMETT

0858. Gow, Gordon. "Pursuit of the Falcon." Films and
       Filming, 20 (March 1974), 56-58.
       On The Maltese Falcon.

0859. Naremore, James. "John Huston and The Maltese Falcon."
       Literature/Film Quarterly, 1 (1973), 239-249.

0860. Scher, Saul N. "The Glass Key: Two Originals and
       Two Copies." Literature/Film Quarterly, 12 (1984),
       147-159.

0861. Tuska, Jon. "The Black Mask." In The Detective
       in Hollywood. New York: Doubleday, 1978, pp. 159-187.
       On Hammett's literary career and the adaptations
       of his fiction.

0862. Wexman, Virginia Wright. "The Transfer from One
       Medium to Another: The Maltese Falcon from Fiction
       to Film." Library Quarterly, 45 (1975), 46-55.

MARK HARRIS

0863.   Childs, James.   "Interview with John Hancock."
        Literature/Film Quarterly, 3 (1975), 109-116.
        The director discusses his adaptation of Harris's
        Bang the Drum Slowly.

0864.   Harris, Mark.   "Flying Elephants: Transformations
        in Literature and Film." In Transformations in
        Literature and Film.   Ed. Leon Golden.   Tallahassee:
        University Presses of Florida, 1982, pp. 98-109.

WILLIAM HARRISON

0865.   Hull, Elizabeth Anne.   "Merging Madness: Rollerball
        as a Cautionary Tale." In Clockwork Worlds:
        Mechanized Environments in Science Fiction.
        Ed. Richard D. Erlich and Thomas P. Dunn.   Westport,
        Conn.: Greenwood Press, 1983, pp. 163-180.
        Harrison's short story "Rollerball Murder" compared
        to Norman Jewison's film adaptation.

NATHANIEL HAWTHORNE

0866.   Allyn, John.   "Hawthorne on Film--Almost." Literature/
        Film Quarterly, 2 (1974), 124-128.
        On Donald Foxe's adaptation of "Young Goodman Brown."

0867.   Baar, Stephen Ronald.   "Novel into Film: The Adaptation
        of American Renaissance Symbolic Fiction." DAI,
        34 (1974), 4186A (The University of Utah).
        On adaptations of The Scarlet Letter, The House
        of the Seven Gables, and Melville's Moby Dick.

0868.   Estrin, Mark Walter.   "Dramatizations of American
        Fiction: Hawthorne and Melville on Stage and
        Screen." DAI, 30 (1970), 3428A (New York
        University).

0869.   _____.   "Triumphant Ignominy: The Scarlet Letter
        on the Screen." Literature/Film Quarterly, 2
        (1974), 110-122.   A shorter version reprinted
        in The Classic American Novel and the Movies.
        Ed. Gerald Peary and Roger Shatzkin.   New York:
        Frederick Ungar, 1977, pp. 20-29.

0870.   Gollin, Rita.   "Hawthorne on Film." Hawthorne Society
        Newsletter, 5, No. 2 (1979), 6-7.

0871.   Kaplan, E. Ann.   "The House of the Seven Gables:
        Hawthorne's `Fancy Pictures' on Film." In The
        Classic American Novel and the Movies.   Ed. Gerald
        Peary and Roger Shatzkin.   New York: Frederick
        Ungar Publishing, 1977, pp. 30-41.

0872.   Smith, Julian.   "Hester, Sweet Hester Prynne--The
        Scarlet Letter in the Movie Market Place."
        Literature/Film Quarterly, 2 (1974), 100-109.

0873.   Welsh, James M. and Richard Keenan.   "Wim Wenders
        and Nathaniel Hawthorne: From The Scarlet Letter
        to Der Scharlachrote Buchstabe."   Literature/Film
        Quarterly, 6 (1978), 175-179.

BEN HECHT

0874.   Brown, Geoff.   "`Better Than Metro Isn't Good Enough:'
        Hecht and MacArthur's Own Movies."   Sight and
        Sound, 44 (1975), 153-155, 196.

0875.   Corliss, Richard.   "Ben Hecht."   In The Hollywood
        Screenwriters.   Ed. Richard Corliss.   New York:
        Avon Books, 1972, pp. 65-92.   Reprinted in Talking
        Pictures: Screenwriters in the American Cinema
        1927-1973.   Woodstock, N.Y.: The Overlook Press,
        1974, pp. 2-24.

0876.   Fetherling, Doug.   "1001 Afternoons in Hollywood"
        and "Shelley in Chains."   In The Five Lives of
        Ben Hecht.   New York: New York Zoetrope, 1977,
        pp. 87-104 and pp. 140-155.

0877.   Fuller, Stephen.   "Ben Hecht: A Sampler."   Film
        Comment, 6 (Winter 1970-1971), 32-39.
        Hecht's comments on his screenplays.

0878.   Hecht, Ben.   A Child of the Century.   New York:
        Simon and Schuster, 1954, pp. 466-514.
        On Hecht's career in Hollywood.

0879.   _____.   "My Testimonial to the Movies: The
        Frank Confessions of a Literary Man Who Puts
        into Words What Others Have Only Dared Think."
        Theatre Magazine, 49 (June 1929), 18.

0880.   Leonard, William T.   "The Scoundrel."   Films in
        Review, 26 (1975), 143-149.
        Making of the Hecht-MacArthur film with Noel Coward.

0881.   Martin, Jeffrey Brown.   Ben Hecht: Hollywood
        Screenwriter.   Ann Arbor: UMI Research Press,
        1985.

JOSEPH HELLER

0882.   Clancy, Jack.   "The Film and the Book: Joseph Heller
        and D.H. Lawrence on the Screen."   Meanjin Quarterly,
        3 (Autumn 1971), 96-97, 99-101.
        On Catch-22 and Women in Love.

0883.   Heller, Joseph.   "On Translating `Catch-22' into
        a Movie."   In A `Catch-22' Casebook.   Ed. Frederick
        Kiley and Walter McDonald.   New York: Thomas
        Y. Crowell, 1973, pp. 346-362.   A shortened version
        reprinted as "Catch-22: Did the Author Catch
        the Movie?"   In The Modern American Novel and
        the Movies.   Ed. Gerald Peary and Roger Shatzkin.
        New York: Fredrick Ungar, 1978, pp. 256-265.

0884.   McHenry, G.B.   "Significant Corn: <u>Catch-22</u>."   <u>Critical</u>
        <u>Review</u>, 9 (1966), 133-144.

0885.   Marcus, Fred H. and Paul Zall.   "<u>Catch-22</u>: Is Fidelity
        an Asset?"   In <u>Film and Literature: Contrasts</u>
        <u>in Media</u>.   Ed. Fred H. Marcus.   Scranton, Pa.:
        Chandler Publishing Co., 1971, pp. 127-136.

0886.   Miller, Wayne Charles.   "`Catch-22': Joseph Heller's
        Portrait of American Culture--The Missing Portrait
        in Mike Nichols' Movie."   In <u>A `Catch-22' Casebook</u>.
        Ed. Frederick Kiley and Walter McDonald.   New
        York: Thomas Y. Crowell, 1973, pp. 383-390.

0887.   Standiford, Les.   "Novels into Film: <u>Catch-22</u> as
        Watershed."   <u>Southern Humanities Review</u>, 8 (1974),
        19-25.   Reprinted in <u>Critical Essays on Joseph</u>
        <u>Heller</u>.   Ed. James Nagel.   Boston: G.K. Hall,
        1984, pp. 227-232.

0888.   Thegze, Chuck.   "`I See Everything Twice': An Examination
        of <u>Catch-22</u>."   <u>Film Quarterly</u>, 24 (Fall 1970),
        7-17.

0889.   Williams, Melvin G.   "<u>Catch:22</u>: What the Movie Audiences
        Miss."   <u>Christianity and Literature</u>, 23, No. 4
        (1974), 21-25.

LILLIAN HELLMAN

0890.   Dick, Bernard.   <u>Lillian Hellman in Hollywood</u>.   East
        Brunswick, N.J.: Associated University Presses,
        1982.
        Works discussed: <u>The Children's Hour</u>, <u>The Little</u>
        <u>Foxes</u>, <u>Dead End</u>, <u>Another Part of the Forest</u>, <u>Watch</u>
        <u>on the Rhine</u>, <u>North Star</u>, <u>The Searching Wind</u>, <u>Toys</u>
        <u>in the Attic</u>, <u>The Chase</u>, and <u>Julia</u>.

0891.   Easton, Carol.   "The North Star."   In <u>The Search</u>
        <u>for Sam Goldwyn</u>.   New York: William Morrow, 1976,
        pp. 218-222.

0892.   Issacs, Edith.   "Lillian Hellman, a Playwright on
        the March."   <u>Theatre Arts</u>, 28 (Jan. 1944), 19-24.
        Analyzes Hellman's plays and scripts.

0893.   McCreadie, Marsha.   "`Julia"--Memory in <u>Pentimento</u>
        and on Film."   <u>Literature/Film Quarterly</u>, 7 (1979),
        260-269.

ERNEST HEMINGWAY

0894.   Adams, Michael.   "Hemingway Filmography."   <u>Fitzgerald/</u>
        <u>Hemingway Annual 1977</u>.   Ed. Margaret M. Duggan
        and Richard Layman.   Detroit: Gale Research,
        1977, pp. 219-232.

0895.   Arnold, Robert, Nicholas Humy, and Ana Lopez. "Rereading
         Adaptations: A Farewell to Arms." Iris, 1, No. 1
         (1983), 101-114.

0896.   Coleman, Arthur. "Hemingway's The Spanish Earth."
         Hemingway Review, 2 (Fall 1982), 64-67.

0897.   Deutelbaum, Marshall. "Showing the Strings That
         Don't Show: Mise-en-scène and Meaning in To Have
         and Have Not." North Dakota Quarterly, 51 (Summer
         1983), 61-77

0898.   Horrigan, William. "Dying Without Death: Borzage's
         A Farewell to Arms." In The Classic American
         Novel and the Movies. Ed. Gerald Peary and Roger
         Shatzkin. New York: Frederick Ungar, 1977,
         pp. 297-304.

0899.   Kaminsky, Stuart M. "The Killers." Take One, 4,
         No. 6 (1974), 17-19.

0900.   _____. "Literary Adaptation: The Killers--
         Hemingway, Film Noir, and the Terror of Daylight."
         In American Film Genres. Chicago: Nelson-Hall,
         1985, pp. 81-96.

0901.   Kaplan, E. Ann. "Hemingway, Hollywood, and Female
         Representation: The Macomber Affair." Literature/
         Film Quarterly, 13 (1985), 22-28.

0902.   Laurence, Frank M. "Death in the Matinee: The Film
         Endings of Hemingway's Fiction." Literature/Film
         Quarterly, 2 (1974), 44-51.

0903.   _____. Hemingway and the Movies. Jackson:
         University Press of Mississippi, 1981.
         Adaptations discussed: A Farewell to Arms (1932
         and 1958), For Whom the Bell Tolls, To Have and
         Have Not, The Killers (1946 and 1964), The Macomber
         Affair (adaptation of "The Short Happy Life of Francis
         Macomber"), Under My Skin (adaptation of "My Old
         Man"), The Breaking Point (adaptation of To Have
         and Have Not), The Snows of Kilimanjaro, The Sun
         Also Rises, The Gun Runners (adaptation of To Have
         and Have Not), The Old Man and the Sea, Hemingway's
         Adventures of a Young Man (adaptation of the Nick
         Adams stories), and Islands in the Stream.

0904.   Lillich, Richard B. "Hemingway on the Screen."
         Films in Review, 10 (1959), 208-218.

0905.   Marcus, Mordecai. "A Farewell to Arms: Novel into
         Film." Journal of the Central Mississippi Valley
         American Studies Association, 2 (1961), 69-71.

0906.   Morsberger, Robert E. "`That Hemingway Kind of
         Love': Macomber in the Movies." Literature/Film
         Quarterly, 4 (1976), 54-59.

0907.   Murphy, Kathleen Ann. "Howard Hawks: An American
          Auteur in the Hemingway Tradition." DAI, 38
          (1978), 5097-5098A (The University of Washington).
        A comparison of Hawks' films with Hemingway's fiction.

0908.   Nadeau, Robert L. "Film and Mythic Heroism: Sturges's
          Old Man." In The Modern American Novel and the
          Movies. Ed. Gerald Peary and Roger Shatzkin.
          New York: Frederick Ungar, 1978, pp. 199-203.
        On The Old Man and the Sea.

0909.   Phillips, Gene D. Hemingway and Film. New York:
          Frederick Ungar, 1980.
        Adaptations discussed: A Farewell to Arms (1932
        and 1958), For Whom the Bell Tolls, To Have and
        Have Not, The Killers (1946 and 1964), The Macomber
        Affair (adaptation of "The Short Happy Life of Francis
        Macomber), Under My Skin (adaptation of "My Old
        Man"), The Breaking Point (adaptation of To Have
        and Have Not), The Snows of Kilimanjaro, The Sun
        Also Rises, The Gun Runners (adaptation of To Have
        and Have Not), The Old Man and the Sea, Hemingway's
        Adventures of a Young Man (adaptation of the Nick
        Adams stories), and Islands in the Stream.

0910.   Pohl, Constance. "For Whom the Bells Toll: The
          `Unmaking' of a Political Film." In The Modern
          American Novel and the Movies. Ed. Gerald Peary
          and Roger Shatzkin. New York: Frederick Ungar,
          1978, pp. 317-324.

0911.   Roth, Phillip. "The Sun Also Rises: Photography
          Does Not a Movie Make." In The Classic American
          Novel and the Film. Ed. Gerald Peary and Roger
          Shatzkin. New York: Frederick Ungar, 1977,
          pp. 268-271.

0912.   Rothman, William. "To Have and Have Not: To Have
          and Have Not Adapted a Novel." In The Modern
          American Novel and the Movies. Ed. Gerald Peary
          and Roger Shatzkin. New York: Frederick Ungar,
          1978, pp. 70-79.

0913.   Wood, Robin. "To Have (written) and Have Not
          (directed)." In Movies and Methods. Ed. Bill
          Nichols. Berkeley: University of California
          Press, 1976, pp. 297-305.
        In an analysis of the auteur theory, Wood analyzes
        Hemingway's novel and the Faulkner-Furthman script
        to determine Howard Hawk's contribution to To Have
        and Have Not.

JOSEPH HERGESHEIMER

0914.   Bodeen, DeWitt. "Joseph Hergesheimer and Films."
          Films in Review, 28 (1977), 538-545.

JAMES LEO HERLIHY

0915. Birdsall, Eric R. and Fred H. Marcus. "Schlesinger's
       Midnight Cowboy: Creating a Classic." In Film
       and Literature: Contrasts in Media. Ed. Fred
       H. Marcus. Scranton, Pa.: Chandler Publishing
       Co., 1971, pp. 178-189.

0916. Fiore, Robert L. "The Picaresque Tradition in Midnight
       Cowboy." Literature/Film Quarterly, 3 (1975),
       270-276.

0917. _____. "Lazarillo de Tormes and Midnight Cowboy:
       The Picaresque Model and Mode." In Studies in
       Honor of Everett W. Hesse. Ed. William C. McCrady
       and Jose Madrigal. Lincoln, Neb.: Society of
       Spanish and Spanish-American Studies, 1981,
       pp. 81-97.

0918. Phillips, Gene D. "Midnight Cowboy." In his John
       Schlesinger. Boston: Twayne Publishers, 1981,
       pp. 112-131.

JAMES HILTON

0919. Hilton, James. "Literature and Hollywood." The
       Atlantic Monthly, 178 (Dec. 1946), 130-136.

0920. _____. "A Novelist Looks at the Screen."
       Screen Writer, 1 (Nov. 1945), 30-34.

JOHN IRVING

0921. Bawer, Bruce. "The World According to Garp: Novel
       to Film." Bennington Review, No. 15 (Summer
       1983), pp. 74-79.

0922. Horton, Andrew. "The World According to Garp."
       In his The Films of George Roy Hill. New York:
       Columbia University Press, 1984, pp. 150-167.

0923. Jones, Henry T. "Checking in While Others Run to
       Check Out of Tony Richardson's Hotel New
       Hampshire." Literature/Film Quarterly, 13 (1985),
       66-69.

HENRY JAMES

0924. Allen, Jeanne Thomas. "Aspects of Narration in
       The Turn of the Screw and `The Innocents.'"
       DAI, 37 (1976), 2846-2847A (The University of
       Iowa).

0925. _____. "Turn of the Screw and The Innocents:
       Two Types of Ambiguity." In The Classic American
       Novel and the Movies. Ed. Gerald Peary and Roger
       Shatzkin. New York: Frederick Ungar, 1977,
       pp. 132-142.

0926. Ashton, Jean. "Reflecting Consciousness: Three
          Approaches to Henry James." Literature/Film
          Quarterly, 4 (1976), 230-239.
       On Bogdanovich's Daisy Miller, Rivette's Celine
       et Julie vont en boteau (loosely based on James's
       "The Other House"), and Chabrol's The Bench of
       Desolation.

0927. Bodeen, DeWitt. "Henry James into Film." Films
          in Review, 28 (1977), 163-170.

0928. Bradbury, Nicola. "Filming James." Essays in Criticism,
          29 (1979), 293-301.
       On James Ivory's The Europeans.

0929. Carlson, Jerry W. "Washington Square and The Heiress:
          Comparing Artistic Forms." In The Classic American
          Novel and the Movies. Ed. Gerald Peary and Roger
          Shatzkin. New York: Frederick Ungar, 1977,
          pp. 95-104.

0930. Dawson, Jan. "The Continental Divide: Filming Henry
          James." Sight and Sound, 43 (Winter 1973-74),
          12-15. Reprinted as "Daisy Miller: An Interview
          with Peter Bogdanovich." In The Classic American
          Novel and the Movies. Ed. Gerald Peary and
          Roger Shatzkin. New York: Frederick Ungar, 1977,
          pp. 83-89.

0931. Grenier, Richard. "The Bostonians Inside Out."
          Commentary, 78 (Oct. 1984), 60-65.
       On James Ivory's adaptation.

0932. Hirsh, Allen. "The Europeans: Henry James, James
          Ivory, `And That Nice Mr. Emerson.'" Literature/Film
          Quarterly, 11 (1983), 112-119.

0933. Klein, Michael. "Truffaut's Sanctuary: "The Green
          Room." Film Quarterly, 34 (Fall 1980), 15-20.
       Film is an adaptation of "The Altar of the Dead"
       and "The Lesson of the Master."

0934. Liggera, J.J. "`She Would Have Appreciated One's
          Esteem': Peter Bogdanovich's Daisy Miller."
          Literature/Film Quarterly, 9 (1981), 15-21.

0935. Long, Robert Emmet. "Adaptations of Henry James'
          Fiction for Drama, Opera, and Films; With a Checklist
          of New York Theatre Critics' Reviews." American
          Literary Realism, 1870-1910 (University of Texas
          at Arlington), 4 (1971), 268-278.

0936. Murphy, Kathleen. "Daisy Miller: An International
          Episode." Movietone News, No. 33 (1974), pp. 13-16.
          Reprinted in The Classic American Novel and the
          Movies. Ed. Gerald Peary and Roger Shatzkin.
          New York: Frederick Ungar, 1977, pp. 90-94.

0937. Palmer, James W.   "Cinematic Ambiguity: James's
         The Turn of the Screw and Clayton's The Innocents."
         Literature/Film Quarterly, 5 (1977), 198-215.

0938. Shields, John C. "Daisy Miller: Bogdanovich's Film
         and James' Nouvelle." Literature/Film Quarterly,
         11 (1983), 105-111.

0939. Tintner, Adeline R.   "Truffaut's La Chambre Verte:
         Homage to Henry James." Literature/Film Quarterly,
         8 (1980), 78-83.

0940. Vendetti, James Anthony. "A Critical Interpretation
         of Jack Clayton's Film The Innocents." DAI,
         36 (1976), 4816-4817A (Columbia University Teachers
         College).

0941. Vineberg, Steve. "The Responsibility of the Adapter:
         The Bostonians on Film." Arizona Quarterly,
         41 (1985), 223-230.

KEN KESEY

0942. Billingsley, Ronald G. and James W. Palmer. "Milos
         Forman's Cuckoo's Nest: Reality Unredeemed."
         Studies in the Humanities, 7, No. 1 (1978), 14-18.

0943. Haskell, Molly. "Kesey Cured: Forman's Sweet Insanity."
         In The Modern American Novel and the Film. Ed. Gerald
         Peary and Roger Shatzkin. New York: Frederick
         Ungar, 1978, pp. 266-271.
         on One Flew Over the Cuckcoo's Nest.

0944. McCreadie, Marsha.   "One Flew Over the Cuckoo's
         Nest: Some Reasons for One Happy Adaptation."
         Literature/Film Quarterly, 5 (1977), 125-131.

0945. Palumbo, Donald. "Kesey's and Forman's One Flew
         Over the Cuckoo's Nest: The Metamorphosis of
         Metamorphoses as Novel Becomes Film." CEA Critic,
         45 (Jan. 1983), 25-32.

0946. Safer, Elaine B.   "`It's the Truth Even If It Didn't
         Happen': Ken Kesey's One Flew Over the Cuckoo's
         Nest." Literature/Film Quarterly, 5 (1977),
         132-141.

STEPHEN KING

0947. Ciment, Michel. "Third Interview: The Shining."
         In Kubrick. Trans. Gilbert Adair. New York:
         Holt, Rinehart and Winston, 1983, pp. 181-197.

0948. Cook, David A. "American Horror: The Shining."
         Literature/Film Quarterly (12), 2-4.

0949.   Ehlers, Leigh A.   "<u>Carrie</u>: Book and Film."   In <u>Ideas</u>
        <u>of Order in Literature and Film</u>.   Ed. Peter Ruppert.
        Tallahassee: University Presses of Florida, 1980,
        pp. 39-50.   Reprinted in <u>Literature/Film Quarterly</u>,
        9 (1981), 32-39.

0950.   Hoile, Christopher.   "The Uncanny and the Fairy
        Tale in Kubrick's <u>The Shining</u>."   <u>Literature/Film</u>
        <u>Quarterly</u>, 12 (1984), 5-12.

0951.   Nelson, Thomas Allen.   "Remembrance of Things
        Forgotten: <u>The Shining</u>."   In his <u>Kubrick: Inside</u>
        <u>a Film Artist's Maze</u>.   Bloomington: Indiana University
        Press, 1982, pp. 197-231.

JOHN KNOWLES

0952.   Heinz, Linda and Roy Huss.   "<u>A Separate Peace</u>: Filming
        the War Within."   <u>Literature/Film Quarterly</u>,
        3 (1975), 160-171.

HANS KONINGSBERGER

0953.   Koningsberger, Hans.   "From Book to Film--Via John
        Huston."   <u>Film Quarterly</u>, 22 (Spring 1969), 2-4.
        On Huston's adaptation of Koningsberger's novel
        <u>A Walk With Love and Death</u>.

JERZY KOSINSKI

0954.   Wilson, Robert F., Jr.   "<u>Being There</u> at the End."
        <u>Literature/Film Quarterly</u>, 9 (1981), 59-62.

JOHN HOWARD LAWSON

0955.   Carr, Gary.   <u>The Left Side of Paradise: The Screenwriting</u>
        <u>of John Howard Lawson</u>.   Ann Arbor: UMI Research
        Press, 1984.

0956.   Lawson, John Howard.   <u>Film: The Creative Process:</u>
        <u>The Search For an Audio-Visual Language and</u>
        <u>Structure</u>.   New York: Hill and Wang, 1964.
        History of film has a chapter on film and theatre
        and a chapter on film and the novel.

0957.   _____.   <u>Theory and Technique of Playwriting</u>
        <u>and Screenwriting</u>.   New York: G.P. Putnam's Sons,
        1949.

SINCLAIR LEWIS

0958.   Bluestone, George.   "Adaptation or Evasion: <u>Elmer</u>
        <u>Gantry</u>."   <u>Film Quarterly</u>, 14 (Spring 1961), 15-19.

0959.   LaValley, Albert J.   "<u>Dodsworth</u>: The Virtues of
        Unfaithfulness."   In <u>The Classic American Novel</u>
        <u>and the Movies</u>.   Ed. Gerald Peary and Roger Shatzkin.
        New York: Frederick Ungar, 1977, pp. 272-285.

0960.   Munden, Kenneth W. "Sinclair Lewis and the Movies."
        Cinema Journal, 12 (Fall 1972), 46-56.

0961.   Smoller, Sanford J. "Babbitt: The `Booboisie' and
        Its Discontents." In The Classic American Novel
        and the Movies. Ed. Gerald Peary and Roger Shatzkin.
        New York: Frederick Ungar, 1977, pp. 226-238.

0962.   Turim, Maureen. "I Married a Doctor: Main Street
        Meets Hollywood." In The Classic American Novel
        and the Movies. Ed. Gerald Peary and Roger Shatzkin.
        New York: Frederick Ungar, 1977, pp. 206-217.

VACHEL LINDSAY

0963.   Lindsay, Vachel. The Art of the Moving Picture.
        New York: The Macmillan Company, 1922; rpt. New
        York: Liveright, 1970. A chapter, "Thirty Differences
        Between the Photoplays and the Stage," reprinted
        in Focus on Film and Theatre. Ed. James Hurt.
        Englewood Cliffs: Prentice-Hall, 1974, pp. 18-28.

0964.   Wolfe, Glenn J. "Vachel Lindsay: The Poet as Film
        Theorist." DA, 26 (1965), 1222 (The State University
        of Iowa).

JACK LONDON

0965.   Flinn, Tom and John Davis. "The Sea Wolf: Warners'
        War of the Wolf." In The Classic American Novel
        and the Movies. Ed. Gerald Peary and Roger Shatzkin.
        New York: Frederick Ungar, 1977, pp. 192-205.

MARY MCCARTHY

0966.   Kael, Pauline. "The Making of The Group." In Kiss
        Kiss Bang Bang. Boston: Little, Brown and Co.,
        1968, pp. 67-100.

0967.   Sirkin, Elliott. "The Group." Film Comment, 8
        (Sept.-Oct. 1972), 66-68.

HORACE MCCOY

0968.   Benair, Jonathan. "They Shoot Horses, Don't They?"
        Film Society Review, 5, No. 9 (1970), 32-37.

0969.   Dempsey, Michael. "Trials and Traumas: James Poe,
        An Interview." Film Comment, 6 (Winter 1970-1971),
        65-73. Reprinted in The Hollywood Screenwriters.
        Ed. Richard Corliss. New York: Avon Books, 1972,
        pp. 181-204.
        Interview concerns Poe's script of They Shoot Horses,
        Don't They?

0970.   Warshow, Paul. "They Shoot Horses, Don't They?:
        The Unreal McCoy." In The Modern American Novel
        and the Movies. Ed. Gerald Peary and Roger Shatzkin.
        New York: Frederick Ungar, 1978, pp. 29-39.

CARSON MCCULLERS

0971.   Aldridge, Robert. "The Heart Is a Lonely Hunter:
        Two Planetary Systems." In The Modern American
        Novel and the Movies. Ed. Gerald Peary and Roger
        Shatzkin. New York: Frederick Ungar, 1978,
        pp. 119-130.

0972.   Giannetti, Louis D. "The Member of the Wedding."
        Literature/Film Quarterly, 4 (1976), 28-38.

0973.   Roud, Richard. "The Empty Streets." Sight and
        Sound, 26 (Spring 1957), 191-195.
        On The Member of the Wedding.

LARRY MCMURTRY

0974.   Degenfelder, E. Pauline. "McMurtry and the Movies:
        Hud and The Last Picture Show." Western Humanities
        Review, 29 (1975), 81-91.

0975.   Folson, James K. "Shane and Hud: Two Stories in
        Search of a Medium." Western Humanities Review,
        24 (1970), 359-372.

0976.   Gerlach, John. "Last Picture Show and One More
        Adaptation." Literature/Film Quarterly, 1 (1973),
        161-166.

0977.   McMurtry, Larry. "Cowboys, Movies, Myths, and Cadillacs:
        Realism in the Western." In Man and the Movies.
        Ed. W.R. Robinson. Baltimore: Penguin Books,
        1967, pp. 46-52.

0978.   _____. "On Learning to Write for the Movies."
        American Film, 1 (Oct. 1975), 9-12.

0979.   Wilson, Robert F., Jr. "Which is the Real Last
        Picture Show?" Literature/Film Quarterly, 1
        (1973), 167-169.

RACHEL MADDUX

0980.   Isaacs, Neil D. "Fiction into Film." In Fiction
        into Film: A Walk in the Spring Rain. Knoxville:
        University of Tennessee Press, 1970, pp. 135-227.
        On the film adaptation of Maddux's novella A Walk
        in the Spring Rain.

NORMAN MAILER

0981.   Jurkiewicz, Kenneth. "Mailer and the Movies: An
        American Writer Confronts the Mass Culture."
        DAI, 40 (1979), 248-249A (The University of Detroit).

0982.   McCardell, William Paul. "The `Existential' Films
        of Norman Mailer: A Comparison of His Fiction
        and His Nonfiction." DAI, 37 (1976), 2185A (Temple
        University).

0983.   Mailer, Norman. "A Course in Filmmaking." In his
        <u>Maidstone: A Mystery</u>. New York: New American
        Library, 1971, pp. 139-180.

0984.   _____. "Some Dirt in the Talk" and "A Course
        in Filmmaking." In his <u>Existential Errands</u>.
        Boston: Little, Brown, and Co., 1972, pp. 89-123,
        123-168.
        First essay is on the filming of Mailer's film <u>Wild
        90</u>; the second is on Mailer's theory of improvisational
        filmmaking.

0985.   _____. "A Transit to Narcissus." <u>New York
        Review of Books</u>, 20 (17 May 1973), 3-10. Reprinted
        in <u>Closeup: Last Tango in Paris</u>. Ed. Kent
        E. Carroll. New York: Grove Press, Inc., 1973,
        pp. 165. Reprinted as "Tango, Last Tango."
        In his <u>Pieces and Pontifications</u>. Boston: Little,
        Brown and Co., 1982, pp. 115-133.
        On Bertolucci's <u>Last Tango in Paris</u>.

0986.   _____. "The Writer and Hollywood." <u>Film Heritage</u>,
        2 (Fall 1966), 23. Reprinted as "<u>Naked and the
        Dead</u>: Naked Before the Camera." In <u>The Modern
        American Novel and the Movies</u>. Ed. Gerald Peary
        and Roger Shatzkin. New York: Frederick Ungar,
        1978, pp. 187-88.

HERMAN MELVILLE

0987.   Atkins, Thomas. "<u>Moby Dick</u>: An Interview with Ray
        Bradbury." In <u>The Classic American Novel and
        the Movies</u>. Ed. Gerald Peary and Roger Shatzkin.
        New York: Frederick Ungar Publishing, 1977, pp. 42-51.
        Bradbury wrote the script for Huston's adaptation.

0988.   Bluestone, George. "<u>Bartleby</u>: The Tale, the Film."
        In <u>Melville Annual 1965, A Symposium: Bartleby
        the Scrivener</u>. Ed. Howard P. Vincent. Kent:
        Kent State University Press, 1966, pp. 45-54.
        Bluestone directed the adaptation of <u>Bartleby</u>.

0989.   Bradt, David Richard. "From Fiction to Film: An
        Analysis of Aesthetic and Cultural Implications
        in the Adaptations of Two American Novellas."
        <u>DAI</u>, 35 (1974), 3671-3672A (Washington State
        University).
        On <u>Billy Budd</u> and West's <u>Miss Lonelyhearts</u>.

0990.   French, Brandon. "<u>Moby Dick</u>: Lost at Sea." In
        <u>The Classic American Novel and the Movies</u>. Ed. Gerald
        Peary and Roger Shatzkin. New York: Frederick
        Ungar Publishing, 1977, pp. 52-61.
        On Huston's adaptation.

0991.   Friel, Joseph C. "Ustinov's Film <u>Billy Budd</u>, a
        Study in the Process of Adaptation: Novel, to
        Play to Film." <u>Literature/Film Quarterly</u>, 4
        (1976), 271-284.

0992.   Fuller, Stanley. "Melville on the Screen." Films in Review, 19 (1968), 358-363.

0993.   Haag, John. "Bartleby-ing for the Camera." In Melville Annual 1965, A Symposium: Bartleby the Scrivener. Ed. Howard P. Vincent. Kent: Kent State University Press, 1966, pp. 55-63.
Haag plays Barleby in Bluestone's adaptation.

0994.   Hillway, Tyrus. "Hollywood Hunts the Whale." Colorado Quarterly, 5 (1957), 298-305.
Huston's adaptation of Moby Dick.

0995.   Nadeau, Robert L. "Billy Budd: Melville's Sailor in the Sixties." In The Classic American Novel and the Movies. Ed. Gerald Peary and Roger Shatzkin. New York: Frederick Ungar, 1977, pp. 124-131.

0996.   Stern, Milton R. "The Whale and the Minnow: Moby Dick and the Movies." College English, 17 (1956), 470-473.
Huston's adaptation.

0997.   Stone, Edward. "Ahab Gets the Girl, or Herman Melville Goes to the Movies." Literature/Film Quarterly, 3 (1975), 172-181.

W.S. MERWIN

0998.   Quinn, Theodore Kinget. "W.S. Merwin: A Study in Poetry and Film." DAI, 33 (1973), 3665-3666A (The University of Iowa).

ARTHUR MILLER

0999.   Benedek, Laslo. "Directing Death of a Salesman for the Screen." Theatre Arts, 36 (Jan. 1952), 36-37, 87.

1000.   _____. "Play into Picture." Sight and Sound, 22 (Oct.-Dec. 1952), 82-84.
The director of Death of a Salesman discusses his adaptation.

1001.   O'Grady, Gerald. "The Dance of The Misfits." Journal of Aesthetic Education, 5 (April 1971), 75-89.

1002.   Press, David P. "The Misfits: The Western Gunned Down." Studies in the Humanities, 8 (1980), 41-44.

HENRY MILLER

1003.   Delpino, Louis. "Transliteration: Joseph Strick's Tropic of Cancer." Film Heritage, 6 (Fall 1970), 27-29.

1004.   Miller, Henry. "The Golden Age" and "Reflections
         on `Extasy.'" In The Cosmological Eye. Norfolk,
         Conn.: New Directions, 1939, pp. 47-62 and pp. 63-74.

1005.   _____. "Raimu." In The Wisdom of the Heart.
         Norfolk, Conn.: New Directions, 1941, pp. 47-62.
         On French and American films.

                    MARGARET MITCHELL

1006.   Behlmer, Rudy, ed. "Gone With the Wind." In Memo
         From: David O. Selznick. New York: The Viking
         Press, 1972, pp. 137-247.

1007.   Curran, Trisha. "Gone With the Wind: An American
         Tragedy." Southern Quarterly, 19 (Spring-Summer
         1981), 47-57.

1008.   Flamini, Roland. "Fade In: Front of Tara: Long
         Shot." In his Scarlett, Rhett, and a Cast of
         Thousands: The Filming of Gone With the Wind.
         New York: Macmillan, 1975, pp. 194-217.
         On the writing of the script of Gone With the Wind.

1009.   Harwell, Richard. "Introduction." In GWTW: The
         Screenplay. New York: Macmillan Publishing,
         1980. pp. 7-44.
         On the writing of the screenplay.

1010.   Lambert, Gavin. "Speaking of Tara." In his GWTW:
         The Making Of Gone With the Wind." Boston:
         Little, Brown and Co., 1973, pp. 157-204.
         Draws some comparison between novel and film.

1011.   Pauly, Thomas H. "Gone With the Wind and The Grapes
         of Wrath as Hollywood Histories of the Depression."
         Journal of Popular Film, 3 (1974), 202-218.
         Reprinted in Movies as Artifacts: Cultural Criticism
         of Popular Film. Ed. Michael T. Marsden, John
         G. Nachbar, and Sam L. Grogg, Jr. Chicago:
         Nelson-Hall, 1982, pp. 164-176. Reprinted in
         Gone With the Wind as Book and Film. Ed. Richard
         Harwell. Columbia: University of South Carolina
         Press, 1983, pp. 218-228.

1012.   Pratt, William. "The Differences." In his Scarlet
         Fever: The Ultimate Pictoral Treasury of Gone
         With the Wind. New York: Macmillan Publishing,
         1977, pp. 204-212.
         On the differences between the novel and the film.

1013.   Richey, Rodney. "The Other Authors of Gone With
         the Wind." American Classic Film, 5, No. 6 (1980),
         14-16.
         On the writing of the script.

1014. Wood, Gerald. "From The Clansman and Birth of a
       Nation to Gone With the Wind: The Loss of American
       Innocence." In Recasting: Gone With the Wind
       in American Culture. Ed. Darden Asbury Pyron.
       Miami: University Press of Florida, 1983, pp. 123-136.

                     WRIGHT MORRIS

1015. Machann, Ginny Brown. "Ceremony at Lone Tree and
       Badlands: The Starkweather Case and the Nebraska
       Plains." Prairie Schooner, 53 (1979), 165-172.

                     VLADIMIR NABOKOV

1016. Appel, Alfred, Jr. "The End of the Road: Dark Cinema
       and Lolita." Film Comment, 10 (Sept.-Oct. 1974),
       25-31.
       Parallels between film noir and Nabokov's novel.

1017. _____. "The Eyehole of Knowledge: Voyeuristic
       Games in Film and Literature." Film Comment,
       9 (May-June 1973), 20-26.
       Film's influence on Lolita.

1018. _____. Nabokov's Dark Cinema. New York: Oxford
       University Press, 1974.
       Influence of film on Nabokov's fiction.

1019. _____. "Nabokov's Dark Cinema: A Diptych."
       TriQuarterly, 3 (1973), 267-273. Reprinted in
       The Bitter Air of Exile: Russian Writers in the
       West. Ed. Simon Karlinsky and Alfred Appel,
       Jr. Berkeley: University of California Press,
       1977, pp. 196-273.
       A portion of Nabokov's Dark Cinema; discussion of
       Kubrick's film of Lolita.

1020. _____. "Tristram in Movielove: Lolita at the
       Movies." Russian Literature Triquarterly, 7
       (1973), pp. 343-388.
       Nabokov's attitude toward film.

1021. Bienstock, Beverly Gray. "Film Imagery in Bend
       Sinister." In Nabokov's Fifth Arc: Nabokov and
       Others on His Life's Work. Ed. J.E. Rivers and
       Charles Nicol. Austin: University of Texas Press,
       1982, pp. 125-138.

1022. Burdick, Dolores M. "'The Line Down the Middle':
       Politics and Sexuality in Fassbinder's Despair."
       In Fearful Symmetry: Doubles and Doubling in
       Literature and Film. Ed. Eugene J. Crook.
       Tallahassee: University Presses of Florida, 1981,
       pp. 138-148.

1023. French, Brandon. "The Celluloid Lolita: A Not-So-Crazy
       Quilt." In The Modern American Novel and the
       Movies. Ed. Gerald Peary and Roger Shatzkin.
       New York: Frederick Ungar, 1978, pp. 224-235.

1024. Galperin, William H. "Kubrick's `Lolita': Humbert
       into Quilty." <u>Bennington Review</u>, No. 15 (Summer
       1983), pp. 65-69.

1025. Nabokov, Vladimir. "Foreward." In <u>Lolita: A
       Screenplay</u>. New York: McGraw-Hill, 1974,
       pp. vii-xiii.
       Nabokov recounts the making of the film.

1026. Nelson, Thomas Allen. "<u>Lolita</u>: Kubrick in Nabokovland."
       In <u>Kubrick: Inside a Film Artist's Maze</u>. Bloomington:
       Indiana University Press, 1982, pp. 54-78.

1027. Niebuhr, Reinhold. "<u>Lolita</u>." <u>Show</u>, 2 (August 1962),
       69.

1028. Schuman, Samuel. "<u>Lolita</u>: Novel and Screenplay."
       <u>College English</u>, 5 (1978), 195-204.

JOHN NICHOLS

1029. Pellow, G. Kenneth. "The Transformation of <u>The
       Sterile Cuckoo</u>." <u>Literature/Film Quarterly</u> 5
       (1977), 252-257.

ANAIS NIN

1030. Scholar, Nancy. "Anais Nin's <u>House of Incest</u> and
       Ingmar Bergman's <u>Persona</u>: Two Variations of a
       Theme." <u>Literature/Film Quarterly</u>, 7 (1979),
       47-59.

FRANK NORRIS

1031. Finler, Joel W. "Norris and <u>McTeague</u>," <u>Greed</u>: Prologue,"
       "<u>Greed</u>: Courtship," <u>Greed</u>: Marriage," "<u>Greed</u>:
       Decline," <u>Greed</u> and Other Stroheim." In <u>Stroheim</u>.
       Berkeley: University of California Press, 1968,
       pp. 23-35, pp. 36-43, pp. 44-53, pp. 54-62, pp. 63-75,
       pp. 76-82.
       Finler's monograph is the only book-length study
       of Stroheim's work that includes a detailed comparison
       of Norris's novel and Stroheim's film.

1032. Fulton, A.R. "Stroheim's <u>Greed</u>." <u>Films in Review</u>,
       6 (1955), 263-268.

1033. Mottram, Ron. "Impulse Toward the Visible: Frank
       Norris and Photographic Representation." <u>Texas
       Studies in Language and Literature</u>, 25 (1983),
       574-596.
       Influence of film and photography on Norris.

1034. Wead, George. "Frank Norris: His Share of <u>Greed</u>."
       In <u>The Classic American Novel and the Movies</u>.
       Ed. Gerald Peary and Roger Shatzkin. New York:
       Frederick Ungar, 1977, pp. 143-151.

1035. Weinburg, Herman G. "Greed." Cinemages, 1, No. 1
       (1955), 4-6. Reprinted In his Saint Cinema:
       Selected Writings 1929-1970. New York: DBS
       Publications, 1970, pp. 128-136. Reprinted as
       "Stroheim's Greed." In Greed: A Film by Erich
       von Stroheim. Ed. Joel W. Finler. New York:
       Simon and Schuster, 1972, pp. 14-21.

1036. _____. "Introduction to Greed." Focus on
       Film, No. 14 (Spring 1973), pp. 51-53.

EDWIN O'CONNOR

1037. Taylor, Robert. "The Last Hurrah: John Ford's Boston."
       In The Modern American Novel and the Movies.
       Ed. Gerald Peary and Roger Shatzkin. New York:
       Frederick Ungar, 1978, pp. 215-223.

FLANNERY O'CONNOR

1038. Archer, Jane Elizabeth. "`This Is My Place': The
       Short Films Made from Flannery O'Connor's Short
       Fiction." Studies in American Humor, 1 (June
       1982), 52-65.
       On "A Good Man is Hard to Find," "The Displaced
       Person," and "A Circle in the Fire."

1039. Menides, Laura Jehn. "John Huston's Wise Blood
       and the Myth of the Sacred Quest." Literature/Film
       Quarterly, 9 (1981), 207-212.

FRANK O'HARA

1040. Fialkowski, Barbara. "The Centrality of Cinema
       in the Poetry of Frank O'Hara." Quarterly Review
       of Film Studies, 3 (Spring 1978), 199-200.

JOHN O'HARA

1041. French, Warren. "O'Hara on Film." John O'Hara
       Journal, 3 (Fall-Winter 1980), 138-140.

EUGENE O'NEILL

1042. Bentley, Byron. "Long Day's Journey into Film."
       Theatre Arts, 46 (Oct. 1962), 16-18, 70-71.

1043. Ben-Zvi, Linda. "Eugene O'Neill and Film." The
       Eugene O'Neill Newsletter, 7 (Spring 1983), 3-10.
       On produced and unproduced screenplays of O'Neill's
       work.

1044. Blesch, Edwin J., Jr. "Lots of Desire, No Elms:
       A Consideration of Eugene O'Neill's Desire Under
       the Elms." Nassau Review, 4, No. 2 (1981), 14-22.

1045. Cutler, Janet Klotman. "Eugene O'Neill on the Screen:
       Love, Hate, and the Movies." DAI, 38 (1977),
       3109A (University of Illinois at Urbana-Champaign).

1046. Frankenheimer, John. "Filming The Iceman Cometh."
      Action, 9 (Jan.-Feb. 1974), 34-37.
      By director of the American Film Theatre production.

1047. Kagan, Norman. "Return of `The Emperor Jones."
      Negro History Bulletin, 34 (Nov. 1971), 160-162.

1048. Kaplan, Abraham. "Realism in the Film: A Philosopher's
      Viewpoint." The Quarterly of Film, Radio, and
      Television, 7 (1953), 370-384.
      On Ford's The Long Voyage Home.

1049. Krafchick, Marcelline. "Film and Fiction in O'Neill's
      Hughie." Arizona Quarterly, 39 (1983), 47-61.
      On O'Neill's use of film on stage.

1050. Luciano, Dale. "Long Day's Journey into Night:
      An Interview with Sidney Lumet." Film Quarterly,
      25 (Fall 1971), 20-29.

1051. Macgowan, Kenneth. "O'Neill and a Mature Hollywood
      Outlook." Theatre Arts, 42 (April 1958), 79-81.
      On Desire Under the Elms.

1052. Orlandello, John Richard. O'Neill on Film. East
      Brunswick, N.J.: Associated University Presses,
      1982.
      Discussions of Anna Christie, Strange Interlude,
      Emperor Jones, Ah,Wilderness!/Summer Holiday, The
      Long Voyage Home, Mourning Becomes Electra, Desire
      Under the Elms, and The Iceman Cometh.

1053. Roman, Robert C. "O'Neill on the Screen." Films
      in Review, 9 (1958), 296-305.
      Annotated filmography.

1054. Sipple, William L. "From Stage to Screen: The Long
      Voyage Home and Long Day's Journey into Night."
      The Eugene O'Neill Newsletter, 7 (Spring 1983),
      10-14.

                    WALKER PERCY

1055. Freshney, Pamela. "The Moviegoer and Lancelot:
      The Movies as Literary Symbol." The Southern
      Review, 18 (1982), 718-727.

1056. Lawson, Lewis A. "Moviegoing in The Moviegoer."
      In Another Generation: Southern Fiction Since
      World War II. Jackson: University Press of
      Mississippi, 1984, pp. 90-108.

1057. Ward, Carol Marie. "Movie as Metaphor in Contemporary
      Fiction: A Study of Walker Percy, Larry McMurtry,
      and John Fowles." DAI, 42 (1982), 3996A (The
      University of Tennessee).
      On Percy's The Moviegoer and Lancelot, McMurtry's
      The Last Picture Show and Somebody's Darling, and
      Fowles's Daniel Martin.

EDGAR ALLAN POE

1058. Bayton, Michael Dewitt. "Poe, the Critics and
        Filmmakers." DAI, 38 (1978), 5472A (Northwestern
        University).

1059. Begnal, Michael H. "Fellini and Poe: A Story with
        a Moral?' Literature/Film Quarterly, 10 (1982),
        130-133.
        On "Never Bet the Devil Your Head."

1060. Roman, Robert C. "Poe on the Screen." Films in
        Review, 12 (1961), 462-473.
        Annotated filmography.

1061. Simper, Deloy. "Poe, Hitchcock, and the Well-Wrought
        Effect." Literature/Film Quarterly, 3 (1975),
        226-231.

1062. Stern, Seymour. "Griffith and Poe." Films in Review,
        2 (1951), 23-28.
        On Griffith's The Avenging Conscience, an adaptation
        of "The Tell-Tale Heart."

THOMAS PYNCHON

1063. Clerc, Charles. "Film in Gravity's Rainbow." In
        Approaches to Gravity's Rainbow. Ed. Charles
        Clerc. Columbus: Ohio State University Press,
        1983, pp. 103-151.

1064. Cowart, David. "Cinematic Auguries of the Third
        Reich in Gravity's Rainbow." Literature/Film
        Quarterly, 6 (1978), 364-370.

1065. _____. "`Making the Unreal Reel': Film in
        Gravity's Rainbow." In Thomas Pynchon: The Art
        of Allusion. Carbondale: Southern Illinois University
        Press, 1980, pp. 31-62.

1066. Grace, Sherrille. "Fritz Lang and the `Para-Cinematic
        Lives' of Gravity's Rainbow." Modern Fiction
        Studies, 29 (1983), 655-670.

1067. Larsson, Donald Foss. "The Film Breaks: Thomas
        Pynchon and the Cinema." DAI, 41 (1981), 4394A
        (The University of Wisconsin at Madison).

1068. Lippman, Bertram. "The Reader of Movies: Thomas
        Pynchon's Gravity's Rainbow." University of
Denver   Quarterly, 12 (1977), 1-46.

1069. Moore, Thomas. "A Decade of Gravity's Rainbow,
        the Incredible Moving Film." Michigan Quarterly
        Review, 22 (1983), 78-94.

1070. Simmon, Scott. "Beyond the Theater of War: Gravity's
       Rainbow as Film." Literature/Film Quarterly,
       6 (1978), 347-363.

1071. Stark, John O. "The Film." In his Thomas Pynchon
       and the Literature of Information. Athens: Ohio
       University Press, 1980, pp. 132-145.

1072. Worley, Joan Yvonne. "Film into Fiction: Thomas
       Pynchon and Manuel Puig." DAI, 44 (1984), 3680A
       (Ohio University).

AYN RAND

1073. McGann, Kevin. "The Fountainhead: Ayn Rand in the
       Stockyard of the Spirit." The Modern American
       Novel and the Movies. Ed. Gerald Peary and Roger
       Shatzkin. New York: Frederick Ungar, 1978,
       pp. 325-335.

WILLIAM SAROYAN

1074. McGilligan, Patrick. "The Human Comedy: Mr. Saroyan's
       Thoroughly American Movie." In The Modern American
       Novel and the Movies. Ed. Gerald Peary and Roger
       Shatzkin. New York: Frederick Ungar, 1978,
       pp. 156-167.

BUDD SCHULBERG

1075. Ciment, Michel. "Working With Schulberg: On the
       Waterfront (1954), A Face in the Crowd (1957)."
       In his Kazan on Kazan. New York: The Viking
       Press, 1974, pp. 102-119.

1076. Georgakas, Dan. "The Screen Playwright as Author"
       An Interview with Budd Schulberg." Cinéaste,
       11, No. 4 (1982), 15, 39.

1077. Hey, Kenneth R. "Ambivalence as a Theme in On the
       Waterfront (1954): An Interdisciplinary Approach
       to Film Study." American Quarterly, 31 (1979),
       666-696. Reprinted in Hollywood as Historian:
       American Film in a Cultural Context. Ed. Peter
       C. Rollins. Lexington: University of Kentucky
       Press, 1983, pp. 159-189.

1078. _____. "On the Waterfront: Another Look."
       Film and History, 9 (Dec. 1979), 82-86.

1079. Pauly, Thomas H. An American Odyssey: Elia Kazan
       and American Culture. Philadelphia: Temple University
       Press, 1983, pp. 179-194.
       On the Waterfront.

1080. Schulberg, Budd. "Afterward." In <u>On the Waterfront</u>.
       Ed. Matthew J. Bruccoli. Carbondale: Southern
       Illinois University Press, 1980, pp. 141-153.

1081. _____. <u>The Four Seasons of Success</u>. New York:
       Doubleday, 1972.
       The Hollywood careers of F. Scott Fitzgerald, Nathanael
       West, Dorothy Parker, John Steinbeck, Thomas Heggen,
       and William Saroyan.

1082. _____. "The Hollywood Novel: The Love-Hate
       Relationship Between Writers and Hollywood."
       <u>American Film</u>, 1 (May 1976), 29-32.

ROBERT SHERWOOD

1083. Fulton, A.R. "From Play to Film." In <u>Motion Pictures:</u>
       <u>The Development of an Art From Silent Films to</u>
       <u>the Age of Television</u>. Norman: University of
       Oklahoma Press, 1960, pp. 201-227.
       On the adaptation of <u>Abe Lincoln in Illinois</u>.

1084. Hagemann, E.R. "An Extraordinary Picture: The Film
       Criticism of Robert Sherwood." <u>Journal of Popular</u>
       <u>Film</u>, 1 (Spring 1972), 81-104.

UPTON SINCLAIR

1085. Mansfield, Joseph. "<u>The Wet Parade</u>: Que Viva
       Prohibition?" In <u>The Modern American Novel and</u>
       <u>the Movies</u>. Ed. Gerald Peary and Roger Shatzkin.
       New York: Frederick Ungar, 1978, pp. 308-316.

1086. Soderbergh, Peter A. "Upton Sinclair and Hollywood."
       <u>Midwest Quarterly</u>, 11 (Jan. 1970), 173-191.
       On Eisenstein's adaptations.

ISSAC BASHEVIS SINGER

1087. Siporin, Stephen Charles. "Story Versus Movie:
       Comments On I.B. Singer's `Zlateh the Goat.'"
       In <u>Studies in Jewish Folklore</u>. Ed. Frank Talmage.
       Cambridge: The Association for Jewish Studies,
       1980, pp. 307-312.

SUSAN SONTAG

1088. Holdsworth, Elizabeth McCaffrey. "Susan Sontag:
       Writer-Filmmaker." <u>DAI</u>, 42 (1982), 4447-4448A
       (Ohio University).

1089. Sontag, Susan. "A Note on Novels and Films." In
       her <u>Against Interpretation</u>. New York: Farrar,
       Straus, and Giroux, 1961, pp. 242-245.

1090. _____. "Theatre and Film." <u>Tulane Drama Review</u>,
      11 (1966), 24-37. Reprinted in her <u>Styles of
      Radical Will</u>. New York: Farrar, Straus, and
      Giroux, 1969, pp. 99-122. Reprinted in <u>Perspectives
      in the Study of Film</u>. Ed. John Stuart Katz.
      Boston: Little, Brown, and Co., 1971, pp. 73-90.
      Reprinted in <u>Film Theory and Criticism: Introductory
      Readings</u>. Ed. Gerald Mast and Marshall Cohen.
      New York: Oxford University Press, 1974, pp. 249-267.
      Reprinted in <u>Film and/as Literature</u>. Ed. John
      Harrington. Englewood Cliffs: Prentice-Hall,
      1977, pp. 76-92.

                    GERTRUDE STEIN

1091. Purdy, Strother. "Gertrude Stein at Marienbad."
      <u>PMLA</u>, 85 (1970), 1096-1105.

                    JOHN STEINBECK

1092. Beatty, Sandra. "Steinbeck's Play-Women: A Study
      of the Female Presence in <u>Of Mice and Men</u>, <u>Burning
      Bright</u>, <u>The Moon Is Down</u>, and <u>Viva Zapata!</u>"
      In <u>Steinbeck's Women: Essays in Criticism</u>. Ed.
      Tetsumaro Hayashi. Muncie: Steinbeck Society
      of America, Ball State University, 1979, pp. 7-16.

1093. Biskind, Peter. "Ripping Off Zapata's Revolution
      Hollywood Style." <u>Cinéaste</u>, 7, No. 2 (1976),
      10-15.

1094. Burrows, Michael. <u>John Steinbeck and His Films</u>.
      Cornwall: Primestyle, 1970.
      Monograph sketches Steinbeck's career and offers
      brief evaluations of the film adaptations of his
      works.

1095. Campbell, Russell. "Trampling Out the Vintage:
      Sour Grapes." In <u>The Modern American Novel and
      the Movies</u>. Ed. Gerald Peary and Roger Shatzkin.
      New York: Frederick Ungar, 1978, pp. 107-118.

1096. Ciment, Michel. "The Political Issues: The HUAC;
      <u>Viva Zapata!</u> (1951), <u>Man on a Tightrope</u> (1952)."
      In his <u>Kazan on Kazan</u>. New York: The Viking
      Press, 1974, pp. 83-101.

1097. Davis, Gary Corbett. "John Steinbeck in Films:
      An Analysis of Realism in the Novel and in the
      Film--A Non-teleological Approach." <u>DAI</u>, 36
      (1975), 3170A (University of Southern California).
      On <u>The Grapes of Wrath</u>, <u>The Pearl</u>, <u>East of Eden</u>,
      <u>The Wayward Bus</u>, and <u>In Dubious Battle</u>.

1098. Ditsky, John. "Words and Deeds in <u>Viva Zapata!</u>"
      <u>Dalhousie Review</u>, 56 (1976), 125-131.

1099. Emory, Doug. "Point of View and Narrative Voice
       in The Grapes of Wrath: Steinbeck and Ford."
       In Narrative Strategies: Original Essays in Film
       and Prose Fiction. Ed. Syndy Conger and Janice
       R. Welsch. Macomb: Western Illinois University,
       1980, pp. 129-135.

1100. Everson, William K. "Of Mice and Men: Thoughts
       on a Great Adaptation." In The Modern American
       Novel and the Movies. Ed. Gerald Peary and Roger
       Shatzkin. New York: Frederick Ungar, 1978, pp. 63-69.

1101. Federle, Steven J. "Lifeboat as Allegory: Steinbeck
       and the Demon of War." Steinbeck Quarterly,
       12 (1979), 14-20.

1102. French, Warren. Filmguide to The Grapes of Wrath.
       Bloomington: University of Indiana Press, 1973.

1103. Georgakas, Dan. "Still Good After All These Years."
       Cinéaste, 7, No. 2 (1976), 10-15.
       On Viva Zapata!

1104. Hayashi, Tetsumaro. "The Theme of Revolution in
       Julius Caesar and Viva Zapata!" In John Steinbeck
       East and West. Ed. Tetsumaro Hayashi, Yasuo
       Hasiguchi, and Richard F. Peterson. Muncie:
       Steinbeck Society, Ball State University, 1978,
       pp. 28-39.

1105. Kline, Herbert. "On John Steinbeck." Steinbeck
       Quarterly, 4 (1971), 80-88.
       On the making of The Forgotten Village by the film's
       director.

1106. McConnel, Frank D. "Film and Writing: The Political
       Dimension." Massachusetts Review, 13 (1972),
       543-562.
       Concerns In Dubious Battle.

1107. Metzger, Charles R. "The Film Version of Steinbeck's
       `The Pearl'." Steinbeck Quarterly, 4 (1971),
       88-92.

1108. Millichap, Joseph. "A Realistic Style in Steinbeck's
       and Milestone's Of Mice and Men." Literature/Film
       Quarterly, 6 (1978), 241-252.

1109. _____. Steinbeck and Film. New York: Frederick
       Ungar, 1983.
       Films discussed: Of Mice and Men, The Grapes of
       Wrath, The Forgotten Village, Tortilla Flat, The
       Moon Is Down, Lifeboat, A Medal for Benny, The Pearl,
       The Red Pony, Viva Zapata!, East of Eden, The Wayward
       Bus, Flight, and Cannery Row.

1110. Morsberger, Robert E. "Adrift in Steinbeck's Lifeboat."
       Literature/Film Quarterly, 4 (1976), 325-338.

1111. _____. "Cannery Row Revisited." Steinbeck
       Quarterly, 16 (1983), 89-95.

1112. _____. "Steinbeck on Screen." In A Study
       Guide to Steinbeck: A Handbook to His Major Works
       (Part I). Ed. Tetsumaro Hayashi. Metuchen,
       N.J.: Scarecrow Press, 1974, pp. 258-298. Reprinted
       as "Steinbeck's Screenplays and Productions."
       In Viva Zapata! The Original Screenplay by John
       Steinbeck. Ed. Robert E. Morsberger. New York:
       Viking Press, 1975, pp. 123-144.

1113. _____. "Steinbeck's Zapata: Rebel vs.
       Revolutionary." In Steinbeck: The Man and His
       Work. Ed. Richard Astro and Tetsumaro Hayashi.
       Corvallis: Oregon State University Press, pp. 43-63.
       Reprinted in Viva Zapata! The Original Screenplay
       by John Steinbeck. Ed. Robert E. Morsberger.
       New York: Viking Press, 1975, pp. xi-xxxviii.

1114. _____. "Viva Zapata!" In A Study Guide to
       Steinbeck (Part II). Ed. Tetsumaro Hayashi.
       Metuchen, N.J.: Scarecrow Press, 1979, pp. 191-209.

1115. Pauly, Thomas H. An American Odyssey: Elia Kazan
       and American Culture. Philadelphia: Temple University
       Press, 1983, pp. 194-202 and pp. 145-156.
       On East of Eden and Viva Zapata!

1116. Pettit, Arthur. "Viva Zapata! A Tribute to Steinbeck,
       Kazan, and Brando." Film and History, 7 (May
       1977), 25-45.

1117. Place, Janey. "The Grapes of Wrath: A Visual Analysis."
       Film Comment, 12, No. 5 (1976), 46-51.

1118. Pulliam, Rebecca. "The Grapes of Wrath." The Velvet
       Light Trap, No. 2 (1971), pp. 3-7.

1119. Scheer, Ronald. "Of Mice and Men: Novel, Play,
       Movie." American Examiner, 6 (Fall-Winter 1978-79),
       6-39.

1120. _____. "Steinbeck into Film: The Making of
       Tortilla Flat." West Virginia University Philological
       Papers, 26 (Aug. 1980), 30-36.

1121. Sheridan, Marion, Harold H. Owen, Jr. Ken Macrorie,
       and Fred Marcus. "Structure of a Film." In
       The Motion Picture and the Teaching of English.
       New York: Appleton Century Crofts, 1965, pp. 103-111.
       On The Grapes of Wrath.

1122. Sobchack, Vivian C. "The Grapes of Wrath: Thematic
       Emphasis Through Visual Style." American Quarterly,
       31 (1979), 596-615. Reprinted in Hollywood as
       Historian: American Films in a Cultural Context.
       Ed. Peter C. Rollins. Lexington: University
       Press of Kentucky, 1983, pp. 68-87.

1123. Tibbetts, John C. "It Happened in Monterey: Cannery
       Row." Literature/Film Quarterly, 10 (1982),
       82-84.

1124. Vanderwood, Paul J. "An American Cold Warrior:
       Viva Zapata! (1952)." In American History/American
       Film: Interpreting the Hollywood Image. Ed. John
       E. O'Connor and Martin A. Jackson. New York:
       Frederick Ungar, 1979, pp. 183-201.

                HARRIET BEECHER STOWE

1125. Andrews, Hannah Page Wheeler. "Theme and Variations:
       Uncle Tom's Cabin as Book, Play, and Film."
       DAI, 40 (1980), 6276-6277A (The University of
       North Carolina at Chapel Hill).

1126. Slout, William L. "Uncle Tom's Cabin in American
       Film History." Journal of Popular Film, 2 (1973),
       137-151.

                 WILLIAM STYRON

1127. Firestone, Bruce M. "A Rose Is a Rose Is a Columbine:
       Citizen Kane and William Styron's Nat Turner."
       Literature/Film Quarterly, 5 (1977), 118-124.

                 RONALD SUKENICK

1128. Sukenick, Ronald. "Film Digression." In his In
       Form: Digressions on the Act of Fiction. Carbondale:
       Southern Illinois University Press, 1985, pp. 83-98.

                 BOOTH TARKINGTON

1129. Cowie, Peter. "The Study of Fading Aristocracy:
       The Magnificent Ambersons." In Ribbon of Dreams:
       The Cinema of Orson Welles. New York: A.S. Barnes
       and Co., 1973, pp. 63-83.

1130. Farber, Stephen. "The Magnificent Ambersons."
       Film Comment, 7 (Summer 1971), 49-50.

1131. Higham, Charles. "The Magnificent Ambersons."
       In The Films of Orson Welles. Berkeley: University
       of California Press, 1970, pp. 48-71.

1132. Naremore, James. "The Magnificent Ambersons."
       In The Magic World of Orson Welles. New York:
       Oxford University Press, 1978, pp. 103-133.

1133. Reitz, Carolyn Lee. "The Narrative Capabilities
       of Prose and Film." DAI, 39 (1978), 1887A (The
       University of Texas at Austin).
       Reitz analyzes both Tarkington's and Welles's The
       Magnificent Ambersons.

1134.   Schwartz, Nancy L.   "Alice Adams: From American
        Tragedy to Small-Town-Dream-Come-True."   In The
        Classic American Novel and the Movies.   Ed. Gerald
        Peary and Roger Shatzkin.   New York: Frederick
        Ungar Publishing, 1977, pp. 218-225.

1135.   Sirkin, Elliott.   "Alice Adams."   Film Comment,
        7 (Winter 1971-1972), 66-69.

B. TRAVEN

1136.   Kaminsky, Stuart.   "The Treasure of the Sierra Madre:
        Gold, Hat, Gold Fever, Silver Screen."   In The
        Modern American Novel and the Movies.   Ed. Gerald
        Peary and Roger Shatzkin. New York: Frederick
        Ungar, 1978, pp. 53-62.   Reprinted as "Literary
        Adaptation: The Treasure of the Sierra Madre--Novel
        into Film."   In American Film Genres.   Chicago:
        Nelson-Hall, 1985, pp. 97-105.

1137.   Naremore, James.   "Introduction: A Likely Project."
        In The Treasure of the Sierra Madre.   Ed. James
        Naremore.   Madison: University of Wisconsin Press,
        1979, pp. 9-32.

JOHN UPDIKE

1138.   Seigel, Gary.   "Rabbit Run: Rabbit Runs Down."
        In The Modern American Novel and the Movies.
        Ed. Gerald Peary and Roger Shatzkin.   New York:
        Frederick Ungar, 1978, pp. 247-255.

KURT VONNEGUT, JR.

1139.   Atwell, Lee. "Two Studies in Space-Time."   Film
        Quarterly, 26, (Winter 1972-73), 2-9.
        On George Roy Hill's Slaughterhouse-Five.

1140.   Dimeo, Stephen.   "Reconciliation: Slaughterhouse-Five--
        the Film and the Novel."   Film Heritage, 8 (Winter
        1972-73), 1-12.   Revised and reprinted as "Novel
        into Film: So It Goes."   In The Modern American
        Novel and the Movies.   Ed. Gerald Peary and Roger
        Shatzkin.   New York: Frederick Ungar, 1978,
        pp. 282-292.

1141.   Horton, Andrew.   "Unstuck in Time: Slaughterhouse-Five."
        In his The Films of George Roy Hill.   New York:
        Columbia University Press, 1984, pp. 81-98.

1142.   Mayer, Peter C.   "Film Ontology and the Structure
        of a Novel."   Literature/Film Quarterly, 8 (1980),
        204-208.
        On Slaughterhouse-Five.

1143.   Nelson, Joyce.   "Slaughterhouse-Five: Novel into
        Film."   Literature/Film Quarterly, 1 (1973),
        149-153.

1144. Sharples, Win. "The Art of Filmmaking: An Analysis
       of <u>Slaughterhouse-Five</u>." <u>Filmmakers Newsletter</u>,
       6, No. 1 (1972), 24-28.

EDWARD LEWIS WALLANT

1145. Lyons, Joseph. "<u>The Pawnbroker</u>: A Study of the
       Flashback in Novel and Film." <u>Western Humanities
       Review</u>, 20 (1966), 243-248.

1146. Petrie, Graham. "A Note on the Novel and the Film:
       Flashbacks in <u>Tristram Shandy</u> and <u>The Pawnbroker</u>."
       <u>Western Humanities Review</u>, 21 (1967), 165-169.
       A response to Lyons's article.

ROBERT PENN WARREN

1147. Walling, William. "<u>All the King's Men</u>: In Which
       Humpty Dumpty Becomes King." In <u>The Modern American
       Novel and the Movies</u>. Ed. Gerald Peary and Roger
       Shatzkin. New York: Frederick Ungar, 1978,
       pp. 168-177.

JESSAMYN WEST

1148. West, Jessamyn. <u>To See the Dream</u>. New York: Harcourt,
       Brace and Co., 1956.
       On the making of the adaptation of West's novel
       <u>The Friendly Persuasion</u>.

NATHANAEL WEST

1149. Cohen, Mitchell S. "Odd Jobs and Subsidies: Nathanael
       West in Hollywood." <u>Film Comment</u>, 11 (May-June
       1975), 44-46.

1150. Gottlieb, Sidney. "<u>The Day of the Locust</u>: The Madding
       Crowd in the Movies." In <u>The Modern American
       Novel and the Movies</u>. Ed. Gerald Peary and Roger
       Shatzkin. New York: Frederick Ungar, 1978,
       pp. 95-106.

1151. Jones, Edward T. "That's Wormwood: <u>The Day of the
       Locust</u>." <u>Literature/Film Quarterly</u>, 6 (1978),
       222-229.

1152. Klein, Michael. "<u>Miss Lonelyhearts</u>: Miss L. Gets
       Married." In <u>The Modern American Novel and the
       Movies</u>. Ed. Gerald Peary and Roger Shatzkin.
       New York: Frederick Ungar, 1978, pp. 19-28.

1153. Lev, Peter and Gary Scharnhorst. "Nathanael West's
       Unproduced Treatment of <u>A Cool Million</u>: A Twice-
       Twisted Tale." <u>Post-Script</u>, 2 (1983), 24-32.

1154. Light, James F. "The Dream Factory." In his <u>Nathanael
       West: An Interpretative Study</u>. Evanston: Northwestern
       University Press, 1971, pp. 151-202.
       West's Hollywood career.

1155.   Lokke, J.L.   "A Side Glance at Medusa: Hollywood,
            the Literature Boys, and Nathanael West."   Southwest
            Review, 46 (1961), 35-45.
         West's career in Hollywood with emphasis on The
         Day of the Locust.

1156.   Martin, Jay.   Nathanael West: The Art of His Life.
            New York: Farrar, Straus and Giroux, 1970.
         In addition to biographical material about West's
         Hollywood career, the book contains an appendix
         on West's screenplays.

1157.   Phillips, Gene D.   "The Day of the Locust."   In
            his John Schlesinger.   Boston: Twayne Publishing,
            1981, pp. 92-108.

1158.   Rapf, Joanna E.   "`Human Need' in The Day of the
            Locust: Problems of Adaptation."   Literature/Film
            Quarterly, 9 (1981), 22-31.

1159.   Zlotnick, Joan.   "The Day of the Locust--Comparing
            John Schlesinger's Film and Nathanael West's
            Novel."   Filmograph, 5, No. 1 (1976), 25-29.

1160.   _____.   "The Day of the Locust, A Night at
            the Movies."   Film Library Quarterly, 6, No. 1
            (1972-1973), 22-26.
         Not a study of the adaptation but film's influence
         on the novel.

1161.   _____.   "Nathanael West and the Pictoral
            Imagination."   Western American Literature, 9
            (1974), 177-185.
         The influence of comic strips, painting and film
         on West's novels.

                         EDITH WHARTON

1162.   Bodeen, DeWitt.   "Films and Edith Wharton."   Films
            in Review, 28 (1977), 73-81.

                          E.B. WHITE

1163.   Apseloff, Marilyn.   "Charlotte's Web: Flaws in the
            Weaving."   In Children's Novels and the Movies.
            Ed. Douglas Street.   New York: Frederick Ungar,
            1983, pp. 171-181.

                         WALT WHITMAN

1164.   Freedman, Florence B.   "A Motion Picture `First'
            for Whitman: O'Connor's `The Carpenter'."   Walt
            Whitman Review, 9 (1963), 31-33.

1165.   Grant, Barry Keith.   "Whitman and Eisenstein."
            Literature/Film Quarterly, 4 (1976), 264-270.

RICHARD WILBUR

1166. Wilbur, Richard. "A Poet and the Movies." In Man
       and the Movies. Ed. W.R. Robinson. Baltimore:
       Penguin Books, 1967, pp. 223-226. Reprinted in
       Film and/as Literature. Ed. John Harrington.
       Englewood Cliffs: Prentice-Hall, 1977, pp. 206-208.

THORNTON WILDER

1167. Wilder, Thornton. "Our Town--From Stage to Screen:
       A Correspondence Between Thornton Wilder a.ld
       Sol Lesser." Theatre Arts, 24 (1940), 815-824.

TENNESSEE WILLIAMS

1168. Asral, Ertem. "Tennessee Williams on Stage and
       Screen." DA, 22 (1961), 1169-1170 (The University
       of Pennsylvania).
       On A Streetcar Named Desire, Suddenly, Last Summer,
       Cat on a Hot Tin Roof, and The Glass Menagerie.

1169. Brandt, George. "Cinematic Structure in the Work
       of Tennessee Williams." In American Theatre.
       Ed. John Russell Brown and Bernard Harris. London:
       Edward Arnold Publishers, 1967, pp. 163-188.

1170. Ciment, Michel. "Tennessee Williams and the South:
       A Streetcar Named Desire (1950), Baby Doll (1956)."
       In his Kazan on Kazan. New York: The Viking
       Press, 1974, pp. 66-82.

1171. Dowling, Ellen. "The Derailment of A Streetcar
       Named Desire." Literature/Film Quarterly, 9
       (1981), 233-240.

1172. Hirsch, Foster. "Tennessee Williams." Cinema (US),
       8, No. 1 (1973), 2-7.
       Survey of adaptations and a discussion of Baby Doll.

1173. MacMullan, Hugh. "Translating The Glass Menagerie
       to Film." Hollywood Quarterly, 5 (1950), 14-32.

1174. Pauly, Thomas H. An American Odyssey: Elia Kazan
       and American Culture. Philadelphia: Temple University
       Press, 1983, pp. 130-137.
       On A Streetcar Named Desire.

1175. Ricci, Frederick. "An Analysis of the Directing
       Techniques of Elia Kazan in Theatre and Film
       as Illustrated in A Streetcar Named Desire."
       DAI, 36 (1975), 35A (Columbia University).

1176. Roberts, Meade. "Williams and Me." Films and Filming,
       6 (Aug. 1960), 7.
       Author, who collaborated with Williams on The Fugitive
       Kind, explains how Williams wrote screenplays.

1177.   Warren, Clifton Lanier.   "Tennessee Williams as
           a Cinematic Writer."   DA, 25 (1964), 489-490
           (Indiana University).
        On The Glass Menagerie, A Streetcar Named Desire,
        The Rose Tattoo, and Baby Doll.

1178.   Yacowar, Maurice.   Tennesse Williams and Film.
           New York: Frederick Ungar, 1977.
        On The Glass Menagerie, The Rose Tattoo, Baby Doll,
        Cat on a Hot Tin Roof, The Fugitive Kind, Summer
        and Smoke, The Roman Spring of Mrs. Stone, Sweet
        Bird of Youth, Period of Adjustment, Night of the
        Iguana, This Property Is Condemned, BOOM, and Last
        of the Mobile Hot-Shots.

                       OWEN WISTER

1179.   Trimmer, Joseph F.   "The Virginian: Novels and Films."
           Illinois Quarterly, 35 (Dec. 1972), 5-18.   Reprinted
           as "The Virginian: Three Treks West."   In The
           Classic American Novel and the Movies.   Ed. Gerald
           Peary and Roger Shatzkin.   New York: Frederick
           Ungar, 1977, pp. 176-191.

                      RICHARD WRIGHT

1180.   Brunette, Peter.   "Native Son: Two Wrights, One
           Wrong."   In The Modern American Novel and the
           Movies.   Ed. Gerald Peary and Roger Shatzkin.
           New York: Frederick Ungar, 1978, pp. 131-142.

1181.   Pyros, John.   "Richard Wright: A Black Novelist's
           Experience in Film."   Negro American Literature
           Forum, 9 (1975), 53-54.

9
Literary Figures
of
the United Kingdom

RICHARD ADAMS

1182. Jordan, Tom. "Watership Down: Breaking Away from
the Warren." In Children's Novels and the Movies.
Ed. Douglas Street. New York: Frederick Ungar,
1983, pp. 227-235.

ERIC AMBLER

1183. Ambler, Eric. "The Film of the Book." Penguin
Film Review, 9 (1949), 22-25; rpt. Totowa, N.J.:
Rowan and Littlefield, 1978.
Satirical account of adaptations of Ambler's novels.

JANE AUSTEN

1184. Lellis, George and H. Philip Bolton. "Pride and
Prejudice: Pride But No Prejudice." In The English
Novel and the Movies. Ed. Michael Klein and
Gillian Parker. New York: Frederick Ungar, 1981,
pp. 44-51.

J.M. BARRIE

1185. Green, Martin. "The Charm of Peter Pan." Children's
Literature, 9 (1981), 19-27.
On the Disney adaptation.

SAMUEL BECKETT

1186. Brater, Enoch. "The Thinking Eye in Beckett's Film."
Modern Language Quarterly, 36 (1975), 166-176.

1187. Dietrich, Richard F. "Beckett's Goad: From Stage
to Film." Literature/Film Quarterly, 4 (1976),
83-89.

1188. Fehsenfeld, Martha. "Beckett's Late Works: An
Appraisal." Modern Drama, 25 (1982), 355-362.
Includes a discussion of Beckett's work for film
and television: Film, Ghost Trio, and Quad.

1189. Fischer, Ernst. "Samuel Beckett: Play and Film." Mosaic,
       2, No. 2 (1969), 96-116.

1190. Gontarski, S.E. "Film and Formal Integrity." In
       Samuel Beckett: Humanistic Perspectives. Ed. Morris
       Beja, S.E. Gontarski, and Pierre Astier. Columbus:
       Ohio State University Press, 1983, pp. 129-136.
       On Film.

1191. Reid, Alec. "Beckett, the Camera, and Jack MacGowan."
       In Myth and Reality in Irish Literature. Ed. Joseph
       Ronsley. Waterloo: Wilfrid Lautier, 1977,
       pp. 219-225.
       Beckett on film: The Goad, Film, Eh Joe, and From
       Beginning to End.

1192. Robinson, Fred M. "Stumbling on a Smooth Road:
       Silent Film Comedy and Beckett's Nouvelles."
       Bucknell Review, 24, No. 2 (1978), 107-119.

1193. Van Wert, William F. "`To Be Is to Be Perceived':
       Time and Point of View in Beckett's Film."
       Literature/Film Quarterly, 8 (1980), 133-140.

JOHN BERGER

1194. Appignanesi, Richard. "The Screenwriter as Collaborator:
       An Interview with John Berger." Cinéaste, 10,
       No. 3 (1980), 14-19.

1195. Tarantino, Michael. "Tanner and Berger: The Voice
       Off-Screen." Film Quarterly, 33 (Winter 1979-80),
       32-43.
       Concerns the writer's novels and his collaborations
       with the Swiss filmmaker.

WILLIAM BLAKE

1196. Blaydes, Sophia B. and Phillip Bordinat. "Blake's
       `Jerusalem' and Popular Culture: The Loneliness
       of the Long-Distance Runner and Chariots of Fire."
       Literature/Film Quarterly, 11 (1983), 211-214.

JOHN BRAINE

1197. Houston, Penelope. "Room at the Top?" Sight and
       Sound, 28 (Spring 1959), 56-59.

CHARLOTTE BRONTE

1198. Ellis, Kate and E. Ann Kaplan. "Jane Eyre: Feminism
       in Bronte's Novel and Its Film Versions." In
       The English Novel and the Movies. Ed. Michael
       Klein and Gillian Parker. New York: Frederick
       Ungar, 1981, pp. 83-94.

1199. Higashi, Sumiko. "Jane Eyre: Charlotte Bronte Vs. the
       Hollywood Myth of Romance." Journal of Popular
       Film, 6 (1977), 13-31.

1200. Palmer, James. "Fiction into Film: Delbert Mann's
       Jane Eyre (An Edited Interview)." _Studies in
       the Humanities_, 5, (Oct. 1976), 3-8.

1201. Riley, Michael. "Gothic Melodrama and Spiritual
       Romance: Vision and Fidelity in Two Versions
       of _Jane Eyre_." _Literature/Film Quarterly_, 3
       (1975), 145-159.

EMILY BRONTE

1202. Harrington, John. "_Wuthering Heights_: Wyler as
       Auteur." In _The English Novel and the Movies_.
       Ed. Michael Klein and Gillian Parker. New York:
       Frederick Ungar, 1981, pp. 67-82.

ROBERT BROWNING

1203. Griffith, Mrs. D.W. (Linda Arvidson). "`Pippa Passes'
       Filmed." In _When the Movies Were Young_. New
       York: E.P. Dutton, 1925, pp. 127-133; rpt. New
       York: Dover, 1970.

1204. Guiliano, Edward and Richard C. Keenan. "Browning
       Without Words: D.W. Griffith and the Filming
       of _Pippa Passes_." _Browning Institute Studies_,
       4 (1976), 125-159.

1205. Hilenski, Ferdinand Alexi. "D.W. Griffith's Film
       Version of Browning's _Pippa Passes_: Some Problems
       in Early Literature to Film Adaptations."
       Literature/Film Quarterly, 4 (1976), 76-82.

JOHN BUCHAN

1206. Camp, Jocelyn. "John Buchan and Alfred Hitchcock."
       Literature/Film Quarterly, 6 (1978), 230-240.

1207. McDougal, Stuart Y. "Mirth, Sexuality, and Suspense:
       Alfred Hitchcock's Adaptation of _The Thirty-Nine
       Steps_." _Literature/Film Quarterly_, 3 (1975),
       232-239.

ANTHONY BURGESS

1208. Aggeler, Geoffrey. "_A Clockwork Orange_." In _Anthony
       Burgess: The Artist as Novelist_. University,
       Alabama: The University of Alabama Press, 1979,
       pp. 169-182.

1209. Boyers, Robert. "Kubrick's _A Clockwork Orange_."
       Sight and Sound, 42 (Winter 1972-73), 44-46.

1210. _____. "Kubrick's _A Clockwork Orange_: Some
       Observations." _Film Heritage_, 7 (Summer 1972),
       1-6.

1211. Burgess, Anthony. "Clockwork Marmalade." _Listener_,
       87 (17 Feb. 1972), 197-199.

1212.   _____. "Juice From a Clockwork Orange."
         Rolling Stone, 8 June 1972, pp. 52-53.
         Burgess discusses why Kubrick did not use the last
         chapter of the British edition of his novel.

1213.   Ciment, Michel. "First Interview: A Clockwork Orange."
         In his Kubrick. Trans. Gilbert Adair. New York:
         Holt, Rinehart and Winston, 1983, pp. 148-165.

1214.   Coale, Samuel. "A Clockwork Orange (1963):'Real
         Horrorshow.'" In his Anthony Burgess. New York:
         Frederick Ungar Publishing, 1981, pp. 84-98.

1215.   Dimeo, Steven. "The Ticking of an Orange." Riverside
         Quarterly, 5 (1973), 318-321.

1216.   Gilbert, Basil. "Kubrick's Marmalade: The Art of
         Violence." Meanjin Quarterly, 33 (1974), 157-162.

1217.   Gow, Gordon. "Novel into Film." In Film Review,
         1974-75. Ed. Maurice Speed. London: W.H. Allen,
         1974, pp. 33-42.
         Discussion of adaptation of A Clockwork Orange.

1218.   Gumenik, Arthur. "A Clockwork Orange: Novel into
         Film." Film Heritage, 7 (Summer 1972), 7-18.

1219.   Isaacs, Neil D. "Unstuck in Time: A Clockwork Orange
         and Slaughterhouse-Five." Literature/Film Quarterly,
         1 (1973), 122-131.

1220.   Kolker, Robert Phillip. "Oranges, Dogs, and Ultra-
         Violence." Journal of Popular Film, 1 (1972),
         159-172.

1221.   McCracken, Samuel. "Novels into Films; Novelist
         into Critic: A Clockwork Orange...Again." Antioch
         Review, 32 (1973), 427-436.

1222.   Mamber, Stephen. "A Clockwork Orange." Cinema,
         7, No. 3 (1973), 49-57.

1223.   Nelson, Thomas Allen. "The Performing Artist: A
         Clockwork Orange." In his Kubrick: Inside a
         Film Artist's Maze. Bloomington: Indiana University
         Press, 1982, pp. 133-164.

1224.   Rice, Susan. "Stanley Klockwork's Cubrick Orange."
         Media and Methods, 8 (March 1972), 39-43.

1225.   Ricks, Christopher. "Horror Show: A Clockwork Orange."
         New York Review of Books, 18 (6 April 1972),
         28-31.

1226.   Roth, Ellen Shamis. "The Rhetoric of First Person
         Point of View in the Novel and Film Forms: A
         Study of Anthony Burgess' A Clockwork Orange
         and Henry James's A Turn of the Screw." DAI,
         39 (1979),4558A (New York University).

1227. Samuels, Charles Thomas. "The Context of A Clockwork
      Orange." American Scholar, 41 (1972), 439-443.
      Reprinted in Mastering the Film and Other Essays.
      Ed. Lawrence Graver. Knoxville: University of
      Tennessee Press, 1977, pp. 171-178.

1228. Sobchack, Vivian C. "Decor as Theme: A Clockwork
      Orange." Literature/Film Quarterly, 9 (1981),
      92-102.

1229. Strick, Phillip and Penelope Houston. "Interview
      with Stanley Kubrick." Sight and Sound, 41 (Spring
      1972), 62-66.
      The director on A Clockwork Orange.

JOYCE CARY

1230. Pearse, James Allen. "Montage in Modern Fiction:
      A Cinematographic Approach to the Analysis of
      Ironic Tone in Joyce Cary's `The Horse's Mouth.'"
      DAI, 34 (1973), 3596-3597A (The University of
      Arizona).

GEOFFREY CHAUCER

1231. Green, Martin. "The Dialectic of Adaptation: The
      Canterbury Tales of Pier Paolo Pasolini."
      Literature/Film Quarterly, 4 (1976), 46-53.

AGATHA CHRISTIE

1232. Atkins, Irene Kahn. "Agatha Christie and the Detective
      Film: A Timetable for Success." Literature/Film
      Quarterly, 3 (1975), 205-212.

1233. Jenkinson, Phillip. "The Agatha Christie Films."
      In Agatha Christie: First Lady of Crime. Ed.
      H.R.F. Keating. New York: Holt, Rinehart and
      Winston, 1977, pp. 155-182.

SAMUEL TAYLOR COLERIDGE

1234. Griggs, Earl Leslie. "The Film Seen and Heard."
      The Quarterly of Film, Radio, and Television,
      8 (1953), 93-99.
      On Shull's The Ancient Mariner.

1235. Shull, William M. "Translating with Film." The
      Quarterly of Film, Radio, and Television, 8 (1953),
      88-92.
      On preparing a film version of The Rime of the Ancient
      Mariner.

1236. Valasopolos, Anca. "Ken Russell's Clouds of Glory:
      the Ruling Passion as Key to the Artist."
      Literature/Film Quarterly, 8 (1980), 2-13.

JOSEPH CONRAD

1237.   Anderegg, Michael A.   "Conrad and Hitchcock: The
          Secret Agent Inspires Sabotage."   Literature/Film
          Quarterly, 3 (1975), 215-225.

1238.   Bogue, Ronald L.   "The Heartless Darkness of Apocalypse
          Now."   Georgia Review, 35 (1981), 611-626.

1239.   Brooks, Richard.   "Forward to Lord Jim."   Movie,
          12 (Spring 1965), 15-16.

1240.   _____.   "On the Thematic Visual Action in Lord
          Jim."   Cinema, 2 (March-April 1965), 4-5.
          Both articles are by the director of Lord Jim.

1241.   Cohen, Hubert.   "The Heart of Darkness in Citizen
          Kane."   Cinema Journal, 12 (Fall 1972), 11-25.
          Influence of Conrad on Orson Welles.

1242.   Davis, Roderick.   "Conrad Cinematized: The Duelists."
          Literature/Film Quarterly, 8 (1980), 125-132.

1243.   Dorall, E.N.   "Conrad and Coppola: Different Centers
          of Darkness."   Southeast Asian Review of English,
          1 (Dec. 1980), 19-26.

1244.   Goodwin, James.   "Conrad and Hitchcock: Secret Sharers."
          In The English Novel and the Movies.   Ed. Michael
          Klein and Gillian Parker.   New York: Frederick
          Ungar, 1981, pp. 218-227.
          Hitchcock's adaptation of The Secret Agent.

1245.   Gould, Eric.   "Great Balls of Fire: Apocalypse Now."
          Denver Quarterly, 14 (Fall 1979), 99-106.

1246.   Hagen, William M.   "Apocalypse Now (1979): Joseph
          Conrad and the Television War."   In Hollywood
          as Historian: American Film in a Cultural Context.
          Ed. Peter C. Rollins.   Lexington: The University
          Press of Kentucky, 1983, pp. 230-245.

1247.   _____.   "Heart of Darkness and the Process
          of Apocalypse Now."   Conradiana, 13 (1981), 45-53.

1248.   Harkness, Bruce.   "Conrad, Graham Greene, and Film."
          In Joseph Conrad: Theory and World Fiction.
          Ed. Wolodymyr T. Zyla and Wendell M. Aycock.
          Lubbock: Texas Technical University, 1974, pp. 71-87.
          Examines film adaptations of the two authors.

1249.   Harrell, Bill J.   "The Social Basis of Root Metaphor:
          An Application to Apocalypse Now and The Heart
          of Darkness."   Journal of Mind and Behavior,
          3 (Summer 1982), 221-240.

1250. Hellmann, John. "Vietnam and the Hollywood Genre
       Film: Inversions of American Mythology in The
       Deer Hunter and Apocalypse Now." American Quarterly,
       34 (1982), 418-439.

1251. Holmes, Cecil. "A Journey With Joseph Conrad."
       Overland, 90 (Dec. 1982), 2-14.
       On Holmes's adaptation of "The Planter of Malta."

1252. Jacobs, Diane. "Coppola Films Conrad in Vietnam."
       In The English Novel and the Movies. Ed. Michael
       Klein and Gillian Parker. New York: Frederick
       Ungar, 1981, pp. 211-217.
       On Apocalypse Now, Coppola's adaptation of Heart
       of Darkness.

1253. Kinder, Marsha. "The Power of Adaptation in Apocalypse
       Now." Film Quarterly, 33 (Winter 1979-80), 12-20.

1254. Kirschner, Paul. "Conrad and the Film." The Quarterly
       of Film, Radio, and Television, 11 (1957), 343-353.
       Demonstrates Conrad's techniques are similar to
       those of film.

1255. Pinsker, Sanford. "Heart of Darkness Through
       Contemporary Eyes, or What's Wrong with Apocalypse
       Now?" Conradiana, 13 (1981), 55-58.

1256. Rosenbaum, Jonathan. "The Voice and the Eye: A
       Commentary on The Heart of Darkness Script."
       Film Comment, 8 (Nov.-Dec. 1972), 27-32.
       On Orson Welles's unfinished scenario.

1257. Stewart, Garrett. "Coppola's Conrad: The Repetitions
       of Complicity." Critical Inquiry, 7 (1980-1981),
       455-474.
       On Apocalypse Now.

1258. Sulik, Boleshaw. A Change of Tack: Making The Shadow
       Line. London: British Film Institute, 1976.

1259. Sundelson, David. "Danse Macabre." Conradiana,
       13 (1981), 41-44.
       On Apocalypse Now.

1260. Thomaier, William. "Conrad on the Screen." Films
       in Review, 21 (1970), 611-621.
       Annotated filmography.

1261. Watson, Wallace S. "Conrad on Film." Conradiana,
       11 (1972), 209-227.

1262. _____. "Willard as Narrator: A Critique and
       a Modest Proposal." Conradiana, 13 (1981), 35-40.
       On Apocalypse Now.

NOEL COWARD

1263.   Anderegg, Michael A.   "Interpreting Noel Coward"
         and "Lean's `Coming of Age': Brief Encounter."
         In his David Lean. Boston: Twayne Publishing,
         1984, pp. 7-23 and pp. 25-35.
         Concerns In Which We Serve, This Happy Breed, and
         Blithe Spirit.

DANIEL DEFOE

1264.   Durgnat, Raymond.   "Robinson Crusoe." In his Luis
         Buñuel. Berkeley: University of California Press,
         1968, pp. 78-82.

1265.   Parker, Gillian.   "Robinson Crusoe: Crusoe Through
         the Looking Glass." In The English Novel and
         the Movies. Ed. Michael Klein and Gillian Parker.
         New York: Frederick Ungar, 1981, pp. 14-27.

CHARLES DICKENS

1266.   Anderegg, Michael A.   "Lean and Dickens." In his
         David Lean. Boston: Twayne Publishing, 1984,
         pp. 37-61.
         Oliver Twist and Great Expectations.

1267.   Buscombe, Edward.   "Dickens and Hitchcock." Screen,
         2, Nos. 4-5 (1970), 97-114.

1268.   Butler, Ivan.   "Dickens on the Screen." In Film
         Review 1972-73. Ed. F. Maurice Speed. New
         York: A.S. Barnes, 1972, pp. 19-25.
         Filmography.

1269.   C., A.E.B.   "David Copperfield on the Screen."
         Dickensian, 31 (1935), 223-225.

1270.   _____.   "On Stage and Screen (1) The Old Curiosity
         Shop Film." The Dickensian, 31 (1935), 137-138.

1271.   _____.   "The Screen Version of Great Expectations."
         The Dickensian, 31 (1935), 62.

1272.   _____.   "Scrooge on the Screen." The Dickensian,
         32 (1936), 59-60.

1273.   C., P.T.   "Drood Vanished into Nowhere." The Dickensian,
         31 (1935), 231-232.

1274.   Clarke, T.E.B.   "Every Word in Its Place." Films
         and Filming, 4 (Feb. 1958), 10, 28.
         Clarke discusses his script of A Tale of Two Cities.

1275.   Crabbe, Katharyn.   "Lean's Oliver Twist: From Novel
         to Film." Film Criticism, 2 (Fall 1977), 46-51.

1276. Curry, George. "Treatment and Script." In his
       Copperfield `70: The Making of the Omnibus-20th
       Century-Fox Film. New York: Ballantine Books,
       1970, pp. 12-24.
On the Delbert Mann adaptation.

1277. Dexter, Walter. "Dickens on Screen and Stage."
       The Dickensian, 31 (1935), 215-218.
On problems with adaptations, particularly David
Copperfield.

1278. Eisenstein, Sergei. "Dickens, Griffith, and the
       Film Today." In his Film Form: Essays in Film
       Theory. Ed. Jay Leyda. New York: Harcourt,
       Brace, and World, 1949, pp. 195-255.
The Russian director draws parallels between the
techniques of the American director and the British
novelist.

1279. Ellin, Stanley. "Mr. Dickens and Mr. Pichel."
       Hollywood Quarterly, 3 (Fall 1947), 87-89.
On Great Expectations.

1280. Fawcett, Frank Dubrez. "Dickens on the Screen."
       In his Dickens the Dramatist on Stage, Screen
       and Radio. London: W.H. Allen, 1952, pp. 193-208.

1281. Finlay, Ian. "Dickens in the Cinema." The Dickensian,
       54 (May 1968), 106-109.

1282. Fulton, A.R. "From Novel to Film." In his Motion
       Pictures: The Development of an Art From Silent
       Films to the Age of Television. Norman: University
       of Oklahoma Press, 1960, pp. 228-248
Discussion of Lean's Great Expectations.

1283. Harlow, Nancy Rex. "Dicken's Cinematic Imagination."
       DAI, 37 (1975), 7307A (Brown University).

1284. Harrington, John and David Paroissien. "Alberto
       Cavalcanti on Nicholas Nickleby." Literature/Film
       Quarterly, 6 (1978), 48-56.

1285. Hunt, Peter. "Research for Films for Dickens."
       The Dickensian, 44 (1948), 94-97.
Hunt was the research director for David Lean's
Oliver Twist.

1286. Keyser, Lester J. "Christmas (1951): A Scrooge
       for All Seasons." In The English Novel and
       the Movies. Ed. Michael Klein and Gillian Parker.
       New York: Frederick Ungar, 1981, pp. 121-131.

1287. Lansbury, Coral. "A Cry from Bergman--A Whisper
       of Dickens." Meanjin Quarterly, 32 (1973), 323-327.
Allusions to Dickens in Cries and Whispers.

1288. Law, Frederick Houk. "A Guide to the Study and
       Discussion of Oliver Twist." Audio-Visual Guide,
       18, No. 1 (1951), 33-38.

1289. Luhr, William. "David Copperfield (1935): Dicken's
       Narrative, Hollywood Vignettes." In The English
       Novel and the Movies.   Ed. Michael Klein and
       Guillian Parker. New York: Frederick Ungar,
       1981, pp. 132-142.

1290. Manchel, Frank. "Dickens in the Film: The Adaptation
       of Three Books." In his Film Study: A Resource
       Guide. Cranbury, N.J.: Associated University
       Presses, 1973, pp. 149-156.
       On David Copperfield (1935), A Tale of Two Cities
       (1935), and Great Expectations (1946).

1291. Mason, A. Stewart. "The Film of A Tale of Two Cities."
       The Dickensian, 32 (1936), 172.

1292. Moynahan, Julian. "Great Expectations: Seeing the
       Book, Reading the Movie." In The English Novel
       and the Movies. Ed. Michael Klein and Gillian
       Parker. New York: Frederick Ungar, 1981, pp. 143-154.

1293. Parker, Cecil. "Success to Dickens on the Screen."
       The Dickensian, (1958), 73-76.
       Author played Jarvis Lorry in A Tale of Two Cities.

1294. Paroissien, David. "Dickens and the Cinema." Dickens
       Studies Annual, Volume 7. Ed. Robert B. Partlow,
       Jr. Carbondale: Southern Illinois University
       Press, 1978, pp. 68-80.

1295. _____. "The Life and Adventures of Nicholas
       Nickleby: Alberto Cavalcanti Interprets Dickens."
       Hartford Studies in Literature, 9 (1977), 17-28.

1296. Petrie, Graham. "Dickens, Godard and the Film Today."
       The Yale Review, 64 (1975), 185-201.
       Argues that Dickens has much to offer the French
       director who is attempting to reconcile realism
       and "illusionism."

1297. Pichel, Irving. "`This Happy Breed' and Great
       Expectations." Hollywood Quarterly, 2 (1947),
       408-411.

1298. Pointer, Michael. "A Dicken's Garland: The Collected
       Film Works Reassessed." American Film, 1 (Dec. 1975),
       14-19.
       Survey of adaptations.

1299. Poole, Mike. "Dickens and Film: 101 Uses of a Dead
       Author." In The Changing World of Charles Dickens.
       Ed. Robert Giddings. Totowa: Barnes and Noble,
       1983, pp. 148-162.

1300. Powell, Dilys. "Postscript: Dickens on Film."
       Dickensian, 66 (1970), 183-185.
       On stage and screen adaptations, particularly George
       Cukor's and Delbert Mann's adaptations of David
       Copperfield.

1301. Riley, Michael M. "Dickens and Film: Notes on
       Adaptation." Dickens Studies Newsletter, 5 (1974),
       110-112.
       On Delbert Mann's and George Cukor's David Copperfield.

1302. Roman, Robert C. "Dickens' `A Christmas Carol.'"
       Films in Review, 10 (1958), 572-574.

1303. Silver, Alain. "The Untranquil Light: David Lean's
       Great Expectations." Literature/Film Quarterly,
       2 (1974), 140-153.

1304. Solomon, Stanley J. "The Nature of Plot Structure:
       Dickens Versus Antonioni." In his The Film Idea.
       New York: Harcourt Brace Javanovich, 1972,
       pp. 363-370.

1305. Stannard, Eliot. "Should Dickens Be Modernized
       for the Cinema?" The Dickensian, 14 (1918),
       126-128.
       Author was scenarist for Dombey and Son. Article
       drew seven responses (pp. 145-152).

1306. Staples, Leslie C. "David Lean's Oliver Twist."
       The Dickensian, 44 (1948), 203-205.

1307. _____. "Great Expectations Realized." The
       Dickensian, 43 (1947), 79-81.

1308. _____. "The New Film Version of A Tale of
       Two Cities." The Dickensian, 54 (1958), 110-120.

1309._____. "Nicholas Nickleby as a Film." The
       Dickensian, 43 (1947), 131-133.

1310. _____. "Pickwick on the Screen." The Dickensian,
       49 (1953), 75-76.

1311. Tharaud, Barry. "Two Film Versions of Oliver Twist:
       Moral Vision in Film and Literature." Dickens
       Studies Newsletter, 11 (1980), 41-46.
       On David Lean's and William J. Cowen's versions.

1312. Tupper, Lucy. "Dickens on the Screen." Films in
       Review, 10 (1959), 142-152.
       Annotated filmography.

1313. Wees, William C. "Dickens, Griffith, and Eisenstein:
       Form and Image in Literature and Film." Humanities
       Association Bulletin, 24 (1973), 266-276.

1314.   Young, Vernon.   "Dickens Without Holly: David Lean's
        Oliver Twist."   New Mexico Quarterly, 22 (1952),
        425-430.

1315.   Zambrano, Ana Laura.   "Audio-Visual Teaching Materials:
        A Dickensian Checklist--Part I."   Dickens Studies
        Newsletter, 7 (1976), 43-46.

1316.   _____.   "Audio-Visual Teaching Materials: A
        Dickensian Checklist--Part II."   Dickens Studies
        Newsletter, 7 (1976), 110-113.

1317.   _____.   "Charles Dickens and Serge Eisenstein:
        The Emergence of Cinema."   Style 9 (1975), 469-487.

1318.   _____.   "David Copperfield: Novel and Films."
        Hartford Studies in Literature, 9 (1977), 1-16.

1319.   _____.   Dickens and Film.   New York: Gordon
            Press, 1977.
        Contains discussions of the relationship of Dickens'
        techniques to film techniques, his relationship
        to D.W. Griffith and Sergei Eisenstein, and modern
        film adaptations of his novels (Great Expectations
        (1934, 1947, and 1974), David Copperfield (1935
        and 1970), A Tale of Two Cities (1935 and 1958),
        Oliver Twist (1948 and 1968), Nicholas Nickleby,
        A Christmas Carol (1951 and 1970), and Pickwick
        Papers.

1320.   _____.   "Feature Motion Pictures Adapted From
        Dickens: A Checklist--Part I."   Dickens Studies
        Newsletter, 5 (1974), 106-109.

1321.   _____.   "Feature Motion Pictures Adapted From
        Dickens: A Checklist--Part II."   Dickens Studies
        Newsletter, 6 (1975), 9-13.

1322.   _____.   "Great Expectations: Dickens and David
        Lean."   Literature/Film Quarterly, 2 (1974),
        154-161.

1323.   _____.   "Great Expectations: Dickens' Style
        in Terms of Film."   Hartford Studies in Literature,
        4 (1972), 104-113.

1324.   _____.   "The Styles of Dickens and Griffith:
        A Tale of Two Cities and Orphans of the Storm."
        Language and Style, 7 (1974), 53-61.

CHARLES LUTWIDGE DODGSON

1325.   McGillis, Roderick.   "Novelty and Roman Cement:
        Two Versions of Alice."   In Children's Novels
        and the Movies.   Ed. Douglas Street.   New York:
        Frederick Ungar, 1983, pp. 15-27.

1326.   Schaefer, David H. "The Film Collector's Alice:
         An Essay and a Checklist." In Lewis Carroll
         Observed. Ed. Edward Guiliano. New York: Clarkson
         N. Potter, 1976, pp. 196-207.

1327.   Schaefer, David and Maxine Schaefer. " The First
         Alice Motion Picture." Jabberwocky, 5 (1976),
         50-51.

1328.   Sibley, Brian. "Alice on the Mountain of Dreams:
         An Appreciation of the 1933 Paramount Film of
         Alice in Wonderland." Jabberwocky, 8 (Summer
         1979), 56-65.

ARTHUR CONAN DOYLE

1329.   Connor, Edward. "Sherlock Holmes on the Screen."
         Films in Review, 12 (1961), 409-418.
         Annotated filmography.

1330.   Haylock, Ron. Deerstalker: Holmes and Watson on
         Screen. Metuchen: Scarecrow Press, 1978.

1331.   Pohle, Robert W., Jr. and Douglas C. Hart. Sherlock
         Holmes on the Screen. New York: A.S. Barnes,
         1977.

LAWRENCE DURRELL

1332.   Haller, Robert. "The Writer and Hollywood.: An
         Interview with Lawrence Durrell." Film Heritage,
         6 (Fall 1970), 25-26.
         On Justine.

T.S. ELIOT

1333.   Richardson, Robert. "La Dolce Vita: Fellini and
         T.S. Eliot." In Federico Fellini: Essays in
         Criticism. Ed. Peter Bondanella. New York:
         Oxford University Press, 1978, pp. 103-112.
         Article is a portion of Richardson's Film and
         Literature.

BARRY ENGLAND

1334.   Taylor, Peter. "Metamorphosis: Novel to Film: Figures
         in a Landscape--the Novel, the Script, the Film."
         Lumiere, No. 31 (Jan.-Feb. 1974), pp. 22-25.

HENRY FIELDING

1335.   Battestin, Martin C. "Osborne's Tom Jones: Adapting
         a Classic." Virginia Quarterly Review, 42 (1966),
         378-393. Reprinted in Man and the Movies. Ed. W.R.
         Robinson. Baltimore: Penguin Books, 1967, pp. 31-45.
         Reprinted in Film and Literature: Contrasts in
         Media. Ed. Fred H. Marcus. Scranton, Pa.: Chandler
         Publishing Co., 1971, pp. 164-177.

1336. Behrens, Laurence. "The Argument of Tom Jones."
       Literature/Film Quarterly, 8 (1980), 22-34.

1337. Dolbier, Maurice, George D. Crothers and Glenway
       Westcott. "Henry Fielding's Tom Jones." In
       Invitation to Learning: English and American
       Novels. Ed. George D. Crothers. New York: Basic
       Books, 1966, pp. 36-43.

1338. Insdorf, Annette and Sharon Goodman. "Tom Jones:
       A Whisper and a Wink." In The English Novel
       and the Movies. Ed. Michael Klein and Gillian
       Parker. New York: Frederick Ungar, 1981, pp. 36-43.

1339. Laban, Lawrence F. "Joseph Andrews: Visualizing
       Fielding's Point of View." In The English Novel
       and the Movies. Ed. Michael Klein and Gillian
       Parker. New York: Frederick Ungar, 1981, pp. 28-35.

1340. Rundus, Raymond J. "The History of Tom Jones in
       Adaptation." DAI, 30 (1969), 1535A (The University
       of Nebraska).

1341. _____. "Tom Jones in Adaptation: A Chronology
       and Criticism." Bulletin of the New York Public
       Library, 77 (1974), 329-341.

                    E.M. FORSTER

1342. Annan, Noel. "The Unmysterious East: A Passage
       to India." New York Review of Books, 31 (17
       Jan. 1985), 5-6.

                    JOHN FOWLES

1343. Almansi, Guido and Simon Henderson. "Different
       Ball Games: The French Lieutenant's Woman and
       Other Places." In their Harold Pinter. London:
       Methuen, 1983, pp. 95-101.

1344. Conradi, Peter J. "The French Lieutenant's Woman:
       Novel, Screenplay, Film." Critical Quarterly,
       24 (Spring 1982), 41-57.

1345. Corbett, Thomas. "Film and the Book: A Case Study
       of The Collector." English Journal, 57 (1968),
       328-333.

1346. Gaston, Georg. "The French Lieutenant's Woman."
       Film Quarterly, 35 (Winter 1981-82), 51-56.

1347. Kennedy, Harlan. "The Czech Director's Woman."
       Film Comment, 17 (Sept.-Oct. 1981), 26-27.
       On The French Lieutenant's Woman.

1348. _____. "Karel Reisz Interviewed." Film Comment,
       17 (Sept.-Oct. 1981), 27-28, 30-31.
       Interview with the director of The French Lieutenant's
       Woman.

1349.   Mazis, Glen A.   "The `Riteful' Play of Time in The
         French Lieutenant's Woman." Soundings, 66 (1983),
         296-318.

1350.   Spitz, Ellen Handler.   "Interpretation of Film as
         Dream: The French Lieutenant's Woman." Post
         Script, 2 (Fall 1982), 13-29.

1351.   Whall, Tony.   "Karel Reisz's The French Lieutenant's
         Woman: Only the Name Remains the Same."
         Literature/Film Quarterly, 10 (1982), 75-81.

1352.   Zimmerman, James Richard.   "John Fowles on Film:
         A Study of the Film Adaptations of The Collector,
         The Magus, and The French Lieutenant's Woman."
         DAI, 44 (1983), 1095A (Ohio State University).

PENELOPE GILLIATT

1353.   Childs, James.   "Interview with Penelope Gilliatt."
         Film Comment, 8 (Summer 1972), 22-26. Reprinted
         in The Hollywood Screenwriters. Ed. Richard
         Corliss. New York: Avon Books, 1972, pp. 229-239.
         Discusses how her novel A State of Change became
         her script for Sunday Bloody Sunday.

1354.   Phillips, Gene D.   "Sunday, Bloody Sunday." In
         his John Schlesinger. Boston: Twayne Publishers,
         1981, pp. 131-144.

GRAHAM GREENE

1355.   Adamson, Jyd.   "Graham Greene as Film Critic."
         Sight and Sound, 41 (Spring 1972), 104-106.

1356.   Adamson, Judith. Graham Greene and Cinema. Norman,
         Ok.: Pilgrim Books, 1984.
         Adaptations of Greene's works: This Gun for Hire,
         The Ministry of Fear, Confidential Agent, The Man
         Within, Brighton Rock, The Fugitive, The Fallen
         Idol, The Third Man, The Heart of the Matter, The
         End of the Affair, The Quiet American, Our Man in
         Havana, and The Comedians.

1357.   Adamson, Judy and Phillip Stratford.   "Looking for
         the Third Man: On the Trail in Texas, New York,
         Hollywood." Encounter, June 1978, pp. 39-46.
         Examines the differences between Greene's story,
         the scripts, and the film.

1358.   Atkins, John.   "The Curse of the Film." In his
         Graham Greene. London: John Calder, 1957, pp. 78-87.
         Reprinted in Graham Greene: Some Critical
         Considerations. Ed. Robert O. Evans. Lexington:
         University of Kentucky Press, 1963, pp. 207-218.
         On Greene as a film critic.

1359. Bedard, B.J. "Reunion in Havana." Literature/Film
       Quarterly, 2 (1974), 352-358.
       Concerns Our Man in Havana.

1360. Diephouse, Daniel Jon. "Graham Greene and the Cinematic
       Imagination." DAI, 39 (1978),3572A (The University
       of Michigan).

1361. Fagin, Steven. "Narrative Design in Travels with
       My Aunt." Literature/Film Quarterly, 2 (1974),
       379-383.

1362. Ginna, Robert Emmett. "Our Man in Havana." Horizon,
       2, No. 2 (1959), 27-31, 122-126.
       Report from the set of Carol Reed's Our Man in Havana.

1363. Gomez, Joseph A. "The Theme of the Double in The
       Third Man." Film Heritage, 6 (Summer 1971),
       7-12.

1364. _____. "The Third Man: Capturing the Visual
       Essence of Literary Conception." Literature/Film
       Quarterly, 2 (1974), 332-339.

1365. Greene, Graham. Graham Greene on Film: Collected
       Film Criticism, 1935-1939. Ed. John Russell
       Taylor. New York: Simon and Schuster, 1972.

1366. _____. "The Novelist and the Cinema--A Personal
       Experience." In International Film Annual, No.
       2. Ed. William Whitebait. London: John Calder,
       1958, pp. 54-61.

1367. _____. "Subjects and Stories." In Footnotes
       to the Film. Ed. Charles Davy. London: Lovat
       and Dickson, 1937, pp. 57-70;rpt. New York: Arno
       Press, 1970.

1368. Keyser, Les. "England Made Me." Literature/Film
       Quarterly, 2 (1974), 364-372.
       Concerns the adaptation of Greene's The Shipwrecked.

1369. Lenfest, David S. "Brighton Rock/Young Scarface."
       Literature/Film Quarterly, 2 (1974), 373-378.

1370. McDougal, Stuart Y. "Visual Tropes: An Analysis
       of The Fallen Idol." Style, 9 (1975), 502-513.

1371. McGugan, Ruth E. "The Heart of the Matter."
       Literature/Film Quarterly, 2 (1974), 359-363.

1372. Mass, Roslyn. "The Presentation of the Character
       of Sarah Miles in the Film Version of The End
       of the Affair." Literature/Film Quarterly, 2
       (1974), 347-352.

1373. Navarro, Lenore Mary. "From Fiction to Film: A
       Critical Analysis of Graham Greene's The Fallen
       Idol, The Third Man, and Our Man in Havana."
       DAI, 37 (1977), 5405-5406A (The University of
       Southern California).

1374. Nolan, Jack Edmund. "Graham Greene's Movies."
       Films in Review, 15 (1964), 23-35. Reprinted
       as "Graham Greene's Films" in Literature/Film
       Quarterly, 2 (1974), 302-309.

1375. Palmer, James and Michael Riley. "The Lone Rider
       in Vienna: Myth and Meaning in The Third Man."
       Literature/Film Quarterly, 7 (1980), 14-21.

1376. Phillips, Gene D. "Graham Greene: On the Screen.
       An Interview." Catholic World, 209 (August 1969),
       218-221. Reprinted in Graham Greene: A Collection
       of Critical Essays. Ed. Samuel Hynes. Englewood
       Cliffs: Prentice-Hall, 1973, pp. 168-176.
Greene discusses adaptations of his works.

1377. _____. Graham Greene: The Films of His Fiction.
       New York: Teachers College Press, 1974.
Adaptations of Greene's works: This Gun for Hire,
The Ministry of Fear, Confidential Agent, The Man
Within, Brighton Rock, The Fugitive, The Fallen
Idol, The Third Man, The Heart of the Matter, The
End of the Affair, The Quiet American, Our Man in
Havana, and The Comedians.

1378. Purcell, James Mark. "Graham Greene and Others:
       The British Depression Film as an Art Form."
       Antigonish Review, No. 15 (1973), pp. 75-82.
On Greene as a film critic.

1379. Samuels, Charles Thomas. "Carol Reed and the Novelistic
       Film." In Mastering the Film and Other Essays.
       Ed. Lawrence Graver. Knoxville: The University
       of Tennessee Press, 1977, pp. 12-41.
On Reed's collaborations with Greene: The Fallen
Idol, The Third Man and Our Man in Havana.

1380. Skerrett, Joseph T., Jr. "Graham Greene at the
       Movies: A Novelist's Experience with the Film."
       Literature/Film Quarterly, 2 (1974), 293-301.

1381. Van Wert, William. "Narrative Structure in The
       Third Man." Literature/Film Quarterly, 2 (1974),
       341-346.

1382. Welsh, James M. and Gerald R. Barrett. "Graham
       Greene's Ministry of Fear: The Transformation
       of an Entertainment." Literature/Film Quarterly,
       2 (1974), 310-323.

1383. Wilmington, Michael. "The Fugitive." Velvet Light
       Trap, No. 5 (Summer 1972), pp. 33-35.
Adaptation of Greene's The Power and the Glory.

1384.   Zambrano, Ana Laura.   "Greene's Visions of Childhood:
        `The Basement Room' and The Fallen Idol."
        Literature/Film Quarterly, 2 (1974), 324-331.

                        THOMAS HARDY

1385.   Beach, Jospeh Warren.   "Movie."   In his The Technique
        of Thomas Hardy.   Chicago: University of Chicago
        Press, 1922, 134-157.
        Cinematic techniques in The Mayor of Casterbridge
        and The Woodlanders.

1386.   Costabile, Rita.   "Far From the Madding Crowd: Hardy
        in Soft Focus."   In The English Novel and the
        Movies.   Ed. Michael Klein and Gillian Parker.
        New York: Frederick Ungar, 1981, pp. 155-164.

1387.   Costanzo, William V.   "Polanski in Wessex: Filming
        Tess of the d'Urbervilles."   Literature/Film
        Quarterly, 9 (1981), 71-78.

1388.   Dickinson, Thorold.   "The Mayor of Casterbridge."
        Sight and Sound, 19 (Jan. 1951), 363-371.
        Includes excerpts of the screenplay of this unmade
        film.

1389.   Grundy, Joan.   "Cinematic Arts."   In her Hardy and
        the Sister Arts.   New York: Harper and Row, 1979,
        pp. 106-133.
        Cinematic techniques in Hardy's fiction.

1390.   Harris, Margaret.   "Thomas Hardy's Tess of the
        d'Urbervilles: Faithfully Presented by Roman
        Polanski?"   Syndey Studies in English, 7 (1981-82),
        115-122.

1391.   Kozloff, Sarah R.   "Where Wessex Meets New England:
        Griffith's Way Down East and Hardy's Tess of
        the d'Urbervilles."   Literature/Film Quarterly,
        13 (1985), 35-41.

1392.   Lodge, David.   "Thomas Hardy and the Cinematographic
        Novel."   Novel, 7 (1974), 246-254.   Revised and
        reprinted in Thomas Hardy After Fifty Years.
        Ed. Lance St. John Butler.   Totowa, N.J.: Rowan
        and Littlefield, 1977, pp. 78-89.   Reprinted
        in his Working With Structuralism: Essays and
        Reviews on Nineteenth and Twentieth-Century
        Literature.   Boston: Routledge and Kegan Paul,
        1981, pp. 95-105.

1393.   Phillips, Gene D.   "Far From the Madding Crowd."
        In his John Schlesinger.   Boston: Twayne Publishers,
        1981, pp. 80-92.

1394.   Waldman, Nell Kozak.   "`All That She Is': Hardy's
        Tess and Polanski's."   Queens Quarterly, 88 (Autumn
        1981), 429-436.

1395. Welsh, James M. "Hardy and the Pastoral, Schlesinger
       and Shepherds: Far From the Madding Crowd."
       Literature/Film Quarterly, 9 (1981), 79-84.

L.P. HARTLEY

1396. Gordon, Lois. "The Go-Between--Hartley and Pinter."
       Kansas Quarterly, 4 (Spring 1972), 81-92.

1397. Grossvogel, David I. "Under the Sign of Symbols:
       Losey and Hartley." Diacritics, 4 (Fall 1974),
       51-56.
       On The Go-Between.

1398. Hirsch, Foster. "The Go-Between." In his Joseph
       Losey. Boston: Twayne Publishing, 1980, pp. 129-141.

1399. Jones, Edward T. "Summer of 1900: A la recherche
       of The Go-Between." Literature/Film Quarterly,
       1 (1973), 154-160.

1400. Riley, Michael and James Palmer. "Time and the
       Structure of Memory in The Go-Between." College
       English, 5 (1978), 219-227.

1401. Roud, Richard. "Going Between." Sight and Sound,
       40 (Summer 1971), 158-159.
       On The Go-Between.

1402. Sinyard, Neil. "Pinter's Go-Between." Critical
       Quarterly, 22 (1980), 21-33.

ALDOUS HUXLEY

1403. Clark, Virginia Martha. "Aldous Huxley and Film."
       DAI, 44 (1984), 3069A (The University of Maryland).
       Concerns Huxley's four major scenarios: Madame Curie,
       Pride and Prejudice, Jane Eyre, and A Woman's Vengeance,
       and his "California" novels: After Many a Summer
       and Ape and Essence.

1404. Gomez, Joseph A. "The Devils--Russell's Major
       Achievement: Sources" and "The Devils--Russell's
       Major Achievement: The Film." In his Ken Russell:
       The Adaptor as Creator. London: Frederick Muller,
       1976, pp. 114-136 and pp. 137-164.

1405. Huxley, Aldous. "Silence Is Golden." Sight and
       Sound, 23 (July-Sept. 1953), 47-48.
       Huxley on The Jazz Singer.

CHRISTOPHER ISHERWOOD

1406. Blades, Joe. "The Evolution of Cabaret." Literature/
       Film Quarterly, 1 (1973), 226-238.
       On the adaptation of Isherwood's Goodbye to Berlin.

1407. Sheed, Wilfrid. "I Am a Cabaret." The New York
       Review of Books, 18 (23 March 1972), 17-18.

JAMES JOYCE

1408. Armour, Robert A. "The `Whatness' of Joseph Strick's
        Portrait." In The English Novel and the Movies.
        Ed. Michael Klein and Gillian Parker. New York:
        Frederick Ungar, 1981, pp. 279-290.

1409. Barrow, Craig W. "Montage in James Joyce's Ulysses."
        DAI, 33 (1971), 1713A (University of Colorado);
        rpt. Madrid and Potomac, Md.: Studia Humanitatis,
        1980.

1410. Barsam, Richard. "Ulysses: When in Doubt Persecute
        Bloom." In The English Novel and the Movies.
        Ed. Michael Klein and Gillian Parker. New York:
        Frederick Ungar, 1981, pp. 291-300.

1411. Costanzo, William V. "Joyce and Eisenstein: Literary
        Reflections on the Reel World." Journal of Modern
        Literature, 11 (March 1984), 175-180.

1412. Deane, Paul. "Motion Picture Techniques in James
        Joyce's `The Dead'." James Joyce Quarterly,
        6 (1969), 231-236.

1413. Hutchins, Patricia. "James Joyce and the Cinema."
        Sight and Sound, 21 (Aug.-Sept. 1951), 9-12.
        Studies Joyce's relationship with Eisenstein; contains
        part of a scenario for "Anna Livia Plurabelle."

1414. Klein, Michael. "Strick's Adaptation of Joyce's
        Portrait of the Artist: Discourse and Containing
        Discourse." In Narrative Strategies: Original
        Essays in Film and Prose Fiction. Ed. Syndy
        M. Conger and Janice R. Welsch. Macomb: Western
        Illinois University, 1980, pp. 37-46.

1415. Lang, Dewey. "Ulysses." Film, No. 49 (1967), pp. 23-26.

1416. McCabe, Bernard. "Ulysses in the Reel World."
        New Catholic World, 204 (March 1967), 346-351.
        Considers the possibilities of adapting Joyce's
        novel; article is not an examination of Strick's
        adaptation.

1417. Parr, Mary. James Joyce: The Poetry of Conscience:
        A Study of Ulysses. Milwaukee: Inland Press,
        1961.
        Sees Chaplin as the inspiration for Leopold Bloom;
        traces Joyce's use of cinematic techniques.

1418. Pearce, Richard. "Experimentation with the Grotesque:
        Comic Collisions in the Grotesque World of Ulysses."
        Modern Fiction Studies, 20 (1974), 378-384.
        Joyce's use of montage.

1419. Perlmutter, Ruth. "Joyce and Cinema." Boundary
        2, 6 (1978), 481-502.

1420.   Ryf, Robert F.   "Joyce's Visual Imagination." Texas
        Studies in Literature and Language, 1 (1959),
        30-43.
        Joyce's use of cinematic techniques in his fiction.

1421.   Slate, Joseph Evans.   "The Reisman-Zukofsky Screenplay
        of Ulysses: Its Background and Significance."
        Library Chronicle of the University of Texas,
        20-21 (1982), 107-139.
        On the unfilmed screenplay by Jerry Reisman and
        Louis Zukofsky.

1422.   Smith, Sarah W. R.   "The World Made Celluloid: On
        Adapting Joyce's Wake." In The English Novel
        and the Movies. Ed. Michael Klein and Gillian
        Parker. New York: Frederick Ungar, 1981,
        pp. 301-312.

1423.   Solomon, Margaret C.   "The Porters: A Square Performance
        of Three Tiers in the Round/Book III, Chapter
        iv." In A Conceptual Guide to Finnegan's Wake.
        Ed. Michael H. Begnal and Fritz Stenn. University
        Park: Pennsylvania State University Press, 1974,
        pp. 201-210.
        Cinematic techniques in Joyce's novel.

1424.   Von Abele, Rudolph.   "Film as Interpretation: A
        Case Study of Ulysses." Journal of Aesthetics
        and Art Criticism, 31 (1973), 487-500.

1425.   Weinberg, Gretchen.   "An Interview with Mary Ellen
        Bute on the Filming of Finnegan's Wake." Film
        Culture, No. 35 (Winter 1964-1965), pp. 25-28.

                    RUDYARD KIPLING

1426.   Beckerman, Jim.   "The Man Who Would Be King: On
        Adapting `The Most Audacious Thing in Fiction'."
        In The English Novel and the Movies. Ed. Michael
        Klein and Gillian Parker. New York: Frederick
        Ungar, 1981, pp. 180-186.

1427.   Blackburn, William.   "All About a Boy: Kipling's
        Novel, M.G.M's Film." In Children's Novels and
        the Movies. Ed. Douglas Street. New York: Frederick
        Ungar, 1983, pp. 101-110.
        On Kim.

1428.   Grella, George.   "The Colonial Movie and The Man
        Who Would Be King." Texas Studies in Literature
        and Language, 22 (1980), 246-262.

                    D.H. LAWRENCE

1429.   Baldanza, Frank.   "Sons and Lovers: Novel to Film
        as a Record of Cultural Growth." Literature/Film
        Quarterly, 1 (1973), 64-70.

1430. Becker, Henry, III.   "`The Rocking-Horse Winner':
       Film as Parable."   Literature/Film Quarterly,
       1 (1973), 55-63. Reprinted in From Fiction to
       Film: D.H. Lawrence's "The Rocking-Horse Winner."
       Ed. Gerald R. Barrett and Thomas L. Erskine. Encino,
       Ca.: Dickenson Publishing Co., 1974, pp. 204-213.

1431. Crump, G.B. "The Fox on Film." D.H. Lawrence Review,
       1 (1968), 238-244.

1432. _____. "Gopher Prairie or Papplewick? The
       Virgin and the Gypsy as Film." D.H. Lawrence
       Review, 4 (1971), 142-153.

1433. _____. "Lawrence and The Literature/Film
       Quarterly." D.H. Lawrence Review, 6 (1973),
       326-332.
       On Literature/Film Quarterly's Lawrence issue, 1
       (1973).

1434. _____. "Women in Love: Novel and Film." D.H.
       Lawrence Review, 4 (1971), 28-41.

1435. DeNitto, Dennis. "Sons and Lovers: All Passion
       Spent." In The English Novel and the Movies.
       Ed. Michael Klein and Gillian Parker. New York:
       Frederick Ungar, 1981, pp. 235-247.

1436. Gerard, Lillian N. "Of Lawrence and Love." Film
       Library Quarterly, 3 (Fall 1970), 6-12.
       On Russell's Women in Love.

1437. _____. "The Virgin and the Gypsy and `D.H. Lawrence
       in Taos.'" Film Library Quarterly, 4 (Winter
       1970-71), 36-42.

1438. Gomez, Joseph A. "Women in Love: Novel Into Film."
       In his Ken Russell: The Adaptor as Creator.
       London: Frederick Muller, 1976, pp. 78-95. Revised
       and reprinted as "Women in Love: Russell's Images
       of Lawrence's Vision." In The English Novel
       and the Movies. Ed. Michael Klein and Gillian
       Parker. New York: Frederick Ungar, 1981,
       pp. 248-256.

1439. Gontarski, S.E. "Filming Lawrence." Modernist
       Studies: Literature and Culture, 4 (1982), 87-95.
       Overview of adaptations.

1440. _____. "Mark Rydell and the Filming of The
       Fox: An Interview with S.E. Gontarski." Modernist
       Studies: Literature and Culture, 4 (1982), 96-104.

1441. _____. "The Virgin and the Gypsy: An English
       Watercolor." In The English Novel and the Movies.
       Ed. Michael Klein and Gillian Parker. New York:
       Frederick Ungar, 1981, pp. 257-267.

1442. _____. "Christopher Miles Interview: The
      Virgin and the Gypsy." Literature/Film Quarterly,
      11 (1983), 249-256.

1443. Hanke, Ken. "The First Controlled Feature: Women
      in Love." In his Ken Russell's Films. Metuchen:
      Scarecrow Press, 1984, pp. 51-74.

1444. Hanlon, Lindley. "Lady Chatterley's Lover: Sensuality
      and Simplification." In The English Novel and
      the Movies. Ed. Michael Klein and Gillian Parker.
      New York: Frederick Ungar, 1981, pp. 268-278.

1445. Kaspars, Candace Brand. "Symbolism in the Film
      Adaptations and Novels of D.H. Lawrence's Sons
      and Lovers, Women in Love, and The Virgin and
      the Gypsy." DAI, 37 (1977), 6113-6114A (The
      University of Michigan).

1446. Knoll, Robert F. "Women in Love." Film Heritage,
      6 (Summer 1971), 1-6.

1447. Lambert, Gavin. "Lawrence: The Script." Films
      and Filming, 6 (May 1960), 9.
      Lambert wrote the screenplay for Sons and Lovers.

1448. Marcus, Fred. "From Story to Screen." Media and
      Methods, 14 (Dec. 1977), 56-58.
      On Lawrence's The Rocking-Horse Winner.

1449. Mellen, Joan. "Outfoxing Lawrence: Novella into
      Film." Literature/Film Quarterly, 1 (1973),
      17-27. Revised and reprinted in Women and Their
      Sexuality in the New Film. New York: Horizon
      Press, 1972, pp. 216-228.

1450. _____. "'The Rocking-Horse Winner as Cinema."
      In From Fiction to Film: D.H. Lawrence's 'The
      Rocking-Horse Winner. Ed. Gerald R. Barrett
      and Thomas L. Erskine. Encino, Ca.: Dickenson
      Publishing Co., 1974, pp. 214-223.

1451. Moore, Harry T. "D.H. Lawrence and the Flicks."
      Literature/Film Quarterly, 1 (1973), 3-11.

1452. Peek, Andrew. "Tim Burstall's Kangaroo." Westerly,
      25 (Dec. 1980), 39-42.
      Interview with Burstall on his proposed adaptation.

1453. Phillips, Gene D. "Sexual Ideas in the Films of
      D.H. Lawrence." Sexual Behavior, 1 (June 1971),
      10-16.

1454. Scott, James F. "The Emasculation of Lady Chatterly's
      Lover." Literature/Film Quarterly, 1 (1973),
      37-45.

1455. Smith, Julian. "Vision and Revision: The Virgin
          and the Gypsy." Literature/Film Quarterly, 1
          (1973), 28-36.

1456. Sobchack, Thomas. "The Fox: The Film and the Novel."
          Western Humanities Review, 23 (1969), 73-78.

1457. Solecki, Sam. "D.H. Lawrence's View of Film."
          Literature/Film Quarterly, 1 (1973), 12-16.

1458. Stacy, Paul H. "Lawrence and Movies: A Postscript."
          Literature/Film Quarterly, 2 (1974), 93-95.
          On the cinematic qualities of Lawrence's poetry.

1459. Tarratt, Margaret. "An Obscene Undertaking." Films
          and Filming, 17 (Nov. 1970), 26-30.
          On Lawrence adaptations, focusing on Russell's Women
          in Love.

1460. Weightman, John. "Trifling with the Dead." Encounter,
          34 (Jan. 1970), 50-53.
          On Russell's Women in Love.

1461. Zambrano, Ana Laura. "Women in Love: Counterpoint
          on Film." Literature/Film Quarterly, 1 (1973),
          46-54.

DORIS LESSING

1462. Sarvan, Charles and Liebetraut Sarvan. "Doris Lessing
          on Film: The Grass is Singing." The Doris Lessing
          Newsletter, 5 (Winter 1981), 4-5.

1463. Schlueter, Paul. "Doris Lessing on Film: Memoirs
          of a Survivor." The Doris Lessing Newsletter,
          5 (Winter 1981), 5-6.

1464. _____. "Lessing on Film (con.)." The Doris
          Lessing Newsletter, 6 (Summer 1982), 5-6.
          On The Grass is Singing and Memoirs of a Survivor.

1465. Taylor, Jenny. "Memoirs Was Made of This: An Interview
          with David Gladwell, Director of Memoirs of a
          Survivor." In Notebooks/Archives: Reading and
          Rereading Doris Lessing. Ed. Jenny Taylor.
          Boston: Routledge, 1982, pp. 227-240.

C.S. LEWIS

1466. Harsh, Donna J. "Aslan in Filmland: The Animation
          of Narnia." In Children's Novels and the Movies.
          Ed. Douglas Street. New York: Frederick Ungar,
          1983, pp. 163-170.
          On The Lion, the Witch, and the Wardrobe.

MALCOLM LOWRY

1467. Binns, Ronald. "The Film of Under the Volcano."
       In his Malcolm Lowry. London: Methuen, 1984,
       pp. 85-88.

1468. Hamill, Pete. "Against All Odds." American Film,
       9 (July-Aug. 1984), 18-26, 28, 61.
       On Under the Volcano.

1469. Knoll, John Francis. "Malcolm Lowry and the Cinema."
       DAI, 34 (1974), 5181A (St. Louis University).

1470. Lowry, Malcolm and Margerie Bonner Lowry. Notes
       on a Screenplay for F. Scott Fitzgerald's Tender
       Is the Night. Intro. Paul Tiessen. Bloomfield
       Hills, Michigan: Bruccoli Clark, 1976.
       Volume includes the authors' commentary on their
       script but not the script itself.

1471. Perlmutter, Ruth. "Malcolm Lowry's Unpublished
       Filmscript of Tender is the Night." American
       Quarterly, 28 (1976), 561-574.

1472. Tiessen, Paul. "The Daily Province, 1939: Malcolm
       Lowry and Film." The Malcolm Lowry Newsletter,
       10 (Spring 1982), 11-13.

1473. _____. "Malcolm Lowry and the Cinema." Canadian
       Literature, 44 (Spring 1970), 38-49.

1474. _____. "Malcolm Lowry: Statements on Literature
       and Film." In The Practical Vision: Essays in
       English Literature in Honour of Flora Roy. Ed. Jane
       Campbell and James Doyle. Waterloo, Ontario:
       Wilfrid Lauier University Press, 1978, pp. 119-32.

                    JAMES VANCE MARSHALL

1475. Boyle, Anthony. "Two Images of the Aboriginal:
       Walkabout, the Novel and Film." Literature/Film
       Quarterly, 7 (1979), 67-76.

                    SOMERSET MAUGHAM

1476. Calder, Robert L. "Somerset Maugham and the Cinema."
       Literature/Film Quarterly, 6 (1978), 262-273.

1477. Curran, Trisha. "Of Human Bondage (1934, 1964):
       Variations on a Theme." In The English Novel
       and the Movies. Ed. Michael Klein and Gillian
       Parker. New York: Frederick Ungar, 1981,
       pp. 228-234.

1478. Maugham, W. Somerset. "On Writing for the Films."
       The North American Review, 213 (1921), 670-675.
       Reprinted in Authors on Film. Ed. Harry M. Geduld.
       Bloomington: Indiana University Press, 1972,
       pp. 181-187.

JOHN MILTON

1479. Fiore, Peter Amadeus. "Milton and Kubrick: Eden's
       Apple or a Clockwork Orange." CEA Critic, 35,
       No. 2 (1973), 14-17.

1480. Greenfield, Concetta Carestia. "S.M. Eisenstein's
       Alexander Nevsky and John Milton's Paradise Lost:
       A Structural Comparison." Milton Quarterly,
       9 (1975), 93-99.

GEORGE ORWELL

1481. Forbes, Jill. "News From Oceania." Sight and Sound,
       53 (Spring 1984), 111-114.
       Concerns the BBC-TV adaptation (1954) and the first
       film adaptation (1955).

JOHN OSBORNE

1482. Durgnat, Raymond. "Loved One." Films and Filming,
       12 (Feb. 1966), 19-23.
       Look Back in Anger and The Entertainer.

1483. Gomez, Joseph A. "The Entertainer: From Play to
       Film." Film Heritage, 8 (Spring 1973), 19-26.

1484. Robinson, David. "Look Back in Anger." Sight and
       Sound, 28 (Summer-Autumn 1959), 122-125, 179.

1485. Walker, Alexander. "The Angry Brigade." In his
       Hollywood U.K.: The British Film Industry in
       the Sixties. New York: Stein and Day, 1974,
       pp. 56-67.
       On Look Back in Anger.

HAROLD PINTER

1486. Brady, Allen. "The Gift of Realism: Hitchcock and
       Pinter." Journal of Modern Literature, 3 (1973),
       149-172.
       The reaction of theatre (Pinter's The Birthday Party)
       to filmic realism (Hitchcock's Shadow of a Doubt).

1487. Brater, Enoch. "Pinter's Homecoming on Celluloid."
       Modern Drama, 17 (1974), 443-448.

1488. Byrne, Jack. "Accident/Novel/Script/Film:
       Mosley/Pinter/Losey." The Review of Contemporary
       Fiction, 2 (Summer 1982), 132-142.

1489. Cavander, Kenneth. "Interview with Harold Pinter
       and Clive Donner." In Behind the Scenes: Theater
       and Film Interviews from the Transatlantic Review.
       Ed. Joseph F. McCrindle. New York: Holt, Rinehart,
       and Winston, 1971, pp. 211-222. Reprinted in
       Focus on Film and Theatre. Ed. James Hurt.
       Englewood Cliffs: Prentice-Hall, 1974, pp. 154-164.
       On the adaptation of The Caretaker.

1490. Deer, Harriet and Irving Deer. "Pinter's The Birthday
        Party: The Film and the Play." South Atlantic
        Bulletin, 45, No. 2 (1980), 26-30.

1491. Esslin, Martin. "Screenplays." In his Pinter:
        The Playwright. London: Methuen, 1978, pp. 227-233.

1492. Feldstein, Elayne P. "From Novel to Film: The Impact
        of Harold Pinter on Robert Maugham's The Servant."
        Studies in the Humanities, 5, No. 2 (1976), 9-14.

1493. Hirsch, Foster. "The Servant" and "Accident."
        In his Joseph Losey. Boston: Twayne Publishers,
        1980, pp. 87-111 and pp. 113-126.

1494. Horne, William Leonard. "`A Starting Point': A
        Critical Approach to the Role of the Screenplay
        in the Adaptation of Novels for the Cinema."
        DAI, 43 (1983), 3444A (The University of Wisconsin
        at Madison).
        Concerns Pinter's screenplay for The Pumpkin Eater.

1495. Houston, Beverle and Marsha Kinder. "The Losey-Pinter
        Collaboration." Film Quarterly, 32, No. 1 (1978),
        17-30.

1496. Hudgins, Christopher C. "Inside Out: Filmic Technique
        and the Theatrical Depiction of Consciousness
        in Harold Pinter's Old Times." Genre, 13 (1980),
        355-376.

1497. King, Noel. "Pinter's Screenplays: The Menace of
        the Past." Southern Review (University of Adelaide),
        14 (March 1981), 78-90.
        On The Servant, The Pumpkin Eater, Accident, and
        The Go-Between.

1498. Klein, Joanne. Making Pictures: The Pinter Screenplays.
        Columbus: Ohio State University Press, 1985.
        The Servant, The Pumpkin Eater, The Quiller Memorandum,
        Accident, The Go-Between, The Proust Screenplay, The
        Last Tycoon, and The French Lieutenant's Woman.

1499. McGarry, Mary Anne. "A Comparative Analysis of
        the Stage and Screen Versions of Three Plays
        by Harold Pinter." DAI, 38 (1978), 6406A
        (Northwestern University).
        The Birthday Party, The Caretaker, and The Homecoming.

1500. Randisi, Jennifer L. "Harold Pinter as Screenwriter."
        In Harold Pinter: You Never Heard Such Silence.
        Ed. Alan Bold. London: Vision Press, 1984,
        pp. 61-73.

1501. Reames, Wilbur Hazel, Jr. "Harold Pinter: An
        Introduction to the Literature of His Screenplays."
        DAI, 39 (1979), 7361A (The University of Georgia).
        On The Servant, The Pumpkin Eater, The Quiller
        Memorandum, Accident, and The Go-Between.

DOROTHY RICHARDSON

1502.   Richardson, Dorothy. "Continuous Performance."
         Close Up, 1 (July 1927), 34-37.

1503.   _____. "Continuous Performance II: Musical
         Accompaniment." Close Up, 1 (Aug. 1927), 58-62.

1504.   _____. "Continuous Performance III: Captions."
         Close Up, 1 (Sept. 1927), 52-56.

1505.   _____. "Continuous Perfomance IV: A Thousand
         Pities." Close Up, 1 (Oct. 1927), 60-64.

1506.   _____. "Continuous Performance V: There's
         No Place Like Home." Close Up, 1 (Nov. 1927),
         44-47.

1507.   _____. "Continuous Performance VI: The
         Increasing Congregation." Close Up, 1 (Dec.
         1927), 61-65.

1508.   _____. "Continuous Performance VII: The Front
         Rows." Close Up, 2 (Jan. 1928), 59-64.

1509.   _____. "Continuous Performance VIII." Close
         Up, 2 (March 1928), 51-55.

1510.   _____. "Continuous Performance IX: The Thoroughly
         Popular Film." Close Up, 2 (April 1928), 44-50.

1511.   _____. "Continuous Performance X: The Cinema
         in the Slums." Close Up, 2 (May 1928), 58-62.

1512.   _____. "Continuous Performance XI: Slow Motion."
         Close Up, 2 (June 1928), 54-58.

1513.   _____. "Continuous Performance XII: The Cinema
         in Arcady." Close Up, 3 (July 1928), 52-57.

1514.   _____. "Continuous Performance: Pictures and
         Films." Close Up, 4 (Jan. 1929), 51-57.

1515.   _____. "Continuous Performance: Almost Persuaded."
         Close Up, 4 (June 1929), 51-57.

1516.   _____. "Continuous Performance: Dialogue in
         Dixie." Close Up, 5 (Sept. 1929), 211-218.

1517.   _____. "Continuous Performance: A Tear for
         Lycidas." Close Up, 7 (Sept. 1930), 196-202.

1518.   _____. "Continuous Performance: Narcissus."
         Close Up, 8 (Sept. 1931), 182-185.

1519.   _____. "Continuous Performance: This Spoon-
         Fed Generation?" Close Up, 8 (Dec. 1931), 304-308.

1520. _____. "Continuous Performance: The Film Gone
      Male." Close Up, 9 (March 1932), 36-38.

1521. _____. "Continuous Performance." Close Up,
      10 (June 1933), 130-132.

1522. _____. "Talkies, Plays, and Books: Thoughts
      on the Approaching Battle Between the Spoken
      Pictures, Literature, and the Stage." Vanity
      Fair 32 (Aug. 1929), 56.

1523. Tiessen, Paul. "A Comparative Approach to the Form
      and Function of Novel and Film: Dorothy Richardson's
      Theory of Art." Literature/Film Quarterly, 3
      (1975), 83-90.

                    GEORGE BERNARD SHAW

1524. Bishop, G.W. "The Living Talkies: An Interview
      with G.B. Shaw." Theatre Guild Magazine, 7
      (Nov. 1929), 32.

1525. Costello, Donald B. "G.B.S.: The Movie Critic."
      Quarterly of Film, Radio, and Television, 11
      (1957), 256-275.

1526. _____. "Pygmalion." In Film and Literature:
      Contrasts in Media. Ed. Fred H. Marcus. Scranton,
      Pa.: Chandler Publishing Co., 1971, pp. 228-242.
      A chapter from The Serpent's Eye.

1527. _____. The Serpent's Eye: Shaw and the Cinema.
      South Bend: University of Notre Dame Press, 1965.
      Discussions of Shaw as screen writer and three
      adaptations: Pygmalion, Major Barbara, and Caesar
      and Cleopatra.

1528. Henderson, Archibald. "Dialogue II: The Drama,
      the Theater, and the Films." In Table-Talk of
      G.B.S.: Conversations on Things in General Between
      George Bernard Shaw and His Biographer. New
      York: Harper and Brothers, 1925, pp. 42-70.
      Excerpt reprinted as "Table-Talk of G.B.S.: The
      Drama, the Theatre, and the Films." In Focus
      on Film and Theatre. Ed. James Hurt. Englewood
      Cliffs: Prentice-Hall, 1974, pp. 149-153.

1529. Mycroft, Walter. "Shaw--and the Devil to Pay."
      Films and Filming, 5 (Feb. 1959), 14-15, 30-31.
      Anthony Asquith's associate on Shaw and film.

1530. Pascal, Gabriel. "Shaw as Scenario Writer." In
      G.B.S. 90: Aspects of Shaw's Life and Work.
      Ed. S. Winsten. New York: Dodd, Mead and Co.,
      1946, pp. 255-260.
      Pascal produced a number of adaptations of Shaw's
      plays.

1531.   Pascal, Valerie. The Disciple and His Devil: Gabriel
        Pascal and Bernard Shaw. New York: McGraw-Hill,
        1970.

1532.   Roll-Hansen, Diderik. "Shaw's Pygmalion: The Two
        Versions of 1916 and 1941." Review of English
        Literature, 8 (July 1967), 81-90.
        The differences between the original theatrical
        script and the film script.

1533.   Roman, Robert C. "G.B.S. on the Screen." Films
        in Review, 11 (1970), 406-418.
        Annotated filmography.

1534.   Rudman, Harry W. "Shaw's St. Joan and Motion Picture
        Censorship." Shaw Bulletin, 2 (Sept. 1959),
        1-14.

1535.   West, E.J. "Hollywood and Mr. Shaw: Some Reflections
        on Shavian Drama-Into-Cinema." Educational Theatre
        Journal, 5 (1953), 220-232.

MARY GODWIN SHELLEY

1536.   Dillard, R.H.W. "Even a Man Who is Pure at Heart:
        Poetry and Danger in the Horror Film." In Man
        and the Movies. Ed. W.R. Robinson. Baltimore:
        Penguin Books, pp. 60-96.

1537.   Douglas, Drake [peseud]. "The Monster." In his
        Horror! New York: Collier Books, 1969, pp. 77-129.

1538.   Friedman, Lester D. "Frankenstein: The Blasted
        Tree." In The English Novel and the Movies.
        Ed. Michael Klein and Gillian Parker. New York:
        Frederick Ungar, 1981, pp. 52-66.

1539.   Glut, Donald F. The Frankenstein Legend: A Tribute
        to Mary Shelley and Boris Karloff. Metuchen:
        Scarecrow Press, 1973.

1540.   Hitchens, Gordon. "`A Breathless Eagerness in the
        Audience'--Historical Notes on Dr. Frankenstein
        and His Monster." Film Comment, 6 (Spring 1970),
        49-51.

1541.   Jackson, Donald G. "The Changing Myth of Frankenstein:
        A Historical Analysis of the Interactions of
        a Myth, Technology, and Society." DAI, 37 (1977),
        4664A (The University of Texas at Austin).
        Contains discussion on adaptations of the novel.

1542.   LaValley, Albert J. "The Stage and Film Children
        of Frankenstein: A Survey." In The Endurance
        of Frankenstein: Essays on Mary Shelley's Novel.
        Ed. George Levine and U.C. Knoepflmacher. Berkeley:
        University of California Press, 1979, pp. 243-289.

1543.   Mank, Gregory William. "<u>Frankenstein</u> (1931)."
        In his <u>It's Alive! The Classic Cinema Saga of</u>
        <u>Frankenstein</u>. San Diego: A.S. Barnes, 1981,
        pp. 1-41.

1544.   Nestrick, William. "Coming to Life: Frankenstein
        and the Nature of Film Narrative." In <u>The Endurance</u>
        <u>of Frankenstein: Essays on Mary Shelley's Novel</u>.
        Ed. George Levine and U.C. Knoepflmacher. Berkeley:
        University of California Press, 1979, pp. 290-315.

1545.   Tropp, Martin. "Re-Creation." In his <u>Mary Shelley's</u>
        <u>Monster</u>. Boston: Houghton Mifflin, 1976, pp. 84-105.

ALAN SILLITOE

1546.   Harcourt, Peter. "I'd Rather Be Like I Am: Some
        Comments on <u>The Loneliness of the Long-Distance</u>
        <u>Runner</u>." <u>Sight and Sound</u>, 32 (Winter 1962-63),
        16-19.

1547.   Quirk, Eugene F. "Social Class as Audience: Sillitoe's
        Story and Screenplay `The Loneliness of the Long-
        Distance Runner.'" <u>Literature/Film Quarterly</u>,
        9 (1981), 161-171.

1548.   Rollins, Janet Buck. "Novel into Film: <u>The Loneliness</u>
        <u>of the Long-Distance Runner</u>." <u>Literature/Film</u>
        <u>Quarterly</u>, 9 (1981), 172-188.

ROBERT LOUIS STEVENSON

1549.   Durgnat, Raymond. "<u>Le Testament du Dr. Cordelier</u>
        (<u>Experiment in Evil</u>)." In his <u>Jean Renoir</u>.
        Berkeley: University of California Press, 1974,
        pp. 331-346.
        On Renoir's adaptation of <u>Dr. Jekyll and Mr. Hyde</u>.

1550.   Kestner, Joseph A. "Stevenson and Artaud: `The
        Master of Ballantrae'." <u>Film Heritage</u>, 7 (Summer
        1972), 19-28.
        Concerns a planned adaptation by Artaud.

1551.   Luhr, William and Peter Lehman. "Narrative Comparison,
        Part One and Part Two." In their <u>Authorship</u>
        <u>and Narrative in the Cinema: Issues in Contemporary</u>
        <u>Aesthetics</u>. New York: G.P. Putnam's Sons, 1977,
        pp. 197-280.
        On the adaptations of <u>Dr. Jekyll and Mr. Hyde</u>.

1552.   Nodelman, Perry. "Searching for <u>Treasure Island</u>."
        In <u>Children's Novels and the Movies</u>. Ed. Douglas
        Street. New York: Frederick Ungar, 1983, pp. 58-68.

1553.   Prawer, S.S. "Book Into Film I: Mamoulian's <u>Dr.</u>
        <u>Jekyll and Mr. Hyde</u>." In his <u>Caligari's Children:</u>
        <u>The Film as Tale of Terror</u>. New York: Oxford
        University Press, 1980, 85-107.

1554. Telotte, J.P. "Dealing with Death: The Body Snatcher."
       In his Dreams of Darkness: Fantasy and the Films
       of Val Lewton. Urbana: University of Illinois
       Press, 1985, pp. 149-167.

1555. _____. "A Photogenic Horror: Lewton Does Robert
       Louis Stevenson." Literature/Film Quarterly,
       10 (1982), 25-37.
       Adaptation of "The Body Snatcher."

1556. Welsch, Janice R. "Dr. Jekyll and Mr. Hyde: The
       Horrific and the Tragic." In The English Novel
       and the Movies. Ed. Michael Klein and Gillian
       Parker. New York: Frederick Ungar, 1981, pp. 165-179.

1557. Zharen, W.M. von. "Kidnapped: Improved Hodgepodge?"
       In Children's Novels and the Movies. Ed. Douglas
       Street. New York: Frederick Ungar, 1983, pp. 81-91.

BRAM STOKER

1558. Roth, Lane. "Dracula Meets the Zeitgeist: Nosferatu
       (1922) as Film Adaptation." Literature/Film
       Quarterly, 7 (1979), 309-313.

1559. Todd, Janet M. "Nosferatu (Herzog): The Class-ic
       Vampire." In The English Novel and the Movies.
       Ed. Michael Klein and Gillian Parker. New York:
       Frederick Ungar, 1981, pp. 197-210.

1560. Welsh, Jim and John Tibbetts. "Visions of Dracula."
       American Classic Screen, 5, No. 1 (1980), 12-16.

1561. Wood, Robin. "Burying the Undead: The Use and
       Obsolescence of Count Dracula." Mosaic, 16
       (Winter-Spring 1983), 175-187.

DAVID STOREY

1562. Milne, Tom. "This Sporting Life." Sight and Sound,
       31 (Summer 1962), 113-115.

J.M. SYNGE

1563. Gerstenberger, Donna. "Bonnie and Clyde and Christy
       Mahon: Playboys All." Modern Drama, 14 (1971),
       227-231.

ALFRED,LORD TENNYSON

1564. Devlin, Francis P. "A `Cinematic' Approach to Tennyson's
       Descriptive Art." Literature/Film Quarterly,
       3 (1975), 132-44.

WILLIAM MAKEPEACE THACKERAY

1565. Bledsoe, Robert. "Kubrick's _Vanity Fair_." _Rocky_
       Mountain Review of Language and Literature, 31
       (1977), 96-99.
       On _Barry Lyndon_.

1566. Bluestone, George. "_Barry Lyndon_: The Book, The
       Film." _Sphinx_, 9 (1979), 16-27.

1567. Carroll, Noel. "_Becky Sharp_ (_Vanity Fair_): Becky
       Sharp Takes Over." In _The English Novel and_
       the Movies. Ed. Michael Klein and Gillian Parker.
       New York: Frederick Ungar, 1981, pp. 108-120.

1568. Ciment, Michel. "Second Interview: _Barry Lyndon_."
       In his _Kubrick_. Trans. Gilbert Adair. New York:
       Holt, Rinehart and Winston, 1983, pp. 167-179.

1569. Colby, R.A. "'Scenes of All Sorts': _Vanity Fair_
       on Stage and Screen." _Dickens Studies Annual,_
       Volume 9. Ed. Michael Timko, Fred Kaplan, and
       Edward Guiliano. New York: AMS Press, 1981-82,
       pp. 163-194.

1570. Dempsey, Michael. "Barry Lyndon." _Film Quarterly_,
       30 (Fall 1976), 49-54.

1571. Feldman, Hans. "Kubrick and His Discontents."
       Film Quarterly, 33 (Fall 1976), 12-19.
       On _Barry Lyndon_.

1572. Grundy, Dominick. "Barry Lyndon." _The Nassau Review_,
       3, No. 3 (1977), 92-97.

1573. Houston, Penelope. "_Barry Lyndon_." _Sight and Sound_,
       45 (Spring 1976), 77-80.

1574. Klein, Michael. "_Barry Lyndon_: Narrative and Discourse
       in Kubrick's Modern Tragedy." In _The English_
       Novel and the Movies. Ed. Michael Klein and
       Gillian Parker. New York: Frederick Ungar, 1981,
       pp. 95-107.

1575. Miller, Mark Crispin. "Kubrick's Anti-Reading of
       The Luck of Barry Lyndon." _Modern Language Notes_,
       91 (1976), 1360-1379.

1576. Nelson, Thomas Allen. "A Time Odyssey: _Barry Lyndon_."
       In _Kubrick: Inside a Film Artist's Maze_. Bloomington:
       Indiana University Press, 1982, 165-196.

1577. Spiegel, Alan. "Kubrick's _Barry Lyndon_." _Salmagundi_,
       Nos. 38-39 (1977), pp. 194-208.

1578. Stephenson, William. "The Perception of 'History'
       in Kubrick's _Barry Lyndon_." _Literature/Film_
       Quarterly, 9 (1981), 251-260.

DYLAN THOMAS

1579.   Sinclair, Andrew.   "The Making of `Under Milkwood.'"
        <u>Filmmakers Newsletter</u>, 6, Nos. 9-10)1973), 32-34.
        Sinclair directed the film.

J.R.R. TOLKIEN

1580.   Hardy, Gene.   "<u>The Hobbit</u>: More Than a Magic Ring."
        In <u>Children's Novels and the Movies</u>. Ed. Douglas
        Street. New York: Frederick Ungar, 1983, pp. 131-140.

1581.   Walker, Steven C.   "Tolkien According to Bakshi."
        <u>Mythlore</u>, 6 (Winter 1979), 36.
        On <u>The Lord of the Rings</u>.

1582.   Ziegler, Dale.   "Ring-Wraith: Or Therein Baskshi
        Again." <u>Mythlore</u>, 6 (Winter 1979), 37-38.
        On the animated feature <u>Lord of the Rings.</u>

HUGH WALPOLE

1583.   Lambert, Gavin.   "Shadow Upon Shadow: Hugh Walpole
        in Hollywood." <u>Sight and Sound</u>, 23 (Oct.-Dec. 1953),
        78-82.

ALEXANDER RABIN (ALEC) WAUGH

1584.   Waugh, Alec.   "The Film and the Future."   The <u>Fortnightly
        Review</u>, 116 (1924), 524-531.

EVELYN WAUGH

1585.   Lane, Calvin W.   "Waugh Incunabula: `The Lost Art
        of the Cinema.'" <u>The Evelyn Waugh Newsletter</u>,
        17 (Autumn 1983), 4.

1586.   McCaffery, Donald W.   "<u>The Loved One</u>--An Irreverent,
        Invective, Dark Film Comedy." <u>Literature/Film
        Quarterly</u>, 11 (1983), 83-87.

1587.   Phillips, Gene D., S.J.   "Big Screen, Little Screen:
        Adaptations of Evelyn Waugh's Fiction."
        <u>Literature/Film Quarterly</u>, 6 (1978), 162-170.

1588.   Southern, Terry. <u>The Journal of The Loved One:
        The Production Log of a Motion Picture</u>. New
        York: Random House, 1965.
        Southern wrote the adaptation of Waugh's novel.

H.G. WELLS

1589.   Davis, Ken.   "<u>The Shape of Things to Come</u>: H.G. Wells
        and the Rhetoric of Proteus." In <u>No Place Else:
        Explorations in Utopian and Dysutopian Fiction</u>.
        Ed. Eric S. Rabkin, Martin C. Greenberg, and
        Joseph D. Olander. Carbondale: Southern Illinois
        University Press, 1983, pp. 110-124.

1590. Jensen, Paul. "H.G. Wells on the Screen." Films
          in Review, 18 (1967), 521-527.

1591. Wasson, Richard. "The Time Machine: Myths of the
          Future." In The English Novel and the Movies.
          Ed. Michael Klein and Gillian Parker. New York:
          Frederick Ungar, 1981, pp. 187-196.

1592. Wykes, Alan. H.G. Wells in the Cinema. London:
          Jupiter Books, 1977.
          Discussions of The Invisible Thief, The First Men
          in the Moon, Kipps (1922 and 1941), The Wheels of
          Chance, The Passionate Friends (1922 and 1948),
          Bluebottles, The Island of Lost Souls, The Invisible
          Man, Things to Come, The Man Who Could Work Miracles,
          Dead of Night (the episode adapted from "The
          Inexperienced Ghost"), The History of Mr. Polly,
          The War of the Worlds, The Door in the Wall, The
          Time Machine, and Half a Sixpence (adaptation of
          Kipps).

OSCAR WILDE

1593. Asquith, Anthony. "Importance of Being Faithful."
          Theatre Arts, 37 (April 1953), 72-74.
          Asquith directed the 1952 film of The Importance
          of Being Earnest.

1594. Davidson, David. "The Importance of Being Ernst:
          Lubitsch's Adaptation of Lady Windemere's Fan."
          Literature/Film Quarterly, 11 (1983), 120-131.

1595. Smith, John Harrington. "Oscar Wilde's Earnest
          in Film." The Quarterly of Film, Radio, and
          Television, 8 (1953), 72-79.
          On Asquith's The Importance of Being Earnest.

1596. Tyler, Parker. "Magic Lantern Metamorphosis I:
          Dorian Gray, Last of the Draculas." In his Magic
          and Myth of the Movies. New York: Simon and
          Schuster, 1970, pp. 55-71.
          On The Picture of Dorian Gray.

P.G. WODEHOUSE

1597. Stephenson, William. "The Wodehouse World of
          Hollywood." Literature/Film Quarterly, 6 (1978),
          190-203.

CHARLES WOOD

1598. Page, Malcolm. "Charles Wood: How I Won the War
          and Dingo." Literature/Film Quarterly, 1 (1973),
          256-262.
          On Wood's play and his adaptation of Patrick Ryan's
          novel.

VIRGINIA WOOLF

1599.   Woolf, Virginia.   "The Cinema."   The Arts, 9 (1926),
        314-316.   Reprinted as "The Movies and Reality"
        in The New Republic, 47 (4 Aug. 1926), 308-310.
        Reprinted as "The Cinema" in her The Captain's
        Death Bed and Other Essays.   New York: Harcourt,
        Brace, and Co., 1950, pp. 180-186.   Abridged
        and reprinted in Sight and Sound, 23 (April-June
        1954), 215-216.   Reprinted in her Collected Essays.
        Volume Two.   London: The Hogarth Press, 1966,
        pp. 268-279.   Reprinted in Authors on Film.
        Ed. Harry M. Geduld.   Bloomington: Indiana University
        Press, 1972, pp. 86-91.

10

William Shakespeare
and Film

A. GENERAL STUDIES

1600. Albert, Richard N. "An Annotated Guide to Audio-Visual
       Materials for Teaching Shakespeare." The English
       Journal, 54 (1965), 704-715.

1601. Anderegg, Michael A. "Shakespeare on Film in the
       Classroom." Literature/Film Quarterly, 4 (1976),
       165-175.

1602. Atkinson, E.J. Rupert. Key to the Adaptation of
       the Best of Shakespeare's Plays to the
       Stage-Cinema-Interaction Process for the Production
       of Drama. New York: The Knickerbocker Press,
       1920.
       Describes how film could be used in stage performances
       of nine Shakespeare plays.

1603. Ball, Robert Hamilton. "The Beginnings of Shakespeare
       Sound Films." Shakespeare Newsletter, 23 (1973),
       48.

1604. _____. "On Shakespeare Filmography." Literature/
       Film Quarterly, 1 (1973), 299-306.

1605. _____. "Pioners and All: The Beginnings of
       Shakespeare Film." Theatre Survey, 1 (1960),
       18-42.

1606. _____. "The Shakespeare Film as Record: Sir
       Herbert Beerbohm Tree." Shakespeare Quarterly,
       3 (1952), 227-236.

1607. _____. "Shakespeare in One Reel." The Quarterly
       of Film, Radio, and Television, 8 (1953), 139-149.

1608. _____. Shakespeare on Silent Film: A Strange
       Eventful History. New York: Theatre Art Books,
       1968.

1609. Belsey, Catherine. "Shakespeare and Film: A Question
        of Perspective." Literature/Film Quarterly,
        11 (1983), 152-158.

1610. Bies, Werner. "Shakespeare on Film: Some German
        Approaches." Literature/Film Quarterly, 11
        (1983), 203-207.

1611. Brinson, Peter. "The Real Interpreter." Films
        and Filming, 1 (April 1955), 4-5.
        Concerns Olivier's Shakespeare films.

1612. Buchman, Lorne Michael. "From the Globe to the
        Screen: An Interpretative Study of Shakespeare
        Through Film." DAI, 45 (1984), 1574A (Stanford
        University).
        On Orson Welles's Macbeth, Othello, and Chimes
        at Midnight and Grigori Kozintsev's Hamlet and
        King Lear.

1613. Camp, Gerald. "Shakespeare on Film." Journal
        of Aesthetic Education, 3 (1969), 107-120.

1614. Clay, James H. and Daniel Krempel. "Plays on Film."
        In their The Theatrical Image. New York:
        McGraw-Hill, 1967, pp. 231-254.
        On Reinhardt's A Midsummer Night's Dream, Welles's
        Macbeth, and Olivier's Hamlet.

1615. Clayton, Bertram. "Shakespeare and the `Talkies.'"
        The English Review, 49 (1929), 739-748, 752.
        On silent film adaptations and speculations about
        how sound might benefit adaptations of Shakespeare.

1616. Clayton, T. "Aristotle on the Shakespearean Film:
        Or Damn Thee, William, Thou Art Translated."
        Literature/Film Quarterly, 2 (1974), 183-189.

1617. Dehn, Paul. "The Filming of Shakespeare." In
        Talking of Shakespeare. Ed. John Garrett.
        Freeport, N.Y.: Books for Libraries Press, 1971,
        pp. 49-72.
        On the educational value of Shakespeare adaptations.

1618. Dworkin, Martin S. "`Stay Illusion!': Having Words
        About Shakespeare on Screen." The Journal of
        Aesthetic Education, 11 (Spring 1977), 51-61.
        On Zeffirelli's Romeo and Juliet and Richardson's
        Hamlet.

1619. Eckert, Charles W., ed. Focus on Shakespearean
        Films. Englewood Cliffs: Prentice Hall, 1972.
        See 1631, 1639, 1652, 1669, 1693, 1697, 1698, 1703,
        1709, 1719, 1724, 1741, 1776, 1812, 1813, 1820,
        1824, 1825, 1827, 1846, 1854, 1856.

1620. Felheim, Marvin. "Criticism and the Films of
        Shakespeare's Plays." Comparative Drama, 9
        (1975), 147-155.

1621. Fuegi, John. "Exploration of No Man's Land:
       Shakespeare's Poetry as Theatrical Film."
       Shakespeare Quarterly, 23 (1972), 37-49.
       The relationship of text to medium in thirteen
       adaptations.

1622. Giesler, Rodney. "Shakespeare on the Screen."
       Films and Filming, 2 (July 1956), 6-7, 31.
       Covers Olivier's adaptations, Welles's Othello,
       and Castellani's Romeo and Juliet.

1623. Greg, W.W. "Shakespeare Through the Camera's Eye:
       1953-54." Shakespeare Quarterly, 6 (1955),
       63-66.
       Television productions of Shakespeare.

1624. Hardison, O.B. "Shakespeare on Film: The Developing
       Canon." Shakespeare's Art From a Comparative
       Perspective. Ed. Wendell M. Aycock. Lubbock:
       Texas Tech Press, 1981, pp. 131-145.
       On Olivier's Hamlet and Henry V. and Polanski's
       and Welles's Macbeth.

1625. Hodgdon, Barbara. "Shakespeare on Film: Taking
       Another Look." Shakespeare Newsletter, 26 (May
       1976), 26.

1626. Homan, Sidney. "A Cinema for Shakespeare."
       Literature/Film Quarterly, 4 (1976), 176-187.
       On teaching adaptations.

1627. _____. "Criticism for the Filmed Shakespeare."
       Literature/Film Quarterly, 5 (1977), 282-290.

1628. Homan, Sidney and Neil Feineman. "The Filmed
       Shakespeare: From Verbal to Visual." In
       Shakespeare's More Than Words Can Witness: Essays
       on Visual and Non-verbal Enactment in the Plays.
       Lewisburg: Bucknell University Press, 1980,
       pp. 207-236.
       Discusses five general approaches to adapting
       Shakespeare.

1629. Hooker, Brian. "Shakespeare and the Movies."
       Century, 93 (1916), 298-304.

1630. Hurtgen, Charles. "The Operatic Character of Background
       Music in Film Adaptations of Shakespeare."
       Shakespeare Quarterly, 20 (1969), 53-64.

1631. Johnson, Ian. "Merely Players: 400 Years of
       Shakespeare." Films and Filming, 10 (April
       1964), 41-48. Reprinted in Focus on Shakespearean
       Films. Ed. Charles W. Eckert. Englewood Cliffs:
       Prentice Hall, 1972, pp. 7-26.
       Survey of film adaptations of Shakespeare.

1632. Jorgens, Jack. "A Course in Shakespeare on Film."
       Shakespeare Newsletter, 23 (May 1973), 43.

1633. _____. Shakespeare on Film. Bloomington:
      Indiana University Press, 1976.
      Adaptations discussed: Reinhardt and Dieterle's
      A Midsummer Night's Dream; Hall's A Midsummer Night's
      Dream; Zeffirelli's Taming of the Shrew and Romeo
      and Juliet; Mankiewicz's Julius Caesar; Welles's
      Chimes at Midnight; Olivier's Hamlet and Richard
      III; Schaefer's, Welles's, Polanski's Macbeth and
      Kurosawa's Throne of Blood; Welles's and Burge
      and Dexter's Othello; Kozintsev's Hamlet; Koztintsev's
      and Brook's King Lear.

1634. _____. "Shakespeare on Film: A Selected
      Checklist." Literature/Film Quarterly, 4 (1976),
      189-193.

1635. Kermode, Frank. "Shakespeare in the Movies."
      The New York Review of Books, 18 (4 May 1972),
      18-21. Reprinted in Film Theory: Introductory
      Readings. Ed. Gerald Mast and Marshal Cohen.
      New York: Oxford University Press, 1974, pp. 422-432.
      On Heston's Antony and Cleopatra, Polanski's Macbeth,
      and Brook's King Lear.

1636. Kitchin, Laurence. "Shakespeare on the Screen."
      The Listener, 71 (1964), 788-790.
      On Olivier's adaptations.

1637. _____. "Shakespeare on the Screen." Shakespeare
      Survey, 18 (1965), 70-74.

1638. Kozintsev, Grigori. Shakespeare: Time and Conscience.
      Trans. Joyce Vining. New York: Hill and Wang,
      1967.
      The director on Hamlet, King Lear, and Henry V.

1639. Lemairtre, Henri. "Shakespeare, the Imaginary
      Cinema, and the Pre-Cinema." In Focus on
      Shakespearean Films. Ed. Charles W. Eckert.
      Englewood Cliffs: Prentice-Hall, 1972, pp. 27-36.

1640. Lillich, Meredith. "Shakespeare on the Screen."
      Films in Review, 7 (1956), 247-260.
      Annotated filmography.

1641. McDonald, N. "The Relationship Between Shakespeare's
      Stagecraft and Modern Film Technique." Australian
      Journal of Film Theory, No. 7 (1980), pp. 18-33.

1642. McNeir, Waldo F. and Michael Payne. "Feature Length
      Sound Films Adapted From Shakespeare's Plays
      Available for Distribution in the U.S." Shakespeare
      Newsletter, 23 (May 1973), 44.

1643. Manvell, Roger. Shakespeare and the Film. New
            York: Praeger Publishers, 1971.
       Adaptations discussed include: Olivier's Henry
       V, Hamlet and Richard III; Welles's Othello, Macbeth
       and Chimes at Midnight; Yutkevitch's Hamlet; Kozintsev's
       Hamlet and King Lear; Mankiewicz's Julius Caesar;
       Burge's Julius Caesar; Zeffirelli's Romeo and Juliet
       and Taming of the Shrew; Castellani's Romeo and
       Juliet; Kurosawa's Throne of Blood; Hall's A Midsummer
       Night's Dream; Reinhardt and Dieterle's A Midsummer
       Night's Dream; Czinner's As You Like It; and Brook's
       King Lear.

1644. Marder, Louis. "Sex in Shakespeare." Shakespeare
            Newsletter, 18 (April 1968), 10-11.
       On Zeffirelli's Romeo and Juliet and The Taming
       of the Shrew.

1645. _____. "The Shakespeare Film: Facts and
            Problems." Shakespeare Newsletter, 23 (1973),
            42, 49.

1646. Millard, Barbara C. "Shakespeare on Film: Towards
            an Audience Perceived and Perceiving."
            Literature/Film Quarterly, 5 (1977) 352-357.

1647. Morris, Peter. Shakespeare on Film: An Index to
            William Shakespeare's Plays on Film. Ottowa:
            Canadian Film Institute, 1972. Reprinted as
            "Shakespeare on Film." Films in Review, 24
            (1973), 132-163.

1648. Parker, Barry M. The Folger Shakespeare Filmography.
       Washington, D.C.: Folger Press, 1979.

1649. Phillips, James E. "By William Shakespeare--With
            Additional Dialogue." Hollywood Quarterly,
            5 (1951), 224-236.
       Concerns Olivier's Hamlet and Welles's Macbeth.

1650. Pring, Beryl. "Shakespeare and the Russian Films."
            Adelphi, 3 (1932), 469-473.

1651. Raynor, Henry. "Shakespeare Filmed." Sight and
            Sound, 22 (July-Sept. 1952), 10-15.
       On Olivier's and Welles's adaptations.

1652. Reeves, Geoffery. "Shakespeare on Three Screens:
            Peter Brook Interviewed." Sight and Sound,
            34 (1965), 66-70. Reprinted as "Finding Shakespeare
            on Film: From an Interview with Peter Brook."
            Tulane Drama Review, 11 (Fall 1966), 117-121.
            Reprinted in Focus on Shakespearean Film.
            Ed. Charles W. Eckert. Englewood Cliffs: Prentice-
            Hall, 1972, pp. 37-41. Reprinted in Film Theory
            and Criticism: Introductory Readings. Ed. Gerald
            Mast and Marshall Cohen. New York: Oxford University
            Press, 1974, pp. 316-321.
       On Kurosawa's Throne of Blood and Kozintsev's Hamlet.

1653. Richmond, Hugh M. "The Synergistic Use of Shakespearean
          Film and Videotape." Literature/Film Quarterly,
          5 (1977), 362-364.

1654. Roemer, Michael. "Shakespeare on Film: A Filmmaker's
          View." Shakespeare Newsletter, 26 (May 1976),
          26.

1655. Sewell, J.B. "Shakespeare on the Screen: II"
          Films in Review, 20 (1969), 419-426.
          Annotated filmography.

1656. Shattuck, Charles H. "Shakespeare on Film: The
          Silent Era; The Advent of Sound; Shakespeare
          Films Since World War II." In The Riverside
          Shakespeare. Ed. G.B. Graves. Boston: Houghton
          Mifflin, 1974, pp. 1819-1825.

1657. Silviria, Dale. Laurence Olivier and the Art of
          Film Making. Cranbury, N.J.: Associated University
          Presses, 1985.
          On Olivier's Shakespeare films (Hamlet, Henry V,
     Richard III).

1658. Singer, Sandra Sugarman. "Laurence Olivier Directs
          Shakespeare: A Study in Film Authorship." DAI,
          40 (1979), 2948-2949A (Northwestern University).
          Auteur analysis of Hamlet, Henry V, and Richard
          III.

1659. Skoller, Donald S. "Problems of Transformation
          in the Adaptation of Shakespeare's Tragedies
          from Play-Script to Cinema." DA, 29 (1969),
          2830A (New York University).
          Adaptations discussed: Cukor's and Renato Castellani's
          Romeo and Juliet, David Bradley's and Joseph
          Mankiewicz's Julius Caesar, Laurence Olivier's
          and Girogi Kozintsev's Hamlet, Orson Welles's,
          Sergei Yutkevich's and Stuart Burges' Othello,
          Welles's, Kurosawa's, and Schaefer's Macbeth.

1660. Staton, Shirley F. "Shakespeare Redivivus:
          Supplementary Techniques for Teaching Shakespeare."
          Literature/Film Quarterly, 5 (1977), 358-361.

1661. Styan, J.L. "Sight and Space: The Perception of
          Shakespeare on Stage and Screen." Educational
          Theatre Journal, 29 (1977), 18-28. Reprinted
          in Shakespeare: The Pattern of Excelling Nature.
          Ed. Jay L. Halio and David Bevington. Cranbury,
          N.J.: Associated University Presses, 1978,
          pp. 198-209.
          On Olivier's Hamlet and Zeffirelli's Romeo and
     Juliet.

1662. Taylor, John Russell. "Shakespeare in Film, Radio,
          and Television." In Shakespeare: A Celebration,
          1564-1964. Ed. T.J.B. Spencer. Baltimore:
          Penguin Books, 1964, pp. 97-113.

1663. Trewin, J.C.   "I Hate the Films!"   *Sight and Sound*,
        7 (Spring 1938), 17-18.

1664. Tucker, Nicholas.   "Shakespeare and Film Technique."
        The Use of English, 14 (1963), 98-104.
        Using film analogies to teach Shakespeare.

1665. Welles, Orson.   "The Third Audience."   *Sight and
        Sound*, 23 (Jan.-March 1954), 120-123.
        Includes Welles's views on Shakespeare adaptations.

1666. Welsh, James M.   "Shakespeare With-and-Without
        Words."   *Literature/Film Quarterly*, 1 (1973),
        84-88.

1667. Whitehead, Peter and Robin Bean.   *Olivier-Shakespeare*.
        London: Lorrimer Films, 1966.
        A forty-page monograph in English, French, and
        German on Olivier's adaptations.

B.   STUDIES OF INDIVIDUAL PLAYS

As You Like It

1668. Poague, Leland A.   "*As You Like It* and *It Happened
        One Night*: The Generic Pattern of Comedy."
        Literature/Film Quarterly, 5 (1977), 346-350.

Hamlet

1669. Alexander, Peter.   "From School in Wittenberg."
        In his *Hamlet: Father and Son*. Oxford: Cambridge
        Press, 1955, pp. 1-39.   Portion reprinted in
        Focus on Shakespearean Films. Ed. Charles
        W. Eckert.   Englewood Cliffs: Prentice Hall,
        1972, pp. 67-70.
        Olivier's *Hamlet*.

1670. Babcock, R. W.   "George Lyman Kittredge, Olivier,
        and the Historical Hamlet."   *College English*,
        11 (1949-50), 256-265.
        Contrasts Olivier's written comments about *Hamlet*
        with the film.

1671. Barbarow, George.   "*Hamlet* Through a Telescope."
        Hudson Review, 2 (1949), 98-117.
        Olivier's *Hamlet*.

1672. Brebach, Emily S.   "From Olivier to Kozintsev:
        Visual Technique in Transforming *Hamlet* into
        Film."   *Shakespeare's Art From a Comparative
        Perspective*.   Ed. Wendell M. Aycock.   Lubbock:
        Texas Tech Press, 1981, pp. 67-81.

1673. Brown, John Mason.   "Olivier's *Hamlet*."   In his
        Still Seeing Things. New York: McGraw-Hill,
        1950, pp. 145-153.

1674. Cottrell, John. "The Film Hamlet." In his Olivier.
       Englewood Cliffs: Prentice-Hall, 1975, pp. 220-232.

1675. Cross, Brenda, ed. The Film Hamlet. London: Saturn
       Press, 1948.
       Articles by those who worked on Olivier's Hamlet.

1676. Dehn, Paul. "The Filming of Shakespeare." In
       Talking of Shakespeare. Ed. John Garrett.
       New York: Theatre Arts Books, 1954, pp. 49-72.
       On Olivier's Hamlet and Henry V.

1677. Dent, Alan, ed. Hamlet: The Film and the Play.
       London: World Film Publishers, 1948.
       Articles on Olivier's Hamlet.

1678. Duffy, Robert A. "Gade, Olivier, Richardson: Visual
       Strategy in Hamlet Adaptations." Literature/Film
       Quarterly, 4 (1976), 141-152.

1679. Eidsvik, Charles. "Thought in Film: The Case of
       Kozintsev's Hamlet." West Virginia University
       Philiological Papers, 26 (Aug. 1980), 74-82.

1680. Grebanier, Bernard. The Heart of Hamlet: The Play
       Shakespeare Wrote. New York: Thomas Y. Crowell,
       1960.
       One of the productions Grebanier discusses throughout
       his book is Olivier's film adaptation.

1681. Griffin, ALice Venezky. "Shakespeare Through the
       Camera's Eye: IV." Shakespeare Quarterly, 17
       (1966), 383-387.
       On Kozintsev's Hamlet and Welles's Othello.

1682. Halio, J. L. "Three Filmed Hamlets." Literature/Film
       Quarterly, 1 (1973), 316-320.

1683. Hirsch, Foster. "Hamlet." In his Laurence Olivier.
       Boston: Twayne Publishers, 1979, pp. 79-93.

1684. Hodgdon, Barbara. "`The Mirror Up to Nature':
       Notes on Kozintsev's Hamlet." Comparative Drama,
       9 (1975), 305-317.

1685. Huntley, John. "The Music of `Hamlet' and `Oliver
       Twist.'" The Penguin Film Review, 8 (1949),
       110-116; rpt. Totowa, N.J.: Rowan and Littlefield,
       1978.
       On music for Olivier's and Lean's adaptations.

1686. Jorgens, Jack J. "Image and Meaning in the Kozintsev
       Hamlet." Literature/Film Quarterly, 1 (1973),
       307-315.

1687. Kliman, Bernice W. "Olivier's Hamlet: A Film-Infused
       Play." Literature/Film Quarterly, 5 (1977),
       305-314.

1688. _____. "A Palimpset for Olivier's Hamlet."
       Comparative Drama, 17 (1983), 243-253.

1689. _____. "The Spiral of Influence: `One Defect'
       in Hamlet." Literature/Film Quarterly, 11 (1983),
       159-166.

1690. Kott, Jan and Mark Mirsky. "On Kozintsev's Hamlet."
       Literary Review, 22 (1979), 383-407.

1691. Kozintsev, Grigori. "Hamlet and King Lear: Stage
       and Film." In Shakespeare 1971: Proceedings
       of the World Shakespeare Congress. Ed. Clifford
       Leech and J.M.R. Margeson. Toronto: University
       of Toronto Press, 1972, pp. 190-199.

1692. _____. "The Hamlet Within Me." Films and
       Filming, 8 (Sept. 1962), 20.

1693. Kurstow, Michael. "Hamlet." Sight and Sound,
       33 (Summer 1964), 144-145. Reprinted in Focus
       on Shakespearean Films. Ed. Charles W. Eckert.
       Englewood Cliffs: Printice-Hall, 1972, pp. 147-149.
       On Kozintsev's adaptation.

1694. Leaming, Barbara. "Hamlet." In her Grigori Kozintsev.
       Boston: Twayne Publishers, 1980, pp. 95-116.

1695. Litton, Gene. "Diseased Beauty in Tony Richardson's
       Hamlet." Literature/Film Quarterly, 4 (1976),
       109-128.

1696. Lordkipandze, Natela. "Hamlet on the Screen."
       Soviet Literature, No. 9 (1964), pp. 170-173.
       On Kozintsev's adaptation.

1697. McCarthy, Mary. "A Prince of Shreds and Patches."
       In her Sights and Spectacles. New York: Farrar,
       Straus and Cudahy, 1956, pp. 141-145. Reprinted
       in Focus on Shakespearean Films. Ed. Charles
       W. Eckert. Englewood Cliffs: Prentice-Hall,
       1972, pp. 64-67.
       On Olivier's adaptation.

1698. Macdonald, Dwight. "Hamlet." In Focus on Shakespearean
       Films. Ed. Charles W. Eckert. Englewood Cliffs:
       Prentice-Hall, 1972, pp. 149-150.
       On Kozintsev's adaptation.

1699. McManaway, James G. "The Laurence Olivier Hamlet."
       Shakespeare Association Bulletin, 24 (Jan. 1949),
       3-11.

1700. McVay, Douglas. "Hamlet to Clown." Films and
       Filming, 8 (Sept. 1962), 16-19.

1701. Manvell, Roger. "The Film of `Hamlet.'" The Penguin
       Film Review, 8 (1949), 16-24; rpt. Totowa, N.J.:
       Rowan and Littlefield, 1978.
       Olivier's version.

1702. Mullin, Michael. "Tony Richardson's Hamlet: Stage
       and Screen." Literature/Film Quarterly, 4 (1976),
       123-133.

1703. Pearson, Gabriel and Eric Rhode. "Screened Culture--
       Letter From Venice." Encounter, 23 (Nov. 1964),
       62. Reprinted in Focus on Shakespearean Films.
       Ed. Charles W. Eckert. Englewood Cliffs: Prentice-
       Hall, 1972, pp. 151-152.
       On Kosintsev's adaptation.

1704. Robinson, W.R. "The Visual Powers Denied and Coupled:
       Hamlet and Fellini-Satyricon as Narratives of
       Seeing." In Shakespeare `More Than Words Can
       Witness': Essays on Visual and Nonverbal Enactments
       in the Plays. Ed. Sidney Homan. Lewisberg:
       Bucknell University Press, 1980, pp. 177-206.

1705. Rowe, Eleanor. "Pasternak and Hamlet." In Hamlet:
       A Mirror on Russia. New York: New York University
       Press, 1976, pp. 147-166.
       On Pasternak's translation and Kosintsev's film.

1706. Silber, Joan Ellyn Frager. "Cinematic Techniques
       and Interpretations in Film and Television
       Adaptations of Shakespeare's Hamlet." DAI,
       34 (1974), 5370A (The University of Michigan).
       Concerns Kosintsev's, Schell's and Olivier's versions.

1707. Tyler, Parker. "Hamlet and Documentary." Kenyon
       Review, 11 (1949), 527-532.
       On Olivier's adaptation.

1708. Wilds, Lillian. "On Film: Maximillian Schell's
       Most Royal Hamlet." Literature/Film Quarterly,
       4 (1976), 134-140.

Henry IV, Henry V, Merry Wives of Windsor
     (Orson Welles's Chimes at Midnight)

1709. Billard, Pierre. "Chimes at Midnight." Sight
       and Sound, 34 (Spring 1965), 64-65. Reprinted
       in Focus on Shakespearean Films. Ed. Charles
       W. Eckert. Englewood Cliffs: Prentice Hall,
       1972, pp. 162-164.

1710. Cobos, Juan and Miguel Rubio. "Welles and Falstaff."
       Sight and Sound, 35 (Autumn 1966), 158-163.

1711. Cowie, Peter. "The Study of Good Companionship:
       Chimes at Midnight." In his Ribbon of Dreams:
       The Cinema of Orson Welles. New York: A.S. Barnes,
       1973, pp. 178-194.

1712. Crowl, Samuel. "The Long Goodbye: Welles and
       Falstaff." Shakespeare Quarterly, 31 (1980),
       369-380.

1713. Higham, Charles. "Chimes at Midnight." In his
       The Films of Orson Welles. Berkeley: University
       of California Press, 1971, pp. 167-177.

1714. Johnson, William. "Othello and Chimes at Midnight."
       Film Quarterly, 21 (1968), 13-24.

1715. McBride, Joseph. "Welles' Chimes at Midnight."
       Film Quarterly, 23 (Fall 1969), 11-20.

1716. McLean, Andrew. "Orson Welles and Shakespeare:
       History and Consciousness in Chimes at Midnight."
       Literature/Film Quarterly 11 (1983), 197-202.

1717. Naremore, James. "Chimes at Midnight." In his
       The Magic World of Orson Welles. New York:
       Oxford University Press, 1978, pp. 257-281.

1718. Poague, Leland. "`Reading' the Prince: Shakespeare
       and Some Aspects of Chimes at Midnight." Iowa
       State Journal of Research, 56 (Aug. 1981), 57-65.

Henry V

1719. Agee, James. "Henry V." In Focus on Shakespearean
       Films. Ed. Charles W. Eckert. Englewood Cliffs:
       Prentice Hall, 1972, pp. 54-62.

1720. Andrew, Dudley. "Realism, Rhetoric, and the Painting
       of History in Henry V." In Film in the Aura
       of Art. Princeton: Princeton University Press,
       1984, pp. 131-151.

1721. Beauchamp, Gorman. "Henry V: Myth, Movie, Play."
       College Literature, 5 (1978), 228-238.

1722. Chang, Joseph S.M. "Shakespeare's Dramatic Self-
       Consciousness on Stage and Film." Iowa State
       Journal of Research, 53 (Feb. 1979), 207-212.
       Appearance and reality in plays and Olivier's
       Henry V and Richard III.

1723. Cottrell, John. "The Making of a Masterpiece."
       In his Olivier. Englewood Cliffs: Prentice-Hall,
       1975, pp. 187-200.

1724. Crowther, Bosley. "Henry V." In Focus on Shakespearean
       Films. Ed. Charles W. Eckert. Englewood Cliffs:
       Prentice-Hall, 1972, pp. 57-62.

1725. Geduld, Harry M. Filmguide to Henry V. Bloomington:
       Indiana University Press, 1973.

1726. Hirsch, Foster. "Henry V." In his Laurence Olivier.
       Boston: Twayne Publishers, 1979, pp. 61-76.

1727. Huntley, John. "Henry V." In British Film Music.
       Ed. John Huntley. New York: Arno Press, 1972,
       pp. 74-76.
       Concerns William Walton's score for the Olivier
       film.

1728. Hutton, C. Clayton. The Making of Henry V.   London:
Ernest J. Day and Co., 1944.
       Monograph on the making of Olivier's film.

1729. Krempel, Daniel. "Olivier's Henry V: Design in
       Motion Picture." Educational Theatre Journal,
       2 (1950), 322-328.

1730. McConnell, Stanlie. "Henry V: An American Analysis
       of the Score." In British Film Music. Ed. John
       Huntley. New York: Arno Press, 1972, pp. 171-176.
       Concerns William Walton's score for the Olivier
       film.

1731. McCreadie, Marsha. "Henry V: Onstage and On Film."
       Literature/Film Quarterly, 5 (1977), 316-321.

1732. Manheim, Michael. "Oliver's Henry V and the Elizabethan
       World Picture." Literature/Film Quarterly,
       11 (1983), 179-184.

1733. Phillips, James E. "Adapted from a Play by W.
       Shakespeare." Hollywood Quarterly, 2 (1946),
       82-90.

1734. Smith, Garland Garvey. "Shakespeare on the Screen."
       Emory University Quarterly, 3, No. 2 (1947),
       88-95.

Julius Caesar

1735. Charney, Maurice and Gordon Hitchens. "On Mankiewicz's
       Julius Caesar." Literary Review, 22 (1979),
       433-459.

1736. Culkin, The Rev. John M., S.J. "Julius Caesar
       as a Play and as a Film: A Study in Comparative
       Communications." In Julius Caesar. New York:
       Scholastic Book Services, 1963, pp. 141-186.
       On Mankiewicz's Julius Caesar.

1737. Griffin, Alice Venezky. "Shakespeare Through the
       Camera's Eye-- Julius Caesar in Motion Pictures;
       Hamlet and Othello on Television." Shakespeare
       Quarterly, 4 (1953), 331-336.
       On Mankiewicz's Julius Caesar.

1738. Houseman, John. "Filming <u>Julius Caesar</u>." <u>Films</u>
       <u>in Review</u>, 4 (1953), 184-188. Reprinted in
       <u>Sight and Sound</u>, 23 (July-Sept. 1953), 24-27.

1739. _____. "This Our Lofty Scene." <u>Theatre Arts</u>,
       37, (May 1953), 26-28.
       Houseman produced Joseph Mankiewicz's film.

1740. Lewin, William. "A Guide to the Discussion of
       the Metro-Goldwyn-Mayer Screen Version of William
       Shakespeare's <u>Julius Caesar</u>." <u>Audio-Visual</u>
       <u>Guide</u>, 19, No. 9 (1953), 35-43.

1741. Pasinetti, P.M. "<u>Julius Caesar</u>: The Role of the
       Technical Advisor." <u>The Quarterly of Film</u>,
       <u>Radio, and Television</u>, 8 (1953), 131-138. Reprinted
       in <u>Focus on Shakespearean Films</u>. Ed. Charles
       W. Eckert. Englewood Cliffs: Prentice-Hall,
       1972, pp. 102-106.
       Author was technical advisor on Mankiewicz's film.

1742. Phillips, James E. "<u>Julius Caesar</u>: Shakespeare
       as a Screen Writer." <u>The Quarterly of Film</u>,
       <u>Radio, and Television</u>, 8 (1953), 125-130.

1743. Sargent, Seymour. "<u>Julius Caesar</u> and the Historical
       Film." <u>English Journal</u>, 61 (1972), 230-233,
       245.
       On Burge's and Mankiewicz's adaptations.

1744. Walker, Roy. "Look Upon Caeser." <u>The Twentieth</u>
       <u>Century</u>, 154 (1953), 469-474.
       On Mankiewicz's version.

<u>King John</u>

1745. Ball, Robert Hamilton. "Tree's <u>King John</u> Film:
       An Addendum." <u>Shakespeare Quarterly</u>, 24 (1973),
       455-459.

<u>King Lear</u>

1746. Acker, Paul. "Conventions for Dialogue in Peter
       Brook's <u>King Lear</u>." <u>Literature/Film Quarterly</u>,
       9 (1980), 219-224.

1747. Anikst, Alexander. "Grigori Kozintsev's <u>King Lear</u>."
       <u>Soviet Literature</u>, No. 6 (1971), pp. 177-182.

1748. Berlin, Normand. "Peter Brook's Interpretation
       of <u>King Lear</u>: `Nothing Will Come of Nothing.'"
       <u>Literature/Film Quarterly</u>, 5 (1977), 299-303.

1749. Braun, Eric. "<u>King Lear</u>." <u>Films and Filming</u>,
       18 (Oct. 1971), 54-56.

1750. Carnovsky, Morris and Paul Barry. "On Kozintsev's
       <u>King Lear</u>." <u>Literary Review</u>, 22 (1979), 408-432.

1751. Chaplin, William. "Our Darker Purpose: Peter Brook's
      King Lear." Arion, no. 1 (1973-74), pp. 168-187.

1752. Condee, Ralph Waterbury. "Goneril Without a White
      Beard." Shakespeare Film Newsletter, 1, No. 1
      (1976), 1, 5, 7.
      On Peter Brook's adaptation.

1753. Hayman, Ronald. "Grigori Kozintsev Talking About
      His `Lear' and `Hamlet.'" Transatlantic Review,
      46-47 (1973), 10-15.

1754. Hodgdon, Barbara. "Kozintsev's King Lear: Filming
      a Tragic Poem." Literature/Film Quarterly,
      5 (1977), 291-298.

1755. _____. "Two King Lears: Uncovering the
      Filmtext." Literature/Film Quarterly, 11 (1983),
      143-151.

1756. Johnson, William. "King Lear and Macbeth." Film
      Quarterly, 25 (Spring 1972), 41-48.
      Brooks's Lear and Polanski's Macbeth.

1757. Jorgens, Jack J. Teaching Manual: "King Lear."
      New York: Audio Brandon Films, 1978.
      A twelve-page manual for use with Brook's adaptation.

1758. Knight, L.H. "Grigori Kozintsev's King Lear."
      Journal of English, 2 (1976), 48-66.

1759. Kozintsev, Grigori. King Lear: The Space of Tragedy:
      The Diary of a Film Drama. Trans. Mary MacKintosh.
      Berkeley: University of California Press, 1977.

1760. Leaming, Barbara. "King Lear." In her Grigori
      Kozintsev. Boston: Twayne Publishers, 1980,
      pp. 119-135.

1761. McNeir, Waldo F. "Grigori Kozintsev's King Lear
      (USSR, 1971)." College Literature, 5 (1978),
      239-248.

1762. Muir, Kenneth. "The Critic, the Director, and
      Liberty of Interpreting." In The Triple Bond:
      Plays, Mainly Shakespearean, in Performance.
      Ed. Joseph G. Price. University Park: Pennsylvania
      State University Press, 1975, pp. 20-29.
      On Kozintsev's Lear.

1763. Mullin, Michael. "Peter Brook's King Lear: Stage
      and Screen." Literature/Film Quarterly, 11
      (1983), 190-196.

1764. Radcliff-Umstead, Douglas. "Order and Disorder
      in Koztintsev's King Lear." Literature/Film
      Quarterly, 11 (1983), 266-273.

1765. Rosenberg, Marvin. The Masks of King Lear. Berkeley:
       University of California Press, 1972.
       On Brook's and Kozintsev's adaptations.

1766. Schoenbaum, Samuel. "Looking for Shakespeare."
       In Shakespeare's Craft: Eight Lectures. Ed. Phillip
       H. Highfill, Jr. Carbondale: Southern Illinois
       University Press, 1982, pp. 156-177.
       Brief comparison of King Lear to Harry and Tonto.

1767. Schupp, Patrick. "King Lear." Sequences, No. 72
       (April 1973), pp. 38-39.
       On Brook's adaptation.

1768. Speaight, Robert. "Shakespeare in Britain."
       Shakespeare Quarterly, 22 (1971), 359-364.
       In part on Brook's adaptation.

1769. Welsh, James M. "To See It Feelingly: King Lear
       Through Russian Eyes." Literature/Film Quarterly,
       4 (1976), 153-158.
       On Kozintsev's adaptation.

1770. Wilds, Lillian. "One King Lear for Our Time: A
       Bleak Film Version by Peter Brook." Literature/Film
       Quarterly, 4 (1976), 159-164.

1771. Wilson, Robert F. "On the Closing of Gloucester's
       Door in the Kozintsev Lear." Shakespeare Film
       Newsletter, 2 (December 1977), 3, 5.

1772. Yutkevitch, Sergei. "The Conscience of the King:
       Kozintsev's King Lear." Sight and Sound, 40
       (Autumn 1971), 192-196.

Macbeth

1773. Barasch, Frances K. "Revisionist Art: Macbeth
       on Film." University of Dayton Review, 14 (1979-
       80), 15-20.
       Welles's and Polanski's adaptations.

1774. Bazerman, Charles. "Time in Play and Film: Macbeth
       and Throne of Blood." Literature/Film Quarterly,
       5 (1977), 333-337.

1775. Berlin, Normand. "Macbeth: Polanski and Shakespeare."
       Literature/Film Quarterly, 1 (1973), 291-298.

1776. Beylie, Claude. "Macbeth or the Magical Depths."
       In Focus on Shakespearean Films. Ed. Charles
       W. Eckert. Englewood Cliffs: Printice-Hall,
       1972, pp. 72-75.

1777.   Blumenthal, J. "Macbeth into Throne of Blood."
        Sight and Sound, 34 (Autumn 1965), 190-195.
        Reprinted in Renaissance of the Film. Ed. Julius
        Bellone. London: Collier Books, 1970, pp. 289-305.
        Reprinted in Film Theory and Criticism: Introductory
        Readings. Ed. Gerald Mast and Marshall Cohen.
        New York: Oxford University Press, 1974, pp. 340-351.

1778.   Clifton, Charles H. "Making an Old Thing New:
        Kurosawa's Film Adaptation of Shakespeare's
        Macbeth." In Ideas of Order in Literature and
        Film. Ed. Peter Ruppert. Tallahassee: University
        Presses of Florida, 1980, pp. 51-58.

1779.   Coursen, H.R. "Polanski's Macbeth: A Dissent."
        University of Dayton Review, 14 (1979-80), 95-97.

1780.   Cowie, Peter. "The Study of Panic: Macbeth."
        In his A Ribbon of Dreams: The Cinema of Orson
        Welles. New York: A.S. Barnes, 1973, pp. 108-115.

1781.   Crowl, Samuel. "Chain Reaction: A Study of Roman
        Polanski's Macbeth." Soundings, 59 (1976),
        226-233.

1782.   Gerlach, John. "Shakespeare, Kurosawa, and Macbeth:
        A Response to J. Blumenthal." Literature/Film
        Quarterly, 1 (1973), 352-359.

1783.   Grossvogel, David I. "When the Stain Won't Wash:
        Polanski's Macbeth." Diacritics, 2 (Summer
        1972), 46-51.

1784.   Heaven, Simon. "Macbeth: A Brief Filmography."
        Theatre Quarterly, 1 (July-Sept. 1971), 53.

1785.   Higham, Charles. "Macbeth." In his The Films
        of Orson Welles. Berkeley: University of California
        Press, 1971, pp. 125-134.

1786.   Hodgdon, Barbara. "Of Time and the Arrow: A Reading
        of Kurosawa's Throne of Blood." University
        of Dayton Review, 14 (1979-80), 63-70.

1787.   Jorgens, Jack J. "Kurosawa's Throne of Blood: Washizu
        and Miki Meet the Forest Spirit." Literature/Film
        Quarterly, 11 (1983), 167-173.

1788.   _____. "The Opening Scene of Polanski's Macbeth."
        Literature/Film Quarterly, 3 (1975), 277-278.

1789.   Kinder, Marsha. "Throne of Blood: A Morality Dance."
        Literature/Film Quarterly, 5 (1977), 339-345.

1790. McDonald, Keiko I. "The Phantasmagorical World
         of Kurosawa's Throne of Blood." In his Cinema
         East: A Critical Study of Major Japanese Films.
         East Brunswick, N.J.: Associated University
         Presses, 1983, 154-167.
       Less a study of the film as an adaptation than
       a study of the influence of Noh drama on the film.

1791. McLean, Andrew M. "Kurosawa and the Shakespearean
         Moral Vision." University of Dayton Review,
         14 (1979-80), 71-76.

1792. Mellen, Joan and Bernice Kliman. "On Kurosawa's
         Throne of Blood." Literary Review, 22 (1979),
         460-489.

1793. Middleton, David. "The Self-Reflective Nature
         of Roman Polanski's Macbeth." University of
         Dayton Review, 14 (1979-80), 89-94.

1794. Mullin, Michael. "Macbeth on Film." Literature/Film
         Quarterly, 1 (1973), 332-342.
       On Polanski's adaptation.

1795. _____. "Orson Welles' Macbeth." In Focus
         on Orson Welles. Ed. Ronald Gottesman. Englewood
         Cliffs: Prentice-Hall, 1976, pp. 136-145.

1796. Naremore, James. "The Walking Shadow: Welles'
         Expressionistic Macbeth." Literature/Film Quarterly,
         1 (1973), 360-366. Revised and reprinted in
         his The Magic World of Orson Welles. New York:
         Oxford University Press, 1978, pp. 164-173.

1797. Ornstein, Robert. "Interpreting Shakespeare: The
         Dramatic Text and the Film." University of
         Dayton Review, 14 (1979-80), 55-61.
       Chiefly concerns Polanski's Macbeth.

1798. Reddington, John. "Film, Play and Idea." Literature/
         Film Quarterly, 1 (1973), 367-371.
       On Polanski's Macbeth and Brook's King Lear.

1799. Richie, Donald. "The Throne of Blood." In his
         The Films of Akira Kurosawa. Berkeley: University
         of Califorina Press, 1970, pp. 115-124.

1800. Rothwell, Kenneth S. "Polanski's Macbeth: Golgotha
         Triumphant." Literature/Film Quarterly, 1 (1973),
         71-75.

1801. _____. "A Reply to Mr. Silverstein."
         Literature/Film Quarterly, 2 (1974), 91-92.
       Defends his article against Silverstein's criticism.

1802. Silverstein, Norman. "The Opening Shot of Macbeth."
         Literature/Film Quarterly, 2 (1974), 88-90.
       On what he believes are errors in Rothwell's article.

1803. Ulbricht, Walt. "Orson Welles' Macbeth: Archetype
         and Symbol." University of Dayton Review, 14
         (1979-80), 21-27.

1804. Wexman, Virginia Wright. "History as Nightmare:
         Macbeth." In her Roman Polanski. Boston: Twayne
         Publishers, 1985, pp. 79-88.

1805. _____. "Macbeth and Polanski's Theme of
         Regression." University of Dayton Review, 14
         (1979-80), 85-88.

1806. Wilson, Richard. "`Macbeth' on Film." Theatre
         Arts, 33, No. 5 (1949), 53-55.
         On Welles's version.

1807. Zambrano, Ana Laura. "Throne of Blood: Kurosawa's
         Macbeth." Literature/Film Quarterly, 2 (1974),
         262-274.

A Midsummer Night's Dream

1808. Crowl, Samuel. "Babes in the Woods; or the Lost
         Boys." Literature/Film Quarterly, 11 (1983),
         185-189.
         On Reinhardt's A Midsummer NIght's Dream and Czinner's
         As You Like It.

1809. Gow, Gordon. "In Search of a Revolution: Peter
         Hall." Films and Filming, 15 (Sept. 1969),
         40-44.

1810. Mullin, Michael. "Peter Hall's Midsummer Night's
         Dream on Film." Educational Theatre Journal,
         27 (1975), 529-534.

1811. Occhiogrosso, Frank. "Cinematic Oxymoron in Peter
         Hall's A Midsummer Night's Dream." Literature/Film
         Quarterly 11 (1983), 174-178.

1812. Watts, Richard, Jr. "Films of a Moonstruck World."
         Yale Review, 25 (1935), 311-320. Portion reprinted
         in Focus on Shakespearean Film. Ed. Charles
         W. Eckert. Englewood Cliffs: Prentice-Hall,
         1972, pp. 47-52.
         Centers on Reinhardt's film.

Othello

1813. Bazin, André. "A Review of Othello." In Focus
         on Shakespearean Films. Ed. Charles W. Eckert.
         Englewood Cliffs: Prentice-Hall, 1972, pp. 77-78.
         Welles's adaptation.

1814. Brown, Constance. "Olivier's Othello." Film Quarterly,
         19 (Summer 1966), 48-50.

1815.   Cowie, Peter. "The Study of Jealousy: Othello."
        In his Ribbon of Dreams: The Cinema of Orson
        Welles. New York: A.S. Barnes, 1973, pp. 116-127.

1816.   Fisher, James E. "Olivier and the Realistic Othello."
        Literature/Film Quarterly, 1 (1973), 321-331.

1817.   Higham, Charles. "Othello." In his The Films
        of Orson Welles. Berkeley: University of California
        Press, 1971, pp. 135-144.

1818.   Jorgens, Jack. "Orson Welles' Othello: A Baroque
        Translation." In Focus on Orson Welles. Ed. Ronald
        Gottesman. Englewood Cliffs: Prentice-Hall,
        1976, pp. 146-156.

1819.   Kozelka, Paul. "A Guide to the Screen Version
        of Shakespeare's Othello." Audio-Visual Guide,
        22, No. 2 (1955), 31-40.
        On Welles's adaptation.

1820.   MacLiammóir, Micheál. Put Money in Thy Pocket:
        The Filming of Orson Welles' Othello. London:
        Methuen, 1952. Selection reprinted in Focus
        on Shakespearean Films. Ed. Charles W. Eckert.
        Englewood Cliffs: Prentice-Hall, 1972, pp. 79-100.
        An account of the making of Welles's version by
        the actor who played Iago.

1821.   Naremore, James. "Othello." In his The Magic
        World of Orson Welles. New York: Oxford University
        Press, 1978, pp. 212-219.

1822.   Nelson, Harland S. "Othello." Film Heritage,
        2 (Fall 1966), 18-22.
        On Olivier's adaptation.

1823.   Plotkin, Frederick. "Othello and Welles: A Fantastic
        Marriage." Film Heritage, 4 (Summer 1969),
        9-16.

1824.   Prouse, Derek. "Othello." Sight and Sound, 26
        (Summer 1956), 30. Reprinted in Focus on
        Shakespearean Films. Ed. Charles W. Eckert.
        Englewood Cliffs: Prentice-Hall, 1972, pp. 126-129.
        On Yutkevich's adaptation.

1825.   Simon, John. "Pearl Throwing Free Style." In
        Focus on Shakespearean Films. Ed. Charles
        W. Eckert. Englewood Cliffs: Prentice-Hall,
        1972, pp. 154-157.
        On Welles's adaptation.

1826.   Yutkevitch, Sergei. "My Way With Shakespeare."
        Films and Filming, 4 (Oct. 1957), 8.

Richard III

1827. Brown, Constance. "Richard III: A Re-evaluation."
       Film Quarterly, 20 (Summer 1967), 23-32. Reprinted
       in Focus on Shakespearean Films. Ed. Charles
       W. Eckert. Englewood Cliffs: Prentice-Hall,
       1972, pp. 131-145.

1828. Cottrell, John. "The Filming of Richard III."
       In his Olivier. Englewood Cliffs: Prentice-Hall,
       1975, pp. 264-273.

1829. Diether, Jack. "Richard III: The Preservation
       of a Film." The Quarterly of Film, Radio, and
       Television, 11 (1957), 280-293.

1830. Griffin, Alice Venezky. "Shakespeare Through the
       Camera's Eye: III." Shakespeare Quarterly,
       7 (1956), 235-240.
       On Welles's Othello, Castellani's Romeo and Juliet,
       but chiefly on Olivier's Richard III.

1831. Hirsch, Foster. "Richard III." In his Laurence
       Olivier. Boston: Twayne Publishers, 1979,
       pp. 95-109.

1832. Jorgens, Jack. "Laurence Olivier's Richard III."
       Literature/Film Quarterly, 4 (1976), 99-107.

1833. Kozelka, Paul. "A Guide to the Screen Version
       of Shakespeare's Richard III." Audio-Visual
       Guide, 22, No. 8 (1956), 51-57.

1834. Leyda, Jay. "The Evil That Men Do." Film Culture,
       2, No. 1 (1956), 21-23.

1835. Phillps, James E. "Some Glories and Some Discontents."
       The Quarterly of Film, Radio, and Television,
       10 (1956), 399-407.

1836. Schein, Harry. "A Magnificent Fiasco?" The Quarterly
       of Film, Radio, and Television, 10 (1956), 407-415.

1837. Thorp, Margaret Farrand. "Shakespeare and the
       Movies." Shakespeare Quarterly, 9 (1958), 357-366.

1838. Walker, Roy. "Bottled Spider." Twentieth Century,
       159 (Jan. 1956), 58-68.

1839. Wood, Charles T. "Whatever Happened to Margaret
       of Anjou or Olivier's Shakespeare and Richard
       III." Iowa State Journal of Research, 53 (Feb.
       1979), 213-217.

Romeo and Juliet

1840.   Cirillo, Albert R.   "The Art of Franco Zeffirelli
        and Shakespeare's Romeo and Juliet." TriQuarterly,
        No. 16 (1969), pp. 69-92. Reprinted in Film
        and Literature: Contrasts in Media. Ed. Fred
        H. Marcus. Scranton, Pa.: Chandler Publishing
        Co., 1971, pp. 205-227.

1841.   Denson, Alan. Franco Zeffirelli's Production of
        William Shakespeare's Romeo and Juliet. Kendal,
        Westmorland: Denson, 1968.
        A four page booklet on the film.

1842.   Halio, Jay L.   "Zeffirelli's Romeo and Juliet:
        The Camera Versus the Text." Literature/Film
        Quarterly, 5 (1977), 322-325.

1843.   Herzberg, Max J.   "A Preliminary Guide to the Study
        and Appreciation of the Screen Version of
        Shakespeare's Romeo and Juliet." In Romeo and
        Juliet: A Motion Picture Edition. New York:
        Random House, 1936, pp. 271-290.
        On the Cukor film.

1844.   Jackson, Robert Darrell.   "Romeo and Juliet on
        Film: A Comparative Analysis of Three Major
        Film Versions of Shakespeare's Play." DAI,
        39 (1978), 1164A-65A (Wayne State University).

1845.   Jennings, Talbot.   "Romeo and Juliet Script."
        In Romeo and Juliet: A Motion Picture Edition.
        New York: Random House, 1936, pp. 251-252.
        Jennings wrote the scenario for the Cukor version.

1846.   Jorgenson, Paul A.   "Castellani's Romeo and Juliet:
        Intention and Response." The Quarterly of Film,
        Radio, and Television, 10 (1955), 1-10. Reprinted
        in Focus on Shakespearean Films. Ed. Charles
        W. Eckert. Englewood Cliffs: Prentice-Hall,
        1972, pp. 108-115.

1847.   Lewin, William.   "Guide to the Technicolor Screen
        Version of Romeo and Juliet." Audio-Visual
        Guide, 21 (Dec. 1954), 19-28.
        On Castellani's version.

1848.   Marks, Louis.   "Shakespeare--Then and Now." Films
        and Filming, 1 (Nov. 1954), 15.
        On Cukor's and Castellani's versions.

1849.   Rothwell, Kenneth S.   "Hollywood and Some Versions
        of Romeo and Juliet: Toward a Substantial Pageant."
        Literature/Film Quarterly, 1 (1973), 343-351.

1850.   _____.   "Zeffirelli's Romeo and Juliet: Words
        into Picture and Music." Literature/Film Quarterly,
        5 (1977), 326-331.

1851. Strunk, William, Jr. "Foreward to Romeo and Juliet."
      In Romeo and Juliet: A Motion Picture Edition.
      New York: Random House, 1936, pp. 19-24.
      General observations on adapting Shakespeare's
      play.

1852. Sypher, Wylie. "Romeo and Juliet Are Dead: Melodrama
      of the Clinical." In Melodrama. Ed. Daniel
      Gerould. New York: New York Literary Forum,
      1980, pp. 179-186.
      Contrasts Shakespeare's play with Last Tango in
      Paris.

1853. Thalberg, Irving G. "Picturizing Romeo and Juliet."
      In Romeo and Juliet: A Motion Picture Edition.
      New York: Random House, 1936, pp. 13-15.
      Thalberg produced the Cukor version.

1854. Walker, Roy. "In Fair Verona." The Twentieth
      Century, 156 (1954), 464-471. Reprinted in
      Focus on Shakespearean Films. Ed. Charles W.
      Eckert. Englewood Cliffs: Prentice-Hall, 1972,
      pp. 115-121.
      On Castellani's version.

The Taming of the Shrew

1855. Ball, Robert Hamilton. "The Taming of the Shrew--With
      `Additional Dialogue.'" In The Triple Bond:
      Plays, Mainly Shakespearean, in Performance.
      Ed. Joseph G. Price. University Park: Pennsylvania
      State University Press, 1975, pp. 203-220.
      On the script for the Mary Pickford-Douglas Fairbanks
      version.

1856. Harrison, Casey. "Taming of the Shrew." Sight
      and Sound, 36 (Spring 1967), 97-98. Reprinted
      in Focus on Shakespearean Films. Ed. Charles
      W. Eckert. Englewood Cliffs: Prentice-Hall,
      1972, pp. 159-160.

1857. Lane, John Francis. "The Taming of the Shrew."
      Films and Filming, 13 (Oct. 1966), 50-52.

1858. Pursell, Michael. "Zeffirelli's Shakespeare: The
      Visual Realization of Tone." Literature/Film
      Quarterly, 8 (1980), 210-218.

1859. Welsh, James M. "The Sound of Silents: An Early
      Shrew." The English Journal, 62 (1973), 754-758,
      767-769.
      On Sam Taylor's 1929 adaptation.

11

Literary Figures
of
Classical Literature

AESCHYLUS

1860. Berlin, Normand. "Easy Rider: Touching the Tragic."
      Hartford Studies in Literature, 3 (1971), 12-18.
      Revised and reprinted as "On the Road and On
      the Rock: Easy Rider and Prometheus Bound."
      In his The Secret Cause: A Discussion of Tragedy.
      Amherst: University of Massachusetts Press,
      1981, pp. 153-172.

EURIPIDES

1861. McDonald, Marianne. Euripides in Cinema: The
      Heart Made Visible. Philadelphia: Centrum
      Philadelphia, 1983.
      Essays on Passolini's Medea, Dassin's Dream of
      Passion, Dassin's Phaedra, Cacoyannis's Iphigenia
      at Aulis, Cacoyannis's The Trojan Women, and
      Cacoyannis's Electra.

OVID

1862. Solomon, Jon. "Fellini and Ovid." Classical and
      Modern Literature, 3 (1982), 39-44.

PETRONIUS

1863. Dick, Bernard F. "Adaptation as Archeology: Fellini
      Satyricon." In Modern European Filmmakers and
      the Art of Adaptation. Ed. Andrew Horton and
      Joan Magretta. New York: Frederick Ungar, 1981,
      pp. 145-157.

1864. Grossvogel, David I. "Fellini's Satyricon."
      Diacritics, 1 (Fall 1971), 51-54.

1865. Highet, Gilbert. "Whose Satyricon--Petronius's
      or Fellini's?" In The Classical Papers of Gilbert
      Highet. Ed. Robert J. Ball. New York: Columbia
      University Press, 1983, pp. 339-348.

1866. Moravia, Alberto. "Dreaming Up Petronius." New
       York Review of Books, 14 (26 March 1970), 40-42.
       Reprinted in Federico Fellini: Essays in Criticism.
       Ed. Peter Bondanella. New York: Oxford University
       Press, 1978, pp. 161-168.

1867. Richardson, Robert D. "Fellini's Satyricon."
       Denver Quarterly, 6 (Spring 1971), 59-71.

1868. Segal, Erich. "Arbitrary Satyricon: Petronius
       and Fellini." Diacritics, 1 (Fall 1971), 54-57.

                          SOPHOCLES

1869. McGinnis, Wayne D. "Chinatown: Roman Polanski's
       Contemporary Oedipus Story." Literature/Film
       Quarterly, 3 (1975), 249-251.

1870. Palmer, R. Barton. "Chinatown and the Detective
       Story." Literature/Film Quarterly, 5 (1977),
       112-117.
       Comparison of the film to Oedipus Rex.

1871. Pasolini, Pier Paolo. "Why That of Oedipus Is
       a Story." In Oedipus Rex. Trans. John Mathews.
       New York: Simon and Schuster, 1971, pp. 5-13.

1872. White, Robert J. "Myth and Mise-en-Scène: Pasolini's
       Edipo Re." Literature/Film Quarterly, 5 (1977),
       30-37.

12

Literary Figures
of
Europe

LEONID ANDREEV

1873. Andreev, Leonid. "Letters on the Theatre." In
      <u>Russian Dramatic Theory From Pushkin to the
      Symbolists</u>. Trans. Laurence Senelick. Austin:
      University of Texas Press, 1981, pp. 223-272.
      The playwright on the connection of film to theatre.

FERNANDO ARRABAL

1874. Brown, Edward G. "Arrabal's <u>Viva la Muerte!</u> From
      Novel to Film script." <u>Literature/Film Quarterly</u>,
      12 (1984), 136-141.

1875. Striker, Ardelle. "From <u>Baal Babylone</u> to <u>Viva
      la Muerte</u>: Reflections on the Visions of Fernando
      Arrabal." <u>West Virginia University Philological
      Papers</u>, 26 (Aug. 1980), 53-59.

ANTONIN ARTAUD

1876. Artaud, Antonin. "On the Cinema." In <u>Antonin
      Artaud: Collected Works</u>. Vol. Three. Trans.
      Alastair Hamilton. London: Calder and Boyars,
      1972, pp. 59-82.
      This section on the collected works contains nine
      essays on film.

1877. Blum, William. "Towards a Cinema of Cruelty."
      <u>Cinema Journal</u>, 10 (Spring 1971), 19-33.

1878. Dozoretz, Wendy. "Dulac Versus Artaud." <u>Wide
      Angle</u>, 3, No. 1 (1979), 46-53.
      On <u>The Sea Shell and the Clergyman</u>.

1879. Greene, Naomi. "Artaud and Film: A Reconsideration."
      <u>Cinema Journal</u>, 23 (Summer 1984), 28-40.

234 Literature as Film

1880. Knapp, Bettina L. "The Life of Usher...." In
       her <u>Antonin Artaud: Man of Vision</u>. New York:
       David Lewis, 1969, pp. 65-83.
       Concerns both Artaud's writing about film and his
       scenarios.

1881. Kovács, Steven. "What the Surrealist Film Might
       Have Been: Artaud and the Cinema." In his <u>From
       Enchantment to Rage: The Story of Surrealist
       Cinema</u>. Cranbury, N.J.: Associated University
       Presses, 1980, pp. 155-182.

1882. Rose, Mark Verlin. "The Actor and His Double:
       Antonin Artaud's Theory and Practice of Movement."
       <u>DAI</u>, 44 (1984), 3543A (The University of California
       at Davis).
       Analyzes both Artaud's film performances and his
       scenarios.

1883. Virmaux, Alain. "Artaud and Film." Trans. Simone
       Sanzenbach. <u>Tulane Drama Review</u>, 11 (1966),
       154-165.

GIORGIO BASSANI

1884. Eskin, Stanley G. "<u>The Garden of the Finzi-Continis</u>"
       <u>Literature/Film Quarterly</u>, 1 (1973), 171-175.

CHARLES-PIERRE BAUDELAIRE

1885. Hagan, John. "Cinema and the Romantic Tradition."
       In <u>Film Before Griffith</u>. Ed. John L. Fell.
       Berkeley: University of California Press, 1983,
       pp. 229-235.
       The literary tradition, exemplified by Baudelaire
       and Poe, during the early years of the film.

1886. Rowe, Carel. <u>The Beaudelairean Cinema: A Trend
       Within the American Avant-Garde</u>. Ann Arbor:
       UMI Research Press, 1982.
       Book draws analogies between the works of Baudelaire
       and other nineteenth century French writers and
       the work of American avant-garde filmmakers.

SIMONE DE BEAUVOIR

1887. Emelson, Margaret A. "The Ambivalence of Survival
       in Ingmar Bergman and Simone de Beauvoir: A
       Perspective on Dying and Death." <u>Journal of
       Evolutionary Psychology</u>, 1 (1979), 58-68.
       On Bergman's <u>The Seventh Seal</u> and de Beauvoir's
       <u>Une Mort très douce</u>.

GEORGES BERNANOS

1888. Andrew, Dudley. "Desperation and Meditation: Bresson's
        Diary of a Country Priest." In Modern European
        Filmmakers and the Art of Adaptation. Ed. Andrew
        Horton and Joan Magretta. New York: Frederick
        Ungar, 1981, pp. 20-37. Revised and reprinted
        as "Private Scribblings: The Crux in the Margins
        around Diary of a Country Priest." In his Film
        in the Aura of Art. Princeton: Princeton University
        Press, 1984, pp. 112-130.

1889. Bazin, André. "Le Journal d'un curé de campagne
        and the Stylistics of Robert Bresson." In his
        What Is Cinema? Vol. I. Trans. Hugh Gray.
        Berkeley: University of California Press, 1967,
        pp. 125-143.

1890. Browne, Nick. "Film Form/Voice Over: Bresson's
        The Diary of a Country Priest." Yale French
        Studies, No. 60 (1980), pp. 233-240.

1891. Feldman, Ellen. "Bresson's Adaptation of Bernanos'
        Diary of a Country Priest." West Virginia University
        Philological Papers, 26 (Aug. 1980), 37-42.

1892. Gerlach, John. "The Diary of a Country Priest:
        A Total Conversion." Literature/Film Quarterly,
        4 (1976), 39-45.

GIOVANNI BOCCACCIO

1893. Bevan, David G. "Pasolini and Boccaccio." Literature/
        Film Quarterly, 5 (1977), 23-29.

1894. Lawton, Ben. "Boccaccio and Pasolini: A Contemporary
        Reinterpretation of The Decameron." In The
        Decameron: A New Translation. Ed. and Trans. Mark
        Musa and Peter E. Bondanella. New York: W.W. Norton,
        1977, pp. 306-322. Revised and reprinted as "The
        Storyteller's Art: Pasolini's Decameron." In
        Modern European Filmmakers and the Art of Adaptation.
        Ed. Andrew Horton and Joan Magretta. New York:
        Frederick Ungar, 1981, pp. 203-221.

1895. _____. "Theory and Praxis in Pasolini's Trilogy
        of Life: Decameron." Quarterly Review of Film
        Studies, 2 (1977), 395-415.

HEINRICH BOLL

1896. Friedman, Lester D. "Cinematic Techniques in The
        Lost Honor of Katharina Blum." Literature/Film
        Quarterly, 7 (1979), 244-252.

1897.   Magretta, William R. and Joan Magretta. "Story
        and Discourse: Schlondörff and von Trotta's
        The Lost Honor of Katharina Blum." In Modern
        European Filmmakers and the Art of Adaptation.
        Ed. Andrew Horton and Joan Magretta. New York:
        Frederick Ungar, 1981, pp. 278-294.

                        PIERRE BOULLE

1898.   Anderegg, Michael A. "Going Hollywood: The Bridge
        on the River Kwai." In his David Lean. Boston:
        Twayne Publishers, 1984, pp. 91-102.

1899.   Joyaux, Georges. "The Bridge Over the River Kwai:
        From the Novel to the Movie." Literature/Film
        Quarterly, 2 (1974), 174-182.

1900.   Watt, Ian. "Bridges Over the Kwai." Partisan
        Review, 26 (Winter 1959), 83-94.

                        BERTOLT BRECHT

1901.   Barthes, Roland. "Diderot, Brecht, Eisenstein."
        In his Image, Music, Text. Trans. Stephen Heath.
        New York: Hill and Wang, 1977, pp. 69-78.

1902.   Brecht, Bertolt. "The Film, the Novel, and the
        Epic Theatre." In Brecht on Theatre. Ed. John
        Willett. New York: Hill and Wang, 1964, pp. 47-50.
        A longer extract from The Threepenny Lawsuit
        can be found in Realism and the Cinema: A
        Reader. Ed. Christopher Williams. London:
        Routledge and Kegan Paul, 1980, pp. 164-170.

1903.   Brewster, Ben. "Brecht and the Film Industry."
        Screen, 16, No. 4 (1975), 16-29.
        On The Threepenny Opera and Hangmen Also Die.

1904.   _____. "The Fundamental Reproach." Cine-Tracts,
        1, No. 2 (1977), 44-53.

1905.   Brewster, Ben and Colin MacCabe. "Editorial: Brecht
        and the Revolutionary Cinema?" Screen, 15,
        No. 2 (1974), 4-6.
        On Kuhle Wampe and Brecht in Hollywood.

1906.   Cook, Bruce. Brecht in Exile. New York: Holt,
        Rinehart and Winston, 1982.
        Brecht's Hollywood experience.

1907.   Fredericksen, Don. "Lessons From Brecht." Screen,
        15 (Summer 1974), 103-128.

1908.   Fuegi, John. "Brecht and the Film Medium." In
        Expression, Communication, and Experience in
        Literature and Language. Ed. Ronald G. Popperwell.
        Leeds: W.S. Manley and Son, 1973, pp. 223-225.

1909.   _____. "Feuchtwanger, Brecht, and the Epic
         Media: The Novel and the Film." In Lion
         Feuchtwanger: The Man, His Ideas, His Work.
         Ed. John M. Spalek. Los Angeles: Hennessey
         and Ingalls, 1972, pp. 307-322.

1910.   _____. "On Brecht's `Theory' of Film." In
         Ideas of Order in Film and Literature. Ed. Peter
         Ruppert. Tallahassee: University Presses of
         Florida, 1980, pp. 107-118.

1911.   Greene, Naomi. "Brecht, Godard, and Epic Cinema."
         Praxis, 1, No. 1 (1975), 19-24.

1912.   Harvey, Sylvia. "Whose Brecht? Memories For the
         Eighties." Screen, 23 (May-June 1982), 45-59.

1913.   Heath, Stephen. "From Brecht to Film--Theses,
         Problems." Screen, 16, No. 4 (1975-76), 34-45.

1914.   _____. "Lessons From Brecht." Screen, 15,
         No. 2 (1974), 103-128.

1915.   Lajtha, Terry. "Brechtian Devices in Non-Brechtian
         Cinema: Culloden." Literature/Film Quarterly,
         9 (1981), 9-14.
         On Peter Watkins's Culloden.

1916.   Lellis, George. "Brecht and Cahiers du Cinema."
         In Bertolt Brecht: Political Theory and Literary
         Practice. Ed. Betty Nance Weber and Herbert
         Heinen. Athens: University of Georgia Press,
         1980, pp. 129-44.

1917.   _____. Bertolt Brecht, Cahiers du Cinema,
         and Contemporary Film Theory. Ann Arbor: UMI
         Research Press, 1982.

1918.   Lesage, Julia. "The Films of Jean-Luc Godard and
         Their Use of Brechtian Dramatic Theory." DAI,
         37 (1976), 1845A-1846A (Indiana University).

1919.   Lovell, Alan. "Brecht in Britain--Lindsay Anderson."
         Screen, 16 (Winter 1975), 62-80.
         Brechtian devices in If and O Lucky Man!.

1920.   Lyon, James K. Brecht in America. Princeton:
         Princeton University Press, 1980.
         Brecht's Hollywood experience.

1921.   _____. "Brecht's Hollywood Years: The Dramatist
         as Film Writer." Oxford German Studies, 6 (1971),
         145-174.

1922.   McCabe, Colin. "Realism and the Cinema: Notes
         on Some Brechtian Theses." Screen, 15 (Summer
         1974), 7-27.

1923.   Polan, Dana.   "Brecht and the Politics of Self-Reflexive
        Cinema."   Jump-Cut, No. 17 (1978), pp. 29-32.

1924.   Schechter, Joel.   "Brecht and Godard in Ten Scenes
        from The Decline and Fall of Aristotle."   Yale/
        Theater, 3 (Fall 1970), 25-30.

1925.   Teuchert, Hans Joachim.   "Bertolt Brecht's Contributions
        to the Screenplay of Hangmen Also Die."   DAI,
        41 (1981), 4410A (The University of California
        at San Diego).

1926.   Thompson, Kristin.   "Sawing Through the Bough:
        Tout va Bien as a Brechtian Film."   Wide Angle,
        1, No. 3 (1976), 38-51.

1927.   Uhde, Jan.   "The Influence of Bertolt Brecht's
        Theory of Distanciation on the Contemporary
        Cinema, Particularly on Jean-Luc Godard."   Journal
        of the University Film Association, 26, No. 3
        (1974), 28-30, 44.

1928.   Walsh, Martin.   The Brechtian Aspect of Radical
        Cinema.   Ed. Keith M. Griffiths.   London: British
        Film Institute, 1981.

1929.   Willett, John.   "Brecht and the Motion Pictures."
        In Brecht in Context: Comparative Approaches.
        New York: Methuen, 1984, pp. 107-128.

1930.   Winge, John H.   "Brecht and the Cinema."   Sight
        and Sound, 26 (Winter 1956-57), 144-147.

                        GEORG BUCHNER

1931.   Bloom, Michael.   "Woyzeck and Kaspar: The Congruities
        in Drama and Film."   Literature/Film Quarterly,
        8 (1980), 225-231.

1932.   Mitgutsch, Waltraud.   "Faces of Dehumanization:
        Werner Herzog's Reading of Buchner's Woyzeck."
        Literature/Film Quarterly, 9 (1981), 152-160.

                        MICHEL BUTOR

1933.   Hedges, Inez Kathleen.   "Temporal and Spatial Structures
        in Film and the Novel: A Comparison Between
        Ozu Yasujiro's Kohayagawa-Ke no Aki and Michel
        Butor's L'Emploi du Temps."   DAI, 37 (1977),
        5805A (The University of Wisconsin at Madison).

                        JEAN CAYROL

1934.   Bortz, Susan Xelia.   "Narrative Structures in a
        Novel and Three Short Films by Jean Cayrol."
        DAI, 41 (1981), 4020A (The University of Wisconsin
        at Madison).
        The novel: Le froid du soleil; the films: Nuit
        et Brouillard, On vous parle, and Madame se meurt.

MIGUEL DE CERVANTES SAAVEDRA

1935. Buck, Tony. "Cherkassov's Don Quixote." Sight and Sound, 27 (Autumn 1958), 320-322.

1936. Leaming, Barbara. "Don Quixote." In her Grigori Kozintsev. Boston: Twayne Publishers, 1980, pp. 77-93.

ANTON CHEKHOV

1937. Funke, Lewis. "`Uncle Vanya'...From Fourth Street to Film." Theatre Arts, 41, No. 10 (1957), 28-29, 84.
On the filming of David Ross' production.

CHRETIEN DE TROYES

1938. Cormier, Raymond J. "Rohmer's Grail Story: Anatomy of a French Flop." Yale French Review, 5 (Winter 1981), 391-396.

1939. Williams, Linda. "Eric Rohmer and the Holy Grail." Literature/Film Quarterly, 11 (1983), 71-82.

JEAN COCTEAU

1940. Amberg, George. "The Testament of Jean Cocteau." Film Comment, 4 (Winter 1971-1972), 23-27.
On The Testament of Orpheus.

1941. Bancroft, David. "Cocteau--Orphée: Film-Maker--Poet." Meanjin Review, 32 (1973), 73-79.

1942. Bishop, John Peale. "A Film of Jean Cocteau." In The Collected Essays of John Peale Bishop. Ed. Edmund Wilson. New York: Charles Scribner's Sons, 1948, pp. 222-226.
On Blood of a Poet.

1943. Callenbach, Ernest. "The Filmed Play: Les Parents Terribles." In his Our Modern Art: The Movies. New York: Center for the Study of Liberal Education for Adults, 1955, pp. 67-76.

1944. Cocteau, Jean. Beauty and the Beast: Diary of a Film. Trans. Ronald Duncan. New York: Dover Publications, 1972.

1945. _____. Cocteau on the Film, Ed. Andre Fraigneau. New York: Dover Publications, 1972.

1946. _____. "Films." In The Journals of Jean Cocteau. Ed. Wallace Fowlie. New York: Criterion Books, 1956, pp. 124-136.

1947. _____. "Le Sang d'une Poète." In Professional
      Secrets: An Autobiography of Jean Cocteau.
      Ed. Robert Phelps. New York: Farrar, Straus,
      and Giroux, 1970, pp. 142-147.

1948. Crowson, Lydia. The Esthetic of Jean Cocteau.
      Hanover: University Press of New England, 1978.

1949. Debrix, Jean R. "Cocteau's `Orpheus' Analyzed."
      Trans. Edith Morgan King. Films in Review,
      2 (June-July 1951), 18-23.

1950. Durgnat, Raymond. "A Great Defect." In Films
      and Feelings. Cambridge: The M.I.T. Press,
      1967, pp. 239-250.
      On Orpheus.

1951. Evans, Arthur B. Jean Cocteau and His Films of
      Orphic Identity. Philadelphia: Philadelphia
      Art Alliance Press, 1977.

1952. Fowlie, Wallace. "The Poet as Filmmaker." In
      his Jean Cocteau: The History of a Poet's Age.
      Bloomington: Indiana University Press, 1966,
      pp. 102-119.

1953. Galef, David. "A Sense of Magic: Reality and Illusion
      in Cocteau's Beauty and the Beast." Literature/Film
      Quarterly, 12 (1984), 96-106.

1954. Gilson, René. Jean Cocteau. Trans. Ciba Vaughan.
      New York: Crown Publishers, 1969.

1955. Hammond, Robert M. "The Authenticity of the Filmscript:
      Cocteau's Beauty and the Beast." Style, 9 (1975),
      514-532.

1956. _____. "Jensen's Gradiva: A Clue to the
      Composition of Cocteau's Orphée." Symposium,
      27 (1973), 126-136.

1957. _____. "The Mysteries of Cocteau's Orpheus."
      Film Journal, 11 (Spring 1972), 26-33.

1958. Hanlon, Lindley. "Cocteau, Cauchemar, Cinema."
      In The Anxious Subject: Nightmares and Daymares
      in Literature and Film. Ed. Moshe Lazar. Malibu:
      Undena Publications, 1983, pp. 107-120.

1959. Harvey, Stephen. "The Mask in the Mirror: The
      Movies of Jean Cocteau." In Jean Cocteau and
      the French Scene. Ed. Alexandra Anderson and
      Caron Saltus. New York: Abbeville Press, 1984,
      pp. 185-207.

1960. Jean, Raymond. "Dialogue Between the Movie-Going
      Public and a Witness for Jean Cocteau." Quarterly
      of Film, Radio, and Television, 10 (Winter 1955),
      160-166.

1961. Keller, Marjorie Elizabeth. "The Theme of Childhood
       in the Films of Jean Cocteau, Joseph Cornell,
       and Stan Brakhage." DAI, 43 (1983), 3444A (New
       York University).

1962. McGowan, Raymond. "Jean Cocteau and Beauty and
       the Beast." New Orleans Review, 8 (Winter 1981),
       106-108.

1963. Oxenhandler, Neal. "Poetry in Three Films of Jean
       Cocteau." Yale French Studies, No. 17 (1956),
       pp. 14-20.

1964. Popkin, Michael. "Jean Cocteau's Beauty and the
       Beast: the Poet as Monster." Literature/Film
       Quarterly, 10 (1982), 100-109.

1965. _____. "The Orpheus Story and the Films of
       Jean Cocteau." DAI, 41 (1980), 1581A (Columbia
       University).

1966. Tomek, James Joseph. "Relationship of Literature
       and Film in Cocteau." DAI, 35 (1974), 3014-3015A
       (Duke University).

1967. Turk, Edward Baron. "The Film Adaptation of Cocteau's
       Les Enfants terribles." Cinema Journal, 19
       (1980), 25-40.

SIDONIE GABRIELLE COLETTE

1968. Virmaux, Alain and Odette Virmaux, eds. "Colette
       and the Cinema" and "Colette the Critic." In
       Colette at the Movies. New York: Frederick
       Ungar, 1980, pp. 1-7 and pp. 9-79.
       Her film criticism.

GABRIELE D'ANNUNZIO

1969. Tintner, Adeline R. "Visconti's Interpretation
       of D'Annunzio's L'Innocente." Literature/Film
       Quarterly, 11 (1983), 132-137.

DANTE ALIGHIERI

1970. Lewalski, Barbara K. "Federico Fellini's Purgatorio."
       Massachusetts Review, 5 (1964), 567-573. Reprinted
       in Federico Fellini: Essays in Criticism. Ed. Peter
       Bondanella. New York: Oxford University Press,
       1978, pp. 113-120.
       Compares Dante's work to 8 1/2.

1971. Welle, John P. "Fellini's Use of Dante in La Dolce
       Vita." Studies in Medievalism, 2 (Summer 1983),
       53-66.

ROBERT DESNOS

1972. Kovács, Steven. "Robert Desnos: The Visionary
as Critic." In his From Enchantment to Rage:
The Story of Surrealist Cinema. Cranbury, N.J.:
Associated University Presses, 1980, pp. 48-64.

DENIS DIDEROT

1973. Konigsberg, Ira. "Cinema of Entrapment: Rivette's
La Religieuse." In Modern European Filmmakers
and the Art of Adaptation. Ed. Andrew Horton
and Joan Magretta. New York: Frederick Ungar,
1981, pp. 115-129.

FEODOR DOSTOYEVSKY

1974. Brooks, Richard. "On Filming `Karamazov.'" Films
in Review, 9 (1958), 49-52.
Brooks directed the film adaptation.

1975. Christensen, Jerome C. "Versions of Adolescents:
Robert Bresson's Four Nights of a Dreamer and
Dostoyevsky's `White Nights.'" Literature/Film
Quarterly, 4 (1976), 222-229.

1976. Hanlon, Lindley. "The `Seen' and the `Said': Bresson's
Une Femme Douce." In Modern European Filmmakers
and the Art of Adaptation. Ed. Andrew Horton
and Joan Magretta. New York: Frederick Ungar,
1981, pp. 158-172.
Film is based on Dostoyevsky's "The Gentle Creature."

1977. Kline, T. Jefferson. "Doubling The Double." In
Fearful Symmetry: Doubles and Doubling in Literature
and Film. Ed. Eugene J. Crook. Tallahassee:
University Presses of Florida, 1981, pp. 65-83.
Concerns Partner, Bertolucci's adaptation of
Dostoyevsky's The Double.

1978. Lawton, Anna M. "The Double: A Dostoevskian Theme
in Polanski." Literature/Film Quarterly, 9
(1981), 121-129.

1979. Rhode, Eric. "Dostoevsky and Bresson." Sight
and Sound, 39 (1970), 82-83.
On Bresson's Une Femme Douce.

1980. Richie, Donald. "The Idiot." In his The Films
of Akira Kurosawa. Berkeley: University of
California Press, 1973, pp. 81-85.

MARGUERITE DURAS

1981. Clarens, Carlos. "India Song and Marguerite Duras."
Sight and Sound, 45 (Winter 1975-1976), 32-35.

1982. Etzkowitz, Janice. <u>Toward a Concept of Cinematic</u>
       <u>Literature: An Analysis of Hiroshima mon amour</u>.
       New York: Garland Publishing, 1983.

1983. Glassman, Debbie. "The Feminine Subject as History
       Writer in <u>Hiroshima Mon Amour</u>." <u>Enclitic</u>, 5
       (Spring 1981), 45-53.

1984. Gollub, Judith. "French Writers Turned Film Makers."
       <u>Film Heritage</u>, 4 (Winter 1968-1969), 19-25.
       On Duras and Robbe-Grillet.

1985. Guers-Villate, Yvonne. "From <u>Hiroshima mon amour</u>
       to <u>India Song</u>: A Novelist's Cinematic Production."
       <u>West Virginia University Philological Papers</u>,
       26 (Aug. 1980), 60-65.

1986. Holmlund, Christine Anne. "Destroy the Old, Suggest
       the New: Image, Sound and Text in Marguerite
       Duras' <u>Détruire, dit-elle</u> Film." <u>DAI</u>, 45 (1985),
       2677A (The University of Wisconsin at Madison).

1987. Kreidl, Francis John. "<u>Hiroshima Mon Amour</u>."
       In his <u>Alain Resnais</u>. Boston: Twayne, 1978,
       pp. 53-64.

1988. Luchting, Wolfgang A. "`Hiroshima Mon Amour,'
       Time, and Proust." <u>The Journal of Aesthetics</u>
       <u>and Art Criticism</u>, 21 (1963), 299-313. Abridgment
       in <u>Renaissance of the Film</u>. Ed. Julius Bellone.
       London: Collier Books, 1970, pp. 105-126.

1989. McKinnis, Joanne Elizabeth Jakle. "Cineliteracy
       Techniques and Their Implications in the Works
       of Marguerite Duras." <u>DAI</u>, 44 (1983), 1099A
       (The University of Texas at Austin).

1990. McNally, Judith. "<u>India Song</u>: An Interview with
       Marguerite Duras." <u>Filmmakers Newsletter</u>, 9,
       No. 3 (1976), 18-21.

1991. McWilliams, Dean. "The Novelist as Filmmaker:
       Marguerite Duras' <u>Destroy, She Said</u>." <u>Literature/</u>
       <u>Film Quarterly</u>, 3 (1975), 264-269.

1992. Medhurst, Martin J. "<u>Hiroshima mon amour</u>: From
       Iconography to Rhetoric." <u>Quarterly Review</u>
       <u>of Speech</u>, 68 (1982), 345-370.

1993. Mercken-Spaas, Godelieve. "Deconstruction and
       Reconstruction in <u>Hiroshima Mon Amour</u>."
       <u>Literature/Film Quarterly</u>, 8 (1980), 244-250.

1994. Monaco, James. "<u>Hiroshima Mon Amour</u>." In his
       <u>Alain Resnais</u>. New York: Oxford University
       Press, 1979, pp. 34-52.

1995. Morgan, Janice. "Marguerite Duras: The Novelist
         as Filmmaker." DAI, 43 (1982), 3444A (Indiana
         University).

1996. Murphy, Carol J. "Duras' New Narrative Regions:
         The Role of Desire in the Films and the Novels
         of Maguerite Duras." Literature/Film Quarterly,
         12 (1984), 122-128.

1997. _____. "Marguerite Duras: `That Obscure Object
         of Desire...'" West Virginia University Philological
         Papers, 26 (Aug. 1980), 89-96.
       Memory in the novels, India Song, and Son Nom de
       Venise dans Calcutta.

1998. Rivette, Jacques and Jean Narboni. "Destruction
         and Language: An Interview with Marguerite Duras."
         Trans. Helen Lane Cumberford. In Destroy, She
         Said by Marguerite Duras. New York: Grove Press,
         1970, pp. 91-133. Reprinted as "Destroy She
         Said: An Interview with Marguerite Duras."
         In Film Festival: Grove International Film Festival
         Book. Ed. Barney Rosset. New York: Grove Press:
         c. 1970, pp. 29-33, 78-81.

1999. Ropars-Wuilleumier, Marie-Claire. "The Disembodied
         Voice." Yale French Studies, No. 60 (1980),
         pp. 241-268.
       On the use of sound in India Song.

2000. Sweet, Freddy. "Hiroshima Mon Amour." In his
         The Film Narratives of Alain Resnais. Ann Arbor:
         UMI Research Press, 1981, pp. 5-33.

2001. Van Wert, William F. "The Cinema of Marguerite
         Duras: Sound and a Voice in a Closed Room."
         Film Quarterly, 33 (Fall 1979), 22-29.

2002. _____. "Point/Counterpoint in Hiroshima Mon
         Amour." Wide Angle, 2, No. 2 (1978), 31-37.

2003. Williams, Linda. "Hiroshima and Marienbad: Metaphor
         and Metonomy." Screen, 17 (Spring 1976), 34-39.

FRIEDRICH DURRENMATT

2004. Brock, D. Heyward. "Dürrenmatt's Der Besuch der
         alten Dame: The Stage and Screen Adaptations."
         Literature/Film Quarterly, 4 (1976), 60-67.

GUSTAVE FLAUBERT

2005. Charney, Hanna. "Images of Absence in Flaubert
         and Some Contemporary Films." Style, 9 (1975),
         488-501.

2006.   Durgnat, Raymond.   "_Madame Bovary_." In his _Jean
        Renoir_. Berkeley: University of California
        Press, 1974, pp. 94-97.

2007.   Gill, Richard.   "The Soundtrack of _Madame Bovary_:
        Flaubert's Orchestration of Aural Imagery."
        Literature/Film Quarterly, 1 (1973), 206-217.

2008.   Sesonske, Alexander.   "_Madame Bovary_." In his
        Jean Renoir: The French Films, 1924-1939. Cambridge:
        Harvard University Press, 1980, pp. 142-164.

2009.   Turnell, Martin.   "Flaubert: The Novel, the Symphony,
        and the Cinema." In his _The Rise of the French
        Novel_. New York: New Directions, 1978, pp. 171-187.
        Less a discussion of Flaubert and film than a discussion
        of film as art.

THEODOR FONTANE

2010.   Borchardt, Edith.   "Leitmotif and Structure in
        Fassbinder's _Effi Briest_." _Literature/Film
        Quarterly_, 7 (1979), 201-207.

2011.   Magretta, William R.   "Reading the Writerly Film:
        Fassbinder's _Effi Briest_." In _Modern European
        Filmmakers and the Art of Adaptation_. Ed. Andrew
        Horton and Joan Magretta. New York: Frederick
        Ungar, 1981, pp. 248-262.

ANDRE GIDE

2012.   Andrew, Dudley.   "Ice and Irony: Delannoy's _La
        Symphonie Pastorale_." In _Modern European Filmmakers
        and the Art of Adaptation_. Ed. Andrew Horton
        and Joan Magretta. New York: Frederick Ungar,
        1981, pp. 7-19. Revised and reprinted as "_La
        Symphonie pastorale_ Performed by the French
        Quality Ochestra." In _Film in the Aura of Art_.
        Princeton: Princeton University Press, 1984,
        pp. 98-111.

JEAN GIONO

2013.   Pomerai, Odile de.   "A Novelist Turns to Films:
        Jean Giono and the Cinema." _Twentieth Century
        Literature_, 12 (1966), 59-65.

2014.   Smith, Maxwell A.   "The Cinema." In his _Jean Giono_.
        Boston: Twayne Publishers, 1966, pp. 166-168.

JOHANN WOLFGANG VON GOETHE

2015.   Frisch, Shelly.   "The Disenchanted Image: From
        Goethe's _Wilhelm Meister_ to Wenders' _Wrong
        Movement_." _Literature/Film Quarterly_, 7 (1979),
        208-214.

2016. Harcourt, Peter. "Adaptation Through Inversion:
       Wenders' Wrong Movement." In Modern European
       Filmmakers and the Art of Adaptation. Ed. Andrew
       Horton and Joan Magretta. New York: Frederick
       Ungar, 1981, pp. 263-277.
       Film is based on Wilhelm Meister's Apprenticeship.

MAXIM GORKY

2017. Durgnat, Raymond. "Les Bas-Fonds (Underworld)."
       In his Jean Renoir. Berkeley: University of
       California Press, 1974, pp. 137-144.
       Renoir's adaptation of The Lower Depths.

2018. Richie, Donald. "The Lower Depths." In his The
       Films of Akira Kurosawa. Berkeley: University
       of California Press, 1973, pp. 125-133.

2019. Sesonske, Alexander. "Las Bas-Fonds." In his
       Jean Renoir: The French Films, 1924-1939. Cambridge:
       Harvard University Press, 1980, pp. 257-281.
       Renoir's adaptation of The Lower Depths.

GUNTHER GRASS

2020. Flasher, John. "The Grotesque Hero in The Tin
       Drum." In Holding the Vision: Essays on Film.
       Ed. Douglas Radcliff-Umstead. Kent, Ohio: The
       International Film Society, 1983, pp. 87-93.

2021. Hughes, John. "The Tin Drum: Volker Schlöndorff's
       `Dream of Childhood'." Film Quarterly, 34,
       (Spring 1981), 2-10.

2022. Rooks, Sharon Elaine. "The Tin Drum: Novel into
       Film. A Phenomenological Approach." DAI, 43
       (1982), 1158A (The Florida State University).

2023. Schinto, Jeanne. "Words into Movies: The Tin Drum
       and The Left-Handed Woman." Cimarron Review,
       No. 55 (April 1981), pp. 57-61.

SACHA GUITRY

2024. Knapp, Bettina. Sacha Guitry. Boston: Twayne
       Publishers, 1981.
       On his work in film.

PETER HANDKE

2025. Brunette, Peter. "Filming Words: Wenders's The
       Goalie's Anxiety at the Penalty Kick." In Modern
       European Filmmakers and the Art of Adaptation.
       Ed. Andrew Horton and Joan Magretta. New York:
       Frederick Ungar, 1981, pp. 188-202.

2026.   Finger, Ellis.   "Kasper Hauser Doubly Portrayed:
        Peter Handke's _Kaspar_ and Werner Herzog's _Every
        Man for Himself and God Against All_."   _Literature/
        Film Quarterly_, 7 (1979), 235-243.

2027.   Handke, Peter.   "Theatre and Film: The Misery of
        Comparison."   In _Focus on Film and Theatre_.
        Ed. James Hurt.   Englewood Cliffs: Prentice-Hall,
        1973, pp. 165-175.

2028.   Kersten, Lee.   "Film Reference as an Imaginative
        Model in Handke's _Der Kurze Brief zum Langen
        Abschied_."   _Journal of the Australian Universities
        Language and Literature Association_, 56 (Nov. 1981),
        152-166.

2029.   Linville, Susan and Kent Casper.   "Reclaiming the
        Self: Handke's _The Left-Handed Woman_."   _Literature/
        Film Quarterly_, 12 (1984), 13-21.

                    E.T.A. HOFFMANN

2030.   Rosen, Robert.   "Enslaved by the Queen of the Night:
        The Relationship of Ingmar Bergman to E.T.A.
        Hoffmann."   _Film Comment_, 6 (Spring 1970), 27-30.

                    BOHUMIL HRABAL

2031.   Hrabal, Bohumil.   "Introduction."   _Closely Watched
        Trains_.   New York: Simon and Schuster, 1971,
        pp. 5-8.

2032.   Skvorecky, Josef.   _Jiri Menzel and the History
        of the Closely Watched Trains_.   New York: Columbia
        University Press, 1982.

                    HENRIK IBSEN

2033.   Alnaes, Karsten.   "Footlights to Film."   _Scandinavian
        Review_, 66, No. 4 (1978), 67-71.
        Annotated filmography of over 50 adaptations of
        Ibsen's plays.

2034.   Brody, Alan.   "Jules and Catherine and Jim and
        Hedda."   _The Journal of Aesthetic Education_,
        5 (April 1971), 91-101.
        Compares Truffaut's _Jules and Jim_ to Ibsen's _Hedda
        Gabler_.

2035.   Steene, Birgitta.   "Film as Theater: Geissendorfer's
        The Wild Duck."   In _Modern European Filmmakers
        and the Art of Adaptation_.   Ed. Andrew Horton
        and Joan Magretta.   New York: Frederick Ungar,
        1981, pp. 295-312.

                    FRANZ KAFKA

2036.   Callenbach, Ernest.   "The Trial."   _Film Quarterly_,
        16 (Summer 1963), 40-43.

2037. Carroll, Noel. "Welles and Kafka." _Film Reader_
       _3_. Evanston: Northwestern University, 1978,
       pp. 180-188.

2038. Cowie, Peter. "The Study of Persecution: _The Trial_."
       In his _Ribbon of Dreams: The Cinema of Orson_
       Welles. New York: A.S. Barnes, 1973, pp. 152-177.

2039. Higham, Charles. "_The Trial_." In his _The Films_
       of Orson Welles. Berkeley: University of California
       Press, 1971, pp. 159-166.

2040. Lev, Peter. "Three Adaptations of _The Trial_."
       Literature/Film Quarterly, 12 (1984), 180-185.
       Concerns Jean-Louis Barrault and André Gide's play,
       Welles's film and an educational film, _The Trials_
       of Franz Kafka (1973).

2041. Martinez, Enrique and Richard Fleischer. "The
       Trial of Orson Welles." _Films and Filming_,
       8 (Oct. 1962), 12-15.
       On Welles's _The Trial_.

2042. Naremore, James. "_The Trial_." In his _The Magic_
       World of Orson Welles. New York: Oxford University
       Press, 1978, pp. 233-256.

2043. Pechter, William S. "Trials." _Sight and Sound_,
       33 (Winter 1963-1964), 4-9.
       On Welles's _The Trial_.

2044. Tyler, Parker. "The Dream-Amerika of Kafka and
       Chaplin." In his _The Three Faces of Film: The_
       Art, the Dream, the Cult. New York: Thomas
       Yoseloff, 1960, pp. 94-101.

                    JOSEPH KESSEL

2045. Stein, Elliot. "Buñuel's Golden Bowl." In _Belle_
       de Jour. New York: Simon and Schuster, 1971,
       pp. 12-20. Reprinted in _The World of Luis Buñuel:_
       Essays in Criticism. Ed. Joan Mellen. New
       York: Oxford University Press, 1978, pp. 278-288.

                  HEINRICH VON KLEIST

2046. Borchardt, Edith. "Eric Rohmer's _Marquise of O_
       and the Theory of the German Novella."
       Literature/Film Quarterly, 12 (1984), 129-135.

2047. Gerlach, John. "Rohmer, Kleist, and _The Marquise_
       _of O_." _Literature/Film Quarterly_, 8 (1980),
       84-91.

2048. Spiegel, Alan. "The Cinematic Text: Rohmer's _The_
       Marquise of O." In _Modern European Filmmakers_
       and the Art of Adaptation. Ed. Andrew Horton
       and Joan Magretta. New York: Frederick Ungar,
       1981, pp. 313-328.

EUGENE LABICHE

2049.   Goodman, Paul. "`Une Chapeau de paille d'Italie':
        Adaptation in Another Medium." In his The Structure
        of Literature. Chicago: University of Chicago
        Press, 1954, pp. 237-245.
        On René Clair's adaptation of Labiche's play.

PIERRE CHODERLOS DE LACLOS

2050.   Fell, John L. "The Correspondents' Curse: Vadim's
        Les Liaisons Dangereuses." In Modern European
        Filmmakers and the Art of Adaptation. Ed. Andrew
        Horton and Joan Magretta. New York: Frederick
        Ungar, 1981, pp. 51-62.

PAR LAGERKVIST

2051.   Jones, Lon, ed. Barabbas. Bologna, Italy: Capelli,
        1962.
        Book is a series of brief essays including discussions
        of the adaptation by Christoper Fry.

GIUSEPPE TOMASI DI LAMPEDUSA

2052.   Tonetti, Claretta. "Dream of a Dying World: The
        Leopard." In her Luchino Visconti. Boston:
        Twayne Publishers, 1983, pp. 95-107.

PIERRE LOUYS

2053.   Flasher, John and Douglas Radcliff-Ulmstead. "The
        Derisive Humor of Luis Buñuel." Perspectives
        on Contemporary Literature, 7 (1981), 7-17.
        On That Obscure Object of Desire, from the novel
        The Woman and the Puppet.

2054.   Kovács, Katherine Singer. "Luis Buñuel and Pierre
        Louys: Two Visions of Obscure Objects." Cinema
        Journal, 19 (Fall 1979), 87-98. Reprinted in
        Cinema Examined: Selections from Cinema Journal.
        Ed. Richard Dyer MacCann and Jack C. Ellis.
        New York: E.P. Dutton, 1982, pp. 222-233.
        On That Obscure Object of Desire.

2055.   Williams, Linda. "That Obscure Object of Desire."
        In her Figures of Desire: A Theory and Analysis
        of Surrealist Film. Urbana: University of Illinois
        Press, 1981, pp. 185-209.

2056.   Wood, Michael. "Buñuel's Private Lessons: That
        Obscure Object of Desire." New York Review
        of Books, 25 (23 Feb. 1978), 39-42. Revised
        and reprinted as "The Corruption of Accidents:
        Buñuel's That Obscure Object of Desire." In
        Modern European Filmmakers and the Art of
        Adaptation. Ed. Andrew Horton and Joan Magretta.
        New York: Frederick Ungar, 1981, pp. 329-340.

ANDRE MALRAUX

2057.   Bazin, André. "On L'Espoir, or Style in the Cinema."
         In his French Cinema of the Occupation and
         Resistance: The Birth of a Critical Esthetic.
         Ed. Francois Truffaut. Trans. Stanley Hochman.
         New York: Frederick Ungar, 1981, pp. 145-157.

2058.   Bevan, David.   "Notes on Sierra de Teruel and the
         Evolution of Malraux's Narrative Tecnhique."
         Twentieth Century Literature, 24 (1978), 351-357.

2059.   Malraux, André. "The Novel and the Film." In
         The Creative Vision. Ed. Haskell M. Black and
         Herman Salinger. New York: Grove Press, 1960,
         pp. 162-164.

2060.   Michalczyk, John J. André Malraux's Espoir: The
         Propaganda Art Film and the Spanish Civil War.
         University of Miss.: Romance Monographs, 1977.

2061.   _____. "The Rediscovered Version of `Sierra
         de Teruel.'" Twentieth Century Literature,
         24 (1978), 344-350.

2062.   Tarica, Ralph.   "Imagery of Human Activity: Literature,
         The Theater, The Cinema." In his Imagery in
         the Novels of André Malraux. Cranbury, N.J.:
         Associated University Presses, 1980, pp. 129-135.

2063.   Thompson, Brian. "Visual Imagination in L'Espoir."
         In André Malraux: Metamorphosis and Imagination.
         Ed. Francoise Dorenlot and Micheline Tison-Braun.
         New York: New York Literary Forum, 1979, pp. 201-208.

HEINRICH MANN

2064.   Firda, Richard Arthur.   "Literary Origins: Sternberg's
         The Blue Angel." Literature/Film Quarterly,
         7 (1979), 126-136.

2065.   Weisstein, Ulrich.   "Translations and Adaptations
         of Heinrich Mann's Novel in Two Media." The
         Film Journal, 1 (Fall-Winter 1972), 53-61.
         On Sternberg's The Blue Angel and the remake by
         Edward Dmytryk.

KLAUS MANN

2066.   Zsugán, István. "Mephisto: A Self-Absolving Character:
         A Conversation with István Szabó." New Hungarian
         Quarterly, 23 (Autumn 1982), 85-89.
         Interview with the director of the film adaptation
         of Mann's novel.

THOMAS MANN

2067. Galerstein, Carolyn. "Images of Decadence in
       Visconti's Death in Venice." Literature/Film
       Quarterly, 13 (1985), 29-34.

2068. Glassco, David. "Films Out of Books: Bergman, Visconti,
       and Mann." Mosaic, 16, Nos. 1-2 (1983), 165-173.
       On Death in Venice.

2069. Gorssvogel, David I. "Death in Venice: Visconti
       and the Too, Too Solid Flesh." Diacritics,
       1 (Winter 1971), 52-55.

2070. Hutchinson, Alexander. "Luchino Visconti's Death
       in Venice." Literature/Film Quarterly, 2 (1974),
       31-43.

2071. Mann, Thomas. "On the Film." In his Past Masters
       and Other Essays. Trans. H.T. Lowe-Porter.
       New York: Alfred A. Knopf, 1933, pp. 263-266.
       Reprinted in Authors on Film. Ed. Harry M. Geduld.
       Bloomington: Indiana University Press, 1972,
       pp. 129-133.

2072. Mazzella, Anthony J. "Death in Venice: Fiction
       and Film." College Literature, 5 (1978), 183-194.

2073. Mellen, Joan. "Death in Venice." Film Quarterly,
       25, (Fall 1971), 41-47. Revised and reprinted
       as "Visconti's Death in Venice: Failing Thomas
       Mann." In her Women and Their Sexuality in
       the New Film. New York: Horizon Press, 1973,
       pp. 203-215.

2074. Singer, Irving. "Death in Venice: Visconti and
       Mann." Modern Language Notes, 91 (1976),
       1348-1359.

2075. Stein, George P. "Death in Venice: From Literature
       to Film." The Journal of Aesthetic Education,
       16 (Fall 1982), 63-70.

2076. Tonetti, Claretta. "Death in Venice: Rational
       Man Among the `Devils.'" In her Luchino Visconti.
       Boston: Twayne Publishers, 1983, pp. 141-151.

2077. Weise, Epi. "Visconti and Renoir: Shadowplay."
       Yale Review, 64 (1974), 202-217.
       On Visconti's Death in Venice and Renoir's Une
       Partie de champagne.

GUY DE MAUPASSANT

2078. Gould, Michael. "Maupassant on Film." West Virginia
       University Philological Papers, 26 (Aug. 1980),
       7-12.

2079. Meilgaard, Manon and Dolores Burdick. "Maupassant
       and Ophuls: The `Real' and The `Ideal' in `La
       Maison Tellier'(Le Plaisir)." Michigan Academician,
       14 (Summer 1981), 63-69.

2080. Sesonske, Alexander. "Une Partie de campagne."
       In his Jean Renoir: The French Films, 1924-1939.
       Cambridge: Harvard University Press, 1980,
       pp. 234-256.

OCTAVE MIRABEAU

2081. Conrad, Randall. "Diaries of Two Chambermaids."
       Film Quarterly, 24 (Winter 1970-71), 48-51.
       On Buñuel's and Renoir's adaptations.

2082. Milne, Tom. "The Two Chambermaids." Sight and
       Sound, 33 (Autumn 1964), 174-178. Reprinted
       in The World of Luis Buñuel: Essays in Criticism.
       Ed. Joan Mellen. New York: Oxford University
       Press, 1978, pp. 257-269.

ALBERTO MORAVIA

2083. Horton, Andrew. "Godard's Contempt: Alberto Moravia
       Transformed." College Literature, 5 (1978),
       205-212.

2084. Kinder, Marsha. "A Thrice-Told Tale: Godard's
       Le Mepris." In Modern European Filmmakers and
       the Art of Adaptation. Ed. Andrew Horton and
       Joan Magretta. New York: Frederick Ungar, 1981,
       pp. 100-114.
       Film is based on A Ghost at Noon.

2085. Kline, T. Jefferson. "The Unconformist: Bertolucci's
       The Conformist." In Modern European Filmmakers
       and the Art of Adaptation. Ed. Andrew Horton
       and Joan Magretta. New York: Frederick Ungar,
       1981, pp. 222-237.

2086. Korte, W. "Godard's Adaptation of Moravia's Contempt."
       Literature/Film Quarterly, 2 (1974), 284-289.

2087. Lopez, Daniel. "Novel into Film: Bertolucci's
       The Conformist." Literature/Film Quarterly,
       4 (1976), 303-312.

2088. Moravia, Alberto. "If You Marry Me I'll Kill You."
       Trans. Salvator Attanasio. In Closeup: Last
       Tango in Paris. Ed. Kent E. Carroll. New York:
       Grove Press, 1973, pp. 101-105.
       On Bertolucci's Last Tango in Paris.

2089. Prigozy, Ruth. "A Modern Pieta: De Sica's Two
       Women." In Modern European Filmmakers and the
       Art of Adpatation. Ed. Andrew Horton and Joan
       Magretta. New York: Frederick Ungar, 1981,
       pp. 78-88.

2090.   Wagstaff, Christopher. "The Construction of Point
        of View of Bertolucci's Il Conformista." Italianist,
        3 (1983), 64-71.

                      PIER PAOLO PASOLINI

2091.   Armes, Roy. "Pier Paolo Pasolini: Myth and Modernity."
        In his The Ambiguous Image: Narrative Style
        in Modern European Cinema. Bloomington: Indiana
        University Press, 1976, pp. 154-164.

2092.   Bachmann, Gideon. "Pasolini Today." Take One,
        4, No. 5 (1973), 72-76.

2093.   Blue, James. "Pier Paolo Pasolini." Film Comment,
        3, No. 4 (1965), 31-45.
        Interview.

2094.   Bragin, John. "Pasolini--A Conversation in Rome,
        June 1966." Film Culture, No. 42 (1966),
        pp. 102-105.

2095.   _____. "Pier Paolo Pasolini: Poetry as
        Compensation." Film Society Review, 4, No. 5
        (1969), 12-18; 4, No. 6 (1969), 18-28; 4, No. 7
        (1969), 35-40.
        Three-part article on Pasolini's film career.

2096.   Durgnat, Raymond. "Pasolini: Equivocations of
        the Androgyne." In Sexual Alienation in the
        Cinema. London: Studio Vista, 1972, pp. 209-42.
        On Oedipus Rex and Teorema.

2097.   Friedrich, Pia. Pier Paolo Pasolini. Boston:
        Twayne Publishing, 1982.
        A study of his poetry, his fiction, and his films.

2098.   McDonald, Susan. "Pasolini: Rebellion, Art, and
        a New Society." Screen, 10, No. 3 (1969), 19-34.
        On Pasolini's films and novels.

2099.   Myrsiades, Kostas. "Classical and Christian Myth
        in the Cinema of Pasolini." College English,
        5 (1978), 213-218.
        On Oedipus Rex, Medea, and The Gospel According
        to St. Matthew.

2100.   Pasolini, Pier Paolo. "The Cinema of Poetry."
        In Movies and Methods. Ed. Bill Nichols. Berkeley:
        University of California Press, 1976, pp. 542-558.

2101.   _____. "Cinematic and Literary Stylistic
        Figures." Film Culture, No. 24 (1962), 42-43.
        Reprinted in Interviews With Film Directors.
        Ed. Andrew Sarris. New York: Avon Books, 1967,
        pp. 366-370.

2102.   _____.   "Pier Paolo Pasolini: An Epical-Religious
         View of the World." Trans. Letzilia MIller
         and Michael Graham. Film Quarterly, 28, No. 4
         (1965), 31-45.
         Interview.

2103.   _____.   "The Scenario as a Structure Designed
         to Become Another Structure." Trans. Michele
         de Cruz-Saenz. Wide Angle, 3, No. 1 (1977),
         40-47.

2104. Radcliff-Umstead, Douglas. "The Hero as Vindication:
         Violence in Pasolini's Films." In Holding the
         Vision: Essays on Film. Ed. Douglas Radcliff-
         Umstead. Kent, Ohio: The International Film
         Society, 1983, pp. 61-78.

2105. Siciliano, Enzo. Pasolini. Trans. John Shepley.
         New York: Random House, 1982.
         Biography.

2106. Snyder, Stephen. Pier Paolo Pasolini. Boston:
         Twayne Publishers, 1980.
         Study of Pasolini's films.

2107. Stack, Oswald. Pasolini on Pasolini. Bloomington:
         Indiana University Press, 1969.
         Interviews covering Pasolini's film theory and
         films through Amore e Rabbica.

2108. Taylor, John Russell. "Pier Paolo Pasolini."
         In his Directors and Directions: Cinema for
         the Seventies. New York: Hill and Wang, 1975,
         pp. 44-69.

2109. Teich, Nathaniel. "Myth into Film: Pasolini's
         Medea and Its Dramatic Heritage." Western
         Humanities Review, 30 (Winter 1976), 53-62.

2110. Willemen, Paul, ed. Pier Paolo Pasolini. London:
         British Film Institute, 1977.
         Essays: "Pasolini's Originality" by Geoffrey Nowell-
         Smith, "De-Liberate Evil" by Don Ranvaud, "Pasolini's
         Semiological Heresy" by Antonio Costa, "Pasolini:
         The Film of Alienation" by Noel Purdon, "Pasolini
         and Homosexuality" by Richard Dyer, "Pasolini's
         Salo: Sade to the Letter" by Roland Barthes, and
         interviews with Pasolini on Medea, The Decameron,
         The Canterbury Tales, and The Arabian Nights.

BORIS PASTERNAK

2111. Anderegg, Michael A. "Dr. Zhivago." In his David
         Lean. Boston: Twayne Publishing, 1984,
         pp. 121-132.

BENITO PEREZ GALDOS

2112.   Buache, Freddy.   "Atheism."   In his The Cinema
        of Luis Buñuel.   Trans. Peter Graham.   New York:
        A.S. Barnes, 1973, pp. 81-102.
        On Nazarin.

2113.   Eidsvik, Charles.   "Dark Laughter: Buñuel's Tristana."
        In Modern European Filmmakers and the Art of
        Adaptation.   Ed. Andrew Horton and Joan Magretta.
        New York: Frederick Ungar, 1981, pp. 173-187.

2114.   Fernández, Henry Cecilio.   "The Influence of Galdós
        on the Films of Luis Buñuel."   DAI, 37 (1976),
        7735A (Indiana University).
        Concerns Nazarin and Tristana.

2115.   Grossvogel, David I.   "Buñuel's Obsessed Camera:
        Tristana Dismembered."   Diacritics, 2 (Spring
        1972), 51-56.

2116.   Miller, Beth.   "From Mistress to Murderess: The
        Metamorphosis of Buñuel's Tristana."   In her
        Women in Hispanic Literature: Icons and Fallen
        Idols.   Berkeley: University of California Press,
        1983, 340-359.

LUIGI PIRANDELLO

2117.   Nulf, Frank Allen, Jr.   "Luigi Pirandello and the
        Cinema."   Film Quarterly, 24 (Winter 1970-71),
        40-48.

2118.   _____.   "Luigi Pirandello and the Cinema:
        A Study of His Relationship to Motion Pictures
        and the Significance of That Relationship to
        Selected Examples of His Prose and Drama."
        DAI, 30 (1970), 4055-4056A (Ohio University).

2119.   Pirandello, Luigi.   "The Cinema Is Digging Its
        Own Grave: The Talking Film Versus the Theatre."
        Illustrated London News, 175 (27 July 1929),
        156.

JACQUES PREVERT

2120.   Durgnat, Raymond.   "Images of the Mind--Part Thirteen:
        Time and Timelessness."   Films and Filming,
        15 (July 1969), 62-67.
        On Prevert's Les Amants de Verone.

2121.   Mancini, Marc Louis.   "Jacques Prévert: Poetic
        Elements in His Scripts and Cinematic Elements
        in His Poetry."   DAI, 37 (1976), 1595-1596A
        (The University of Southern California).

MARCEL PROUST

2122. Brater, Enoch. "Time and Memory in Pinter's Proust
       Screenplay." Comparative Drama, 13 (1979),
       121-126.

2123. Graham, Mark. "The Proust Screenplay: Temps perdu
       for Harold Pinter?" Literature/Film Quarterly,
       10 (1982), 38-52.

2124. Hirsch, Foster. "The Losey-Pinter Collaboration:
       Sequels." In his Joseph Losey. Boston: Twayne
       Publishers, 1980, pp. 143-154.
       On the Proust screenplay.

2125. Pasquale-Maguire, Therese. "Narrative Voices and
       Past Tenses in Novel and Film: Proust's A la
       Recherche du Temps perdu and the Pinter Screenplay."
       DAI, 43 (1982), 1139A (The University of
       Massachusetts).

ALEXANDER PUSHKIN

2126. Manvell, Roger, Thorold Dickinson and Michael Bell.
       "A Symposium on `The Queen of Spades.'" The
       Cinema 1950. Ed. Roger Manvell. Harmondsworth,
       Middlesex: Penguin Books, 1950, 46-77.

RAYMOND QUENEAU

2127. Horton, Andrew. "Growing Up Absurd: Malle's Zazie
       dans le Métro." In Modern European Filmmakers
       and the Art of Adaptation. Ed. Andrew Horton
       and Joan Magretta. New York: Frederick Ungar,
       1981, pp. 63-77.

FRANCOIS RABELAIS

2128. Yacowar, Maurice. "Ken Russell's Rabelais."
       Literature/Film Quarterly, 8 (1980), 41-51.
       On Russell's unproduced script of Gargantua.

ERICH MARIA REMARQUE

2129. Klinger, Werner. "Proposed Continuity for the
       Ending of `All Quiet on the Western Front.'"
       Experimental Cinema, 1, No. 2 (1930), 23-27;
       rpt. New York: Arno Press, 1969.

2130. Millichap, Joseph R. "All Quiet on the Western
       Front." In his Lewis Milestone. Boston: Twayne
       Publishers, 1981, pp. 37-53.

2131. Taylor, Harley U., Jr. "Erich Maria Remarque's
       Im Western nichts Neues and the Movie All Quiet
       on the Western Front: Genesis, Execution, and
       Reception." West Virginia University Philological
       Papers, 26 (Aug. 1980), 13-20.

ALAIN ROBBE-GRILLET

2132.   Alter, Jean V.   "Alain Robbe-Grillet and the
        `Cinematographic Style.'"   Modern Language Journal,
        48 (1964), 36-66.

2133.   Armes, Roy.   "Alain Robbe-Grillet: The Reality
        of Imagination."   In his The Ambiguous Image:
        Narrative Style in Modern European Cinema.
        Bloomington: Indiana University Press, 1976,
        pp. 131-140.

2134.   _____.   The Films of Alain Robbe-Grillet.
        Amsterdam: John Benjamins B.V., 1981.

2135.   _____.   "The Opening of L'Immortelle."   Film
        Reader 4.   Evanston: Northwestern University,
        1979, pp. 154-165.

2136.   _____.   "Robbe-Grillet, Ricardou, and Last
        Year at Marienbad."   Quarterly Review of Film
        Studies, 5 (Winter 1980), 1-17.

2137.   Ashmore, Jerome.   "Symbolism in Marienbad."   The
        University Review (Kansas City), 30 (1964),
        225-233.

2138.   Bishop, Tom and Helen Bishop.   "The Man Who Lies:
        An Interview with Alain Robbe-Grillet."   In
        Film Festival: Grove International Film Festival
        Book.   Ed. Barney Rosset.   New York: Grove Press,
        c. 1970, pp. 41-44, 87-89.

2139.   Blumenberg, Richard.   "Ten Years After Marienbad."
        Cinema Journal, 10 (Spring 1971), 40-43.

2140.   Blumenberg, Richard Mitchell.   "The Manipulation
        of Time and Space in the Novels of Alain Robbe-
        Grillet and in the Narrative Films of Alain
        Resnais, with Particular Reference to Last Year
        at Marienbad."   DAI, 30 (1970), 4051A (Ohio
        University).

2141.   Brunius, Jacques.   "Every Year at Marienbad, or
        The Discipline of Uncertainty."   Sight and Sound,
        31 (Summer 1962), 122-127, 153.   Reprinted in
        Renaissance of the Film.   Ed. Julius Bellone.
        London: Collier Books, 1970, pp. 127-146.

2142.   Burdick, Dolores M.   "Lisa, Lola, and I: The Woman
        Unknown as the Woman Immortal in Ophuls and
        Robbe-Grillet."   Michigan Academician, 12 (1980),
        251-259.
        On Letter From an Unknown Woman, Lola Montes, and
        L'Immortelle.

2143.   Dumont, Lillian and Sandi Silverberg.   "An Interview
        with Alain Robbe-Grillet."   Filmmakers Newsletter,
        9, No. 9 (1976), 22-25.

2144.   Evans, Calvin. "Cinematography and Robbe-Grillet's
         Jealousy." In Nine Essays in Modern Literature.
         Ed. Donald Stanford. Baton Rouge: Louisiana
         State University Press, 1965, pp. 117-128.

2145.   Gollub, Judith. "Trans-Europ Express." Film
         Quarterly, 22 (Spring 1969), 40-44.

2146.   Gow, Gordon. "Travelling Fast: The Cinema of Alain
         Robbe-Grillet." Films and Filming, 20 (Jan. 1974),
         54-56.

2147.   Hellerstein, Marjorie Hope. "Ideas Into Art: Alain
         Robbe-Grillet's Concept of Description as Practiced
         in His Novels and His Films." DAI, 42 (1982),
         5516-5517A (New York University).

2148.   Holland, Norman. "Film, Metafilm, and Un-Film."
         Hudson Review, 15 (1962), 406-412.
         On Last Year at Marienbad.

2149.   Houston, Beverle and Marsha Kinder. "Subject and
         Object in Last Year at Marienbad (1961) and
         The Exterminating Angel (1962): A Mutual Creation."
         In their Self and Cinema: A Transformationalist
         Perspective. Pleasantville, N.Y.: Redgrave
         Publishing, 1980, pp. 241-277.

2150.   Houston, Penelope. "Resnais/Antonioni: L'Année
         dernière à Marienbad." Sight and Sound, 31
         (Winter 1961-1962), 26-28.

2151.   Kreidl, John Francis. "Last Year at Marienbad."
         In his Alain Resnais. Boston: Twayne Publishers,
         1978, pp. 67-76.

2152.   Leki, Illona. "The Films." In her Alain Robbe-
         Grillet. Boston: Twayne Publishers, 1983,
         pp. 160-165.

2153.   McGlynn, Paul. "Last Year at Marienbad: The Aesthetic
         of `Perhaps.'" University of Windsor Review,
         16 (Fall-Winter 1981), 5-12.

2154.   Mathieu-Kerns, Lyliane Denise. "Black and White
         as a Symbolic Device: An Approach to Varda's
         Cleo From Five to Seven and Resnais' Last Year
         at Marienbad." In Holding the Vision: Essays
         on Film. Ed. Douglas Radcliff-Umstead. Kent,
         Ohio: The International Film Society, 1983,
         pp. 127-130.

2155.   Michalczyk, John J. "Robbe-Grillet, Michelet and
         Barthes: From La Sorcière to Glissements progressifs
         du plaisir." French Review, 51 (Dec. 1977),
         233-244.

2156.   _____.   "Recurrent Imagery of the Labyrinth
         in Robbe-Grillet's Films." Stanford French
         Review, 2 (1978), 115-128.

2157.   _____.   "Structural and Thematic Configurations
         in Robbe-Grillet's Films." American Society
         Legion of Honor Magazine, 48 (1977), 17-44.

2158.   Miller, Lynn Christine. "The Subjective Camera
         and Staging Psychological Fiction." Literature
         in Performance, 2 (April 1982), 35-42.
         On Last Year at Marienbad.

2159.   Monaco, James. "Last Year at Marienbad." In his
         Alain Resnais. New York: Oxford University
         Press, 1979, pp. 53-73.

2160.   Morrissette, Bruce. "Games and Game Structures
         in Robbe-Grillet." Yale French Studies, No. 41
         (1968), pp. 159-167. Reprinted in his Novel
         and Film: Essays in Two Genres. Chicago: University
         of Chicago Press, 1985, pp. 157-164.

2161.   _____.   "Last Year at Istanbul." Film Quarterly,
         20 (Winter 1966-67), 38-42.
         On L'Immortelle.

2162.   _____.   "Monsieur X on the Double Track: Last
         Year at Marienbad" and "Toward a New Cinema:
         L'Immortelle." In his The Novels of Alain Robbe-
         Grillet. Ithaca: Cornell University Press,
         1971, pp. 185-212 and pp. 213-236.

2163.   _____.   "Theory and Practice in the Work of
         Robbe-Grillet." Modern Language Notes, 77 (1962),
         257-267.

2164.   Oxenhandler, Neal. "Marienbad Revisited." Film
         Quarterly, 17 (Autumn 1963), 30-35.

2165.   Pechter, William S. "Last Year at Marienbad."
         Kenyon Review, 25 (1963), 337-343.

2166.   Resnais, Alain. "Trying to Understand My Own Film."
         Trans. Raymond Durgnat. Films and Filming,
         8 (Feb. 1962), 9-10, 41. Reprinted in Film
         Makers on Film Making. Ed. Harry M. Geduld.
         Bloomington: Indiana University Press, 1969,
         pp. 155-163.

2167.   Resnais, Alain and Alain Robbe-Grillet. "Last
         Words on Last Year." Trans. Raymond Durgnat.
         Films and Filming, 8 (March 1962), 39-41.
         Reprinted in Film Makers on Film Making. Ed. Harry
         M. Geduld. Bloomington: Indiana Unviersity
         Press, 1969, pp. 164-174.

2168. Robbe-Grillet, Alain. For a New Novel: Essays
          on Fiction. Trans. Richard Howard. New York:
          Grove Press, 1965.
       Robbe-Grillet often uses film as his point of reference
       in these essays on contemporary fiction.

2169. _____. "Images and Texts: A Dialogue." Trans.
          Karlis Racevskis. In Generative Literature
          and Generative Art: New Essays. Ed. David Leach.
          Fredericton, N.B.: York Press, 1983, pp. 38-47.

2170. _____. "L'Anée Dernière à Marienbad." Sight
          and Sound, 30 (Autumn 1961), 176-179.

2171. _____. "Last Year at Marienbad." Réalités
          (English Edition), 6 Oct. 1961, pp. 73-75.

2172. _____. "Order and Disorder in Film and Fiction."
          Trans. Bruce Morrissette. Critical Inquiry,
          4 (1977), 1-20.

2173. Stoltzfus, Ben. "L'Eden et après: Robbe-Grillet's
          Twelve Themes." New Orleans Review, 10 (Summer-Fall
          1983), 129-135.

2174. _____. "Subversive Play: Fantasy in Robbe-
          Grillet's Films." In Shadows of the Magic Lamp:
          Fantasy and Science Fiction in Film. Ed. George
          Slusser and Eric S. Rabkin. Carbondale: Southern
          Illinois University Press, 1985, pp. 30-40.

2175. _____. "This Year at Marienbad--Film or Novel?"
          In his Alain Robbe-Grillet and the New French
          Novel. Carbondale: Southern Illinois University
          Press, 1964, pp. 102-121.

2176. Sturdza, Paltin. "The Rebirth Archetype in Robbe-
          Grillet's L'Immortelle." French Review, 48
          (May 1975), 990-995.

2177. _____. "The Structures of Actants in Robbe-
          Grillet's L'Immortelle." Language Quarterly,
          12 (Spring-Summer 1974), 26-28.

2178. Sweet, Freddy. "Last Year at Marienbad." In his
          The Film Narratives of Alain Resnais. Ann Arbor:
          UMI Research Press, 1981, pp. 35-65.

2179. Tiher, Allen. "L'Année dernière à Marienbad: The
          Narration of Narration." In his Cinematic Muse:
          Critical Studies in the History of French Cinema.
          Columbia: University of Missouri Press, 1979,
          pp. 166-179.

2180. Van Wert, William F. The Film Career of Alain
          Robbe-Grillet. Boston: G.K. Hall, 1977.

2181. _____. "Intertextuality and Redundant Coherence
       in Robbe-Grillet." Romanic Review, 73 (March
       1982), 249-257.

2182. _____. "Structures of Mobility and Immobility
       in the Cinema of Alain Robbe-Grillet." Sub-Stance,
       No. 9 (1974), pp. 79-95.

2183. Ward, John. "Alain Robbe-Grillet: The Novelist
       as Director." Sight and Sound, 37 (Spring 1968),
       86-90.

2184. _____. "L'Annee derniere à Marienbad." In
       Alain Resnais or the Theme of Time. New York:
       Doubleday, 1968, pp. 39-62.

2185. Weightman, J.G. "The New Wave in French Culture."
       Commentary, 30, No. 3 (1966), 230-240.
       The influence of film on Robbe-Grillet's novels.

2186. Westerbeck, Colin L., Jr. "Infrastructures: The
       Films of Alain Robbe-Grillet." Artforum, 14
       (March 1976), 54-57.

HENRI-PIERRE ROCHE

2187. Eidsvik, Charles. "Films From Fiction; Jules and
       Jim and Blow-Up: Two Ways Toward the Future?"
       In Cineliteracy: Film Among the Arts. New York:
       Random House, 1978, pp. 189-230.

2188. Grossvogel, David I. "Truffaut and Roché: Diverse
       Voices of Novel and Film." Diacritics, 3 (Spring
       1973), 47-52.

2189. McDougal, Stuart Y. "Adaptation of an Auteur:
       Truffaut's Jules et Jim." In Modern European
       Filmmakers and the Art of Adaptation. Ed. Andrew
       Horton and Joan Magretta. New York: Frederick
       Ungar, 1981, pp. 89-99.

DONATIEN ALPHONSE FRANCOIS SADE

2190. Bachmann, Gideon. "Pasolini and the Marquis de
       Sade." Sight and Sound, 45 (Winter 1975-1976),
       50-54.

2191. _____. "Pasolini on de Sade: The Filming
       of `The 120 Days of Sodom.'" Film Quarterly,
       29 (Winter 1975-76), 39-45.

2192. _____. "The 220 Days of Salo." Film Comment,
       40, No. 2 (1976), 38-47.

2193. Calvino, Italo. "Sade is Within Us." Trans. Mark
       Pietralunga. Stanford Italian Review, 2 (Fall
       1982), 107-111.

2194.   Sciascia, Leonardo. "God Behind Sade." Trans. Beverly
        Allen. Stanford Italian Review, 2 (Fall 1982),
        104-106.

ANTOINE DE SAINT-EXUPERY

2195.   Arnold, James W. "Musical Fantasy: The Little
        Prince." In Shadows of the Magic Lamp: Fantasy
        and Science Fiction in Film. Ed. George Slusser
        and Eric S. Rabkin. Carbondale: Southern Illinois
        University Press, 1985, pp. 122-140.

2196.   Breedlove, Karin Else. "From Life to Fiction:
        Novels and Screenplays of Saint-Exupery." DAI,
        45 (1985), 2541A (The University of Texas at
        Austin).
        On the adaptations of Courrier Sud and Vol de nuit.

2197.   Casper, Joseph Andrew. "I Never Met a Rose: Stanley
        Donen and The Little Prince." In Children's
        Novels and the Movies. Ed. Douglas Street.
        New York: Frederick Ungar, 1983, pp. 141-150.

NATHALIE SARRAUTE

2198.   Sarraute, Nathalie. "The Age of Suspicion." In
        her The Age of Suspicion: Essays on the Novel.
        Trans. Maria Jolas. New York: George Braziller,
        1963, pp. 53-74.
        Sarraute discusses the impact of film on the novel.

JEAN-PAUL SARTRE

2199.   Contat, Michel and Michel Rybalka. "Appendix on
        the Cinema." In The Writings of Jean-Paul Sartre,
        Volume One. Evanston: University of Illinois
        Press, 1974, pp. 601-612.

2200.   Kellman, Steven G. "Everybody Comes to Roquentin's:
        La Nausée and Casablanca." Mosaic, 16 (Winter-Spring
        1983), 103-112.

2201.   Sartre, Jean-Paul. "The Art of Cinema." In The
        Writings of Jean-Paul Sartre, Volume 2. Trans.
        Richard C. McCleary. Evanston: Northwestern
        University Press, 1974, pp. 53-59.

2202.   _____. "On Dramatic Style," "Theater and
        Cinema," and "In the Mesh (L'Engrenage)." In
        Sartre on Theatre. Ed. Michel Contat and Michel
        Rybalka. Trans. Frank Jellinek. New York:
        Random House, 1976, pp. 6-29, pp. 59-63, and
        pp. 316-319.

ARTHUR SCHNITZLER

2203. Williams, Alan. "Keeping the Circle Turning: Ophuls'
       La Ronde." In Modern European Filmmakers and
       the Art of Adaptation." Ed. Andrew Horton and
       Joan Magretta. New York: Frederick Ungar, 1981,
       pp. 38-50.

2204. _____. "Literary Adaptation: La Ronde and
       Le Plaisir." In his Max Ophuls and the Cinema
       of Desire: Style and Spectacle in Four Films.
       New York: Arno Press, 1980, pp. 71-103.
       Studies the adaptation of Schnitzler's play and
       three Maupassant stories: "The Mask," "Madame Tellier's
       Establishment," and "The Model."

GEORGES SIMENON

2205. Magretta, William R. and Joan Magretta. "The
       Clockmaker: From Novel to Film." Literature/Film
       Quarterly, 7 (1979), 277-284. Reprinted as
       "Private `I': Travernier's The Clockmaker."
       In Modern European Filmmakers and the Art of
       Adaptation. Ed. Andrew Horton and Joan Magretta.
       New York: Frederick Ungar, 1981, pp. 238-247.

2206. Nolan, Jack Edmund. "Simenon on the Screen."
       Films in Review, 16 (1965), 419-437.
       Filmography

ALEXANDER SOLZHENITSYN

2207. Curtis, James M. "Dos Passos, Eisenstein and Film."
       In his Solzhenitsyn's Traditional Imagination.
       Athens: University of Georgia Press, 1984,
       pp. 143-168.

2208. Harwood, Ronald. "Introduction." In his The Making
       of One Day in the Life of Ivan Denisovich.
       New York: Ballantine Books, 1971, pp. 3-24.
       Harwood wrote the screenplay for the film adaptation.

STENDHAL
(HENRI BEYLE)

2209. Kline, T. Jefferson. "The Absent Presence: Stendhal
       In Bertolucci's Prima della Rivoluzione." Cinema
       Journal, 23 (Winter 1984), 4-28.

2210. Williams, Linda L. "Stendhal and Bertolucci: The
       Sweetness of Life Before the Revolution."
       Literature/Film Quarterly, 4 (1976), 215-221.

AUGUST STRINDBERG

2211. Blackwell, Marilyn Johns. "The Chamber Plays and
       the Trilogy: A Revaluation of the Case of Strindberg
       and Bergman." In Structures of Influence: A
       Comparative Approach to August Strindberg.
       Ed. Marilyn Johns Blackwell. Chapel Hill: University
       of North Carolina Press, 1981, pp. 49-64.

2212. Deer, Irving. "Strindberg's Dream Vision: Prelude
       to Film." Criticism, 14 (1972), 253-265.

2213. DePaul, Brother C.F.X. "Bergman and Strindberg:
       Two Philosophies of Suffering." College English,
       26 (1965), 620-630.

2214. Fletcher, John. "Bergman and Strindberg." Journal
       of Modern Literature, 3 (1973), 173-190.

2215. Holden, David F. "Three Literary Sources for Through
       a Glass Darkly." Literature/Film Quarterly,
       2 (1974), 22-29.
       Influence of Strindberg's Easter, Chekhov's The
       Seagull, and Charlotte Gilman's "The Yellow Wallpaper"
       on Ingmar Bergman's film.

2216. Johns, Marilyn. "Dream Reality in August Strindberg's
       A Dreamplay and Ingmar Bergman's Wild Strawberries:
       A Study in Structure." Proceedings of the Pacific
       Northwest Council on Foreign Languages, 27,
       Part 1 (1976), 122-125.

2217. _____. "Journey into Autumn: Oväder and
       Smultrönstället." Scandinavian Studies, 50
       (1978), 292-303.
       Strindberg's influence on Wild Strawberries.

2218. _____. "Kindred Spirits: Strindberg and Bergman."
       Scandinavian Review, 64 (1976), 16.

2219. _____. "Strindberg's Folkungasagan and Bergman's
       Det sjunde inseglet: Medieval Epic and Psychological
       Drama." Scandanavica, 18 (1979), 21-34.
       Strindberg's influence on The Seventh Seal.

2220. _____. "Strindberg's Influence on Bergman's
       Det sjunde inseglet, Smultrönstället, and Persona."
       DAI, 38 (1977), 1401A (The University of Washington).
       Strinberg's influence on Bergman's The Seventh
       Seal, Wild Stawberries, and Persona.

2221. Rowland, Richard. "Miss Julie." Quarterly of
       Film, Radio, and Television, 6 (Summer 1952),
       414-420. Reprinted in Renaissance of the Film.
       Ed. Julius Bellone. London: Collier Books,
       1970, pp. 173-181.

COUNT ALEKSEY NIKOLAYEVICH TOLSTOY

2222.   Karaganov, Alexander. "History on the Screen."
        Soviet Literature, No. 1 (1983), pp. 172-178.
        On adaptations of Tolstoy's works, including Peter
        the First.

COUNT LEV NIKOLAYEVICH TOLSTOY

2223.   Silbajoris, Frank R. "War and Peace on the Screen."
        College English, 18 (1956), 41-45.
        On King Vidor's adaptation.

2224.   Simone, R. Thomas. "The Mythos of `Sickness Unto
        Death: Kurosawa's Ikiru and Tolstoy's The Death
        of Ivan Ilych." Literature/Film Quarterly,
        3 (1975), 2-12.

IVAN TURGENEV

2225.   Dickinson, Thorold and Roger Manvell. "A Film
        is Made." In The Cinema 1951. Ed. Roger Manvell.
        Harmondsworth, Middlesex: Penguin Books, 1951,
        pp. 9-56.
        On a proposed adaptation of The Torrents of Spring.

MIGUEL DE UNAMUNO

2226.   Lacy, Allen. "The Unbelieving Priest: Unamuno's
        Saint Emmanuel the Good, Martyr and Bergman's
        Winter Light." Literature/Film Quarterly, 10
        (1982), 53-61.

FRANK WEDEKIND

2227.   Elsaesser, Thomas. "Lulu and the Meter Man: Louise
        Brooks, Pabst and `Pandora's Box.'" Screen,
        24 (July-Oct. 1983), 4-36.

EMILE ZOLA

2228.   Braudy, Leo. "Zola on Film: The Ambiguities of
        Naturalism." Yale French Studies, No. 42 (1969),
        pp. 68-88.

2229.   Cousins, R. F. "Adapting Zola for the Silent Cinema:
        The Example of Marcel L'Herbier." Literature/Film
        Quarterly, 12 (1984), 42-49.

2230.   Durgnat, Raymond. "Nana" and "La Bête Humaine."
        In his Jean Renoir. Berkeley: University of
        California Press, 1974, pp. 36-41 and pp. 172-184.

2231.   Hjerpe, Cynthia Susan. "Emile Zola: Novel to Film."
        DAI, 41 (1981), 5119-5120A (Brown University).
        Concerns adaptations of Le Bête Humaine and
        L'assommoir.

2232. Rotha, Paul. "The Revival of Naturalism: Émile
         Zola and the Cinema." In his <u>Celluloid: The
         Film To-Day</u>. London: Longmans, Green and Co.,
         1931, pp. 215-226.

2233. Sesonske, Alexander. "<u>Nana</u>" and "<u>La Bête humaine</u>."
         In his <u>Jean Renoir: The French Films, 1924-1939</u>.
         Cambridge: Harvard University Press, 1980, pp. 19-37
         and pp. 351-377.

STEFAN ZWEIG

2234. Grossberg, Mimi. "Zweig in Film." In <u>Stefan Zweig:
         The World of Yesterday's Humanist Today</u>. Ed. Marion
         Sonnenfeld. Albany: State University of New
         York Press, 1983, pp. 314-319.

2235. Koch, Howard. "Script to Screen with Max Ophuls."
         <u>Film Comment</u>, 6 (Winter 1970-1971), 41-43.
         On <u>Letter From an Unknown Woman</u>.

2236. Salerno, Harry, Carol Brownson, Robert Deming,
         David Meerse and James Shokoff. "Comments on
         <u>Letter From an Unknown Woman</u>." In <u>Stefan Zweig:
         The World of Yesterday's Humanist Today</u>. Ed. Marion
         Sonnenfeld. Albany: State University of New
         York Press, 1983, pp. 320-323.

13

Literary Figures
of
Latin America

MARIO DE ANDRADE

2237. Johnson, John Randal. "Macunaíma: From Modernism
to Cinema Novo." DAI, 38 (1978), 4193A (The
University of Texas at Austin).
Concerns Joaquim Pedro de Andrade's adaptation
of Mario de Andrade's novel.

MACHADO DE ASSIS

2238. Dow, Carol L. "Cinematographic Characteristics
in the Prose of Machado de Assis." Hispania,
65 (1982), 12-19.

JAMIE TORRES BODET

2239. Miller, Judy Held. "The Development of Cinematographic
Techniques in Three Novels of Jamie Torres Bodet."
DAI, 36 (1975), 2791A (The State University
of New York at Albany).
The novels discussed are Margarita de niebla, Proserpina
rescatada, and Estrella de día.

JORGE LUIS BORGES

2240. Bennett, Maurice J. "`Everything and Nothing':
The Myth of Personal Identity in Jorge Luis
Borges and Bergman's Persona." In Transformations
in Literature and Film. Ed. Leon Golden.
Tallahassee: University Presses of Florida,
1982, pp. 17-28.

2241. Borges, Jorge Luis. "Borges as Film Critic."
Trans. Gloria Waldman and Ronald Christ. Sight
and Sound, 45 (1976), 230-233.

2242. Cozarinsky, Edgardo. "Borges on and in Film."
Sight and Sound, 45 (Winter 1975-1976), 41-45.

2243. Gomez, Joseph A. "Performance and Jorge Luis Borges."
Literature/Film Quarterly, 5 (1977), 147-153.

2244. Wicks, Ulrich. "Borges, Bertolucci, and Metafiction."
       In Narrative Strategies: Original Essays in
       Film and Prose Fiction. Ed. Syndy M. Conger
       and Janice R. Welsch. Macomb: Western Illinois
       University, 1980, pp. 19-36.
       On The Spider's Stratagem, an adaptation of Borges's
       "Theme of the Traitor and the Hero."

JULIO CORTAZAR

2245. D'Lugo, Marvin. "Signs and Meaning in Blow-Up:
       From Cortázar to Antonioni." Literature/Film
       Quarterly, 3 (1975), 23-29.

2246. Fernández, Henry. "From Cortázar to Antonioni:
       Study of an Adaptation." Film Heritage, 4 (Winter
       1968-1969), 26-30. Reprinted in Focus on Blow-Up.
       Ed. Roy Huss. Englewood Cliffs: Prentice-Hall,
       1971, pp. 163-167.

2247. Ferrua, Pietro. "Blow-Up from Cortázar to Antonioni."
       Literature/Film Quarterly, 4 (1976), 68-75.

2248. Francis, Richard Lee. "Transcending Metaphor:
       Antonioni's Blow-Up." Literature/Film Quarterly,
       13 (1985), 42-49.

2249. Freccero, John. "Blow-Up: From the Word to the
       Image." Yale/Theatre, 3, (Fall 1970), 15-24.
       Reprinted in Focus on Blow-Up. Ed. Roy Huss.
       Englewood Cliffs: Prentice-Hall, 1971, pp. 116-128.

2250. Goldstein, Melvin. "Antonioni's Blow-Up: From
       Crib to Camera." American Imago, 32 (1975),
       240-263.

2251. Grossvogel, David I. "Blow-Up: The Forms of an
       Aesthetic Itinerary." Diacritics, 2 (Fall 1972),
       49-54.

2252. Isaacs, Neil D. "The Triumph of Artifice: Antonioni's
       Blow-Up." In Modern European Filmmakers and
       the Art of Adaptation. Ed. Andrew Horton and
       Joan Magretta. New York: Frederick Ungar, 1981,
       pp. 130-144.

2253. Palmer, William J. "Blow-Up: THe Game with No
       Balls." Literature/Film Quarterly, 7 (1979),
       314-321.

2254. Peavler, Terry J. "Blow-Up: A Reconsideration
       of Antonioni's Infidelity to Cortázar." PMLA,
       94 (1979), 887-893.

2255. Zamora, Lois Parkinson. "Movement and Stasis,
       Film and Photo: Temporal Structures in Recent
       Fiction of Julio Cortázar." Review of Contemporary
       Fiction, 3 (Fall 1983), 51-65.
       Discussion of Deshoras and Libro de Manuel.

EDMUNDO DESNOES

2256. Burton, Julianne. "Individual Fulfillment and
       Collective Achievement: An Interview with Tomas
       Guiérrez Alea." Cinéaste, 7, No. 1 (1977),
       8-15, 59.
    On Memories of Underdevelopment.

2257. _____. "Memories of Underdevelopment in the
       Land of Overdevelopment." Cinéaste, 7, No. 1
       (1977), 16-21, 58.
    On Memories of Underdevelopment.

2258. Fernandez, Henry, David I Grossvogel, and Emir
       Rodriguez Monegal. "3 On 2: Desnoes, Gutiérrez
       Alea." Diacritics, 4 (Winter 1974), 51-64.
    Three views of the adaptation of Inconsolable
    Memories by Tomás Gutiérrez Alea.

CARLOS FUENTES

2259. Gyurko, Lanin A. "La muerte de Artemio Cruz and
       Citizen Kane: A Comparative Analysis." In Carlos
       Fuentes: A Critical View. Ed. Robert Brody
       and Charles Rossman. Austin: University of
       Texas Press, 1982, pp. 64-94.

2260. Tyler, Joseph Vergara. "Cinematic Techniques in
       the Novels of Carlos Fuentes." DAI, 39 (1978),
       1611-1612A (The University of California at
       San Diego).

BEATRIZ GUIDO

2261. Gibson, Christine Mary. "Cinematic Techniques
       in the Prose Fiction of Beatriz Guido." DAI,
       36 (1975), 310-311A (Michigan State University).
    Concerns her novels, her short stories and her
    script, Días de odio.

JOSE HERNANDEZ

2262. McCaffrey, William Mark. "The Gaucho From Literature
       to Film: Martin Fierro and Juan Moreira." DAI,
       44 (1983), 1466-1467A (The University of California
       at San Diego).
    Concerns the poem Martin Fierro by José Hernández
    and the play Juan Moreira by Eduardo Gutiérrez.

VICENTE HUIDOBRO

2263. De Costa, René. "Huidobro: From Film to the Filmic
       Novel." Review: Latin American Literature and
       the Arts, 29 (May-Aug. 1981), 13-20.
    On the Chilean poet's two "filmic novels," Cagliostro
    and Mío Cid Campeador.

MANUEL PUIG

2264.   Maldonado, Armando. "Manuel Puig: The Aesthetics
        of Cinematic and Psychological Fiction." DAI,
        38 (1977), 2156-2157A (The University of Oklahoma).
        Concerns three novels by the Argentine writer:
        La traición de Rita Hayworth, Boquitas pintadas,
        and The Buenos Aires Affair.

NELSON RODRIGUES

2265.   Johnson, Randal. "Nelson Rodrigues as Filmed by
        Arnaldo Jabor." Latin American Theatre Review,
        16 (Fall 1982), 15-28.
        On the adaptation of Rodrigues's play Toda Nudez
        Será Castigada.

14

Literary Figures
of
Asia and Africa

KOBO ABE

2266. Mancia, Adrienne Johnson. "Woman in the Dunes."
      Film Comment, 3 (Winter 1965), 55-60.

RYUNOSUKE AKUTAGAWA

2267. Davidson, James F. "Memory of Defeat in Japan:
      A Reappraisal of Rashomon." In Focus on Rashomon.
      Ed. Donald Richie. Englewood Cliffs: Prentice-Hall,
      1972, pp. 119-128.

2268. McDonald, Keiko I. "Light and Darkness in Rashomon."
      Literature/Film Quarterly, 10 (1982), 120-129.

2269. Richie, Donald. "Rashomon." In his The Films
      of Akira Kurosawa. Berkeley: University of
      California Press, 1973, pp. 70-80.

BIBHUTI BHUSHAN BANDAPADDHAY

2270. Das Gupta, Chidananda. "A Search and a Finding:
      From Pather Panchali to Charlulata." In his
      The Cinema of Satyajit Ray. Sahibabad: Vikas
      Publishing House, 1980, pp. 20-39.
      On the Apu Trilogy, Ray's adaptations of Bandapaddhay's
      novels.

2271. Ray, Satyajit. "A Long Time on the Little Road."
      Sight and Sound, 11 (Spring 1957), 203-205.
      Reprinted in Film Makers on Film Making. Ed. Harry
      M. Geduld. Bloomington: Indiana University
      Press, 1969, pp. 264-270. Reprinted in Pather
      Panchali. Ed. Parimal Mukhopadhyay. Trans. Lila
      Roy. Calcutta: Cine Central, 1984, pp. 34-40.
      On Pather Panchali.

2272.   Seton, Marie. "Ray as Scenarist." In her Portrait
         of a Director: Satyajit Ray. Bloomington: Indiana
         University Press, 1971, pp. 213-229.
         On Abhijan, Ray's adaptation of Bandapaddhay's
         novel.

                    OUSMANE SEMBENE

2273.   Harrow, Kenneth. "Ousmane Sembene's Xala: The
         Use of Film and Novel as a Revolutionary Weapon."
         Studies in Twentieth Century Literature, 4 (Spring
         1980), 177-188.

2274.   Okore, Ode. "The Film World of Ousmane Sembene."
         DAI, 45 (1985), 3015A (Columbia University).

2275.   Perry, G.M. and Patrick McGilligan. "Ousmane   Sembene:
An Interview." Film Quarterly, 26   (Spring 1973),
36-42.

2276.   Pfaff, Francoise. The Cinema of Ousmane Sembene,
         A Pioneer of African Film. Westport, Conn.:
         Greenwood Press, 1984.
         Contains discussions of Borom Street, Black Girl
         (Le Noire De...), Mandabi, Emitai, Xala, and Ceddo.

15

Scripts by Literary Figures
Scripts of Adaptations

2277. Agee, James. "Man's Fate." Films: A Quarterly
         of Discussion and Analysis, 1 (Nov. 1939), 51-60;
         rpt. New York: Arno Press, 1968. Reprinted
         in The Collected Short Prose of James Agee.
         Ed. Robert Fitzgerald. Boston: Houghton Mifflin,
         1968, pp. 205-217.
       Notes for a treatment of Malraux's novel.

2278. _____. "Notes for a Moving Picture: The House."
         Cinemages, No. 9 (1958), 5-18. Reprinted in
         The Collected Short Prose of James Agee. Ed.
         Robert Fitzgerald. Boston: Houghton Mifflin,
         1968, pp. 151-173.

2279. _____. "Noa Noa," "The African Queen," "The
         Night of the Hunter," "The Bride Comes to Yellow
         Sky," and "The Blue Hotel." In Agee on Film:
         Volume 2. New York: Grosset and Dunlap, 1969,
         pp. 1-147, 149-259, 261-354, 355-390, and 391-488.
       Agee's adaptations of C.S. Forester's novel, Davis
       Grubb's novel, and two Stephen Crane stories.

2280. Alea, Tomás Gutiérrez and Edmundo Desnoes. "Memories
         of Underdevelopment." In Memories of
         Underdevelopment: The Revolutionary Films of
         Cuba. Ed. Michael Myerson. New York: Grossman
         Publishers, 1973, pp. 51-107.
       Adaptation of the novel by Desnoes.

2281. Anderson, Maxwell and Andrew Solt. Joan of Arc.
         New York: William Sloane Associates, 1948.

2282. Anobile, Richard J., ed. Dr. Jekyll and Mr. Hyde.
         Screenplay by Samuel Hofenstein and Percy Heath.
         New York: Avon Books, 1975.
       Book is a rendering of Rouben Mamoulian's adaptation
       of Robert Louis Stevenson's novel through frame
       enlargements.

2283. _____ . Frankenstein. Screenplay by Garrett
       Fort and Francis Edward Farogoh. New York:
       Avon Books, 1974.
       Book is a rendering of James Whale's adaptation
       of Mary Shelley's novel through frame enlargements.

2284. _____ . The Maltese Falcon. Screenplay by
       John Huston. New York: Avon Books, 1974.
       Book is a rendering of John Huston's adaptation
       of Dashiell Hammett's novel through frame enlargements.

2285. Antonioni, Michelangelo and Tonino Guerra. Blow-Up.
       New York: Simon and Schuster, 1971.
       Adaptation of Julio Cortazar's short story.

2286. Artaud, Antonin. "Scenarios." In Antonin Artaud:
       Collected Works. Vol. Three. Trans. Alastair
       Hamilton. London: Calder and Boyars, 1972,
       pp. 11-55.
       Includes the following scenarios: "Eighteen Seconds,"
       "Two Nations on the Borders of Mongolia," "The
       Shell and the Clergyman," "Thirty-Two," "The Butcher's
       Revolt," "Flights," and "The Master of Ballantrae."

2287. Baldwin, James. One Day When I Was Lost. New
       York: The Dial Press, 1973.
       Adaptation of The Autobiography of Malcolm X.

2288. Barrett, Gerald R. and Thomas L. Erskine. "Shot
       Analysis: `The Bridge' (`The Spy')." In From
       Fiction to Film: Ambrose Bierce's "An Occurrence
       at Owl Creek Bridge." Ed. Gerald R. Barrett
       and Thomas L. Erskine. Encino, Cal.: Dickenson
       Publishing, 1973, pp. 87-106.
       Shot analysis of Charles Vidor's film.

2289. _____ . "Shot Analysis: `An Occurrence at
       Owl Creek Bridge." In From Fiction to Film:
       Ambrose Bierce's `An Occurrence at Owl Creek
       Bridge. Ed. Gerald R. Barrett and Thomas L.
       Erskine. Encino, Cal.: Dickenson Publishing,
       1973, pp. 107-154.
       Shot analysis of Robert Enrico's film.

2290. _____ . "Shot Analysis: `Silent Snow, Secret
       Snow." In From Fiction to Film: Conrad Aiken's
       Silent Snow, Secret Snow. Ed. Gerald R. Barrett
       and Thomas L. Erskine. Encino, Cal.: Dickenson
       Publishing, 1972, pp. 105-152.
       Shot analysis of Gene Kearney's film.

2291. Barrie, James M. "Peter Pan." In Fifty Years
       of Peter Pan. Ed. Roger Lancelyn Green. London:
       Peter Davies, 1954, pp. 171-218.

2292. Beckett, Samuel. Film. New York: Grove Press,
       1969.

2293.   Benêt, Stephen Vincent.   From Earth to the Moon.
        New Haven: Privately Printed, 1958.
        An unfilmed scenario.

2294.   Blatty, William Peter.   "The First Draft Screenplav
        of The Exorcist" and "Transcript with Scene
        Settings [of The Exorcist]" In William Peter
        Blatty on The Exorcist. New York: Bantam Books,
        1974, pp. 45-270 and pp. 287-367.

2295.   Bolt, Robert. Doctor Zhivago. New York: Random
        House, 1965.
        Adaptation of Boris Pasternak's novel.

2296.   Brackett, Charles and Billy Wilder.   "The Lost
        Weekend." In Best Film Plays 1945. Ed. John
        Gassner and Dudley Nichols. New York: Crown
        Publishers, 1946, pp. 1-56.
        Adaptation of Charles Jackson's novel.

2297.   Brackett, Leigh, William Faulkner and Jules Furthman.
        "The Big Sleep--Screenplay." In Film Scripts
        One.   Ed. George Garrett, et al. New York:
        Appleton, 1971, pp. 137-329.
        Adaptation of Raymond Chandler's novel.

2298.   Brogger, Frederick and Jack Pulman. "David
        Copperfield." In Copperfield `70: The Making
        of the Omnibus-20th Century Fox Film by George
        Curry. New York: Ballantine Books, 1970,
        pp. 107-210.
        Screenplay of the Delbert Mann adaptation.

2299.   Buchman, Sidney. "Over Twenty-One." In Best Film
        Plays 1945. Ed. John Gassner and Dudley Nichols.
        New York: Crown Publishers, 1946, pp. 521-588.
        Film is an adaptation of Ruth Gordon's play.

2300.   Buñuel, Luis. Belle de Jour. Trans. Robert Adkinson.
        New York: Simon and Schuster, 1971.
        Film is an adaptation of the novel by Joseph Kessel.

2301.   Buñuel, Luis and Julio Alejandro. "Nazarin."
        In The Exterminating Angel, Nazarin, and Los
        Olvidados: Three Films by Luis Bunuel.
        Trans. Nicholas Fry. New York: Simon and Schuster,
        1972. pp. 114-205.
     Film is an adaptation of the novel by Benito Perez
     Galdos.

2302.   _____. Tristana. Trans. Nicholas Fry. New
        York: Simon and Schuster, 1971.
        Adaptation of the novel by Benito Perez Galdos.

2303.   Burroughs, William S. The Last Words of Dutch
        Schultz: A Fiction in the Form of a Film Script.
        New York: The Viking Press, 1975.

2304. Butler, Frank and Jack Wagner. "A Medal for Benny."
         In Best Film Plays 1945. Ed. John Gassner   and
         Dudley Nichols. New York: Crown Publishers,
         1946, pp. 589-648.
       From a story by Jack Wagner and John Steinbeck.

2305. Cacoyannis, Michael. The Trojan Women. New York:
         Bantam Books, 1971.
       Adaptation of play by Euripides.

2306. Capote, Truman, Frank Perry and Eleanor Perry.
         Trilogy. New York: The Macmillan Co., 1969.
       Contains Eleanor Perry's adaptations of three Capote
       stories: "Miriam," "Among the Paths to Glory,"
       and "A Christmas Memory" and comments on the adaptations
       by Eleanor Perry.

2307. Chandler, Raymond. The Blue Dahlia: A Screenplay.
         Ed. Matthew J. Bruccoli. Carbondale: Southern
         Illinois University Press, 1975.

2308. _____. Raymond Chandler's Unknown Thriller:
         The Screenplay of Playback. Ed. Robert B. Parker.
       New York: The Mysterious Press, 1985.

2309. Chandler, Raymond and Billy Wilder. "Double
         Indemnity." In Best Film Plays 1945. Ed. John
         Gassner and Dudley Nichols. New York: Crown
         Publishers, 1946, pp. 115-174.
       From the novel by James M. Cain.

2310. Chayefsky, Paddy. The Bachelor Party. New York:
         New American Library, 1957.

2311. _____ . The Goddess. New York: Simon and
         Schuster, 1958.

2312. Clair, René. "The Italian Staw Hat." In Masterworks
         of the French Cinema. Trans. Marianne Alexandre.
         New York: Harper and Row, 1974, pp. 20-70.
       From the play by Eugène Labiche.

2313. Cocteau, Jean. Beauty and the Beast. Ed. Robert
         M. Hammond. New York: New York University Press,
         1970.

2314. _____. The Blood of a Poet. Trans. Lily
         Pons. New York: Bodley Press, 1949.

2315. _____. Three Screenplays: Orpheus, The Eternal
         Return, and Beauty and the Beast. Trans. Carol
         Martin-Sperry. New York: Grossman Publishers,
         1972.

2316. _____. Two Screenplays: Blood of a Poet and
         The Testament of Orpheus. Trans. Carol Martin-
         Sperry. New York: Grossman Publishers, 1961.

2317. Colette, Sidonie Gabrielle. "Dialogue and Scenario
          by Colette." In Colette at the Movies. Ed. Alain
          Virmaux and Odette Virmaux. Trans. Sarah W.R.
          Smith. New York: Frederick Ungar, 1980, pp. 89-168.
       Lac-aux-Dames and Divine.

2318. Collier, John. Milton's Paradise Lost: A Screenplay
          for the Cinema of the Mind. New York: Alfred
          Knopf, 1973.

2319. Connelly, Marc. The Green Pastures. Ed. Thomas
          Cripps. Madison: University of Wisconsin Press,
          1978.

2320. Coward, Noel. "Brief Encounter." In Masterworks
          of the British Cinema. New York: Harper and
          Row, 1974.

2321. Dent, Alan, ed. Hamlet: The Film and the Play.
          London: World Film Publications, 1948.
       The book contains essays by Laurence Olivier and
       Dent and the complete text of Shakespeare's play
       with deletions made for the film noted and film
       directions rather than stage directions.

2322. Dent, Alan, Laurence Olivier, and Dallas Bower.
          Henry V. London: Two Cities Films, 1945.

2323. _____. "Henry V." In Film Scripts One.
          Ed. George Garrett, O.B. Hardison, Jr. and Jane
          R. Gelfman. New York: Appleton-Century Crofts,
          1971, pp. 37-136.

2324. DeSica, Vittorio. The Bicycle Thief. Trans. Simon
          Hartog. New York: Simon and Schuster, 1968.
       DeSica's film is a loose adaptation of a novel
       by Luigi Bartolini; screenplay by Cesare Zavattini.

2325. Dickey, James. Deliverance. Ed. Matthew J. Bruccoli.
          Carbondale: Southern Illinois University Press,
          1982.

2326. Dreyer, Carl Theodor. "Vampyr," "Day of Wrath,"
          and "Ordet." In Carl Theodor Dreyer: Four
          Screenplays. Trans. Oliver Stallybrass.
          Bloomington: University of Indiana Press, 1970,
          pp. 77-129, pp.131-235, and pp. 237-298.
       Films are adaptations of le Fanu's "Carmilla,"
       Anne Pedersdotter by Hans Wiers-Jenssen, and a
          play by Kaj Munk.

2327. Dunne, Phillip. "How Green Was My Valley." In
          Twenty Best Film Plays. Ed. John Gassner and
          Dudley Nichols. New York: Crown Publishers,
          1943, pp. 370-431.
       Adaptation of Richard Llewellyn's novel.

2328. Duras, Marguerite. Hiroshima Mon Amour. Trans. Richard
          Seaver. New York: Grove Press, 1961.

2329. _____. Hiroshima Mon Amour and Une Aussi
      Longue Absence. Trans. R. Seaver and B. Wright.
      London: Calder and Boyars, 1966.

2330. Eisenstein, Sergei, Ivor Montagu, and Grigory
      Alexandrov. "An American Tragedy." In With
      Eisenstein in Hollywood. Berlin: Seven Seas
      Publishers, 1968, pp. 207-341.
      Adaptation of Theodore Dreiser's novel.

2331. Eliot, T.S. and George Hollering. The Film of
      Murder in the Cathedral. New York: Harcourt,
      Brace, and Co., 1952.

2332. Faragoh, Francis Edward. "Little Caesar." In
      Twenty Best Film Plays. Ed. John Gassner and
      Dudley Nichols. New York: Crown Publishers,
      1943, pp. 477-520. Reprinted in Little Caesar.
      Ed. Gerald Peary. Madison: University of Wisconsin
      Press, 1981.
      From the novel by W.R. Burnett.

2333. Fast, Howard. The Hill. Garden City: Doubleday,
      1964.

2334. Faulkner, William. Faulkner's MGM Screenplays.
      Ed. Bruce Kawin. Knoxville: The University
      of Tennessee Press, 1982.
      Four treatments ("Manservant," "The College Widow,"
      "Absolution," and "Flying the Mail") and three
      scripts ("Turn About/Today We Live," "War Birds/Ghost
      Story" and "Mythical Latin American Kingdom Story").

2335. Faulkner, William and Joel Sayre. The Road to
      Glory. Ed. Matthew J. Bruccoli. Carbondale:
      Southern Illinois University Press, 1981.

2336. Faulkner, William and Jules Furthman. To Have
      and Have Not. Ed. Bruce F. Kawin. Madison:
      University of Wisconsin Press, 1980.
      Adaptation of Ernest Hemingway's novel.

2337. Fellini, Federico and Bernardino Zapponi. Fellini
      Satyricon. Ed. Dario Zanelli. New York: Ballantine
      Books, 1970.
      Adaptation of Petronius's Satyricon.

2338. Fitzgerald, F. Scott. F. Scott Fitzgerald's Screenplay
      for Three Comrades by Erich Maria Remarque.
      Ed. Matthew J. Bruccoli. Carbondale: Southern
      Illinois University Press, 1978.

2339. _____. "The Feather Fan." In Hemingway/Fitgerald
      Annual 1977. Ed. Margaret M. Duggan and Richard
      Layman. Detroit: Gale Research, 1977, 3-8.
      Prose from Fitzgerald's college days believed by
      Matthew Bruccoli to be a film scenario.

2340.   _____. "Infidelity." Esquire, 80 (Dec. 1973),
         193-200, 290-304.

2341.   Foote, Horton. The Screenplay of To Kill a
         Mockingbird. New York: Harcourt, Brace and
         World, 1964.
         Adaptation of Harper Lee's novel.

2342.   _____   . "The Film: Tomorrow." In Tomorrow
         and Tomorrow and Tomorrow. Ed. David G. Yellin
         and Marie Connors. Jackson: University Press
         of Mississippi, 1985, pp. 109-161.
         Adaptation of William Faulkner's short story.

2343.   Fry, Christopher. "The First Treatment," "The
         Step-Sheet," "The Final Treatment," "The Beginning
         of the Script," and "The End of the Script."
         In Barabbas: The Story of a Motion Picture.
         Ed. Lon Jones. Bologna, Italy: Capelli, 1962,
         pp. 37-44, pp. 45-55, pp. 57-63, pp. 75-97,
         and pp. 113-128.
         The film is an adaptation of Pär Lagerkvist's novel.

2344.   _____ . The Bible. New York: Pocketbooks,
         1966.

2345.   Gilbert, Stuart. "Sketch for a Scenario of `Anna
         Livia Plurabelle." In A James Joyce Yearbook.
         Ed. Maria Jolas. Paris: Transition Press,   1949,
         pp. 10-19.

2346.   Gilliatt, Penelope. Sunday Bloody Sunday. New
         York: The Viking Press, 1971.

2347.   Goldman, James. The Lion in Winter. New York:
         Dell Publishers, 1968.

2348.   Gorky, Maxim. "Descent to the Lower Depths."
         Trans. Alexander Bakshy. Films: A Quarterly
         of Discussion and Analysis, 1 (Nov. 1939), 40-50;
         rpt. New York: Arno Press, 1968. Reprinted
         in Cinemages, No. 9 (1958), pp. 29-37.

2349.   Greene, Graham. The Third Man. New York: Simon
         and Schuster, 1968. Reprinted in Masterworks
         of the British Cinema. New York: Harper and
         Row, 1974, pp. 89-194.

2350.   Hammett, Dashiell. "Watch on the Rhine." In Best
         Film Plays of 1943-44. Ed. John Gassner and
         Dudley Nichols. New York: Crown Publishers,
         1945, pp. 299-356.
         Play by Lillian Hellman.

2351.   Harwood, Ronald. "One Day in the Life of Ivan
         Denisovich: Screenplay." In The Making of One
         Day in the Life of Ivan Denisovich. New York:
         Ballentine Books, 1971, pp. 177-271.
         Adaptation of Alexander Solzhenitsyn's novel.

2352. Hecht, Ben. "Spellbound." In Best Film Plays--1945.
       Ed. John Gassner and Dudley Nichols. New York:
       Crown Publishers, 1946, pp. 57-113.

2353. Hecht, Ben and Charles MacArthur. "Wuthering Heights."
       In Twenty Best Film Plays. Ed. John Gassner
       and Dudley Nichols. New York: Crown Publishers,
       1943, pp. 293-331.
       Adaptation of Emily Bronte's novel.

2354. Hellman, Lillian. The North Star. New York: Viking,
       1943.

2355. Howard, Sidney. GWTW: The Screenplay. Ed. Richard
       Harwell. New York: Macmillan, 1980.
       Adaptation of Margaret Mitchell's Gone With the
       Wind.

2356. Hrabal, Bohumil and Jiri Menzel. Closely Watched
       Trains. Trans. Josef Holzbecher. New York:
       Simon and Schuster, 1971.
       Adaptation of the novel by Hrabal.

2357. Huston, John. The Treasure of the Sierra Madre.
       Ed. James Naremore. Madison: University of
       Wisconsin Press, 1979.
       Adaptation of B. Traven's novel.

2358. Huston, John and W.R. Burnett. High Sierra. Ed.
       Douglas Gomery. Madison: University of Wisconsin
       Press, 1979.
       From a story by W.R. Burnett.

2359. Inge, William. "Splendor in the Grass." In
       Scholastic's Literature of the Screen: Men and
       Women. Ed. Richard A. Maynard. New York: Scholastic
       Book Services, 1974, pp. 11-74.

2360. Jennings, Talbot. "The Good Earth." In Twenty
       Best Film Plays. Ed. John Gassner and Dudley
       Nichols. New York: Crown Publishers, 1943,
       pp. 875-950.
       Adaptation of Pearl Buck's novel.

2361. _____. "Romeo and Juliet: Scenario Version."
       In Romeo and Juliet: A Motion Picture Edition.
       New York: Random House, 1936, pp. 141-229.
       Book contains Jennings's script and essays by the
       cast and crew of the film.

2362. Johnson, Nunnally. "The Grapes of Wrath." In
       Twenty Best Film Plays. Ed. John Gassner and
       Dudley Nichols. New York: Crown Publishers,
       1943, pp. 333-77.
       Adaptation of John Steinbeck's novel.

2363. Kerouac, Jack. Pull My Daisy. New York: Grove
       Press, 1961.

2364. Kubrick, Stanley. A Clockwork Orange. New York:
           Abelard-Schuman, 1972.
       Adaptation of Anthony Burgess's novel.

2365. Kurosawa, Akira and Shinohu Hashimoto. Rashomon.
           Trans. Donald Richie. New York: Grove Press,
           1969.
       Adaptation of stories by Ryunosuke Akutagawa.

2366. Lania, Leo; Béla Balász and Ladislaus Vajda. "The
           Threepenny Opera." In Masterworks of the German
           Cinema. New York: Harper and Row, 1973,
           pp. 179-276.
       Adaptation of Bertolt Brecht's play.

2367. Launder, Frank and Sidney Gilliat. The Lady Vanishes.
           Ed. Andrew Sinclair. London: Lorrimer Publishing,
           1984.
       From the novel The Wheel Spins by Ethel Lina White.

2368. Loos, Anita and Jane Murfin. "The Women." In
           Twenty Best Film Plays. Ed. John Gassner and
           Dudley Nichols. New York: Crown Publishers,
           1943, pp. 61-130.
       Adaptation of Clare Boothe's play.

2369. MacDougall, Ranald. Mildred Pierce. Ed. Albert
           J. LaValley. Madison: University of Wisconsin
           Press, 1980.
       Adaptation of James M. Cain's novel.

2370. McGuane, Thomas. The Missouri Breaks. New York:
           Ballentine Books, 1976.

2371. Maddow, Ben. "Intruder in the Dust." In Faulkner's
           Intruder in the Dust: Novel into Film. Ed. Regina
           K. Fadiman. Knoxville: University of Tennessee
           Press, 1978, pp. 93-303.
       Adaptation of William Faulkner's novel.

2372. Maddow, Ben and John Huston. The Asphalt Jungle.
           Ed. Matthew J. Bruccoli. Carbondale: Southern
           Illinois University Press, 1980.
       Adaptation of W.R. Burnett's novel.

2373. Mailer, Norman. Maidstone: A Mystery. New York:
           New American Library, 1971.

2374. Marcus, Fred H., ed. Short Story/ Short Film.
           Englewood Cliffs: Prentice-Hall, 1977.
       Contains brief scripts or portions of scripts for
       adaptations of "The Lottery," "Young Goodman Brown,"
       "Bartleby, the Scrivener," "Dr. Heidegger's Experiment,"
       "The Legend of Sleepy Hollow," and "The Masque
       of the Red Death."

2375. Marion, Frances. "The Scarlet Letter." In Motion
           Picture Continuities. New York: Columbia University
           Press, 1929, pp. 89-156.

2376. Mason, Sarah and Victor Heerman. "Little Women."
       In Four Star Scripts. Ed. Lorraine Noble.
       Garden City: Doubleday, Doran and Co., 1936.
       pp. 213-319.
       Adaptation of Louisa May Alcott's novel.

2377. Maugham, W. Somerset. Encore. Garden City: Doubleday
       and Co., 1952.
       Book contains adaptations of Maugham's stories:
       "The Ant and the Grasshopper" (T.E.B. Clarke),
       "Gigolo and Gigolette" (Eric Ambler), and "Winter
       Cruise" (Arhtur Macrae).

2378. _____. Quartet. Garden City: Doubleday and
       Co., 1949.
       Contains adaptations by R.C. Sherriff: "The Facts
       of Life," "The Alien Corn," "The Kite," and "The
       Colonel's Lady."

2379. _____. Trio. Garden City: Doubleday and
       Co., 1950.
       Contains adaptations by Maugham, R.C. Sherriff
       and Noel Langley of "The Verger," "Mr. Know-All,"
       and "Sanitorium."

2380. Mazursky, Paul and Leon Capetanos. Tempest: A
       Screenplay. New York: Performing Arts Journal
       Publications, 1982.
       Loosely based on Shakespeare's play.

2381. Miller, Arthur. The Misfits. New York: The Viking
       Press, 1961.

2382. Miller, Henry. "Scenario: A Film Without Sound."
       In The Cosmological Eye. Norfolk, Conn.: New
       Directions, 1939, pp. 75-106. Reprinted in
       Cinemages, No. 9 (1958), pp. 39-56.
       Treatment inspired by Anais Nin's The House of
       Incest.

2383. Murnau, F.W. and Henrik Galleen. "Nosferatu."
       In Masterworks of the German Cinema. New York:
       Harper and Row, 1973, pp. 52-95. Murnau's copy
       of this adaptation of Stoker's Dracula is printed
       in Murnau by Lotte Eisner. Berkley: University
       of California Press, 1973, pp. 227-272.

2384. Nabokov, Vladimir. Lolita: A Screenplay. New
       York: McGraw-Hill, 1974.

2385. Nin, Anais. "House of Incest." Cinemages, No. 9
       (1958), pp. 38-39.
       The scenario is the first chapter of House of Incest,
       which was used as the basis for Bells of Atlantis,
       a film by Ian Hugo and Anais Nin.

2386. Odets, Clifford. "None But the Lonely Heart."
          In Best Film Plays 1945. Ed. John Gassner and
          Dudley Nichols. New York: Crown, 1946, pp. 261-330.
       Script is an adaptation of the Richard Llewellyn
       novel.

2387. Ophuls, Max and Jacques Nathanson. "La Ronde."
          In Masterworks of the French Cinema. Trans. NIcholas
          Fry. New York: Harper and Row, 1974, pp. 152-225.
       Adaptation of Arthur Schnitzler's play.

2388. Osborne, John. Tom Jones. New York: Grove Press,
          1964.
       Adaptation of Henry Fielding's novel.

2389. Pasolini, Pier Paolo. Oedipus Rex. Trans. John
          Mathews. New York: Simon and Schuster, 1971.
       Adaptation of Sophocles's play.

2390. Pellissier, Anthony. "The Film: `The Rocking-Horse
          Winner'." In From Fiction to Film: D.H.Lawrence's
          "The Rocking-Horse Winner." Ed. Gerald R. Barrett
          and Thomas L. Erskine. Encino, Cal.: Dickenson
          Publishing, 1974, pp. 75-201.
       The final shooting script of Pellissier`s film.

2391. Pinter, Harold. "The Basement." In The Lover,
          The Tea Party, and The Basement. New York:
          Grove Press, 1967.

2392.   . Five Screenplays. London: Methuen
          and Co., 1971.
       Contains "The Servant," "The Pumpkin Eater," "The
       Quiller Memorandum," "Accident," and "The Go-Between."

2393.   . A la Recherche du Temps Perdu: The
          Proust Screenplay. New York: Grove Press, 1977.

2394.   . The Screenplay of The French Lieutenant's
          Woman. London: Jonathan Cape, 1981.
       Adaptation of John Fowles's novel.

2395. Rawlinson, Arthur and Dorothy Farnum. Jew Süss.
          London: Methuen, 1935; rpt. New York: Garland
          Publishing, 1978.
       Adaptation of Lion Feuchtwanger's novel.

2396. Ray, Stayajit. Pather Panchali. Trans. Lila Roy.
          Calcutta: Cine Central, 1984.
       Adaptation of the novel by Bibhuti Bhushan Bandapaddhay.

2397. Reisman, Philip H., Jr. "All the Way Home." In
          The Creative Arts: Four Representative Types.
          Ed. Michael E. Keisman and Rodney E. Sheratsky.
          New York: Globe Book Co., 1968, pp. 299-489.
       Adaptation of James Agee's novel A Death in the
       Family.

2398.   Robbe-Grillet, Alain. The Immortal One. Trans.
         A.M. Sheridan Smith. London: Calder and Boyars,
         1971.

2399.   _____. Last Year at Marienbad. Trans. Richard
         Howard. New York: Grove Press, 1962.

2400.   Roberts, Marguerite and Jane Murfin. "Dragon Seed."
         In Best Film Plays of 1943-1944. Ed. John Gassner
         and Dudley Nichols. New York: Crown Publishers,
         1945, pp. 357-449.
         Adaptation of Pearl Buck's novel.

2401.   Rohmer, Eric and Heinrich von Kleist. The Marquise
         of O. Trans. Stanley Hochman and Martin
         Greenberg. New York: Frederick Ungar, 1984.
         Volume contains both Rohmer's script and Kleist's
         short story.

2402.   Rolland, Romaine. "The Revolt of the Machines."
         Trans. William A. Drake. Cinemages, No. 9 (1958),
         pp. 57-70.

2403.   Rossen, Robert. "All the King's Men." In Three
         Screenplays: All the King's Men, The Hustler,
         and Lilith. Garden City: Doubleday, 1972,
         pp. 1-108.
         Adaptation of Robert Penn Warren's novel.

2404.   Rudolph, Alan and Robert Altman. Buffalo Bill
         and the Indians, Or Sitting Bull's History Lesson.
         New York: Bantam Books, 1976.
         Film is a loose adaptation of Arthur Kopit's play,
         Indians.

2405.   Sartre, Jean Paul. In the Mesh. Trans. Mervyn
         Savill. London: Andrew Dakers, 1954.

2406.   Schulberg, Budd. A Face in the Crowd. New York:
         Random House, 1957. Reprinted in Scholastic's
         Literature of the Screen: Power. Ed. Richard
         A. Maynard. New York: Scholastic Book Services,
         1974, pp. 89-168.

2407.   _____. On the Waterfront. Ed. Matthew J.
         Bruccoli. Carbondale: Southern Illinois University
         Press, 1980.

2408.   Sen, Mrinal. In Search of Famine. Trans. Samik
         Bandyopadhyay. Calcutta: Seagull Books, 1983.
         From a novel by Amalendo Chakraborty.

2409.   Shaw, George Bernard. The Collected Screenplays
         of Bernard Shaw. Ed. Bernard F. Duckore. Athens:
         University of Georgia Press, 1980.
         Contains St. Joan, The Devil's Disciple, Major
         Barbara, Arms and the Man, and Caesar and Cleopatra.

2410. _____. Major Barbara: A Screen Version.
New York: Penguin Books, 1946.

2411. _____. Pygmalion. New York: Dodd, Mead,
and Co. 1939.

2412. _____. Saint Joan: An Unfilmed Script. Ed.
Bernard F. Dukore. Seattle: University of Washington
Press, 1968.

2413. Shaw, Irwin. In the French Style. New York:
Macfadden-Bartell, 1963.
Contains Shaw's script for the 1963 film.

2414. Sherwood, Robert E. "A First Treatment of The
Ghost Goes West" and "The Finished Scenario
of The Ghost Goes West." In Successful Film
Writing As Illustrated By The Ghost Goes West
by Seton Margrave. London: Methuen, 1936, pp. 53-67
and pp. 69-216.

2415. Sherwood, Robert E. and Joan Harrison. "Rebecca."
In Twenty Best Film Plays. Ed. John Gassner
and Dudley Nichols. New York: Crown Publishers,
1943, pp. 233-291.
Adaptation of Daphne du Maurier's novel.

2416. Silliphant, Stirling. "A Walk in the Spring Rain."
In Fiction into Film. Knoxville: University
of Tennessee Press, 1970, pp. 56-132.
Adaptation of a novella by Rachel Maddux.

2417. Sillitoe, Alan. "The Loneliness of the Long-Distance
Runner." In Scholastic's Literature of the
Screen: Identity. Ed. Richard A. Maynard.
New York: Scholastic Book Services, 1974, pp. 27-78.

2418. _____. "Saturday Night and Sunday Morning."
In Masterworks of the British Cinema. New York:
Harper and Row, 1974, pp. 165-327.

2419. Slesinger, Tess and Frank Davis. "A Tree Grows
in Brooklyn." In Best Film Plays 1945. Ed. John
Gassner and Dudley Nichols. New York: Crown
Publishers, 1946, pp. 175-260.
Adaptation of Betty Smith's novel.

2420. Sontag, Susan. Brother Carl. New York: Farrar,
Straus, and Giroux, 1974.

2421. _____ . Duet for Cannibals. New York: Farrar,
Straus, and Giroux, 1970.

2422. Steinbeck, John. The Forgotten Village. New York:
Viking Press, 1941.

2423. _____. Viva Zapata! Ed. Robert E. Morsberger.
New York: Viking Press, 1975.

2424.   Teshiqahara, Hiroshi. <u>Woman in the Dunes</u>. New
         York: Phaedra Publishers, 1966.
         From the novel by Kobo Abe.

2425.   Thomas, Dylan. <u>The Beach at Falesa</u>. New York:
         Stein and Day, 1964.
         Unfilmed script is an adaptation of a Robert Louis
         Stevenson short story.

2426.   _   . <u>The Doctor and the Devils</u>. London:
         J.M. Dent and Sons, 1953. Portion reprinted
         in <u>Cinemages</u>, No. 9 (1958), pp. 71-80.

2427.   _____. <u>Me and My Bike</u>. New York: McGraw-Hill,
         1965.
         Unfilmed screenplay.

2428.   _____. <u>Rebecca's Daughters</u>. Boston: Little,
         Brown, 1966.
         A novel adapted from Thomas's screenplay.

2429.   Thomas, Dylan and Andrew Sinclair. <u>Under Milk
         Wood</u>. New York: Simon and Schuster, 1972.

2430.   Thompson, Robert E. "They Shoot Horses, Don't
         They?" In <u>They Shoot Horses, Don't They?</u> New
         York: Avon Books, 1966, pp. 137-319.
         Volume contains text of Horace McCoy's novel and
         an introduction to the screenplay by director Sydney
         Pollack.

2431.   Totheroh, Dan and Stephen Vicent Benét. "All That
         Money Can Buy." In <u>Twenty Best Film Plays</u>.
         New York: Crown Publishers, 1943, pp. 951-994.
         Adaptation of Benét's short story.

2432.   Trotti, Lamar. "The Ox-Bow Incident." In <u>Best
         Film Plays of 1943-1944</u>. Ed. John Gassner and
         Dudley Nichols. New York: Crown Publishers,
         1945, pp. 511-560.
         Adaptation of Walter Van Tilburg Clark's novel.

2433.   Truffaut, Francois and Jean Gruault. <u>Jules and
         Jim</u>. Trans. Nicholas Fry. New York: Simon
         and Schuster, 1968.
         Adaptation of Henri-Pierre Roche's novel.

2434.   Vadim, Roger, Roger Vailland, and Claude Brulé.
         <u>Les Liaisons Dangereuses</u>. New York: Ballentine
         Books, 1962.
         Adaptation of Choderlos de Laclos's novel.

2435.   Vajda, Ladislaus and G.W. Pabst. <u>Pandora's Box
         (Lulu)</u>. Trans. Christopher Holme. New York:
         Simon and Schuster, 1971.
         Adaptation of Frank Wedekind's plays.

2436. Vidal, Gore. "The Best Man." In Film Scripts
         Four. Ed. George P. Garrett, O.B. Hardison,
         Jr. and Jane R. Gelfman. New York: Appleton-
         Century-Crofts, 1972, pp. 146-296.

2437. Visconti, Luchino and Suso Cecchi d'Amico. "White
         Nights" and "The Job." In Luchino Visconti:
         Three Screenplays. Trans. Judith Green. New
         York: Grossman Publishers, 1970, pp. 1-91 and
         pp. 273-313.
       Based on short stories by Dostoyevsky and de Maupassant.

2438. Von Sternberg, Josef and Robert Liebmann. The
         Blue Angel. New York: Simon and Schuster, 1968;
         rpt. New York: Frederick Ungar, 1979.
       Based on the novel by Heinrich Mann. The Ungar
       edition contains both the film script and the novel.

2439. Von Stroheim, Erich. Greed. Ed. Joel W. Finler.
         New York: Simon and Schuster, 1972.
       Based on Frank Norris's McTeague.

2440. Wajda, Andrzej. The Wajda Trilogy: Ashes and Diamonds,
         A Generation, Kanal. Trans. Boleslaw Sulik.
         New York: Simon and Schuster, 1973.
       A Generation is an adaptation of the novel by Bohdan
       Czeszko; Kanal is an adaptation of the short story
       by Jerzy Stefan Stawinski; Ashes and Diamonds is
       an adaptation of the novel by Jerzy Andrzejewski.

2441. Weinberg, Herman G., ed. The Complete Greed of
         Eric von Stroheim. New York: E.P. Dutton, 1972.
       The Finler edition contains von Stroheim's original
       shooting script. The Weinberg edition is a rendering
       of the film through stills, some representing deleted
       and subsequently lost sections.

2442. Welles, Orson. The Trial. Trans. Nicholas Fry.
         New York: Simon and Schuster, 1970.
       Adaptation of Franz Kafka's novel.

2443. Wells, H.G. The Man Who Could Work Miracles.
         New York: The Macmillan Co., 1936.

2444. _____ . The Man Who Was King. Garden City:
         Doubleday, Doran, and Co., 1929.

2445. _____. Things to Come. New York: The Macmillan
         Co., 1935; rpt. Boston: Gregg Press, 1975.

2446. Williams, Tennessee. Baby Doll. New York: New
         Directions, 1956.

2447. _____. Stopped Rocking and Other Screenplays.
         New York: New Directions, 1984.
       Contains "All Gaul is Divided," "The Loss of a
       Teardrop Diamond," "One Arm," and "Stopped Rocking."

2448. Witcombe, Eleanor. <u>The Getting of Wisdom</u>. Richmond,
           Victoria: Heinemann Educational Australian Pty.,
           1978.
       From the novel by Henry Handel Richardson.

2449. Zarkhy, Nathan. "Mother." In <u>Two Russian Film
           Classics</u>. Trans. Gillon R. Aitken. New York:
           Simon and Schuster, 1973, pp. 5-54.
       Based on the novel by Maxim Gorky.

16

Literature/Film
in the
Classroom

2450. Adams, Dale Talmadge. "Film Study in the Discipline of English." DAI, 37 (1977), 7373A (The University of Texas at Austin).

2451. Admussen, Richard L., Edward J. Gallagher, and Lubbe Levin. "Novel into Film: An Experimental Course." Literature/Film Quarterly, 6 (1978), 66-72.

2452. Armour, Robert. "Poetry and Film for the Classroom." The English Journal, 66 (Jan. 1977), 88-91.

2453. Bartell, Shirley Miller. "The Chinese Bandit Novel and the American Gangster Film: A Theoretical Model for Crosscultural and Interdisciplinary Teaching." DAI, 37 (1977), 5554A (Florida Atlantic University).

2454. Buzzard, David Bruce. "Humanizing the Secondary English Curriculum Through the Use of Film." DAI, 34 (1973), 2155A (The Ohio State University).

2455. Chittister, Joan. "The Perception of Prose and Filmic Fiction." DAI, 32 (1972), 6580A (Pennsylvania State University).

2456. Dayton, Joyce Arlene. "Literature and Film: An Interdisciplinary Course for College Undergraduates." DAI, 37 (1977), 6455-6456A (The State University of New York at Albany).

2457. Donelson, Ken. "Getting at Literary Terms Through Short Films." Literature/Film Quarterly, 11 (1983), 56-65.

2458. English Study Committee. The Uses of Film in the Teaching of English. Toronto: Ontario Institute for Studies in Education, 1971.

2459. Erickson, James. "Teaching Literature and Film:
       Some Useful Examples." Kansas Quarterly, 4
       (Spring 1972), 21-29.

2460. Gollin, Richard. "Film as Dramatic Literature."
       College English, 30 (1969), 424-429. Reprinted
       in The Compleat Guide to Film Study. Ed. G. Howard
       Poteet. Urbana, Ill.: National Council of Teachers
       of English, 1972, pp. 55-62.

2461. Goodwin, James. "Film Study in a Literature Program?"
       College Literature, 5 (1978), 174-182.

2462. Hartley, Dean Wilson. "'How Do We Teach It?'
       A Primer for the Basic Film/Literature Course."
       Literature/Film Quarterly. 3 (1975), 60-69.
       Reprinted in Film and the Humanities. Ed. John
       E. O'Connor. New York: Rockefeller Foundation,
       1977, pp. 39-44.

2463. Holladay, John McKinley. "Trends in the Use of
       Film Among English Teachers at Selected Colleges
       and Universities in Michigan." DAI, 33 (1973),
       6235-6236A (The University of Michigan).

2464. Kallich, Martin and Michael Marsdin. "Teaching
       Film Dramas as Literature." The Quarterly of
       Film, Radio, and Televsion, 11 (1956), 39-48.

2465. Kennedy, Keith. "Film and Literature." In Film
       in Teaching. London: Batsford Ltd., 1972,
       pp. 74-105.

2466. Kinder, Marsha. "Establishing a Discipline for
       the Teaching of Film: Criticism and the Literary
       Analogue." Quarterly Review of Film Studies,
       1 (1976), 424-429.

2467. Lesage, Julia. "Teaching the Comparative Analysis
       of Novels and Films." Style, 9 (1975), 453-468.

2468. Mallery, David. The School and the Art of Motion
       Pictures. Boston: National Association of
       Independent Schools, 1965.

2469. Maynard, Richard A. "Movies and Literature."
       In his The Celluloid Curriculum. New York:
       Hayden Books, 1971, pp. 88-101.

2470. _____ . "The Cross-Media Message: Teaching
       Literature with Film." In his Classroom Cinema.
       New York: Teachers College Press, 1972, pp. 81-91.

2471. Probst, Robert E. "Visual to Verbal." English
       Journal, 61 (1972), 71-75.

2472. Rule, Phillip C., S.J. "Teaching the Film as
       Literature." Soundings, 53 (1970), 77-87.

2473.   Schneider, Harold W.   "Literature and Film: Marking
        Out Some Boundaries." Literature/Film Quarterly,
        3 (1975), 30-44.

2474.   Sheridan, Marion, Harold H. Owen, and Fred Marcus.
        The Motion Picture and the Teaching of English.
        New York: Appleton-Century-Crofts, 1965.

2475.   Sullivan, Sister Bede, O.S.B.   "How a Screen Play
        Differs from a Stage Play--Raisin in the Sun"
        and "A Screen Play is Different from a Novel--
        Barabbas." In her Movies: Universal Language;
        Film Study in High School. Notre Dame, Indiana:
        Fides Publishers, 1967, pp. 42-47 and pp. 47-51.

2476.   Weales, Gerald.   "Teaching Film Drama as Film Drama."
        The Quarterly of Film, Radio, and Television,
        11 (1957), 394-398.

2477.   Weeks, Ruth Mary.   "Use Films--Yes, But Keep It
        English." The English Journal, 40 (1951), 139-143.

17

Research Tools:
Bibliographies and Filmographies

2478. Bowers, Nancy Brooker. The Hollywood Novel and
      Other Novels About Film. New York: Garland
      Publishing, 1985.
      Synopses of 500 novels.

2479. Clay, James H. and Daniel Krempel. "An Annotated
      List of Twenty-Two Filmed Plays." In their
      The Theatrical Image. New York: McGraw-Hill,
      1967, pp. 255-261.

2480. Daisne, Johan. Filmographic Dictionary of World
      Literature. New York: Humanities Press, 1970.
      Filmographies arranged by author.

2481. DeMarco, Norman. "Selected Bibliography of Books
      on Literature and Film." Style, 9 (1975), 593-607.
      Reprinted in Stories into Film. Ed. William
      Kittredge and Steven M. Krauzer. New York:
      Harper and Row, 1979, pp. 259-273.

2482. Emmens, Carol A. Short Stories on Film. Littleton,
      Ohio: Libraries Unlimited, 1978.
      List of short stories adapted for film.

2483. Esner, A.G.S. Filmed Books and Plays. New York:
      London House and Maxwell, 1968.
      List of adaptations from 1928 to 1967.

2484. Gottesman, Ronald and Harry M. Geduld. "Adaptation."
      In their Guidebook to Film: An Eleven-in-One
      Reference. New York: Holt, Rinehart, and Winston,
      1972, pp. 30-35.

2485. Kotzkin, Miriam. "A Bibliographic and Filmographic
      Guide to Teaching Literature/Film." College
      Literature, 5 (1978), 249-262.

2486. Leonard, William Torbert. Theatre: From Stage
         to Screen to Television. Two Volumes. Metuchen:
         Scarecrow Press, 1981.
       Plays adapted to film; volumes contain stage histories,
       casts, credits, and descriptions of plays.

2487. Lindell, Richard L. III. "Literature/Film
         Bibliography." Literature/Film Quarterly, 8
         (1980), 267-276.

2488. Magill, Frank. Cinema: The Novel into Film. Pasadena:
         Salem Softbacks, 1980.
       Plot summaries of novels and their film adaptations.

2489. Manchel, Frank. "Comparative Literature." In
         his Film Study: A Resource Guide. Cranbury,
         N.J.: Associated University Presses, 1973,
         pp. 143-168.

2490. Pickard, Roy. "Novels into Films" and "Plays into
         Films." In his A Companion to the Movies: From
         1903 to the Present Day. New York: Hippocrene
         Books, 1972, pp. 219-236 and pp. 237-246.
       List with brief credits of adaptations.

2491. Ross, Harris. "A Selected Bibliography of Articles
         on the Relationship of Film to Literature."
         Style, 9 (1975), 564-592. Reprinted in Stories
         into Film. Ed. William Kittredge and Steven
         M. Krauzer. New York: Harper and Row, 1979,
         pp. 233-259.

2492. Smith, Julian. "Short Fiction on Film: A Selected
         Filmography." Studies in Short Fiction, 10
         (1973), 397-409.

2493. Welch, Jeffrey Egan. Literature and Film: An
         Annotated Bibliography, 1909-1977. New York:
         Garland Publishing, 1981.

2494. Wendell, Daniel. "A Researcher's Guide and Selected
         Checklist to Film as Literature and Language."
         Journal of Modern Literature, 3 (1973), 323-350.

2495. Wicks, Ulrich. "Literature/Film: A Bibliography."
         Literature/Film Quarterly, 6 (1978), 135-143.

Author Index

Subject Index

Mukarovsky, Jan p.28,
p.29, p.33
Munk, Kaj 0566, 2326
Munsterberg, Hugo p.28,
p.29, p.43
Murder in the Cathedral
(play, T.S. Eliot; film,
George Hollering) 2331
Murder, My Sweet (film,
Edward Dmytryk; novel,
Farewell, My Lovely,
Raymond Chandler) 0694,
0702
Murray, Edward p.28,
p.56
My Brilliant Career (novel,
Miles Franklin; film,
Gillian Armstrong) 0548
"My Old Man" (short story,
Ernest Hemingway)
See Under My Skin
Mystery of Edwin Drood,
The (novel, Charles
Dickens; film, Stuart
Walker) 1273
Nabokov, Vladimir 0112,
0537, 1016-1028
Naked and the Dead, The
(novel, Norman Mailer;
film, Raoul Walsh)
0986
Nana (novel, Emile Zola;
film, Jean Renoir)
2230, 2233
Nash, Mark p.14
Nathan, George Jean 0603
Nathan, Robert p.5
Native Son (novel, Richard
Wright; film, Pierre
Chenal) 0537, 1180,
1181
Nazarin (novel, Benito
Pérez Galdós; film,
Luis Buñuel) 2112,
2114, 2301
Niaye (film, Sembene Ousmane;
novella, Vebi Ciosane
ou Blanche-Genèse)
0574
Nicholas Nickleby (novel,
Charles Dickens; film,
Alberto Cavalcanti)
1284, 1295, 1309, 1319
Nichols, Dudley 0601
Nichols, John 0176, 1029
Nicoll, Allardyce p.28,
p.52, p.55, 0452
Night of the Hunter, The
novel, Davis Grubb;

film, Charles Laughton)
0610, 0617, 0856, 0857
Night of the Iguana (play,
Tennessee Williams;
film, John Huston) 1178
1984 (novel, George Orwell;
film, Michael Anderson)
0584, 1481
Nin, Anais 1030, 2382
Noire de..., Le (story,
Ousmane Sembene; film,
Ousmane Sembene) 2276
None But the Lonely Heart
(novel, Richard Llewellyn;
film, Clifford Odets)
2386
Norris, Frank 0502, 0523,
0577, 0584, 1031-1036,
2439, 2441
North Star, The (film,
Lewis Milestone) 0890,
2354
Nosferatu (film, F.W. Murnau)
See Dracula
Not Reconciled (film,
Jean-Marie Straub; novel,
Billiards at Half Past
Nine, Heinrich Böll)
0507
Notte, La (film, Michelangelo
Antonioni) 0144
Novel
See Prose Fiction
O Lucky Man! (film, Lindsay
Anderson) 1919
Oboler, Arch 0601
Occurrence at Owl Creek
Bridge, An (short story,
Ambrose Bierce; films,
Robert Enrico and Charles
Vidor) 0486, 0560,
0652-0656, 2288, 2289
O'Connor, Edwin 1037
O'Connor, Flannery 0486,
0503, 1038, 1039
Odets, Clifford 0575,
0601, 0602
Oedipus Rex (play, Sophocles;
film, Pier Paolo Pasolini)
p.28, 1869-1872, 2096,
2099, 2389
O'Flaherty, Liam 0498
O'Hara, Frank 0479, 1040
O'Hara, John 0265, 0595,
0608, 1041
Of Human Bondage (novel,
Somerset Maugham; films,
John Cromwell, Ken Hughes)
1477

About the Author

HARRIS ROSS is Assistant Professor of English at the University of Delaware. He has published articles in *Style* and *D. H. Lawrence Review*.